and Montmartre

National Gallery of Art, Washington · The Art Institute of Chicago · in association with Princeton University Press

The exhibition was organized by the National Gallery of Art, Washington, and the Art Institute of Chicago.

Time Warner Inc. is the corporate sponsor of the exhibition at the National Gallery of Art.

The Catherine B. Reynolds Foundation is proud to be the foundation sponsor for the exhibition in Washington.

The Sara Lee Foundation is the exclusive corporate sponsor of the exhibition at the Art Institute of Chicago.

The exhibition is supported by an indemnity from the Federal Council on the Arts and the Humanities.

Exhibition dates

National Gallery of Art, Washington
March 20 – June 12, 2005

The Art Institute of Chicago
July 16 – October 10, 2005

Note to the Reader: Caption numbers in orange denote objects in the exhibition; venues appear in the checklist on page 255. Dimensions are given in centimeters, height preceding width, followed by inches in parentheses.

Produced by the Publishing Office, National Gallery of Art, Washington
www.nga.gov

Editor in Chief, Judy Metro
Designer, Wendy Schleicher Smith
Production Manager, Chris Vogel
Project Editor, Gail Spilsbury
Production Editor, Mariah Shay

Edited by Tam Curry Bryfogle, Chestertown, Maryland

Typeset in Mrs. Eaves and Fago Condensed by Duke & Company, Devon, Pennsylvania and printed on Phoenix Motion Xantur by Grafisches Zentrum Drucktechnik, Ditzingen-Heimerdingen, Germany

Front cover and title page: Henri de Toulouse-Lautrec, *At the Moulin Rouge* (detail), 1892/1895, oil on canvas, 123 x 141 cm. The Art Institute of Chicago, Helen Birch Bartlett Memorial Collection (fig. 66)

Back cover: Henri de Toulouse-Lautrec, *Moulin Rouge: La Goulue,* 1891, color lithograph, 191 x 117 cm (sheet). The Art Institute of Chicago, Mr. and Mrs. Carter H. Harrison Collection (fig. 10)

Endpapers / inside cover adapted from: Anonymous, *The Dance Hall of the Moulin Rouge,* illustration in *Le Panorama: Paris La Nuit,* c. 1898, photorelief. The Jane Voorhees Zimmerli Art Museum, Rutgers, The State University of New Jersey, Anonymous Donation (fig. 139)

Map of Montmartre, page xii, from Karl Baedeker, *Paris and Environs with Routes from London to Paris,* Leipzig, 1904. Courtesy of Library of Congress

Library of Congress
Cataloging-in-Publication Data

Thomson, Richard, 1953 –
Toulouse-Lautrec and Montmartre / Richard Thomson, Phillip Dennis Cate, Mary Weaver Chapin ; with assistance from Florence E. Coman.
       p.   cm.
Catalog of an exhibition to be held Mar. 20 – June 12, 2005, National Gallery of Art, Washington, and July 16 – Oct. 10, 2005, Art Institute of Chicago. Includes bibliographical references and index.

ISBN 0-691-12337-3 (hardcover : alk. paper)
ISBN 0-89468-320-9 (pbk. : alk. paper)

1. Toulouse-Lautrec, Henri de, 1864 – 1901 – Exhibitions. 2. Montmartre (Paris, France) – In art – Exhibitions. 3. Montmartre (Paris, France) – Intellectual life – 19th century – Exhibitions. 4. Arts, French – France – Paris – 19th century – Exhibitions. I. Cate, Phillip Dennis. II. Chapin, Mary Weaver. III. National Gallery of Art (U.S.) IV. Art Institute of Chicago. V. Title.

N6853.T6A4 2005
760'.092 – dc22
2004022870

Hardcover edition published in 2005 by the National Gallery of Art, Washington, in association with Princeton University Press

Princeton University Press, 41 William Street, Princeton, New Jersey 08540

In the United Kingdom: Princeton University Press, 3 Market Place, Woodstock, Oxfordshire OX20 1SY

pup.princeton.edu

10 9 8 7 6 5 4 3 2 1

CONTENTS

Henri de Toulouse-Lautrec (1864–1901) remains one of the most popular French painters of the late nineteenth century, largely because his art has transmitted such a compelling image of fin-de-siècle Paris, particularly its entertainment district of Montmartre. Born into an aristocratic provincial family in Albi, Toulouse-Lautrec divided his childhood and adolescent years between Albi and Paris, but in 1881 he settled into an artistic career in the capital. By the mid-1880s he was frequenting the cabarets and cafés-concerts in the bohemian district of Montmartre, notably the Chat Noir and the Mirliton cabarets, the latter run by the entertainer and impresario Aristide Bruant from 1885. Bruant encouraged artists to show their work at the Mirliton, giving them public exposure while simultaneously decorating his premises. Lautrec showed paintings of the various types seen in and around Montmartre and adopted the titles of Bruant's songs, thus becoming identified with Montmartre's entertainment industry. He was, in any case, a brilliant painter of portraits. He made illustrations for the house paper, *Le Mirliton,* and other contemporary journals, such as *Paris illustré* and *Figaro illustré;* many of his greatest drawings were made as studies for such ephemeral publications. He also produced independent prints for the albums of *L'Estampe originale,* collected by connoisseurs of the contemporary print.

In 1891 Toulouse-Lautrec won the commission for a large lithographic poster to publicize the Moulin Rouge dance hall and its star performer, can-can dancer La Goulue. The great success of this bold image fully launched his public career, and he went on to design some of the most striking and brilliant publicity prints of the 1890s. These posters and prints linked his name with many of the entertainment stars of the day, such as Bruant at the Ambassadeurs, Jane Avril at the Jardin de Paris, and Yvette Guilbert wherever she performed. Others, such as May Belfort or May Milton, are remembered today mainly because of Toulouse-Lautrec's representations of them. He partook in the contemporary fascination with the dancer Loïe Fuller, devoting to her a brilliant series of about sixty lithographs, each colored differently. Toulouse-Lautrec was one of the greatest of printmakers, and he remains as well known for his posters' striking design and imagery as for his incisive lithographic observations of contemporary life.

Toulouse-Lautrec was an outsider who preferred to frequent the demimonde he depicted rather than the world of his own social class. He was often at the bars, cabarets, cafés-concerts, and bordellos of Montmartre, from whence he drew his cast of colorful characters, be it the performers, famous or not, their clientele, or the anonymous figures who inhabited that nocturnal world. Toulouse-Lautrec's paintings, drawings, and prints often candidly explore the seedier side of late nineteenth-century Paris, yet with deep empathy for the unenviable lot of its dissolute characters. Toulouse-Lautrec's physical, and later mental health was always precarious, and in 1899 he was confined to a nursing home. To prove his mental abilities, he made a moving series of drawings devoted to the circus, melancholy souvenirs of the performances he had enjoyed in Montmartre and elsewhere in Paris.

The exhibition explores the work of Toulouse-Lautrec along with that of his contemporaries and the ways in which they depicted the decadent life of Montmartre in the 1890s. It includes more than 250 works of art in many media—including paintings, drawings, posters, prints, and sculptures—along with other printed matter such as advertisements, invitations, and admission tickets. While the art of Toulouse-Lautrec is the main focus of the exhibition, predecessors Edouard Manet and Edgar Degas are represented, as are contemporaries such as Vincent van Gogh, Edouard Vuillard, Pierre Bonnard, and Pablo Picasso; poster artists such as Jules Chéret and others; and a variety of lesser known figures. Together their work presents a lively picture of the ambivalent glamour and the licit and illicit pleasures of Montmartre at the turn of the twentieth century.

As always, we thank our lenders for their thoughtfulness and generosity in sharing their treasures with our audiences in Washington and Chicago. Without their support such an exhibition would not be possible.

We were fortunate to engage the distinguished Toulouse-Lautrec scholar Richard Thomson, Watson Gordon Professor of Fine Art, The University of Edinburgh, as our guest curator. He conceived the thematic approach of the exhibition and wrote the principal essay for the catalogue, which illuminates the social, historical, and intellectual stage for Toulouse-Lautrec and Montmartre. We are also grateful to Phillip Dennis Cate, director emeritus, supervisor of curatorial and academic activities, The Jane Voorhees Zimmerli Art Museum at Rutgers, The State University of New Jersey, for contributing an essay to the catalogue, and for facilitating the loan of many of the works of art and ephemera produced in Paris during the 1890s, which he so assiduously collected for his museum over many years. The exhibition was overseen in Washington by Philip Conisbee, senior curator of European paintings, and its mass of detail was ably coordinated by Florence E. Coman, assistant curator of French paintings. In Chicago, the exhibition was supervised by Douglas Druick, Searle Curator of European Painting and Prince Trust Curator of Prints and Drawings, and Gloria Groom, David and Mary Winton Green Curator, drawing on the expertise of Mary Weaver Chapin, Andrew W. Mellon Curatorial Fellow in the Department of European Painting, who contributed an essay to the catalogue. We are indebted to them all.

The National Gallery of Art is extremely grateful to Time Warner Inc. for its generous financial support, which made the exhibition possible in Washington. We would like especially to thank Richard D. Parsons, chairman of the board and CEO, and Robert M. Kimmitt, executive vice president, global public policy, Time Warner Inc.

The National Gallery gratefully acknowledges the Catherine B. Reynolds Foundation for its role as foundation sponsor for the exhibition in Washington and wishes particularly to thank Catherine and Wayne Reynolds for their ongoing commitment.

The Art Institute of Chicago graciously thanks the Sara Lee Foundation for its generous support in making the exhibition possible in Chicago. The Art Institute would like to extend a special thanks to C. Steven McMillan, chairman, president, and executive officer of the Sara Lee Corporation, and to Robin S. Tryloff, president and executive director of the Sara Lee Foundation.

An indemnity from the Federal Council on the Arts and the Humanities has assisted substantially with insurance costs: the American public is enormously indebted to the Council's continuing support of exhibitions such as this one.

Earl A. Powell III
Director
National Gallery of Art

James Cuno
President and Eloise W. Martin Director
The Art Institute of Chicago

ACKNOWLEDGMENTS

———

The National Gallery of Art, the Art Institute of Chicago, our curators, and the authors of the catalogue would like to thank the many people who have offered valuable information and advice in matters both curatorial and scholarly, and who have facilitated the loan of crucial works: Götz Adriani; Cathleen Anderson; Irina Antonova; João da Cruz Vicente de Azevedo; Joseph Baillio; Jed Bark; Laurence Barret; Mary Bartow; Heike Biedermann; Henry S. Bienen; Ulrich Bischoff; Doreen Bolger; the late Philippe Brame; Sylvie Brame; Emily Braun; Christian Briend; Eduard Carbonell i Esteller; Derrick Cartwright; Thierry Cazaux; Michael Conforti; Alain Daguerre de Hureaux; Philippe de Montebello; Nina del Rio; Danièle Devynck; Elizabeth Easton; Eugênia Gorini Esmeraldo; Christopher Eykyn; Suzannah Fabing; Sabine Fehlemann; Walter Feilchenfeldt; Flemming Friborg; Cristina Mendoza Garriga; Jay Gates; Raphaël Gérard; Claude Ghez; Léonard Gianadda; Barbra Goering; Judy Greenberg; Deborah Gribbon; Dorothee Hansen; Robert Herbert; Wulf Herzogenrath; Sinclair Hitchings; Danielle Hodel; Willard Holmes; Jan Howard; James J. Kamm; Thomas Krens; Mark Krisco; Elizabeth S. Kujawski; Fred Leeman; Arnold Lehman; John Leighton; Serge Lemoine; Thomas W. Lentz; Jean-Marc Léri; David C. Levy; Susana López; Marilyn McCully; Caroline Mathieu; R. Russell Maylone; Leena Ahtola-Moorhouse; Charles S. Moffett; Peter Nathan; Esty Neuman; David Norman; Maureen O'Brien; Inna Orn; Harry S. Parker III; Gregory J. Perry; Lionel Pissarro; Eliza Rathbone; Katherine Lee Reid; Andrea Rich; Malcolm Rogers; Martin Roth; Hélène de Saint-Phalle; Kevin Salatino; Josep Sampera i Aramon; Manuel Schmit; Robert Schmit; Sir Nicholas Serota; George Shackelford; Lauren Shadford; J.P. Sigmond; Michael Simpson; Soili Sinisalo; MaryAnne Stevens; Deborah Swallow; John Tancock; Matthew Teitelbaum; Pierre Théberge; Belinda Thomson; Gary Tinterow; Anna Llanes Tuset; Lora S. Urbanelli; Alice Whelihan.

At the National Gallery of Art we thank deputy director Alan Shestack, D. Dodge Thompson, chief of exhibitions; Jennifer Cipriano, exhibition officer; Jennifer Overton, assistant for exhibition administration; Susan Arensberg, head of department of exhibition programs; Lynn Matheny, assistant curator of exhibition programs; Carroll Moore, film and video producer; Mark Leithauser, chief of design; Donna Kirk, design coordinator; Mari Forsell, design coordinator; Bill Bowser, production coordinator; Judy Metro, editor in chief; Tam Curry Bryfogle, catalogue editor; Gail Spilsbury, project editor; Wendy Schleicher Smith, catalogue designer; Chris Vogel, catalogue production manager; Mariah Shay, production editor; Phyllis Hecht, Web manager; Michelle Fondas, registrar for exhibitions; Alicia Thomas, loan officer; Michael Pierce, senior conservator for loans and exhibitions; Julian Saenz, assistant general counsel; Ira Bartfield and Sara Sanders-Buell, permissions coordinators for photography; Kristen Quinlan Boyce, digital imaging specialist; Christine Myers, chief corporate relations officer; Susan McCullough, corporate relations associate; Andrew Robison, senior curator of prints and drawings; Margaret Morgan Grasselli, department head, Old Master Drawings, and curator of drawings; Peter Parshall, department head, Old Master Prints, and curator of prints; Kimberly Jones, associate curator of French paintings; Benedict Leca, Andrew W. Mellon curatorial fellow; Michelle Bird and Virginia Sweet Dupuy, assistants, and Trevor Boyd, intern, in the department of French paintings; Deborah Ziska, chief press and public information officer; and Anabeth Guthrie, publicist.

At the Art Institute of Chicago the curators thank our colleagues in various departments. Department of European Painting: Jennifer Paoletti, exhibition coordinator and curatorial research assistant; Adrienne Jeske, collection manager; Tiffany L. Johnson, research assistant; Geri Banik, department secretary; Darren Burge, preparator; Carolyn L. Collins, intern. Department of Prints and Drawings: Suzanne Folds McCullagh, Anne Voght Fuller and Marion Titus Searle Curator of Earlier Prints and Drawings; Mark Pascale, associate curator; Jay Clarke, associate curator; Barbara Hinde, collection manager; Harriet Stratis, paper conservator; Margo McFarland, former associate paper conservator; Kristi Dahm, assistant paper conservator; Cæsar Citraro, conservation technician; Christine Conniff-O'Shea, conservation technician; and interns Dionne Ng and Anthony Gibart. Conservation: Frank Zuccari, executive director of conservation; Faye Wrubel, conservator of paintings; Kristin Lister, conservator of paintings; and Allison Langley, assistant curator of paintings. Director's Office: James Cuno, President and Eloise W. Martin Director; Dorothy Schroeder, associate director for exhibitions and museum administration; Edward W. Horner, Jr., executive vice president for development and public affairs; Lisa Key, vice president for development; Eileen Harakal, vice president for audience development; John Hindman, associate director of public affairs; James N. Wood, former Director and President. Registrar: Mary K. Solt, executive director, museum registration; Tamra Yost, associate registrar, loans and exhibitions. Organizational Giving: Amy Katherine Radick, assistant director, sponsorship. Museum Education: Robert Eskridge, Woman's Board Endowed Executive Director of Museum Education; David Stark, director administration and interpretive media. Publications: Susan F. Rossen, executive director of publications; Amanda W. Freymann, associate director of production; Katherine Reilly, assistant editor, scholarly publications; Annie Feldmeier, photography editor. Graphics: Lyn DelliQuadri, department head, graphic design & communication services; Joe Cochand, senior exhibition designer. Imaging: Chris Gallagher, acting director; Greg Williams, photographer; Lisa Dwyer, color image specialist; Caroline Nutley, production coordinator. Copy Center: Donna Forrest, manager; Christian Serig, assistant manager; Jelena Belrenc, color specialist.

Anonymous lender

Art Gallery of Ontario, Toronto

The Art Institute of Chicago

Ateneum Art Museum, Finnish National
   Gallery, Helsinki

The Baltimore Museum of Art

Boston Public Library, Print Department

Brooklyn Museum

The Cleveland Museum of Art

Consorcio del Patrimonio de Sitges, Museo
   Cau Ferrat

The Corcoran Gallery of Art, Washington, D.C.

The Dixon Gallery and Gardens, Memphis,
   Tennessee

Gail and Richard Elden

The Fine Arts Museums of San Francisco

Fogg Art Museum, Harvard University Art
   Museums, Cambridge, Massachusetts

Galerie Neue Meister, Staatliche Kunstsammlungen Dresden

Galerie Schmit, Paris

Francey and Dr. Martin L. Gecht

The J. Paul Getty Museum, Los Angeles

Alex Hillman Family Foundation

Carleton Holstrom and Mary Beth Kineke

The Jane Voorhees Zimmerli Art Museum,
   Rutgers, The State University of New Jersey

The Kreeger Museum, Washington, D.C.

Kunsthalle Bremen

Los Angeles County Museum of Art

The Metropolitan Museum of Art, New York

Mugrabi Collection

Musée Carnavalet—Histoire de Paris

Musée de Montmartre, Paris

Musée des Augustins, Toulouse

Musée des Beaux-Arts de Lyon

Musée d'Orsay, Paris

Musée Toulouse-Lautrec, Albi

Museu de Arte de São Paulo Assis Chateaubriand, São Paulo, Brazil

Museu Nacional d'Art de Catalunya, Barcelona

Museum of Fine Arts, Boston

National Gallery of Art, Washington

National Gallery of Canada, Ottawa

Northwestern University Library, Evanston,
   Illinois

Ny Carlsberg Glyptotek, Copenhagen

The Henry and Rose Pearlman Foundation, Inc.

Petit Palais, Musée d'Art Moderne Genève

The Phillips Collection, Washington, D.C.

A. Carter Pottash

Private collection, Courtesy Brame &
   Lorenceau, Paris

Private collection, Courtesy of Wildenstein & Co.

Private collection, Courtesy of G.P.S.

Private collections

Museum of Art, Rhode Island School of Design,
   Providence

Rijksmuseum, Amsterdam

Phyllis Rothschild

San Diego Museum of Art

Smith College Museum of Art, Northampton,
   Massachusetts

Solomon R. Guggenheim Museum, New York

State Pushkin Museum of Fine Arts, Moscow

Michael and Judy Steinhardt

Sterling and Francine Clark Art Institute,
   Williamstown, Massachusetts

Tate

Van Gogh Museum, Amsterdam (Vincent
   van Gogh Foundation)

Arthur E. Vershbow

Von der Heydt-Museum, Wuppertal

Wadsworth Atheneum Museum of Art,
   Hartford, Connecticut

Richard Thomson

Toulouse-Lautrec & Montmartre:
Depicting Decadence in Fin-de-Siècle Paris

―――――

The philosophy of vice that he sometimes flaunts with
provocative ostentation nevertheless takes on, because of
the strength of his drawing and the gravity of his
diagnosis, the instructive value of a clinical class in morality.

Gustave Geffroy, *La Justice*, 1893

―――――

The hub of Henri de Toulouse-Lautrec's career was Montmartre. It was on those sloping streets to the north of Paris' metropolitan center that he trained in the studio of Fernand Cormon during the early and mid-1880s. It was in that *quartier* that he had his studios, first in the rue Caulaincourt and then in the rue Frochot. Montmartre was where he made his first artistic friends, initially fellow southerners finding their feet in the capital such as Henri Rachou and François Gauzi, then more radical individuals like Louis Anquetin and Emile Bernard as well as the intense Dutchman Vincent van Gogh. At the cabarets of Montmartre Lautrec learned the vocabularies of innovation and disruption that would underlie much of his art. The Chat Noir's shadow plays taught him the expressive force of the silhouette, while the obstreperously anti-establishment values of its performances and songs alerted him to the younger generation's reading of the decadence of contemporary life and schooled him in a satirical approach to it. At Aristide Bruant's cabaret, the Mirliton, Lautrec made his first contact with a rising "star" of the Montmartre entertainment industry, absorbing the low-life atmosphere and the gritty naturalism used to describe it. It was the stimulus of the complex subcultures of Montmartre that provided the subjects of many of Lautrec's early exhibition paintings. And they in turn led to commissions for posters, images such as *Moulin Rouge: La Goulue* and *Ambassadeurs: Aristide Bruant* (see figs. 10 and 113), which not only made an indelible impact on this new medium, so hitched to the momentum of the modern world, but also gave Lautrec an impressive and lasting reputation.

MONTMARTRE AND THE "DECADENT" REPUBLIC

Lautrec's Montmartre years loosely fit the decade 1885 to 1895, and it is on this span that the present exhibition concentrates.[1] It takes us from Lautrec's emergence as a mature artist after several years of academic training in the teaching ateliers of Léon Bonnat and then Cormon, to the mid-1890s when, with new friends among the Nabi circle of artists and the writers of *La Revue blanche,* Lautrec's work shifted upmarket to the theater and city center bars. It can be argued that 1885–1895 offers the best period of Lautrec's short career. His work was of consistently high quality, he covered his widest range of subjects,

and he was at his most experimental with different media. It is also the phase of his career in which his art engaged most intricately with contemporary society. This was, specifically, Montmartre. To hyperbolize about Lautrec as the quintessential chronicler of the belle époque is to exaggerate. Living in, and taking most of his subjects from, a defined *quartier* of Paris, Lautrec focused his art on its social geography, subcultures, and local economy. But this is not to say that Lautrec approached Montmartre like some systematic sociologist or anthropologist. He was an artist, working by instinct, attracted to what caught his eye. Thus he made particular choices for his work, even developed particular specialities. Lautrec was a social painter, then, but we need to define this further. Thus we will explore the aspects of contemporary society with which Lautrec's work interacted, examine the visual culture of Montmartre, and assess Lautrec's images alongside those of others. This is in contrast to a strictly biographical angle, which might emphasize Lautrec the aristocrat, the handicapped, the alcoholic.[2] The objective here is to explore the modernity of Lautrec and how it was formed by social and cultural circumstances.

Born in 1864, Lautrec lived his formative and professional years during the early decades of the Third Republic. The republic had been born in 1870 from disaster, with the collapse of the preceding regime, the Second Empire of Napoleon III, in the face of German invasion. The new republic was confronted within its first few months with both negotiating a humiliating peace with the now united German Empire and repressing a fratricidal civil war, for the lower-class population of Paris, which had doggedly withstood a siege throughout the bitter winter of 1870–1871, was riled by the new government's conservative complexion and concessions to the Germans. Its insurgent Commune, of which Montmartre had been a center, was fiercely put down by the republic's troops in "Bloody Week" of May 1871, which left some 25,000 Parisians dead (fig. 1). The Third Republic had deep flaws. During the 1870s when Lautrec was a schoolboy, conservative politicians came close to returning France to monarchy. It was only in 1879 that a genuine republican, Jules Grévy, was elected president.

During the 1880s successive governments passed reforms—legalizing trade unions and easing the divorce law, for instance—but the republic was under pressure. On the right the Catholic Church resisted republican attempts to wrest education from its traditional grasp, both sides realizing that their future influence, even survival, depended on their ability to inculcate their own values, whether religious and hierarchical or scientific and egalitarian, in the next generation. In addition, nationalists resented France's ceding of Alsace and much of Lorraine to Germany in 1871, urging an eventual war of revenge and reclamation. On the left socialism took root among the growing populations of France's industrializing cities. Although socialists won seats in parliament, some on the left felt that the pace of reform was too sluggish, the republic insufficiently progressive. Strikes and mass demonstrations proliferated. During the early 1890s anarchists even unleashed a terrorist campaign, which saw a bomb thrown into the Chamber of Deputies and, in 1894, the assassination of President Sadi Carnot, after which harsh repression followed. The Third Republic was embattled, nervous, and corrupt. Grévy himself had departed in 1887 after misdemeanors involving trafficking in honors, while

1892 saw the Panama Scandal, revealing that senior politicians had been bribed to keep the struggling canal project alive.

These shifts and stresses in French social and political life should not be seen as merely the backdrop against which Lautrec's career unfolded. They had direct impact on it. These processes involved the gradual repositioning within French society of two major social groups, women and the urban proletariat, both of which were central to Lautrec's subject matter. The liberalizing of censorship in 1881 was a republican reform that released the shackles of satire, sparking the cabarets, illustrated magazines, and climate of irreverence on which Lautrec's art thrived. Toulouse-Lautrec's generation had grown up under the flawed Third Republic. The artists and writers of his age group, coming into their maturity around 1890, were concerned to take the measure of their contemporary culture. How was this to be done?

By the late 1880s naturalism was the established form of representation favored by the Third Republic. It was legible, "democratic," and scientific, thus suiting the regime's progressive and egalitarian rhetoric. The work of senior artists like Lautrec's teachers fitted this mold by the 1880s, with Bonnat's portraits of dignitaries and even his history paintings especially noted for his detailed scrutiny. Lautrec's early mature works and representations of Montmartre

life were in this idiom. Bonnat's *Madame Kahn* (fig. 2), painted in the year Lautrec was his pupil, may represent a woman of the upper bourgeoisie standing formally, while Lautrec's later *"A la Bastille" (Jeanne Wenz)* (fig. 3) shows the sister of a fellow student seated at a café table rigged up in his studio. But both set the sitters' faces against casually brushed dark brown backgrounds, designed not to detract from the women's direct, strongly lit gaze and palpably modeled presence.

Naturalism was also the mode of representation that suited foreign artists working in Paris, such as the Catalans Ramón Casas and Santiago Rusiñol. Visiting Paris in 1889 for the Exposition Universelle, they too gravitated to Montmartre, with its cheap lodgings and reputation as an artistic *quartier*. Excited as they were by their alien surroundings, their paintings settled into the reassuring aesthetic of accuracy, charting sites such as the church of the Sacré-Coeur, seen under construction above the shanties of the rear slopes of the butte Montmartre, and the garden of the Moulin de la Galette dance hall (figs. 4 and 125). As foreigners, they tended to observe from a distance.

Lautrec's aesthetic had been rooted in the dominant naturalism. His teachers had taught him to study the model unflinchingly. The work of more radical artists, notably Edgar Degas, instructed him in subtle pictorial devices to give greater actuality to the fiction of the image: off-center compositions, the active use of empty space, the figure cut off by the edge of the frame as if it were on the periphery of our field of vision (see fig. 159). But despite Lautrec's deep-seated commitment to art that observed the everyday world and set about finding ways to represent it that paralleled the modern perception of the quotidian, he and others sought to extend the frontiers of naturalism into more expressive territory, to make it sharper and more dangerous.

This creative drive was also linked to wider cultural forces. Lautrec's generation drew attention to, and revelled in, what they construed as society's decadence. Their target, the Third Republic and its bourgeois power base, claimed to be progressive—introducing universal manhood suffrage, enacting social and labor reforms, improving women's rights—but public debate identified recurrent problems. Issues as varied as the French army's abject defeat at the hands of the Germans, the stagnant birth rate,

2
—
Léon Bonnat, *Madame Kahn*,
1882, oil on canvas, 212 x 123 cm.
Musée Bonnat, Bayonne

3
—
Henri de Toulouse-Lautrec,
"A la Bastille" (Jeanne Wenz),
1888, oil on canvas, 72.5 x
49.5 cm. National Gallery of Art,
Washington, Collection
of Mr. and Mrs. Paul Mellon

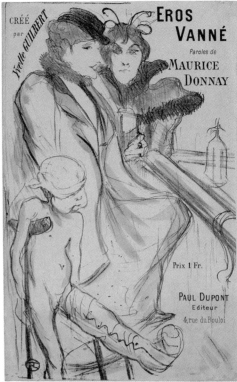

4

Ramón Casas, *The Sacré-Coeur, Montmartre,* c. 1890, oil on canvas, 67 x 55.5 cm. Museu Nacional d'Art de Catalunya, Barcelona

5

Henri de Toulouse-Lautrec, *"Eros vanné,"* 1894, lithograph, heightened in watercolor, 27.5 x 18 cm. Bibliothèque Nationale de France, Paris, Département des Estampes et de la Photographie

and rising alcoholism all seemed to point, in the terms of the social Darwinism so prevalent at the time, to a nation evolving not positively but rather in decadence.

The critique of decadence—drawing attention to society's class divisions, moral corruption, and sexual exploitation—came from various quarters. Conservative forces might use it to condemn modernity in relation to the superior values of the past, while the left used it to promote its own radical agenda.[3] The republic reacted defensively, with moralizing propriety allied to a degree of censorship. This collided with Lautrec's own areas of operation. Songs performed in the cafés-concerts were controlled, Yvette Guilbert being obliged to drop a verse about lesbians from Maurice Donnay's song "Eros vanné" (Clapped-out Cupid), while the song sheet Lautrec designed included that very allusion (fig. 5).[4] In 1896, writing in the establishment *Revue des deux mondes,* Maurice Talmeyr accused contemporary posters of being a corrupting

influence, typically modern and decadent in their feverish commercialism and lack of respect for women, religion, and authority, calling for them to promote more elevated values.[5] In riposte, it was argued that the recent proliferation of the multicolored poster was a lively counter to the regime's stuffiness; hitherto the Parisian street had been "straight, regular, chaste, and republican."[6]

The decadent critique was central to the "Montmartre" culture of cabarets, illustrated periodicals, and popular song within which Lautrec's work developed and to which it contributed. The easing of the censorship laws in 1881 gave scope for the younger generation's perception of the bourgeois republic as corrupt and venal, stuffy and hypocritical. During the early 1880s Montmartre rapidly developed into the locale where such anti-establishment attitudes were stridently voiced. There were a number of reasons why Montmartre, rather than some other *quartier,* nurtured this subculture. Its history of independence counted; it had only become officially incorporated into the administration of Paris in 1860, and its record in the Commune gave it a whiff of danger.[7] Its lower slopes, nearer the city center, already housed the studios of important artists such as Degas, Pierre Puvis de Chavannes, and Gustave Moreau, and alongside the studios was an infrastructure of models, dealers in

6

Adolphe Léon Willette,
Parce Domine, c. 1884, oil on
canvas, 200 x 390 cm. Musée
Carnavalet – Histoire de Paris

artists' materials, and so on. Toward the top of the Montmartre hill, "the butte," rents were cheaper for younger artists because it was a more proletarian district, and the combination of low life and low costs suited Lautrec and his peers. Finally, Montmartre already had its vernacular entertainments: working-class bars and dance halls. And as a porous frontier where there was seepage between the smarter classes of central Paris and the proletariat of the outer suburbs, where the two might meet in the commerce of leisure and prostitution, it was a habitat where the egalitarian rhetoric of the Third Republic came under scrutiny. Class mixture was less an expression of fraternity than nervous, temporary cross-*quartier* tourism, less an expression of equality than evidence of the hypocrisy and exploitation of much social exchange. In any event, Montmartre was the ideal terrain for the development of up-to-the-minute cultural forms.

The cabaret culture, described in detail in Dennis Cate's essay in this catalogue, developed visual vocabularies strongly phrased in decadent terms. Adolphe Willette's decorations for the Chat Noir

cabaret are a case in point. Trained by the celebrated history painter Alexandre Cabanel, Willette adapted his academic training in *Parce Domine*, a large decorative canvas with a multitude of figures pitched in a vertiginous neobaroque torrent (fig. 6). This spate flows between Montmartre, identified by the windmills to the upper right, and downtown Paris, with the Opéra and Notre Dame silhouetted on the horizon. It consists of Montmartrois types, headed by Willette's alter ego, Pierrot: cancan dancers, revelers from a masked ball, prostitutes, the inevitable black cat, and men on the razzle.[8] The crowd is unruly, suffering from a "contagion" or "hysteria," to use the terms borrowed from medicine and psychology, as the discourse of decadence was so wont to do in its analysis of the ailments of modern society.[9] The momentum of this surge of pleasure seekers is downward—it is, literally, decadent—and the moon in the nocturnal sky above takes the form of a skull, a salutary warning. *Parce Domine* was an ironic inversion of the patriotic and rhetorical imagery of the mural paintings commissioned by the Third Republic to decorate its town halls and other public buildings, an irony echoed when Victor Meusy's guide to Montmartre in 1900 suggested that the state itself purchase the subversive painting.[10]

This visual vocabulary was soon raided by artists who worked outside the immediate circles of the cabarets. At the Salon des Indépendants in 1890 Georges Seurat exhibited his large canvas *Chahut* (fig. 7). A complex casting of Montmartrois nightlife into the avant-garde neo-impressionist style, it suited Seurat (who had certainly visited the Chat Noir) to recycle the compositional idea from Willette's stained-glass *Le Veau d'or* (see fig. 34) of the decadent spectacle being conducted.

Of even more vital pictorial importance was the Chat Noir's shadow plays, developed by Henri Rivière, Henry Somm, and others from Japanese prototypes. The subjects of these were various. While some took uplifting themes—such as Rivière's *Marche à l'étoile (Journey Following the Star)* and Caran d'Ache's *L'Epopée (The Epic)*, about the Nativity and Napoleon's grande armée, respectively—others favored decadent subjects, like Louis Morin's *Pierrot pornographe* (1893), set, of course, in Montmartre (fig. 8).[11] The black silhouette that derived from the experience of watching these shadow plays was not just a pictorial convenience, a simple, dramatic dark form. The silhouette was suggestive; it did not describe the whole figure but reduced it, even distorted it. With its lack of exact definition, it expected the viewer to make assumptions about what it defined, to bring into play their knowledge of the shadows.

Thus the silhouette was an ideal pictorial device for the decadent imagination. Anquetin, a close friend of Lautrec's, used it in a large pastel made in 1889 (fig. 9). Although set in central Paris, on the Champs-Elysées, the image is Montmartrois both in its use of the silhouette and in the allusions that it makes about single women with poodles in this particular part of the city: this was the clandestine identification and cruising ground for lesbians.[12] Not everyone looking at Anquetin's pastel—exhibited, it seems, as *Soir (Evening)* at the 1891 Indépendants— would know that, but to do so would require specific inside knowledge of "decadent" codes and behavior. When Lautrec himself came to design his first poster, *Moulin Rouge: La Goulue*, he also turned to the silhouette (fig. 10). The black forms create a dark backdrop to offset the dancer's blonde hair and dotted blouse, but they also characterize the typical spectators. Their smart bonnets and top hats reveal them as bourgeois;

7
—
Georges Seurat, *Chahut*, 1889–1890, oil on canvas, 169 x 139 cm. Kröller-Müller Museum, Otterlo

8
—
Louis Morin, *Décor for the first tableau*, silhouette for the shadow play *Pierrot pornographe*, 1893, zinc, 116 x 114 cm. Musée d'Orsay, Paris

Louis Anquetin, *The Rond-Point of the Champs-Elysées*, 1889, pastel, 153 x 99 cm. Musée départemental du Prieuré, Saint-Germain-en-Laye

Henri de Toulouse-Lautrec, *Moulin Rouge: La Goulue,* 1891, color lithograph, 191 x 117 cm (sheet). The Art Institute of Chicago, Mr. and Mrs. Carter H. Harrison Collection

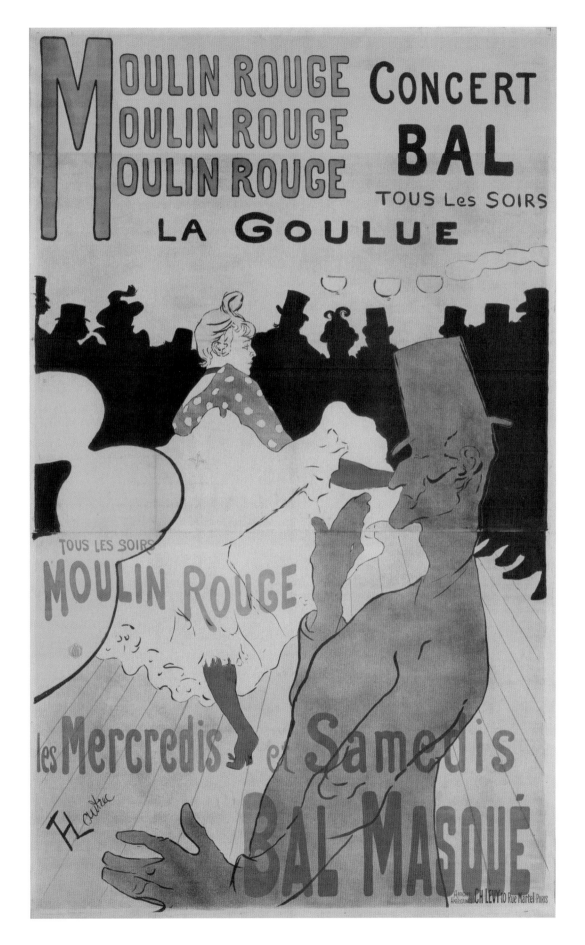

their fictive presence in a dance hall watching a working-class woman dancing provocatively suggests the decadence that the Montmartre entertainment industry so assiduously marketed.

The decadent critique, taken from wider social debate and geared into commercial entertainment—first by the cabaret culture led by the Chat Noir, then by professionally crafted leisure organizations such as the Moulin Rouge—became what typified Montmartre in the eyes of Parisians, French, and foreigners. By the time Pablo Picasso arrived in Paris in 1900, the gambit was a stale one, but the young Spaniard eagerly adopted it. In a self-portrait from his second visit he took on the persona of a smart bourgeois, lining the background with brazenly bare-breasted tarts (fig. 11). It is an image that, with all the hollow confidence of youthful knowledge, proclaims the clichéd Montmartre nostrum that creativity has its roots in decadence.

How might we define Lautrec's relationship with and contributions to this Montmartre culture?

First, it may be useful summarily to map the two trajectories of the subculture and the artist. In simple terms the opening of the Chat Noir in 1882 initiated the vogue for the "cabaret artistique." It was followed by a burgeoning number, typically with their own individual identity, such as Bruant's Mirliton, opened in 1885, or Maxime Lisbonne's Taverne du Bagne. By the later 1880s the dance halls of Montmartre were attracting more and more audiences from outside the *quartier,* and in 1889 Oller and Zidler launched the Moulin Rouge to capitalize on this by presenting a wide range of attractions. Growing activity and increasing investment led to greater media coverage and to still greater momentum within what could now be defined as the Montmartrois entertainment industry.

That momentum is evinced by the rapidity with which the promotional machinery settled on a new "star" and propelled him or her into instant celebrity. Take the case of Yvette Guilbert, a nobody performing in the provincial cafés-concerts of Lyon in the summer of 1889. Yet by December 1890 she was being lauded by the influential journalist Jean Lorrain as a deluxe product: "the *article de Paris* most in fashion."[13] Success led to over-exploitation: a constant appetite for novel and not necessarily better acts, yet more shadow theaters, and cabarets with themes such as Heaven or Hell. But by the mid-1890s momentum and originality were waning. The Moulin Rouge was increasingly a tourist trap; the Chat Noir and the Mirliton both closed their doors in 1897. The lively posters made at the turn of the century by artists such as Jules Grün and Maxime Dethomas (see figs. 95 and 96) were advertising a faded "Montmartre," in Grün's case explicitly, for the foreigner.

For Lautrec's part, despite having arrived in Paris as an art student in 1882, it was not until four years later that we have evidence of his visiting the Chat Noir and beginning the relationship with Bruant that acted as his main portal into the Montmartre culture. By 1886 he had had illustrations published in two of the *quartier*'s periodicals, *Le Courrier français* and *Le Mirliton.* But although the Moulin Rouge seems to have hung some of his paintings from its opening, it was not until two years later, in December 1891, that the dance hall commissioned a poster from him. And for all the intensity of Lautrec's identification of his art with Montmartre in the early 1890s, by mid-decade that had begun to fade, for reasons discussed at the end of this

Jean-François Raffaëlli, *The
Ragpicker,* 1879, oil on wood,
21 x 9 cm. Musée des Beaux-Arts,
Reims

essay. The trajectory of Lautrec's Montmartrois work
does not exactly overlap with that of the entertainment
industry; it was briefer.

THE TYPOLOGY OF MONTMARTRE

In his representations of the varied populations of
Montmartre Lautrec used the standard system of the
type, adapting it acutely to suit his own requirements.
Since at least the seventeenth century the type—the
descriptive schema of the physical attributes and perhaps professional accessories typifying a particular
social grouping—had been common in literature and
the visual arts. In the nineteenth century, as the populations of cities swelled and conurbations became less
easy to "read," the type flourished in journalism, illustration, and photography as a means of identifying
people within social hierarchies, as a means of order-
ing a shifting world. It still flourished at the end of
the century.

An important aspect of the Third Republic's
modernity was its promotion of science as a progressive
means of understanding the world. Since its publication in French in 1862, Darwin's *Origin of Species* had
exerted a significant impact on analyses of how society
was ordered, while the contributions of intellectuals
such as Emile Durkheim, whose *Rules of Sociological Method*
appeared in 1894, made France a leader in the new
science of sociology. The process of categorization that
characterized such scientific thinking deeply marked
the aesthetic of naturalism, in both fiction and the
visual arts. An example of collaboration between those
two forms at this period is the volume *Les Types de Paris,*
published in 1889. Taking types such as the flower
seller and the cobbler, the book combined texts by
naturalist authors such as Guy de Maupassant and
Octave Mirbeau with drawings by Jean-François Raffaëlli. Raffaëlli had made his name during the 1880s
with images of the proletarian and lower middle-class
populations of the Paris suburbs, usually executed in
thin layers of paint that emphasized the graphic quality
of the work, a technique that Lautrec much admired
(fig. 12). At the one-man show Raffaëlli held in 1890
at the Boussod & Valadon gallery, later to be Lautrec's
dealer, the opening exhibits were *Portraits-types de gens du
peuple* and *Portraits-types de petits-bourgeois.*[14] The imagery
of the type was often associated with the lower classes,
and it fascinated, frightened, and offended the bour-

geoisie. Writing in the stolidly bourgeois *Le Monde illustré*
in 1893, the conservative art critic Olivier Merson
dismissed Raffaëlli's work: "I absolutely refuse to recognize as human beings what he offers us as figures."[15]
When Lautrec told his grandmother in December
1886, "I'd like to tell you a little bit about what I'm
doing, but it's so special, so 'outside the law,' Papa
would call me an outsider," he was probably referring
to a combination of factors.[16] All of these—his immer-
sion in the cabaret world as an habitué of Bruant's
Mirliton, his new allegiance to the decadent viewpoint, his adoption of proletarian subjects—divorced
him from the class assumptions of his provincial aristocratic family.

The type was commonly used by artists working
in a variety of media to represent the Parisian, and
often specifically Montmartrois, populations. Théophile-Alexandre Steinlen's large color lithograph
advertising Charles Verneau's poster company, made
in 1896, presented a frieze of types (fig. 13). It combined working-class women—the nanny, the laundress,

15
—
Henri Paul Royer, *A pequena
colina de Montmartre (On the
Slope)*, 1891, oil on canvas,
72.5 x 60 cm. Museu Nacional
de Belas Artes, Rio de Janeiro,
Gift of Conde de Figueredo,
1891

16
—
Henri de Toulouse-Lautrec,
The Laundress, c. 1886,
oil on canvas, 91.4 x 72.4 cm.
Private collection

the maid, and the delivery girl—and male manual
laborers with smartly bonneted bourgeoises and a
paunchy businessman. Pierre Vidal's cover for Georges
Montorgeuil's book *La Vie à Montmartre*, published the
following year to capitalize on an already failing vogue,
depicted an array of types cavorting vertiginously
before the Montmartre skyline: this time the cancan
dancer, the artist, the street girl, the nattily dressed
pimp, and to the right a Bruant-like figure hand-in-
hand with a butch woman (fig. 14).

The type was not only used in such illustrative
forms with a relatively genial tone. It was also a common device in paintings, often intended for public
exhibition. The failure of the Third Republic to resolve *la question sociale*, that complex of issues related to
modern industrial labor such as working hours, insurance, and conditions, was seen as another example
of national decadence. In 1896 the sociologist Alfred
Fouillée published an important article in the *Revue des
deux mondes* entitled "Degeneration?" an analysis of the
state of the nation, which he feared to be in a state
of "reverse Darwinism." Industrial progress, he diagnosed, had disrupted patterns of life, and one of the
results of this was growing vice and alcoholism.[17]

Artists addressing these kinds of problems
in their work often turned to the type. Henri Royer's
On the Slope of 1891 (fig. 15) is a hard-hitting image of
urban poverty: a truculent-looking pubescent girl in
old boots and a grubby dress staring out over her grim
quartier, perhaps even the rear slopes of Montmartre.
The critic of the left-wing newspaper *Le Progrès de l'Est*
imagined that one day this girl would be a beautiful
dancer and would get her revenge for the appalling
conditions of her childhood, implicitly by exploiting
the rich through prostitution.[18] Some five years
before, influenced by the social critique of Aristide
Bruant's songs, Lautrec had launched his career as a
naturalist painter with paintings of types. *The Laundress*,
made about 1886, may have neither the physiognomic
exactitude nor the descriptive setting to the extent of
Royer's picture (fig. 16). But Lautrec suggests, by the
rooftops glimpsed through the window, that this is a
low-rent garret and, by the redhead's distracted gaze,
that she sees something beyond it. Her bony hand,
coarsened by her labors, contrasts with the lithe body
he implies under her cheap clothing. Lautrec seems
to have charged his anonymous type with something of
the longing *Le Progrès de l'Est* imputed to Royer's girl.

Foreign artists in Paris noticed both vice and deprivation as symptoms of France's social problems. At the Salon of 1888 the Finnish artist Eero Järnefelt exhibited *Le Franc, Wine Merchant, Boulevard de Clichy* (fig. 17). The painting represents an *estaminet*, a cheap drinking shop for a working-class clientele. Only a few years later the leftist journalist Henry Leyret reckoned that there were some 25,000 of these in Paris, one per hundred head of population.[19] Järnefelt staffed his scene with two types: the aproned proprietor lighting his pipe; and a down-at-heel man seated at a table with a bottle of cheap wine, a shot of spirits, and a *mazagran* (a hangover cure).[20] The painting operates both as frank naturalism—this is how it is—and as a critique of French society. At the Salon des Indépendants in 1891 Lautrec submitted a very new painting *hors catalogue*. Like Järnefelt's canvas, *A la Mie* operates around types (fig. 18). Lautrec used his friend the champagne merchant and excellent amateur photographer Maurice Guibert to act out a drink-sodden petit-bourgeois,

17

Eero Järnefelt, *Le Franc, Wine Merchant, Boulevard de Clichy*, **1888, oil on canvas, 61 x 74 cm. Ateneum Art Museum, Collection Antell, Finnish National Gallery, Helsinki**

18

Henri de Toulouse-Lautrec, *A la Mie*, **c. 1891, watercolor and gouache on paper mounted on millboard mounted on panel, 53 x 67.9 cm. Museum of Fine Arts, Boston. S.A. Denio Collection, and General Income**

Henri de Toulouse-Lautrec,
Alfred la Guigne, 1894, oil
on cardboard, 65.6 x 50.4 cm.
National Gallery of Art,
Washington, Chester Dale
Collection

posing him with his mistress Mariette Berthaud, who appears as a puffy-faced and swollen-handed woman in worker's clothes. In the fiction of his painting they typify a low-life liaison, cemented by shared alcoholism, in some backstreet *estaminet*. Taking a cue from Bruant, Lautrec's title played with the proletarian slang. "Un mie," an abbreviation for "amie," was a

woman of a lower class. "Un miché à la mie" was slang for a client who dodges paying a prostitute, so Lautrec employed language apt for his types to give the picture a tang of working-class authenticity.[21]

Lautrec's use of types both in his somber-toned naturalistic painting of the mid-1880s and in the more lightly painted and graphic touch of his mature work of the 1890s indicates how important this form of representation remained to him. An outstanding example of Lautrec's later use of types is the painting titled *Alfred la Guigne* (fig. 19). To the public who saw it on exhibition at the Indépendants in 1894, it would have read quite directly as a lower-class bar, the three main characters in which are a blowsy woman in a broad hat and boa, a nattily dressed man, and another woman in a quasi-masculine jacket and tie. Lautrec's fiction invites viewers to use our knowledge, or prejudices, about Parisian low-life to specify those types: probably old-hand prostitute, petty criminal or pimp, and cruising lesbian. "Alfred la Guigne" (Bad Luck Alfred), is the title of a short story in a volume, *La Lutte pour l'amour,* published by Oscar Méténier in 1891. Lautrec's dedication on the painting—"for Méténier after his Alfred la Guigne"—specifies this. The story begins by Alfred losing at cards with his fellow pimps, which he blames on the 13th always being his unlucky day. Tipped off that the police are rounding up prostitutes in the streets between Montmartre and the *grands boulevards,* Alfred goes to look for his girl Louisa and, finding her in the rue Montmartre, sends her back to her lodgings. Relieved at escaping his bad luck, he then goes to a bar. There Alfred pinches "the cheeks of Ernestine Gamahut while whispering in her ear some smutty words. The fat tart laughed." (This could be the moment Lautrec may have loosely used for his painting.) But in the end Alfred falls foul of his *guigne:* on going to Louisa's room in the rue Saint-Sauveur, both are arrested.[22]

Oscar Méténier was an interesting figure. Lautrec may have met him through Bruant's Mirliton. Méténier knew Bruant well and published an extended article on the singer in *La Plume,* also in 1891.[23] Like Bruant, Méténier had a deep knowledge both of proletarian life and its slang. This fascination tied in with both his day job—as a senior civil servant in the Paris Police Commission—and his plays and prose. As early as 1886 Méténier had been acclaimed in decadent circles for his expertise in argot, and his writing used low-life themes as a means of criticizing society.[24] Alfred la Guigne, for instance, condemns bourgeois hypocrisy in using prostitutes and at the same time demanding that they be arrested. This combination of naturalist exactitude, inside knowledge of low-life, and implicit critique of society's decadence brought Méténier's aesthetic close to Lautrec's.

By 1890 Lautrec's art had developed means of expression that articulated a modernity encompassing all these aspects. He had found a thematic topography for his work—Montmartre, with its dance halls, bars, cafés-concerts, and circuses—along with the populations of that habitat. He had inherited and adapted a visual language to represent it: naturalism, with its close observation of the everyday world; and decadence, its offspring, with its more critical slant and its use of exaggeration to articulate this. And he had learned and contributed to a particular phrasing of that language: satire, hard-hitting wit. Essentially Lautrec had honed his gifts as a caricaturist. These were apparently instinctive to him. Perhaps they had been formed by a certain wry detachment in his aristocratic class, or by adolescent resentment at being side-lined by his physical restrictions, or by the high-spirited eccentricities of his family circle.

Whatever their causes, Lautrec's caricatural instincts had been evident from the drawings he had made as an adolescent.[25] They did not abate during his days as an art student. Studios were not just industrious and competitive but also lively places. Prankish insolence toward established senior painters, especially rivals of one's *chef d'atelier,* was common practice. At the Salon of 1884 Puvis de Chavannes exhibited *The Sacred Grove, Beloved of the Arts and Muses* (fig. 20). This was the centerpiece of three mural paintings destined for the stairwell of the Musée des Beaux-Arts in Lyon, France's second city. Representing time-honored cultural forms via allegorical figures and executed in Puvis' characteristic combination of exquisitely poised composition and muted tones, the large painting aptly conveyed the Third Republic's rhetoric about contemporary republicanism's inheritance of the values of the classical past. For art students, particularly those trained in the more naturalistic atmosphere of Cormon's studio, this was pomposity to be pricked. Apparently in a couple of afternoons Lautrec and his fellow students painted a spoof of Puvis' allegory on a similarly grand scale (fig. 21). The painting was evidently teamwork—someone else would surely have brushed in the diminutive figure of Lautrec seen from behind—and it was irreverent. On the left the figure of the Prodigal Son was drafted in from another of Puvis' paintings from 1879 (Bührle Foundation, Zürich) to stare wanly at a painting signed Mackay. This was a reference to a recent dispute between the celebrated French artist Ernest Meissonier and Mrs. John W. Mackay, wife of a Nevada silver magnate, who had initially refused to pay for his portrait of her, which she disliked. (Prevailed upon to concede, she is said to have hung the offending portrait in her lavatory.)[26] On the right of what for Puvis had been a "sacred grove" the Cormon students painted a shambolic file of intruders in modern dress. Among them we can only reliably identify Lautrec and the bearded Maisonneuve, so named by another Cormon student François Gauzi.[27] Nevertheless, the point of this inappropriate gang is that it is illicit—and kept in order by a gendarme. Modernity breaks in on the muses; satirical youth interrupts the rhetoric of the republic. The weapon is wit.

The caricatural element in Lautrec's repertoire was not at the fore in the more directly naturalistic work that he made in the later 1880s, in paintings of types such as *The Laundress* or in portraits like those of Jeanne Wenz, Hélène Vary, or Vincent van Gogh (see figs. 3, 87, 88). These are pictures about scrupulous observation. But from about 1890 onward the caricatural had a very present identity in Lautrec's creative imagination, in his ways of seeing and recording. There were two predominant reasons for this, and again they require us to look out of the studio window, so to speak, into the wider world. The burgeoning of the Montmartre culture after the liberalizing of censorship in 1881 was crucial. Satire and irreverence manifested themselves in forms as diverse as the personæ of cabaret hosts such as Rodolphe Salis and Aristide Bruant: sarcastically polite and bullyingly rude, respectively; the cartoon strips of illustrators such as Steinlen and Willette; the crazy images of the Salon des Incohérents; or the lyrics of Donnay, Alphonse Allais, and Léon Xanrof. It was the voice of the younger generation, a means of taking on the bourgeoisie and the republic.

In addition, there was an increasing perception that modern life was speeding up. This had been a French anxiety for some time, and it was often blamed on "Yankeesme," or American influence. Raoul Ponchon, an habitué of the Chat Noir and contributor to *Le Courrier français*, typified this anxiety in a satirical

20
——

Pierre Puvis de Chavannes, reduced version of *The Sacred Grove, Beloved of the Arts and Muses*, 1884–1889, oil on canvas, 93 x 231 cm. The Art Institute of Chicago, Potter Palmer Collection

21
——

Henri de Toulouse-Lautrec, *Parody of "The Sacred Grove" by Puvis de Chavannes*, 1884, oil on canvas, 172 x 380 cm. The Henry and Rose Pearlman Foundation, Inc.

poem imagining a Paris criss-crossed by trains and trams and with tubes, rails, and wires all over the place: modern technology run riot because Paris must not lag behind Chicago.[28] The 1890s were, after all, the decade in which the telephone and the elevator became ever more common, when the motor car was introduced, and when the Lumière brothers showed the first moving pictures on their *cinématographe*.

By using the methods of caricature—exaggeration, speed, wit, acerbity—Lautrec's art appeared cutting-edge in its handling of modern issues: decadence, nervousness, celebrity. In his painting *Alfred la Guigne* Lautrec's economy of touch, specifically the way in which the main male character's back is left almost blank, is the equivalent to the rapidity of the urban gaze, the pictorial counterpart of taking something in with a momentary glance. (Indeed, Méténier's own plays had a reputation for being short and uncompromising.[29]) Lautrec made certain facial features tell: Alfred's sunken cheekbones, the twisted head and slit eyes of the woman wearing a cravat, the porky nose and pursed lips of the prostitute. Rapid execution and exaggerated features are, of course, quintessential to caricature, and they were two of the main characteristics of Lautrec's mature work. It was typical of his personality—Jane Avril remembered his "witty and mordant banter"—and regularly identified in his work by critics.[30] Reviewing the 1891 Indépendants, where *A la Mie* was shown, Raoul Sertat spoke of how Lautrec's work manifested a "delicate vision, a humorous spirit," while Gustave Geffroy, who knew the artist, wrote of his 1896 one-man show in similar but sharper tones: "In Lautrec there is an innate caricatural sense which it would be a shame to restrain, because it is rich in justified revelations of social pretensions and moral defects."[31]

While such responses to Lautrec's work were commonplace in the early and mid-1890s, the most coherent attempt to categorize it came from a political journalist, not an art critic. In May 1894 a regional newspaper, *La Dépêche de Toulouse,* staged an art exhibition in its offices. The project was the brainchild of the paper's new director, Arthur Huc. His objectives seem to have been to show his provincial readership that the *Dépêche* was open to the new, to support the work of young artists, and, if possible, to develop a taste for contemporary art in the southwest of France, the paper's territory. Huc selected the exhibitors from young

artists, almost all based in Paris, who had made their reputations at the Salon des Indépendants since 1890. Among those invited were a few landscape painters, notably Maxime Maufra and Achille Laugé; members of the Nabis group; Lautrec and friends such as Charles Maurin and Louis Anquetin; and the decorative artist Eugène Grasset. In sum, it was a good spread of recently emerged, innovative artists active in a range of media.[32] Huc needed to explain these unfamiliar names and their work to his provincial readership. He used two articles in the *Dépêche* to do this.[33]

Huc clustered one group of artists—essentially the Nabis: Maurice Denis, Pierre Bonnard, Edouard Vuillard, Paul Ranson, and Ker-Xavier Roussel—under the term "Neo-Traditionists." This was the neologism coined by Denis himself in an article of 1890 when he had defined his and his colleagues' objectives as bringing subject matter into a more equitable relationship with the mark-making processes of painting.[34] If Huc ratified Denis' category by recycling it, he adopted another term for Lautrec, Anquetin, Maurin, Henri-Gabriel Ibels, and Hermann-Paul: these he grouped under the term "Neo-Realists." What linked them, Huc argued, was drawing, the way they would try to catch the "dominant note" of their subject with "a single line, a sure, decisive, rapid, and concise line": in essence a "caricatural procedure."

This tallied with what Lautrec had submitted to the *Dépêche*'s exhibition. He showed two paintings—one of La Goulue (probably the one now in the Museum of Modern Art, New York: fig. 22) and one of a lesbian subject (in all likelihood the one owned by his fellow exhibitor Maurin)—and two posters: *Ambassadeurs: Aristide Bruant* and *Jane Avril* (see figs. 113 and 175). In their varied media these works justified Huc's definition and typified Lautrec's preoccupations: emphatically drawn figures, their characteristics acutely delineated and enhanced by lively but economical brushwork or striking flat color. Huc's arguments were also borne out by the catalogue produced for the exhibition. Each artist submitted a lithograph to accompany the list of their works, and the caricatural was primary in the images of the "Neo-Realists." That term, however, was not of Huc's own invention. Just as he had followed Denis' concept of "Neo-Traditionism," he appropriated "Neo-Realism" from the volume of interviews with literary figures that the journalist Jules Huret had

to keep in touch with the new, and the rapid transmission of ideas through the media.

The intersection of Lautrec's art with other complex patterns of modernity reveals itself in his representation of facial expression and body language. This, I think it can be argued, suggests an awareness of *la nouvelle psychologie*. Since Philippe Pinel at the time of the French Revolution, France had been a pioneer in the treatment of mental illness. This had developed apace under the Third Republic. The regime's progressive, scientific bent gave doctors the opportunity to become celebrities. Jean-Martin Charcot was one who made much of this. Director of the Salpétrière, one of Paris' mental hospitals for women, he staged public demonstrations in the 1870s and 1880s at which he hypnotized patients to explain his theories about the subconsciousness' susceptibility to suggestion.[36] Charcot's clinical practice was supported by modern, visual means. Large drawings by his pupil Dr. Paul Richer charting the stages of hysterical fits illustrated Charcot's lectures and were published in clinical texts by Richer himself.[37]

Other advances were being made at the same time. In 1889, for instance, Dr. Pierre Janet, who used free association to explore the subconscious, first defined psychological analysis.[38] Encouraged by the Third Republic's progressive rhetoric and promoted in the press, thinking about modern society in psychological terms increasingly spread from the clinical to the lay world. The successful novelist Paul Bourget gave his books a diagnostic slant, analyzing modern decadence. His *Physiologie de l'amour moderne* (Physiology of Modern Love), published in 1891, includes "scientific" chapter headings such as "The Therapeutics of Love" and "The Physiology of Physiologists." The pressures and temptations of modern life are blamed for rendering young Parisian men neurotic wrecks.[39] The art world also took on these ideas, with the critic Thiébault-Sisson couching an account of recent decorative art in terms of the "exalted neuroses" brought about by new technology and the accelerating pace of life.[40]

These ideas were current in Lautrec's circle. According to the art critic Arsène Alexandre in the newspaper *Paris* on 23 July 1887, when Maurin needed a model with crazed eyes for a painting of Joan of Arc, he sought one at the Salpétrière.[41] The dancer Jane Avril, a great favorite of Lautrec's around 1892, had

22

Henri de Toulouse-Lautrec, *La Goulue Entering the Moulin Rouge*, 1891–1892, oil on cardboard, 79.4 x 59 cm. The Museum of Modern Art, New York

undertaken for *L'Echo de Paris* and had published in 1891 as *Enquête sur l'évolution littéraire* (Inquiry into Literary Evolution). Huret had used the term "Neo-Realists" to differentiate younger, more cutting, and even satirical writers such as Geffroy, Mirbeau, and Lucien Descaves, from older naturalist novelists like Maupassant and Emile Zola.[35] Like Huret, Huc had an urge to detect "evolutionary" progress that was typical of the "scientific" modernity of the 1890s. His recognition of the caricatural edge to the work of Lautrec and his colleagues, as well as his light-fingered lifting of ideas from a fellow journalist, was characteristic of the period, with its appetite for typologies, its frantic instinct

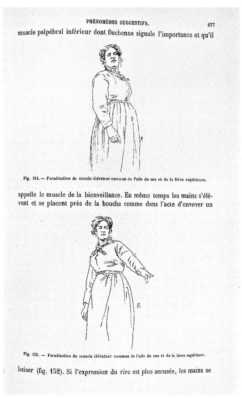

herself been treated there by Charcot for two years. In her memoirs she explained that it was the creative therapy of dancing the *courtille,* in a dress lent her by Charcot's daughter, which cured her.[42] I suspect that this underlies Lautrec's painting of *Jane Avril Dancing* (fig. 23). He divided her image into two halves. Above the waist the primly bloused body seems almost steady, her face placid, introverted, even dreamy. Below the waist a clawlike hand grasps her skirts high, while her spindly legs career and gyrate at what seem to be tortuously distorted angles, not unreminiscent of the physical contortions of hysterical patients in Dr. Richer's drawings. Lautrec's painting makes explicit, with its bifurcation of apparent emotional calm and frantic nervous physicality, how Jane Avril's expressive dancing was a form of therapy.

Another aspect of modernity was the notion that life was more and more fluid and continuous. Scientific developments of various kinds demonstrated, with increasing precision, how things evolved, grew, decayed. That incessant mobility demanded new kinds of representation. If the world was in constant flux, how was this to be understood, explained, and, if possible, pictured? Richer's 1881 study on hysteria, based on his research under Charcot, included a number of drawings, possibly based on photographs, of hysterical women in different manifestations of their symptoms (fig. 24).[43] There is a performative quality to these drawings, the women acting out various states of mind via gesture and expression. The ludic dimension to hysteria was recognized by psychiatrists, Richer naming one manifestation the "clowning" phase. We do not know the extent to which Lautrec knew such material, though he certainly evinced an interest in Richard Krafft-Ebbing's *Psychopathia Sexualis.*[44] Lautrec's images for his *Yvette Guilbert* album may not form a sequence, but they record the *diseuse* making gestures and pulling faces that record specific phases or features of her performance. So too do the photographs that Guilbert herself published in an article in the *Revue illustré* in 1897: "How one becomes a star" (figs. 25 and 26).[45] Both of these sets of images catch the same *artiste* in different expressive modes or states of mind. Because Guilbert's remarkable gifts enabled her to articulate such a medley of moods and actions, it was self-defeating to try to picture her in one. As changeable as one of Charcot or Richer's patients, her personæ required novel means of representa-

Henri de Toulouse-Lautrec,
Yvette Guilbert, plate 10 in the
album *Yvette Guilbert*, 1894,
lithograph in olive green,
38.6 x 38.7 (sheet, folded
approx.) cm. National Gallery
of Art, Washington, New Century
Fund, Gift of Edwin L. Cox—
Ed Cox Foundation

(See also figs. 190 a–q)

tion: in the case of Lautrec's album, a staccato, quasi-sequential process. Such was Lautrec's complex grasp of modernity that he could combine his acute powers of observation and the contemporary instinct for caricature with the malleable performance of the brilliant Montmartre *diseuse* and even the clinical approach of contemporary psychology. All of these were idioms for pictorially registering the flux and momentum of the modern urban experience.

LEAVING MONTMARTRE

During the mid-1890s Montmartre slipped out of Lautrec's focus. This was a gradual process, but the subjects of that particular environment and culture began to lose their appeal for him, although he continued to live in the *quartier* until his death in 1901. The reasons for this shift are various, a combination of the personal, professional, and more broadly social. Lautrec made new friendships. He became close to Thadée Natanson, one of the wealthy proprietors of the innovative periodical *La Revue blanche*, and his wife Misia. They lived in the central rue Saint-Florentin, near the place de la Concorde, and their sophisticated, largely Jewish circle of writers such as Tristan Bernard and Romain Coolus was one motive for Lautrec's gradual shift of interest toward the more highbrow theater.

The Montmartre entertainment industry was also in the process of change. Stars such as Bruant and Guilbert, who had made their names on the outer boulevards, had been drawn to the center of Paris. By 1893 both had enjoyed seasons at the major café-concert the Ambassadeurs on the Champs-Elysées, and in 1892 and 1895, respectively, both had given private performances at soirées held by the prestigious publisher Georges Charpentier, a mark of cultural endorsement. The entertainment entrepreneur Joseph Oller had followed the success of the Moulin Rouge by opening another entertainment complex, the Olympia, in 1893; this time on the central boulevard des Capucines.[46]

As the center of gravity of popular entertainment tipped toward central Paris, Montmartre became tawdrier. Brunois and Camilla Stéphani, for example, were rank imitators of Bruant and Guilbert. Finally, the assassination of President Carnot in 1894, the climax of a period of anarchist terrorism, combined with the progress of the socialists in the 1893 elections

to encourage republicans to rally to the center. This centripetal pull in politics may have had a discouraging effect on the bourgeoisie's fascination with the working classes, itself a trend that had underpinned the Montmartre entertainment industry. By the mid-1890s Lautrec, whose images had in a short span done so much to promote vital aspects of its entertainment culture, had drained Montmartre. On occasion he returned to it, as in the splendidly seedy *At the Rat Mort* (fig. 27), with its suggestive fruits, overblown tart, and faceless client. No doubt he could sense that the *quartier*'s subculture, based as it had been on a critique of contemporary society's decadence, had itself become shallow, exploitative, and decadent.

1. The last major retrospective of Lautrec's whole career was *Toulouse-Lautrec*, held at the Hayward Gallery in London and the Grand Palais in Paris, 1991–1992.

2. For the best recent biography see Frey 1994.

3. Tierstein 2001, 56; Thomson 2004, chap. 1.

4. Condemi 1992, 48; Guilbert 1927, 171–172.

5. Talmeyr 1896, 201–216.

6. Carrère 1893, 495.

7. Willette 1919, 115.

8. Goudeau 1886, 452.

9. Thomson 2004, 84–85.

10. Meusy and Depas 1900, 71.

11. Abelès 2003, 36–47.

12. Thomson 2002, 77–84.

13. "Yvette," *L'Echo de Paris* (22 December 1890), in Lorrain 1932, 221.

14. *Catalogue de Quelques Peintures, Sculptures et Dessin de J.-F. Raffaëlli.* Boussod & Valadon, Paris, May–June 1890, nos. 1–7.

15. Merson 1893, 303.

16. Schimmel ed. 1991, 107, no. 137, 28 December 1886.

17. Fouillée 1896, 816, 818–819.

18. *Le Progrès de l'Est* (6 May 1890), quoted in Nancy 1999, 139.

19. Leyret 1895 (2000 ed.), 8.

20. I am grateful to Robert Herbert for information about the *mazagran*.

21. Littré 1883, 707; and Bruant 1905, 18. For additional analysis of this painting see London and Paris 1991, 23–25; and Murray 1991, 207–210.

22. Méténier 1891a, 29–39.

23. Méténier 1891b, 39–42. A biography followed in 1893.

24. *Petit Bottin,* 1886, 97.

25. For Lautrec's adolescent caricatures see Anne Roquebert in London and Paris 1991, 84–91.

26. Hungerford 1999, 197–198.

27. Gauzi 1954, 116.

28. *Le Journal* (22 March 1897), in Velter 1996, 416–419.

29. Thalasso 1909, 128–129.

30. Avril 1933.

31. Sertat 1891; Gustave Geffroy, "H. de Toulouse-Lautrec," *La Justice* (14 January 1896), in Geffroy 1900, 293.

32. Thomson 1994, 117–123.

33. Huc 1894.

34. Louis 1890, 540–542.

35. Huret 1891.

36. Silverman 1989, chap. 5.

37. Paris 1986, esp. 69–78.

38. Alain Corbin, "Cries and Whispers," in Perrot 1990, 661.

39. Bourget 1891, 81–83; Nye 1993, 95.

40. Thiébault-Sisson 1897, 100.

41. Ward 1996, 189.

42. Avril 1933.

43. Richer 1881, e.g. 676–678.

44. Natanson 1951, 79.

45. Guilbert 1897, 79–81.

46. Anonymous 1893.

Phillip Dennis Cate

The Social Menagerie of Toulouse-Lautrec's Montmartre

———

Both flaneurs and dedicated night owls, they knew nocturnal Paris wonderfully well; going to bed very late, hardly ever before dawn, they spent their nights roaming the city, traversing the capital from one end to the other, in all directions, from Batignolles to Montparnasse, Villette to Neuilly. But it was Montmartre they were crazy about, Montmartre they both loved best, like a little homeland, like a large dwelling where one feels at home.

Victor Joze, *La Ménagerie sociale. L'Homme à femmes,* 1890

———

In the early 1880s Montmartre was a new frontier for an expanding, complex menagerie of artists, writers, musicians, composers, and performers who had forsworn established Paris and the student or Latin Quarter on the Left Bank and had dedicated themselves to being "modern." In fact, the Latin Quarter, famous for its romantic poets and artists of the 1830s, had become briefly revitalized in 1878 with the founding by the young poet Emile Goudeau of the eclectic group of poets, musicians, and artists called the Hydropathes. There was a *pre*-fin-de-siècle tradition, based primarily in the Latin Quarter, of cafés serving as regular gathering places for small groups of artists, writers, and poets with similar æsthetics to discuss and spontaneously perform their work.[1] Yet it was the modern imagination and organizational skills of Goudeau that transformed this kind of casual get-together into a grander scale of group entertainment, collaboration, and self-promotion. Starting in the fall of 1878 and officially existing until the fall of 1881, when Goudeau and his associates changed the group's name to the Hirsutes, the Hydropathes preceded by six years the equivalent, democratic forum for the visual arts: the Société des Artistes Indépendants. Unlike the latter, however, which exhibited annually, the Hydropathes met each Wednesday and Saturday at a Latin Quarter café and published, for nearly a year and a half, their self-promoting bimonthly journal, *L'Hydropathe.* In the aftermath of the greatly destabilizing and demoralizing Franco-Prussian War of 1870–1871, the Hydropathes formalized and intensified the role of the café as the noninstitutional showplace for emerging and recognized members of an increasingly close-knit segment of the Parisian literary-artistic community. As Goudeau stated, behind the foundation of the Hydropathes was *fumisme,* a form of tongue-in-cheek and at times macabre humor based on skepticism and on the debunking of hypocrisy in society.

At that time, two distinct classes were emerging in Paris society: on the one hand, there were the *artists,* on the other, the *bourgeois*....The bourgeois imagined that the artist passed his days in the arms of scantily dressed women and spent his rent money on cocktails, particularly the dreaded absinthe. The artist saw the bourgeois as having no other ideal than his "bourgeoisie," necessarily arid in body and spirit. And these two species of men lived in the same city without knowing one another.... when, by chance, they happened to rub shoulders, they turned away in mutual disdain, the bourgeois murmuring "What a bohemian!" and the artist crying "What a shopkeeper!" And the bourgeois knew nothing of the clubs and cafés of the Left Bank, where the artists gathered.[2]

The Hydropathes included young poet/writers such as Alphonse Allais, Félicien Champsaur, Jules Lévy, Eugène Bataille (alias Sapeck), and Georges Lorin (alias Cabriol), the latter two doubling as illustrators; of composer/performers such as Georges Fragerolle, Maurice Mac-Nab, Maurice Rollinat, and Charles de Sivry; and of artists such as Emile Cohl and Eugène Mesplès; as well as the older poet/caricaturist André Gill. Gill had gained great fame with his unrelenting, one-artist battle against the status quo of the Second Empire and, after 1870, the Third Republic. His caustic satirical illustrations and *portraits-charges*— comic depictions of individuals—in *La Lune* and *L'Eclipse* brought him the respect of liberal republicans and earned him a place, in the minds of the avant-garde, as the successor to Honoré Daumier. Gill was the mentor to many in the new generation of humorist/ illustrators, in particular Cohl, who at the end of the 1870s attended the former's popular soirées at his atelier on the avenue Denfert Rochereau at the top of the boulevard Saint-Michel.

The "terrible year" of 1870–1871—with the defeat of Napoleon III by the Prussians on 4 September, with the immediate establishment of the conservative and fragile government of the Third Republic, with the final surrender of France in March, and with the horrendous massacre in May by the French army of its own citizens in the Paris Commune—was a major line of demarcation between what was often referred to as the "Ancients" or "Antiques" and the "Moderns." Goudeau, a modern, stated that "One felt a bit revolutionary in the clan of the new, of those after the war; it seemed that a moat separated the two perfectly distinct periods."[3] With the fall of the Second Empire, institutional support of the arts had been greatly weak-

ened, leading to a greater degree of artistic independence. The concept of "modern life," extolled first by Baudelaire in 1859, benefited greatly by the disintegration of the Second Empire and by the subsequent psychological, political, and economical changes thrust on French society.[4] Goudeau defined "modernisme" as: "the search for the present moment, for the passing moment at the exclusion of antique legends and medieval recitals."[5] When the Hydropathes, under the leadership of Goudeau, migrated up to Montmartre at the end of 1881 and found their home in Rodolphe Salis' newly opened Chat Noir cabaret, Montmartre began to evolve as the primary theater of modernist activity in Paris at the expense of the Latin Quarter and in conflict with the ancients.

The decades of the 1880s and 1890s were the period in which artists and writers slowly, and not without inward struggles, weaned themselves from their imposed penchants for academic themes and styles. For the most part, the moderns of Montmartre, such as the young Toulouse-Lautrec, committed their art to the representation of their own everyday reality rather than to the ancients' academic emphasis on portraying biblical stories, glorious historical events, or classical allegories. In Paul Adam's 1886 novel *Soi,* the young bride Marthe Grellon, on her honeymoon in Venice, expressed to her writer husband, Luc Polskoff, how refreshing it was for her to be in the old city with its ancient architecture and its rich history. She was shocked when Luc countered her opinion: "He launched into a defense of modernism. He was carried away by his enthusiasm for horse-drawn carriages, for road sweepers, for paved streets after the rain. He declared the Seine and its banks to be the most beautiful spectacle on earth."[6]

From the early part of the century Montmartre had been home to many painters and sculptors, including, among others, Carle Vernet, Théodore Géricault, Paul Garvarni, Georges Michel, Eugène Delacroix, Gustave Moreau, Pierre Puvis de Chavannes, Thomas Couture, Alfred Stevens, Pierre-Auguste Renoir, and Edgar Degas, the last remaining there throughout his life.[7] As Goudeau explained, however, the move of the Hydropathes from the Latin Quarter "was an invasion of these two arts: poetry and music, in the sanctuary of painting, in Montmartre, the land of the plastic arts."[8]

One Hydropathe invader was Félicien Champsaur (b. 1859). In 1882, at the age of twenty-three, he published his first novel, a "roman moderniste" entitled *Dinah Samuel* (fig. 28). In the preface he states: "I have tried to portray a world I knew. If some people recognize themselves, so much the better for them, or so much the worse, for I had the idea, rightly or wrongly, of using features from several people to create a character."[9] Champsaur's long and convoluted tale, some of its autobiographical elements scarcely veiled, drags its readers from the Left Bank of Hydropathian Paris to Montmartre and back again, all the time dropping real names—Goudeau, Sapeck, Emile Cohl, etc.—or pseudonyms of these same and other contemporary artists, writers, and actors. The male protagonist of the story, Patrice Montclar, is loosely based on Champsaur himself, while "Lindor" recalls the poet/illustrator Georges Lorin (Cabriol), "Carolus Zeph" the poet Charles Cros, "the illustrious Pasteck" the *fumiste* Eugène Bataille (Sapeck), and "Albert Max" André Gill.

FÉLICIEN CHAMPSAUR

DINAH SAMUEL

Preface:
LE
MODERNISME

PAUL OLLENDORFF, ÉDITEUR

PARIS

The story is obviously self-referential, but as Champsaur implies in his preface, reality and fantasy often cross lines, and one character may take on the qualities and idiosyncrasies of several real individuals. Thus the main character, Dinah Samuel, is a very popular Jewish actress/sculptor who openly loves both men and women, lives in an exotically decorated home on the border of Montmartre, and is clearly based on Sarah Bernhardt (one of the few female Hydropathes, if, in fact, only honorary). Champsaur's modernist approach to literature, however, was immediately criticized by the press for its naivete and awkwardness:

Poor Félicien! After ten years of hanging around with poets, journalists, illustrators, and second-rate actors, he still doesn't know how to make a book! His is a real ragbag, a strange motley of personal recollections and bits of gossip that have appeared hundreds of times in the press.... In order to spice up this rather stale mixture, he has added a sprinkling of ridiculous verses, slang words, gangster and art vocabulary borrowed from Goncourt, Zola, and Richepin.... Is it necessary to identify any more clearly the actress whose transparent pseudonym serves to advertise the book? If it's true that she sometimes bestowed her favors on him, she's paying for it dearly now. And he needn't imagine he's been clever in giving his fellow journalists such absurd pen names. My goodness, how brilliant to have called Rochefort *Bechefort*, Richepin *Pauvrepin*, Paul Alexis *Paul Corydon*, P. Bourget *P. Courget*, Mme. Adam *Mme. Eve*, etc.[10]

In the preface of the 1889 "definitive edition" of *Dinah Samuel*, the author entitles his preface "Le Modernisme" and explains that "this new term—modernist—which is used routinely today (although without recalling its source or any sense of what it means) is at the heart of the literary battle between romantics and naturalists.... I raise my torch high: modernism ... modernism is not an innovation but a return to realism. In this century, Balzac was the great modern visionary; he saw what was around him; his work is modeled on life."[11] Thus Champsaur's *Dinah Samuel* is an early effort by a member of the young generation of postwar writers and artists, following in the naturalist footsteps of Honoré Balzac, Gustave Flaubert, the de Goncourt brothers, Emile Zola, and J. K. Huysmans, at documenting the social/artistic menagerie of contemporary Paris—but more and more focusing specifically on their own literary artistic community of Montmartre as it became increasingly populated and sophisticated and as it emerged as the primary vortex of avant-garde Parisian activities.

Montmartre, once a commune on the northern outskirts of Paris, was annexed by the city in 1860. It is officially defined by the boulevards de Clichy, de Rochechouart, and de la Chapelle to the south; by the boulevard de Ney to the north; by the avenues de Saint-Ouen and de Clichy to the west, and by the rue d'Aubervilliers to the east. In reality Paris had two Montmartres: "the official Montmartre, classified for administrative purposes as the eighteenth arrondissement;...the other is an arbitrary Montmartre whose limits may change depending on the vogue for certain establishments, but whose center always remains the Butte."[12] Champsaur describes Montmartre in *Dinah Samuel* just at the time that Salis opens his Chat Noir cabaret and attracts the Hydropathes to the butte:

The boundaries [of Montmartre] are, to the south, Notre-Dame de Lorette; to the north, on the hill's other slope, a tavern where people drink on Sundays, the Assassins, whose sign is André Gill's *Le Lapin Agile,* at the intersection of the rue Saint-Vincent and the rue des Saules; to the west, Dinah Samuel's house, at the intersection of the avenue de Villiers and the rue de Charny; and finally, to the east, the rue Rochechouart. The principal landmarks are the Reine Blanche and Boule Noire dance halls, the Elysée-Montmartre, known familiarly as the Présidence, the Fernando circus and its café, the Montmartre theater, the larger of the two Bocks, the Du Caprice brasserie, the Orsel tavern, the Perroquet gris, the nightclub on the rue de la Chaussée-Clignancourt, the Rat Mort and Nouvelle-Athènes cafés, the Grand'Pinte, the Fontaine brasserie, the Des Phocéens brasserie, run by a woman from Marseilles, the Lauer brasserie, on the rue Condorcet, the de la Rochefoucault café, and, of course, the Moulin de la Galette, whose great sails, which have not moved for centuries, tower over Paris and its forest of chimneys, spires, and domes, spreading across the sky and, on Sundays, bestowing their blessing on little girls between fourteen and sixteen, a few of whom will one day own mansions on the avenue de Villiers.[13]

Later, there was the Chat Noir cabaret...in this bizarre land swarmed a host of colorful artists, writers, painters, musicians, sculptors, architects, a few with their own places but most in furnished lodgings, surrounded by the workers of Montmartre, the starchy ladies of the rue Bréda, the retired folk of Batignolles, sprouting up all over the place, like weeds. Montmartre was home to every kind of artist.[14]

LE CHAT NOIR

L'ancien Chat Noir

DESSIN DE HENRI RIVIERE

THE CHAT NOIR AND THE INCOHÉRENTS

In November 1881 Goudeau by chance met Rodolphe Salis, an unsuccessful painter of Swiss origin, at the Grande Pinte cabaret. Founded in 1878, the Grande Pinte was the first in a line of Montmartre "cabarets artistiques" that were decorated in pseudo-Gothic furnishings, expressing the growing nostalgia for France's Rabelaisian past, and that little by little began to acquire and display contemporary art (fig. 29). The Rat Mort, the Café Guerbois, the Bon Bock, and the Nouvelle-Athènes were also popular gathering spots in Montmartre at this time, drawing as customers the impressionists and other artists and intellectuals of their generation. Each place had its own character and attractions. For instance, at five in the evening the Rat Mort, decorated with its distinctive painting of a dead rat by Léon Goupil, "begins to fill up with a special crowd of artists and women enticed in from the street. The women, dressed to the nines and even better, are nobody in particular. The artists are

Messrs. Degas, Pissarro, Manet, Pierre [*sic*] Carrier-Belleuse, Cabaner, Tivoli, Goeneutte, Detouche, Cézanne, Paul Alexis, Métra, and Vallès—in general, the modernists."[15]

It was in a similar atmosphere at the Grande Pinte that Salis, looking for a means to distinguish his soon-to-be-opened, Louis-XIII-style, two-room Chat Noir cabaret at 84 boulevard Rochechouart and to build its clientele, invited Goudeau to develop an alliance between the former's new cabaret and the ex-Hydropathes. This chance meeting at the end of 1881 initiated the highly creative and prolific collaboration at the Chat Noir between the new generation of writers and artists, which quickly expanded beyond the Hydropathes to include such integral participants as the artists Caran d'Ache, Henri Pille, Henry Somm, Henri Rivière, Théophile-Alexandre Steinlen, and Adolphe Willette as well as composer/performers Aristide Bruant, Jules Jouy, Maurice Mac-Nab, and others. Within a short time Salis was

able to gain permission from the local police to install a piano, normally not permitted in such watering spots, and thus added music and song to the Chat Noir's repertoire of poetry readings. In a *fumiste* parody on the Académie française and as a means to attract more clientele, Salis dubbed the Chat Noir's dingy backroom the "Institut" and reserved it for a select group of poets, artists, and other regulars of the cabaret. This strategy made the normally unattractive space in great demand. The front room was for less illustrious customers. In January 1882 Salis began promoting the cabaret with the *Chat Noir* journal: "The Chat Noir is the most extraordinary cabaret in the world. You rub shoulders with the most famous men of Paris, meeting there with foreigners from every country in the globe. Victor Hugo, Emile Zola, Barbey d'Aurevilly, the inseparable Mr. Brisson, and the austere Gambetta talk buddy-to-buddy with Messrs. Gaston Vassy and Gustave Rothschild. People hurry in, people crowd in. It's the greatest success of the age! Come on in!! Come on in!!"[16]

On 8 October 1882 *Le Chat Noir* published as its supplement the one-page, two-sided catalogue for an extremely bizarre exhibition entitled *Arts incohérents,* which included work by artists and, surprisingly enough, by nonartists (fig. 30). The exhibition was organized by the ex-Hydropathe Jules Lévy and held in his tiny Left Bank apartment. Over a period of four hours the display drew two thousand visitors, including Renoir, Edouard Manet, Camille Pissarro, and Richard Wagner. Champsaur reviewed it a week later in the journal *Panurge:* "If you didn't see it, you haven't seen anything. It was extraordinary. Ferdinandus enjoyed enormous success with a painting in relief, *Le Facteur rural* [The Rural Postman]. It really was painting in relief, because the mailman's shoe, a real shoe that had very visibly been worn, vigorously thrust back, protruded from the canvas.... Miss Chabot, a dancer at the Opéra, told me that she had exhibited a landscape on the sole of her ballet slipper. It's so small that I didn't see it."[17]

Lévy's Incohérent exhibitions, illustrated catalogues, and costume balls took place irregularly in Paris and in the provinces for eleven years (1882–1893), with the participation of numerous ex-Hydropathes and members of the Chat Noir such as Allais, Cohl, Rivière, Salis, and Somm. The Incohérents carried the *fumiste* nonsensical, antibourgeois

30

Henri Gray, cover for *Catalogue illustré de l'exposition des arts incohérents* (Paris, 1884), photorelief. The Jane Voorhees Zimmerli Art Museum, New Brunswick, Rutgers, The State University of New Jersey, Herbert D. and Ruth Schimmel Purchase Fund

humor to the extreme, producing extraordinary works of art that predict dada, surrealism, and conceptual art of the twentieth century. Incohérent exhibitions were filled with astonishing works that relied primarily on visual, word-and-image puns, such as Allais' monochromatic 1884 red painting entitled *Tomato Harvest by Apoplectic Cardinals on the Shore of the Red Sea* and Cohl's 1886 portrait *The Assembly Was Hanging on His Lip.*

Nothing was sacred; Sapeck's 1887 illustration of *Mona Lisa Smoking a Pipe* (fig. 31) predates Marcel Duchamp's Mona Lisa with a goatee by thirty years![18] The Incohérents' anarchic form of thumbing one's nose at all things serious is one of the group's greatest legacies to the Montmartre avant-garde mentality of the 1880s and 1890s. In the twentieth century Incohérent *fumisme*'s most able inheritor and practitioner was Duchamp.

In 1882, soon after the Chat Noir opened and the same year that the Incohérents were founded and that Champsaur published *Dinah Samuel*, the eighteen-year-old Toulouse-Lautrec moved to Paris and lived with his father at the Hotel Pérey, just off the fashionable rue du faubourg Saint-Honoré. In March the young artist entered the Montmartre painting studio of the academician Léon Bonnat, where he met the slightly older student Louis Anquetin with whom he formed what was to be a life-long friendship. With the closing of Bonnat's studio in the fall of 1882, Lautrec, Anquetin, and fellow students René Grenier and Henri Rachou moved only a few blocks away to the studio of Fernand Cormon. In May 1884, now ensconced in his own Montmartre apartment, Toulouse-Lautrec ventured down from the butte accompanied by fellow Cormon artists and other young friends to view the official academic Salon of the Société des Artistes Français held at the Palais de l'Industrie. There they came across the immense painting by Puvis de Chavannes entitled *Le Bois Sacré, cher aux arts et aux muses (The Sacred Grove, Beloved of the Arts and Muses)* (see fig. 20). Their response to the allegorical world of Puvis was the equally large *Parody of "The Sacred Grove" by Puvis de Chavannes* (see fig. 21).

Although undoubtedly a group effort, the latter painting was located for a number of years in Toulouse-Lautrec's studio and is primarily his work. The parody pokes fun at Puvis' pastoral scene in several ways. Most important is the replacement of a few of the allegorical muses of art and literature on the right with the depictions of Lautrec with back turned and perhaps urinating, with possibly Anquetin in coveralls, writers Edouard Dujardin with blond beard and Maurice Barrès in top hat, as well as other contemporaries (Anquetin would return the favor by including Lautrec in his own parody, *Meeting of Friends at Bourgueil*, of 1893 [fig. 32]). Modernism à la Champsaur enters Puvis' "Sacred Grove" and illuminates the emerging social menagerie of Toulouse-Lautrec's Montmartre. Indeed, much of Lautrec's art throughout his relatively short career is self-referential; he, in the manner of Alfred Hitchcock in the next century and in the new medium of film, often inserted himself into his images of contemporary Montmartre and Paris.

Lautrec's *Parody* is quite prescient. In addition to himself, the three other apparently recognizable Montmartre personalities—Anquetin, Barrès, and Dujardin—played significant roles in fin-de-siècle Paris, although the future fame of each was not predictable in 1884. Toulouse-Lautrec eventually developed as an accomplished and innovative poster artist and prolific printmaker whose art, often modernist in style, focused on the depiction of modern life. Anquetin, Barrès, and Dujardin were each fundamental participants in major ideological movements in France: Anquetin led the way in the development of cloisonism/synthetism in painting; Dujardin was a

33

Théophile-Alexandre Steinlen, *"Les Quat'Pattes,"* cover of *Le Mirliton* (9 June 1893), color photorelief depicting Maurice Barrès looking at Lautrec's poster of Aristide Bruant. The Jane Voorhees Zimmerli Art Museum, New Brunswick, Rutgers, The State University of New Jersey, Herbert D. and Ruth Schimmel Purchase Fund

prime mover in literary symbolism; and Barrès formulated the arguments for a type of insidious right-wing nationalism based on anti-Semitism and revenge against Germany. During the 1890s Lautrec, Dujardin, and Barrès, each at separate times, were featured as the personality of the week in issues of *Les Hommes d'aujourd'hui* (see fig. 33).[19] Begun in 1878 by Champsaur and Gill, the journal for twenty years irregularly published a four-page, chatty biographical sketch of a noted representative of the arts or politics; the cover of each issue was illustrated in color with a portrait of the featured personality drawn by Gill and, after 1881, by artists such as Cohl, Lautrec, Maximilien Luce, and Georges Seurat, among others.

In 1886 Anquetin is depicted in two Lautrec paintings of Montmartre subjects: *The Quadrille of the Louis XIII Chair at the Elysée Montmartre* and *The Refrain of the Louis XIII Chair at the Mirliton* (see figs. 49 and 50). Both were displayed on walls in Aristide Bruant's Mirliton cabaret, and the former is reproduced on the cover of the 29 December 1886 issue of Bruant's journal *Le Mirliton*. From 1884 to 1887 Anquetin's painting style evolved from impressionism and pointillism to "cloisonism," a word coined by his Rouen Lycée schoolmate, Dujardin. Within a few years he retreated to a more conservative, old master style of painting and replaced much of his interest in contemporary subject matter with a greater commitment to allegorical themes. Yet the artist's bold abstract cloisonist style predates that of Emile Bernard and Paul Gauguin at Pont Aven and permits him a place of honor and influence in fin-de-siècle avant-garde art.

From November 1886 to November 1888 the poet and critic Dujardin along with Téodor de Wyzewa and Félix Fénéon published the influential symbolist journal *La Revue indépendante*, which had its first office at Dujardin's and Wyzewa's apartment at 79 rue Blanche in Montmartre. Among Dujardin's other literary achievements, he founded the *Revue wagnérienne* in 1885 and published his canonical symbolist novel *Les Lauriers sont coupés* in 1887, which is credited as being the first stream-of-consciousness novel and which directly influenced James Joyce's use of this monologue writing style.[20] Lautrec's 1892 poster for the Divan Japonais poses Dujardin next to the popular café-concert dancer Jane Avril just above the cabaret's orchestra pit during a performance by singer Yvette Guilbert.

But of the three colleagues Lautrec apparently depicted in the *Parody*, it was Barrès who had the greatest, if not the most positive, impact on the world. By transforming his initial philosophy of the cult of the individual Self *(Moi)* into a cult of the collective Self—the State—in the 1890s, Barrès argued for protecting French historical national identity, unity, and security from foreign influences at all costs. The xenophobic nationalism he professed urged revenge against Germany, declared capitalists and Jews anti-French, equated the military with the French nation, and as such placed the military above the law at the expense of truth and of individual rights. The litmus test for Barrès' proto-Fascist, anti-Semitic thesis came at the end of the century with the Dreyfus Affair. Although he lost this battle, Barrès helped set the stage for the conflict that would consume the world in the second quarter of the twentieth century.[21]

MONEY AND PREJUDICE

With Salis' entrepreneurial direction and the fresh talent of writers, artists, and performers, the Chat Noir and its journal became popular and financial successes. By June 1885 Salis was able to move his operation into a three-floor, elaborately furnished *hôtellerie* on the rue Victor Massé (the old rue Laval), just a few blocks from the old Chat Noir that Bruant took over and renamed the Mirliton.

That same year Goudeau published his first novel, *La Vache enragée*. The protagonist, Tignassou, is a down-and-out, failed poet who is just at the point of committing suicide when he demonstrates life-saving entrepreneurial skills in a small business transaction with the factory owner Roumégous. The latter advises Tignassou to take his newly earned money and to play the stock market, but he also tells him: "Always remember that it [the stock market] is a game of the Jews, the circumcised, the 'youddi!' A Christian must have a better target: put the money earned into industry, agriculture, or the arts." Tignassou was not a Parisian by birth. He, like Goudeau and many other artists and writers of their generation, came to Paris from the provinces seeking fame and wealth. But what they often experienced was "la vache enragée," taken from the idiomatic expression "manger de la vache enragée," which means to be deprived or destitute, to have a hard time of it. A basic initiation right of artists

and poets was to suffer for one's art. On the other hand, the taste of success brought with it the danger of giving up one's ideals by succumbing to the temptation to worship *le veau d'or* (the Golden Calf), to seek only wealth and, thus, in the language of stereotypes, to play the "game of the Jews."

This dilemma of choosing between art and wealth, between good and evil, is an underlying theme of the writer/poet Goudeau and of his artist counterpart Adolphe Willette. Both were very critical of Montmartre's rapid transition from its innocent bohemian origins, with the opening of Salis' first, rather modest Chat Noir, into a flamboyant, commercial world of entertainment, as exemplified by the cabaret's relocation in 1885 to deluxe accommodations. Goudeau even withdrew his association with the Chat Noir in 1885 because of Salis' apparent sellout to wealth:

Far from wanting to detach itself from the rest of the universe, Montmartre made conciliatory advances to Paris; having sufficiently disdained wealth, it turned to the Golden Calf and offered it ironic, licentious, and waggish excuses, but the Golden Calf, who is very cunning, pretended to accept these jests as candid speech, and it came to Montmartre to cover the Artists, the Poets, the Musicians, with jingling écus, with daily bread, even with tuxedos and polished shoes.

The cabarets saw at their formerly modest doors the throng of emblazoned carriages and the wealthiest bankers contributing their subsidy to this former Golgotha transformed into Gotha of the silly songs.[22]

In 1896 and 1897 Goudeau and Willette copublished the only two issues of *La Vache enragée* magazine to appear, which announced and described the two elaborate artists' processions or parades that took place in Montmartre in those years. Toulouse-Lautrec's 1896 poster *La Vache enragée* promoted that year's publication. The two events were organized to raise funds for impoverished artists—those suffering from "la vache enragée." But the parades, with their lavish floats and costumes, were a financial failure and were thus discontinued.

Willette's six-panel stained-glass window *Le Veau d'or* (fig. 34) was, ironically, commissioned in 1885 by Salis for the new Chat Noir. It is an allegorical narrative criticizing Montmartre's fall from innocence and, as such, is a pictorial equivalent to Goudeau's *La Vache enragée*, published that same year. In the far left panel a young, nude female holding a lily, a symbol

34

Fernand Fau after Adolphe Léon
Willette, stained-glass window,
Le Veau d'or, 1885, stencil-
colored photorelief in John
Grand Carteret's *Raphaël et
Gambrinus* (Paris, 1886), 89.
The Jane Voorhees Zimmerli
Art Museum, New Brunswick,
Rutgers, The State University
of New Jersey, Herbert D. and
Ruth Schimmel Purchase Fund

of virtue, seems to be in shock as a black cat (the Chat Noir) jumps onto her shoulder threatening her innocence (*virginitas*) by pushing her in the direction of the Golden Calf. In the next panel, in front of a background of factories, workers have broken their chains of capitalistic oppression. They rush toward the third panel, where the Golden Calf has the word "Israel" inscribed on its halo, behind which are the guillotine and the Bourse, the Paris stock exchange. (Below the Golden Calf is a man only partly visible because of the leading of the glass, but in a new rendition of the stained glass, which Willette created in 1895 as the cover design for Paul Delmet's *Nouvelles Chansons,* a man with Semitic features is depicted wearing a fez and holding a coffer of coins.) Below the impassive Golden Calf, a young mother strangles her newborn child as a sacrifice to avarice. At the top of the fourth panel, representing idyllic Montmartre, are the Moulin de la Galette and the word *Poésie;* just below stands a winged Saint Joan of Arc whose legs are clutched by an impoverished *cul-de-jatte,* or legless cripple, as if seeking salva-

tion or a cure. The fifth panel shows a man of wealth and power with royal crown and robe, a Herod-like capitalist king or banker behind whom is seen a perspective view of a Haussmann boulevard. In the sixth and final panel the hand of the capitalist king grasps a ballet dancer, a femme fatale like Salomé, who holds in her left hand a platter with the decapitated head of a man. The head, however, is that of Pierrot, Willette's alter ego, not that of John the Baptist. The dancer has given herself to the man of wealth in exchange for the death of the personification of innocence (Pierrot). Death in the guise of a skeleton conducts this moral narrative and an orchestra of partially hidden musicians.

The early anti-Semitism found in the work of Goudeau and Willette preceded by at least five years the development of Barrès' similar views and appeared on the eve of Edouard Drumont's *La France juive* (1886). This seminal publication laid the foundation for the future arguments of the xenophobic, anti-Semitic nationalism of Barrès and of other anti-Dreyfusards of the 1890s. While Goudeau's book may have been expressing a kind of generic form of popular anti-Semitism of the time, Willette over the next few years raised the decibel of the rhetoric to an extremely high pitch, with hateful, anti-Jewish illustrations in *Le Courrier français* and in the short-lived journal *Le Pierrot* (1888–1889), which Willette copublished with Goudeau in the artist's Montmartre apartment at 79 boulevard Rochechouart, across the street from Bruant's Mirliton cabaret.[23]

In September 1879 Drumont founded the Ligue nationale antisémitique de France. Its headquarters were at 48 rue Lepic just below the Moulin de la Galette dance hall. Willette's anti-Semitic activities culminated that fall in his stand as the Ligue's candidate for the legislative assembly. His election campaign was based totally on a nationalist, anti-Semitic platform. Although he lost the election, his art played an important role in reinforcing negative cultural and pictorial stereotypes of Jews such as the ugly, fat, hook-nosed banker or capitalist: "A million! She cried, joyously. That's nice ... it's awfully decent of you! ...

Starting to rise she wrapped her naked arms around the neck of the baron. And, as her lips, in straining toward the mouth of the old man, found an obstacle in his large Semitic hooked nose, it was there that she planted a kiss."[24] So speaks Alice Lamay, the demimonde star of Victor Joze's 1892 novel *Reine de joie*.[25] Alice is depicted by Lautrec in his poster for the book at the very moment she learns that her new protector, the wealthy financier Baron Rozenfeld, has bought her a mansion on the avenue de la Bois de Boulogne.

In 1890 Joze, a young naturalist writer, initiated investigations into what he referred to as the "social menagerie" of contemporary Paris. His emphasis was on the titillating aspects of the lives of the literary-artistic avant-garde, of which he was a member and which was centered by this time primarily in Montmartre. *Reine de joie. Moeurs du demi monde* (*Queen of Joy: Manners of the Demi Monde*) (fig. 35) is the third book in Joze's series "La Ménagerie sociale," which, as he stated, "would be a faithful account of things seen and sensations felt by myself, and not a rehash based

35

Pierre Bonnard, front and back covers for Victor Joze's *Reine de joie* (Paris, 1892), color lithograph. The Jane Voorhees Zimmerli Art Museum, New Brunswick, Rutgers, The State University of New Jersey

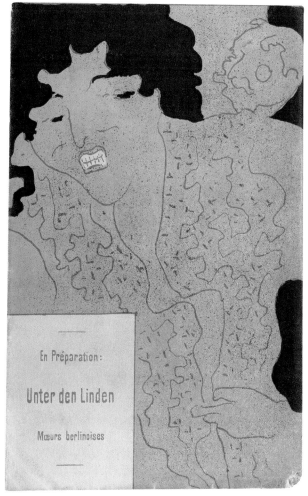

on other people's accounts."[26] Inspired by the writings of Balzac, Flaubert, the de Goncourts, and Zola, and much in the manner of Champsaur's 1882 novel *Dinah Samuel,* Joze began his series of "naturalist sketches" and "Parisian novels" with *Lever de Rideau (Raise the Curtain),* a collection of provocative short stories.[27] This was followed the same year by *L'Homme à femmes (The Ladies' Man),* for which Seurat designed the cover illustration (fig. 36). The "ladies' man," a writer/journalist named Charles de Montfort, is most likely modeled on Joze himself, while his friend Georges Legrand, "an impressionist painter of outstanding talent," has been identified as Seurat by Richard Thomson.[28] Thomson also points out that some characters are real-life associates of Joze, such as the realist writers Paul Alexis and Oscar Méténier, while others, such as the symbolist writers Dujardin and Wyzewa, are only thinly disguised.

Georges Seurat, cover for Victor Joze's *L'Homme à femmes* (Paris, 1890), photorelief. The Jane Voorhees Zimmerli Art Museum, New Brunswick, Rutgers, The State University of New Jersey

L'Homme à femmes relates a year in the life of de Montfort as he experiences the love of five women of decidedly different backgrounds, including Alice Lamay, in different degrees of seriousness. In fact, *Reine de joie* is the sequel to *L'Homme à femmes.* In both books much of the action takes place in Montmartre. De Montfort (Joze) and Legrand (Seurat) are flaneurs who love Montmartre "like a little homeland, like a large dwelling where one feels at home." And while making the rounds of Paris nightlife, Alice, the "Queen of Joy," and her friends stop by the Jardin de Paris dance hall where "La Goulue is applauded like a queen, and Nina-Sauterelle, Clair-de-lune, Georgette-la-Vadrouille are sure of a great evening. Valentin-le-Désossé, though as serious as ever, deigns to smile at the tarts who greet him.... The band plays a wild quadrille, the audience presses forward to get a better look at the legs and raised skirts. La Goulue, lifting her skirts, shows onlookers her bottom draped in a pair of transparent knickers. It's the high point of the modern cancan."[29]

At the entrance of the second Chat Noir a yellow-and-black sign welcomed potential patrons not only with a tongue-in-cheek, modern/antique exegesis of four political leaders of the Third Republic (President Jules Grévy and ministers Charles de Freycinet, Allain-Targé, and Charles Floquet) and two of the Roman Empire but also with the admonition to "be modern": "Passerby, stop! This building by the will of Destiny, under the protectorate of Jules Grévy, Freycinet, and Allain-Targé being archontes, Floquet tétrarque, and Gragnon, chief archer, was consecrated to the Muses and to joy, under the auspices of the *Chat Noir.* Passerby, be modern!"[30] Once inside, Salis, with *fumiste* sarcasm, would berate his clients:

Foolish bourgeois fellows, who listen to me with the astonished eyes of a cat doing its business in the dust or a cow gazing at a passing train, drink my too-good beer for which I don't charge you enough, or I'll throw you out!...Notorious imbeciles that you are, empty your pockets; you'll get your money's worth, and for the first time in my life I shan't be ungrateful! For I'll give you as many kicks in the backside as it takes to make you into intelligent people....In the meantime, drink, 'nunc est bibendum'! So that Montmartre, capital of this Paris of which you are the pudendum, so that Montmartre, I say, shines like the beacon of the Eiffel Tower, the capital's phallus, just as the Chat Noir is the brain and the Moulin de la Galette the soul! Amen. Waiter, beer![31]

Henri Rivière, *The Shadow Theater at the Chat Noir*, c. 1888, pen, ink, and gouache, 20.5 x 20 cm. The Jane Voorhees Zimmerli Art Museum, New Brunswick, Rutgers, The State University of New Jersey, Mindy and Ramon Tublitz Purchase Fund

37

Our national theater, the old art of Molière, Corneille, and Racine, has at last achieved a formula that will bring it new life.... Go hang yourself, Zola! The revolution whose apostle you claimed to be has taken place without you, worlds away from the vulgarities of your naturalism, in the realm of fantasy and dreams, in the pictorial theater anticipated by Somm and recently presented by Rivière in its definitive form in *The Temptation of Saint Anthony*, which far outdoes the splendors of *L'Epopée* [*The Epic*, by Caran d'Ache], acclaimed last year by all of Paris.[32]

The plays produced at the Chat Noir varied from outright *fumiste* humor, such as Somm's *Le Fils de l'eunuque* (1887), to the mix of realism and fantasy found in Rivière's *Temptation of Saint Anthony*, to the serious symbolist, religious play *La Marche à l'étoile* (*Journey Following the Star*) (1890) by Rivière and Georges Fragerolle. Rivière's intricate productions required the participation of twelve mechanics and many of his friends and colleagues as script writers, singers, musicians, and technical assistants. Rivière described his invention and how he obtained his extraordinary Japanese-inspired visual effects to Paul Eudel, the author of a book on traditional shadow theater plays, during a performance of the production of *Phryné*:

I employ no projections. The oxyhydric light I use burns as an open flame, without a reflector, about three meters from the screen.... Before striking the screen the light passes through three cagelike structures, composed of frames and grooves. Thus imprisoned, it has to go through this tunnel before illuminating the screen.

In the first light box can be slid thirty glass sheets, each of a single color. This gives me an initial palette from which, depending on the distance, I select particular tones.

The second box, also designed to hold thirty glass sheets, is used to portray the skies, landscapes, and accessories. By combining these plates with the preceding ones and maneuvering them in different directions, I obtain remarkable shadings: dawns, sunsets, moonrises, delicate mists, and movements of the sea.

The third box, higher than the others to accommodate the spread of the light, contains the backgrounds, zinc cutouts set in small frames. It serves to create dense silhouettes: fogs, mountain ranges fading into the horizon....

Reflections on water are created by superimposing gauze fabric, the rain is represented with sand, snow with spotted muslin, lightning with nitrated paper that we set alight and throw. We obtain the movement of the sea with our hands, onto which we attach little fins, of varying shapes; by direct superimposition, we simulate the swell of the waves.

SUCCESS OF THE SHADOW

Regardless of the complaints of commercialism by Goudeau, Willette, and others, the Chat Noir offered much to the artistic environment of Paris. Perhaps its most important and influential contribution was the sophisticated shadow theater at the cabaret in 1886 by the artists Henri Rivière and Henry Somm (fig. 37). The shadow theater became the greatest realization of the cabaret's exhortation to "be modern." It began by expanding on the theatrical possibilities of the small puppet theater that Georges Auriol and Somm had set up at the Chat Noir the previous year. By the end of 1887, with *La Tentation de Saint Antoine* (*The Temptation of Saint Anthony*), Rivière had transformed the traditional, simple silhouette shadow play normally performed in France as domestic, family entertainment into an elaborate, technically complicated theater production, which included all the future components of cinema: movement, color, sound (instruments and voice):

38

Henri Rivière, *The Sky*, illustration in Rivière's shadow theater album *La Tentation de Saint Antoine*, 1888, stencil-colored photorelief. The Jane Voorhees Zimmerli Art Museum, New Brunswick, Rutgers, The State University of New Jersey, Norma B. Bartman Purchase Fund

39

Interior of the Chat Noir cabaret with (left to right) Jan Rictus, Rodolphe Salis, Louise France, and Henri Rivière; illustration in *Le Figaro illustré* (June 1896), 113, photorelief. The Jane Voorhees Zimmerli Art Museum, New Brunswick, Rutgers, The State University of New Jersey

EUDEL: . . . It requires a year of painstaking art work and over 25,000 francs to achieve an ensemble of effects that delights the public for barely a moment![33]

Rivière controlled the quality of each performance. He was "the soul, the driving force. Everywhere at once, at the light, on the stage, on the catwalks, at the percussion instruments, he saw everything, supervised everything, directed everything. Regardless of whether it was his own play or someone else's, not a single detail escaped him."[34]

The Temptation of Saint Anthony has forty scenes:

As the curtain rises, Saint Anthony is at prayer in the midst of an austere and lonely landscape. The saint's prayer is so fervent, so absorbing and lengthy, that the hours pass and he remains in his ecstatic state; begun at first light, the invocation lasts into the night, allowing a spider the time to spin its web between two rocks behind the holy man. But all of a sudden the devil appears, a devil in priest's clothing, quintessentially modern, conjuring the troubling visions of wealth and glory offered to the saint by Paris, the great city, whose red silhouette stands out against the background landscape, expanding until it is swallowed entirely. And so begins Saint Anthony's journey. We seem him visit Les Halles, where he is exposed to the temptation of gluttony, the Stock Exchange, where he is offered riches and the power of a ministerial position (a suggestion of Sadi Carnot). The scene and its disturbing mysteries pass before the saint's astonished

eyes; then come the depths of the ocean and its hidden riches, after, the immensity of the heavens — a most remarkable tableau for which H. Jouard, theater director, the most important of Henri Rivière's collaborators, has had the patience to reconstruct the celestial chart, with its countless stars and various heavenly bodies.[35]

The æsthetics of the Chat Noir shadow theater — in particular the flat silhouettes and subtle color variations (fig. 38) — resonated with the nascent modernist concerns of Lautrec, Anquetin, Bernard, Gauguin, and especially with the future Nabis: Pierre Bonnard, Edouard Vuillard, Félix Vallotton, and Henri-Gabriel Ibels, who lived and/or worked in Montmartre. For more than ten years Rivière's innovative shadow theater produced more than forty plays. It was the cabaret's star attraction, and during the 1890s Salis shadow theater company toured throughout France and other parts of the world. It was widely imitated at other cabarets artistiques in Montmartre, and in 1897 it directly inspired the shadow theater at the Quatre Gats cabaret in Barcelona that was created by Ramón Casas and Miguel Utrillo and frequented by the young Pablo Picasso.

In the fall of 1893 the Chat Noir opened its new season of shadow plays with a renovated and enlarged theater (fig. 39): "On the walls, the panels of Jules Chéret, the color prints of Rivière, Louis Morin, Lautrec, Auriol."[36] In addition to Willette's *Le Veau d'or*, the stained-glass window in the front, the façade was elaborately decorated by Eugène Grasset with two fifteenth-century-style lanterns and an enormous heraldic, bronze black cat surrounded by golden sunbursts. Over the entrance was Willette's bronze *Black Cat on a Half Moon*. On the ground floor was a large plaster cast of Houdon's nude *Diana*. On the walls of stairwells and of rooms throughout the cabaret were an assortment of antiquities, Japanese masks, portraits by Antonio de la Gandara, and many of the original drawings for the *Le Chat Noir* by Auriol, Rivière, Salis, Steinlen, Somm, Caran d'Ache, and other artists. In the Salle des Fêtes was a group of forty-five drawings, including work by Degas, Lautrec, Camille and Lucien Pissarro, Claude Monet, and Théophile-Pierre Wagner, the enigmatic friend of Seurat and Paul Signac. The Salle des Fêtes housed the shadow theater and accommodated 150 guests.

Grasset's redesign of the façade of the theater framed the screen along the bottom and sides with a painted frieze of cats. Hanging over the center was a large plaster head of a black cat, above which hung eight monochromatic, Japanese-inspired masks by Grasset representing the major Chat Noir personalities: Salis (yellow), Tinchant (green), Mac-Nab (gray), Caran d'Ache (off-white), Steinlen (blue), Rivière (red), Somm (scarlet), and Willette (a "Pierrot" white). At the top was the Chat Noir's motto: "Montjoye et Montmartre!" The Salle des Fêtes also contained two of Willette's designs for the old Chat Noir: *Parce Domine*, the large allegorical painting of the death of Pierrot (see fig. 6); and the oil on canvas study for Willette's stained-glass *Virgin with a Cat* or *Green Virgin* (see fig. 97). In addition to many drawings, Steinlen was represented by his three-meter-wide mural, *Apotheosis of Cats* (see fig. 99). In fact, because of the quantity and variety of art in the Chat Noir, it was considered by many of its habitués "the Louvre of Montmartre."[37]

In the spring of 1887 André Antoine founded the Théâtre Libre, with its office at 96 rue Blanche. As an experimental theater, the Théâtre Libre (1887–1896) broke with the stilted, dramatic repertoire of traditional French theater by producing naturalist plays based on novels by Zola, the de Goncourts, Paul Alexis, and others, and it introduced the work of foreign authors such as the Norwegians Björnstjerne Björnson and Henrik Ibsen.

The eclectic avant-garde activities of the Théâtre Libre were complemented by the symbolist plays performed by the Théâtre de l'Oeuvre at its various rented sites in and around Montmartre.[38] Founded in 1893 by Aurélien Lugné-Poe, Camille Mauclair, and Edouard Vuillard, the Théâtre de l'Oeuvre is probably best remembered for Alfred Jarry's December 1896 production of *Ubu Roi* (fig. 40). The groundbreaking play's *fumiste*, scatological script, amoral premise of avarice and war, and marionette-like performances by noted actors in effect announced the advent of the theater of the absurd. The stage set and masks (Jarry preferred that the actors disguise their human appearance, movements, and voices to suggest that of puppets) were designed and painted by Bonnard, Jarry, Toulouse-Lautrec, Vuillard, Paul Ranson, and Paul Sérusier. Claude Terrasse, the brother-in-law of Bonnard, composed the music; Fermin Germier played the part of Ubu, while Louise France, the Montmartroise comedienne of the Théâtre Libre and the Grand Guignol, was Mère Ubu. Throughout their existence both the Théâtre Libre and Théâtre de l'Oeuvre commissioned many of the local Montmartre artists—Anquetin, Auriol, Bonnard, Ibels, Rivière, Signac, Toulouse-Lautrec, Vuillard, Willette, and others—to illustrate the covers of their playbills and to design stage sets. In fact, the presence of the Théâtre Libre and Théâtre de l'Oeuvre energized and expanded the collaborative, experimental environment of the Chat Noir, which had initially attracted artists, writers, and performers to Montmartre.

Before his death in 1907 Jarry was able to direct two other productions of *Ubu Roi*, both of them puppet shows that took place in makeshift theaters in Montmartre. The first ran for five weeks in early 1898 at the Théâtre des Pantins. It was a brief collaboration among Bonnard, Jarry, Terrasse, and the writers Franc-Nohain and A. F. Hérold, which led to the pup-

40

Alfred Jarry, *Ubu Roi*, program for Le Théâtre des Pantins, December 1897, lithograph. The Jane Voorhees Zimmerli Art Museum, New Brunswick, Rutgers, The State University of New Jersey, David A. and Mildred H. Morse Art Acquisition Fund

pet performance of several Jarryesque plays at Terrasse's apartment on the "rue Ballu, at the end of a courtyard, on the second floor, a minuscule theater holding a handful of people [fifty].... The hall is small, but pleasingly decorated by Edouard Vuillard with pyrotechnics of superb colors, and by Bonnard with black and gray silhouettes drawn with great virtuosity."[39] Beginning on the evening of 27 November 1901, Jarry directed a total of sixty-four marionette performances of *Ubu Roi* at the Quat'z'Arts cabaret, 62 boulevard de Clichy. It was a reduced, two-act version of the original five-act play and was adapted specifically to Quat'z'Arts by including within a humorous prologue the character of François Trombert, the owner of the cabaret.

Francisque Sarcey, the well-known writer and often-feared theater critic for *Le Temps* and other journals, lived in Montmartre on the rue Douai. He was an early supporter of the Hydropathes, and soon after he met Salis, at the time of the opening of the Chat Noir, the latter dubbed him "our uncle Sarcey." It was an affectionate title that stuck with the critic until his death in 1899. In a sense Sarcey became a kind of mascot for the Chat Noir and the Montmartre artists' community: throughout the last two decades of the century his image appears frequently and incidentally in illustrations for journals and books and in prints and posters (fig. 41). More problematic for the critic was the confusion caused by Alphonse Allais when

he signed Sarcey's name to articles that he, Allais, had written for *Le Chat Noir* and other publications, beginning in 1886 and for the next ten years, appropriating Sarcey's writing style.[40] Many writers and illustrators regularly used pseudonyms: Goudeau at times signed himself "A'Kempis," while Toulouse-Lautrec and Steinlen at early stages of their careers signed their published illustrations "Tréclau" (reversing the two syllables in "Lautrec") and "Petit Pierre" (the German *Steinlen* means "petit pierre" in French, or "little stone"). But the false "Sarcey" act is an example of a sustained *fumiste* performance.

Similarly, Elie Calmé (which translates "he is drugged") was a fictive character created as an alter ego or persona of the illustrator Henry Somm.[41] Calmé existed from the late 1870s until the death of Somm in 1907. Calmé was a make-believe personality, like Duchamp's Rose Sélevy or Max Ernst's Lop Lop, which for years fooled many of Somm's friends and colleagues. Both Rodolphe Salis and the *Chat Noir* artist Georges Tiret-Bognet knew the true identity of Calmé (fig. 42). In fact, Tiret-Bognet was with Somm at a café on the place Clichy in the late 1870s when this alter ego was first created. Somm revitalized Calmé at the Chat Noir in 1885 when the poets Henri Beauclair and Gabriel Vicaire published their parody on decadent poetry entitled *Les Déliquescences. Poèmes décadents d'Adoré Floupette.*[42] Inspired by the fact that Adoré Floupette was a figment of the two poets' imaginations, Somm made Calmé another of the numerous sustained *fumiste* activities at the Chat Noir. When Somm entered the cabaret, Salis would announce that "Elie Calmé was here earlier; he left a note for you," or when a new customer came to the Chat Noir, Somm, Salis, or someone else who knew the secret would inform customers that the new customer was Elie Calmé, thus maintaining the deception and ambiguity for years. Somm never publically admitted that Calmé was only an invention.

Allais' Sarcey and Somm's Calmé are examples of the confusion between fact and fiction, true and false, past and present, that Montmartre artists and writers imposed on themselves and on their art as a means of separating themselves from the bourgeois establishment and, perhaps, as a *fumiste* way to deal with an ever-more complicated and ambiguous world. In *Le Chat Noir*, for instance, all kinds of make-believe situations were elaborately reported as fact, including

the premature death of Salis or the siege of Montmartre by Léon Gambetta, the republican hero of
the 1870–1871 siege of Paris.[43] The *Chat-Noir Guide*
published in 1888 is a detailed factual description of
the interior decoration of the Chat Noir—its spaces,
its furnishings, and the art on its walls—and as such
is essential as a record of the contents of the cabaret.
But the credibility of the guide can easily be ques-
tioned on reading the many bizarre, annotated prov-
enances for the items listed. In one example Willette's
painting for the *Green Virgin* is described as follows:
"This painting was intended for the queen of Belgium's bathroom, but a malicious hand snatched
it from the artist's studio before it was finished. It
was thought to be lost forever, when, in 1885, it was
discovered in the possession of the publisher Kiste-
mæckers, who restored it to the Chat Noir for the
sum of 3,500 francs."[44] The existence and location of
the items listed in the *Guide* are, however, corroborated
by the auction catalogue of the "Collection du Chat
Noir," which took place in 1898 after Salis' death
the previous year.[45]

STAGING THE SHOCKING

The erection of the Eiffel Tower in 1889 for the
Exposition Universelle added a new—and almost immediately an internationally recognized—architectural
symbol to the skyline of Paris. Up to this point in
history Notre Dame, the Arc de Triomphe, and the
Panthéon had been the primary structural icons of
the city. Yet, as Salis claimed, the Chat Noir was the
"brain of Paris," and the Moulin de la Galette was
the city's "soul." The latter was a colorful but notorious
working-class dance hall, perched atop the butte
Montmartre and identified from afar by its two flank-
ing old windmills, and it became the first architectural
symbol of bohemian Montmartre. To reach it at
night from either the first or the second Chat Noir
could be dangerous. The steep, badly lit climb from
the boulevard Rochechouart up crooked narrow
streets to the intersection of rue Girardon and
rue Lepic was difficult, and the dance hall attracted
prostitutes, pimps, and thieves to the area.

The iconography of Montmartre expanded at
the end of the 1880s, as the scaffold-enclosed Sacré-
Cœur slowly emerged in the east at the highest point
on the butte and the newly built Moulin Rouge opened

in 1889 at the bottom of the hill on the place Blanche.
The construction of Sacré-Cœur was authorized in
1873 by the conservative Third Republic as official
penitence for France's defeat in the 1870–1871 war.
Located at one of the epicenters of the brutally quelled
Paris Commune, however, this mammoth symbol of
religion and right-wing nationalism was the antithesis
of the social and artistic freedom professed by the
Montmartre community.

The Moulin Rouge could not be seen from
a distance; it was only visible as one entered the place
Blanche. Yet, as depicted in the shadow theater play
Pierrot pornographe, it made a visual and psychological
connection with the windmills of the Moulin de la
Galette above it (fig. 43). The Moulin Rouge—like the
older Elysée-Montmartre dance hall, located two doors
down from the original Chat Noir (and the Casino de
Paris that would open in 1891 at 15 rue de Clichy)—
catered to an upscale clientele and promoted a degree
of uninhibited sexuality, as suggested by Lautrec's
poster. The Moulin de la Galette charged each couple
eighty centimes per dance, whereas the Moulin Rouge
charged each customer, male or female, a high entrance fee of two to three francs just to watch the titillating performances of the *chahut* or cancan by the
exotically named professional dancers who had previ-
ously performed at the Elysée-Montmartre and
the Jardin de Paris: dancers such as La Goulue, Valentin le Désossé, La Tonkinoise, La Môme-Cri-Cri,
La Sauterelle, Reine-des-Prés, Rayon-d'or, L'Etoile-
Filante, and Fin-de-Siècle. Joze's description in
Reine de joie of the high-kicking cancan is confirmed
by the following observation: "It's then that one sees

whether they are really blondes or brunettes, these daughters of Eve who, just like many socialites, have adopted the stupid mania of coloring their hair with mixtures which give it incredible colors! The old English ladies and the young misses wrapped up in warm furs even in the middle of summer and who sit always in the front row in order to better ascertain the immorality of French dances, cover their faces when it's over, and then utter their properly indignant 'Shockings.'"[46] Thus, although the Moulin de la Galette served as the landmark, literally representing the height of bohemian Paris, the Moulin Rouge served as the symbol of its fin-de-siècle decadence.

When François Trombert established the Quat'z'Arts cabaret in 1893, with its "revue Chatnoiresque," the ex-Incohérent Abel Trouchet created its stained-glass window and promotional poster. Goudeau, Willette, and the young artist Auguste Roedel were the force behind the Quat'z'Arts' organization of Montmartre's two *La Vache enragée* artists' processions in 1896 and 1897. The walls of the Quat'z'Arts were filled with art: "[Charles] Léandre and Guirand

de Scévola are profusely present here with admirable caricatures, portraits, or sketches of artists and actors [fig. 44]. They hang alongside Willette, Roedel, Redon, Pelez, E. Vincent, Toulouse-Lautrec, Markous, Brunner, Cohl, etc.... Among them a portrait by Guirand of Louise France in the role of Frochard in *Deux Orphelines* and another of the same by Chahine are two notably strange masterpieces."[47]

A number of the Quat'z'Arts' habitués— including the actress Louise France of *Ubu Roi* fame (fig. 45), the poster artists Jules Grün and Auguste Roedel, the poet/writers Edmond Teulet and Charles Quinel, and the singer Yon Lug—for ten years, off and on, took turns serving as "editors" of the cabaret's ephemeral journal *Le Mur*. In fact, *Le Mur* was not a printed journal. It was a sort of Happening in which childlike drawings, poems, edited newspaper clippings, collective serial stories, similar to the "exquisite corpse" medium of the surrealists, were pinned to the wall of the cabaret. Continuing the practice of the Hydropathes, the Incohérents, and the Chat Noir, much of the material was self-referential and filled with in-house puns, sexual innuendoes, and scatological jokes. But even more relevant to the Montmartre spirit of subterfuge is the fact that signatures were constantly forged and the authorship of artwork falsified, creating an ongoing tension between truth and fiction. Drawings signed "Ibels" and "Vallotton" and imitative of those artists' works are, in reality, false. *Le Mur*, like Allais' Sarcey, was a ten-year performance of *fumiste* deception. This is not surprising, for many of the players from the earlier groups, including Allais, Goudeau, Willette, and Charles de Sivry, were regular participants or spectators at Quat'z'Arts in the 1890s, along with a new generation of *fumistes*. The cabaret served as a crucial link between the creative and rebellious generation following the Franco-Prussian War and the artists and writers who came to maturity during the decade prior to the First World War. Quat'z'Arts permitted the transmission of Montmartre's radical but often ephemeral art, à la *Le Mur* and *Ubu Roi*, to a new avant-garde that included Duchamp, Picasso, and Guillaume Apollinaire.

At the time of the 1900 Paris Exposition Universelle, promoters of Montmartre boasted that the butte and its surroundings offered more than forty places of entertainment—cabarets, cafés-concerts, balls, music halls, theaters, circuses—two and a half times the number described around two decades

earlier by Champsaur in *Dinah Samuel*.[48] In 1884, as a candidate from Montmartre for the legislative election, Rodolphe Salis ran on the audacious platform to separate Montmartre from Paris. His campaign poster rhetorically stated: "WHAT IS MONTMARTRE? NOTHING! WHAT SHOULD IT BE? EVERYTHING!" It then went on to proclaim: "MONTMARTRE IS THE CRADLE OF HUMANITY. MONTMARTRE IS THE CENTER OF THE WORLD." Although Salis' claims for Montmartre's cultural hegemony were premature in 1884, by the end of the century, with nearly two decades of intense participation by the numerous and diverse personalities that constituted *la ménagerie sociale* of Henri de Toulouse-Lautrec, those assertions had a real validity.

1. Raymond de Casteras, *Avant le Chat Noir. Les Hydropathes* (Paris, 1945), 35–45.

2. Fernand Weyl, "Le Chat Noir," *Revue d'art dramatique* (April 1897): 26–27.

3. Goudeau 1888, 11.

4. Johnathan Mayne, trans. and ed., *The Painter of Modern Life and Other Essays by Charles Baudelaire* (London, 1965), xviii.

5. Goudeau 1888, 52.

6. Paul Adam, *Soi* (Paris, 1886), 97.

7. Philippe Jullian, *Montmartre* (New York, 1977).

8. Goudeau 1888, 259.

9. Félicien Champsaur, *Dinah Samuel* (Paris, 1882), ii [hereafter Champsaur 1882a].

10. *Le Livre* (10 July 1882): 440.

11. Champsaur 1882a, iii, vii, xxvii.

12. Meusy and Depas 1900, 9.

13. As Champsaur was writing his novel in 1881, Degas included in the impressionist exhibition his realist wax sculpture of *The Fourteen-Year-Old Dancer*, which J.K. Huysmans referred to as a "terrible reality" in *L'Art moderne* (Paris, 1883), 226.

14. Champsaur 1882a, 248–249.

15. Félicien Champsaur, "Le Rat Mort," *La Presse parisienne* (2 April 1882): 2.

16. *Le Chat Noir* (8 April 1882).

17. Félicien Champsaur, "Courrier de Paris," *Panurge*, no. 2 (8 October 1882): 2.

18. For all these examples and more see New Brunswick 1996.

19. *Les Hommes d'aujourd'hui*, no. 340 (c. 1889), with a cover portrait of Barrès by an unidentified artist; no. 388 (n.d.), with a portrait by Anquetin; no. 460 (1898), with a cover portrait of Toulouse-Lautrec by Cohl.

20. Halpern 1988, 194.

21. For the evolution of Barrès' social/political philosophy see Zeev Sternhell, *Maurice Barrès. La France entre nationalisme et fascisme* (Paris, 2000).

22. Emile Goudeau in Meusy and Depas 1900, 7–8.

23. See Phillip Dennis Cate, Norman Kleeblatt, et al., *The Dreyfus Affair* (Berkeley, 1987), 67–68.

24. As translated in Gale B. Murray, "Toulouse-Lautrec's Illustrations for Victor Joze and Georges Clemenceau and Their Relationship to French Anti-Semitism of the 1890s," in Linda Nochlin and Tamar Garb, eds., *The Jew in the Text: Modernity and the Contruction of Identity* (London, 1995), 60.

25. Victor Joze, *Reine de joie* (Paris, 1892), 159.

26. Victor Joze, *L'Homme à femmes* (Paris, 1890), vii–viii.

27. Victor Joze, *Lever de Rideau* (Paris, 1890).

28. Thomson 1985, 214.

29. Joze 1892, 84–85.

30. As quoted in Paul Eudel, "L'Auberge du Chat Noir," *La Lecture illustrée* (1897): 242.

31. As quoted in Darzens 1889, 112–113.

32. Edouard Norès, "La Tentation de Saint Antoine," *Les Premières illustrées* (28 December 1887), 173.

33. Paul Eudel, *Le Théâtre du Chat Noir* [1895?], 573.

34. Norès 1887, 179.

35. Norès 1887, 180–181.

36. Georges Auriol, "Le Théâtre au Chat-Noir," *Revue encyclopédique* (February 1894): 2.

37. Eudel 1897, 365.

38. Washington 1998.

39. *L'Echo de Paris* (1 April 1898), as quoted in Francis Bouvet, *Bonnard: The Complete Graphic Work* (New York, 1981), cat. 46.

40. François Caradec, *Alphonse Allais* (Paris, 1994), 260–270.

41. The information on Elie Calmé derives from an unpublished letter in the collection of the Zimmerli Art Museum written by Tiret-Bognet to "Mon cher Paul" soon after the death of Henry Somm. "Paul" is most likely Paul Eudel, an intimate and chronicler of the Chat Noir.

42. Henri Beauclair and Gabriel Vicaire, *Les Déliquescences. Poèmes décadents d'Adoré Floupette* (Paris 1885).

43. *Le Chat Noir* (1 April 1882), 1.

44. *Le Chat-Noir Guide* [1887?], 53.

45. *Catalogue de la collection du Chat Noir* (Paris, 1898), 4.

46. Maurice Delsol, *Paris-Cythère* (Paris, [1896?]), 148.

47. Jacques Ferny, "Le Cabaret des Quat'z'Arts," *Les Chansonniers de Montmartre* (special issue, 1906), n.p.

48. Meusy and Depas 1900, 107–109.

Mary Weaver Chapin

Toulouse-Lautrec & the Culture of Celebrity

———

The queens of the quadrille, the monarchy of the
chahut are embodied in the personalities of La Goulue
and Grille-d'Egout. They command more attention
than the utterances of the president.

Abel Hamel, "Chronique parisienne," *La Vie Moderne*, 1886

———

By the time Henri de Toulouse-Lautrec arrived in Montmartre in the 1880s, the lust for celebrity—both to achieve and to behold it—had reached a feverish pitch. Once the province of rulers, politicians, and great men, celebrity was now an equal-opportunity venture, open to all classes of entertainers, courtesans, dandies, artists, and writers. Esteemed ancestry or heroic deeds no longer defined the modern star; instead the ability to generate publicity, shock society, and remain in the coveted limelight were the new keys to success. In 1886, when the scandalous cancan dancers La Goulue (the Glutton) and Grille-d'Egout (Sewer Grating) were said to attract more attention than the president, it signaled a sea change in the cult of personality.[1]

Toulouse-Lautrec was the most acute observer and promoter of the luminaries of Montmartre. He was fascinated by the larger-than-life personalities who performed there and by the spectacle of their public and private lives. Lautrec's keen eye, expert draftsmanship, and intuitive understanding of the new rules of celebrity helped him craft unique images to promote his favorite stars and further their careers. By choosing and befriending a few particular entertainment personalities of Montmartre, he created an important synergy between their work and his. Thus by the end of the century he not only had contributed to the fame of these stars but had become one himself. In the process he helped elevate the cult of celebrity to new heights.

To understand Lautrec's contribution to the intersecting worlds of art, publicity, and celebrity, it is useful to consider the wider changes in society that inspired the fin-de-siècle obsession with public personalities. It is also important to try to recapture the novelty of the situation; contemporary American life, steeped as it is in visual culture, popular entertainment, and movie-star politicians, has normalized the condition of celebrity to the point of banality. Trappings that we take for granted—photography, color posters, entertainment magazines, high art and low, biographies of stars (in other words, mass media)—were bold innovations that helped create and fuel the culture of celebrity that survives and indeed thrives to this day. Once we appreciate the broader changes, Lautrec's specific contribution comes into sharp relief.

The trend that vaulted cancan dancers like La Goulue and Grille-d'Egout into the pantheon of Parisian celebrity was part of several larger shifts that destabilized modern life and made way for new icons. Perhaps the most important change was the unprecedented surge in population around 1850, when peasants and rural workers flocked to the capital. Uprooted from their native villages and confronted with the fast-paced life of the metropolis—a city of strangers—the new city-dwellers lost some of their older beliefs. By 1870 nearly two million people crowded into Paris, more than twice the number that had populated the city just forty years before.[2] Beginning in 1852, Paris underwent a physical transformation as well. Napoleon III and his prefect of the Seine, Baron Georges Haussmann, instituted a massive municipal reconstruction to accommodate the swelling population, to add sewer systems, modern markets, and improved street lighting, and to prevent insurrection. The controversial project destroyed the medieval character of the capital and displaced hundreds of thousands of people, yet it also gave Paris the wide boulevards, open parks, and harmonious architecture that define it today.

Haussmann's *grands boulevards* established thoroughfares between major points of interest and facilitated transportation and communication. But they also served another vital purpose: as a stage for daily life. Department stores, restaurants, stylish shops, and entertainments such as the café-concert lined the boulevards, creating a virtual catwalk for the chic and up-to-date. Life became a spectacle in which Parisians tried to decode subtle and shifting clues in status, wealth, and fashion. Ready-made clothing available at the new department stores further confused the boundaries between aristocratic women in their couture designs and *cocottes* (prostitutes), who initially copied the dress of these "honest" women, then began to replace them as the new trendsetters in fashion.[3] Courtesans, businessmen, entertainers, shop assistants, milliners, politicians, and the elites of society all came into contact in the bustling city, slowly breaking down rigid class divisions and blurring the lines of identity. Private life grew increasingly public, as even contemporary guidebooks noted: "We need publicity, daylight, the street, the cabaret, the café, the restaurant.... We like to *pose,* to make a spectacle of ourselves, to have a public, a *gallery,* witnesses to our life."[4]

It is not surprising that this new society—enamored of ostentation, focused on public display, and increasingly democratic and intermingled—found new heroes to worship that embodied this age. A shift occurred away from fame (that is, renown earned by heroic actions or outstanding character) toward celebrity, the condition of being a well-known personality.[5] Unlike fame, which suggested enduring value, individual accomplishment, and lasting prestige, celebrity was subject to general approval and, as such, was often fleeting and capricious. Whereas fame was based on integrity and inner qualities, celebrity glorified the surface and outer appearance. Thus an actress more beautiful than talented, a fashionable courtesan, an outrageous writer, or a scandalous cancan dancer from the lowest echelon of society could rise to unprecedented heights.

The first wave of celebrity culture depended on these upheavals in society and demographics in the years before Toulouse-Lautrec's birth in 1864. The entertainment world was undergoing important changes at this time as well. The number of pleasure establishments in Paris and the amount of revenue they generated increased exponentially in the second half of the nineteenth century. The café-concert, a forerunner of the music hall that featured singing and vaudeville acts, was another key entertainment that would become a prime source for new celebrities. It first gained a foothold as a new urban spectacle in the 1840s and 1850s and was firmly rooted as a Paris institution by the 1860s.

Café-concert and dance hall performers occupied a special place within this new arena of display and celebrity. Their rise to prominence was greatly aided by an ever larger arsenal of publicity tools, foremost among them photography. Photographs of the stars were first circulated in the popular *carte de visite* format soon after A.A.E. Disdéri patented the process in 1854.[6] Beginning with likenesses of statesmen, rulers, and other notables, by the 1870s the *carte de visite* craze had expanded to include all manner of entertainers, from the loftiest *tragédiennes* to the lowliest café-concert personalities. Theatergoers collected these images and pasted them into private albums alongside photographs of family and friends, setting up a composite of the familial and the famous, mingling side by side. Beginning in the 1850s, these celebrity portraits appeared in the streets as well, when

46

Anonymous, *Grand Concert du Cadran*, n.d., color lithograph, 82.5 x 61 cm. Musée de la publicité, Paris

47

Jules Chéret, *Concert des Ambassadeurs*, 1881, color lithograph, 125 x 88 cm. Musée de la publicité, Paris

merchants placed photographs of actresses in their storefronts as a means of attracting attention for both their businesses and the performers, a symbiotic relationship that served both parties well.[7]

Photography alone, however, was not enough to establish and maintain a star's reputation. Biographies, then autobiographies, were a new and potent source of fuel for the publicity machine. Since at least the beginning of the nineteenth century biographical sketches of actors and actresses from the traditional theater had been published. Yet as the culture of celebrity intensified around midcentury, biographies of individual performers became more commonplace, and some audacious entertainers produced book-length autobiographies. Rigolboche, the first star of the cancan, and Thérésa, the preeminent diva of the café-concert, both published their memoirs in the 1860s. Gossipy and wide-ranging, these books kept the stars' names before audiences while serving up a healthy dose of mythmaking. As ordinary as this may sound to us today, it was shocking then for a performer from the lower rungs of the entertainment world to consider herself a subject worthy of personal memoirs.[8] Nonetheless, these publications (many written with the help of journalists) were hugely popular, and many went through multiple editions and printings, attesting to the public's appetite for such fare.[9] By the fin de siècle the celebrity biography was no longer an anomaly but a necessity, and it was central to Toulouse-Lautrec's Montmartre.

Another important trend was the proliferation of entertainment posters, which emerged in tandem with the dance halls and cafés-concerts that they advertised beginning in the 1860s.[10] These early posters were more informative than alluring. Most employed text-heavy designs that emphasized the venue rather than the performers. Some listed entertainers by name in small print, but the primary purpose of these early *affiches* (posters) was to inform viewers of the features of the magnificent concert hall, as in the case of an anonymous poster for the Grand Concert du Cadran (fig. 46).

As particular performers gained celebrity and became bigger attractions than the locations at which they appeared, poster designers responded. Prime examples can be seen in the work of Jules Chéret, the influential "father of the poster," who opened his first printing house in Paris in 1866.[11] Chéret's innovations in color printing and his imaginative designs based on the rococo revival revolutionized the entertainment poster, brought colorful *affiches* to the hoardings and Morris columns throughout Paris, and increased the exposure of numerous stars of the day. In an 1881 design for the Ambassadeurs café-concert Chéret included twenty-one small, labeled cameo portraits of performers arranged around two playful putti (fig. 47). Although Chéret's poster placed greater emphasis on the entertainers than the venues, the tiny portraits did little to convey the unique aspects of individuals, nor did they suggest the powerful lure of celebrity that Lautrec would capture so well just ten years later. Nonetheless, Chéret's role should not be underestimated; his designs initiated an artistic appreciation for this commercial medium, which would reach a pinnacle in the work of Toulouse-Lautrec.

TOULOUSE-LAUTREC AND THE CELEBRITIES OF MONTMARTRE

When Toulouse-Lautrec settled in Montmartre in 1882 to begin his artistic career, the emergent celebrity culture stood poised for a second wave of intense fascination. Major demographic shifts, the growth of the entertainment industry, and publicity tools such as photographs, biographies, autobiographies, and posters formed the basis for this development. The rise of Montmartre as a pleasure center (discussed by Dennis Cate in the preceding essay) and the increasingly intertwined worlds of fine art and consumerism contributed to a surge in celebrity worship. Lautrec arrived at a decisive moment, with his dazzling hybrid creations of art and publicity.

One of the most significant changes to foster the culture of celebrity was the relaxation of censorship laws in July 1881 that had kept newspapers and journals under strict control. Publishing of all varieties skyrocketed, including journals that focused on specific venues, ranging from state-sponsored theaters near the Opéra to luxurious cafés-concerts in central Paris and seedy cabarets perched on the slopes of Montmartre. Gillotage, a form of relief printing developed in the 1850s, allowed these journals to incorporate illustrations into their pages and further disseminate visual information about the stars and entertainment of "the butte." Some enterprising impresarios did not wait to win attention in the press but produced their

Tous les Clients sont des Cochons !...

own publications: Rodolphe Salis, founder of the Chat Noir cabaret artistique, and Aristide Bruant, star and owner of the Mirliton, each published eponymous journals for their cabarets that served as brilliant publicity organs, not only for their business establishments but for their entertainers as well (fig. 48).

Toulouse-Lautrec's first introduction to the luminaries of Montmartre probably came through such periodicals. *Le Courrier français,* founded by Jules Roques in 1884 and among the most influential of these journals at the fin de siècle, devoted itself to the divertissements of Montmartre. Significantly, Roques came from the advertising and entertainment industries rather than publishing or journalism, and he was keenly attuned to the publicity value of his journal.[12] Featuring reviews, notices, interviews, and lithographs by Montmartrois artists, *Le Courrier français* both mirrored and stoked public interest in the celebrities of the dance hall, cabaret, and café-concert. It also provided an alternative forum for young artists—Lautrec's first published images appeared in this journal in 1886—and forged important links between the realms of art and publicity.

The role of *Le Courrier français* in creating celebrities and promoting the myth of Montmartre cafés-concerts was substantial. It was also controversial. For that reason, Roques frequently denied the star-making power of his journal, even as it formed an active part of the system. In one article he addresses café-concert hopefuls who dream of becoming famous at any price. He simultaneously warns them of the impossibility of "achieving celebrity with neither effort nor talent" while he inventories the media that makes this very thing possible. Roques' description is a handy summation of the resources available at the fin de siècle: "[Aspiring stars] lacked nothing in terms of publicity: reporters have interviewed them and written their biographies; their portraits have been distributed; large-format posters made by followers of Chéret have announced their venue to the world; prospectuses, announcements, gossip columns, publicity carts, sandwich-board men, illuminated signs, lighted columns where their names flame in letters of fire in the night of the boulevards, their merits shouted out, announced with a trumpet blast to Paris, in the provinces, even abroad: everything has been put in place!"[13] Ironically, although his putative intention was to discourage *aspirantes-étoiles* and distance his publication from the charge that journalists have undue influence in star-making, Roques' article in fact encourages the belief that publicity does create the celebrity.

Lautrec embraced the culture of celebrity described by the journals, visiting dance halls, cabarets, and cafés-concerts, and befriending those who performed there. His first images of Montmartre personalities, however, give little indication of the innovation that would mark his mature career. Like other young artists, he began by contributing drawings and lithographs to the wide variety of journals that covered the entertainments of the city. Among his earliest depictions is *The Quadrille of the Louis XIII Chair at the Elysée-Montmartre,* a photomechanically reproduced illustration based on his grisaille painting (Private collection, Paris), which was published on the cover of Bruant's journal *Le Mirliton* in December 1886 (fig. 49). Here Lautrec followed the style of established Montmartre illustrators such as Ferdinand Lunel,

Jean-François Raffaëlli, and Adolphe Willette,[14] depicting the stars of the quadrille, La Goulue and Grille-d'Egout, in the throes of the dance's famous high kick, but he gave no sense of their individual charisma. Likewise, his early images of Aristide Bruant, the rising celebrity of the Montmartre cabaret scene, are much in the manner of other Montmartre illustrators. In *The Refrain of the Louis XIII Chair at the Mirliton*, 1886 (fig. 50), Lautrec suggests the general mood of the club and its patrons, with Bruant standing atop a table, arms in the air, but there is little hint of the imposing icon the actor would become in Lautrec's posters of the 1890s.

Toulouse-Lautrec was still quite young at this point. Only twenty-two years old and fresh out of the atelier of Fernand Cormon, he was still finding his way as an artist. Yet in five short years he would make the transition from being just one of many illustrators to the master of the publicity poster, a friend and collaborator of the Montmartre entertainment aristocracy, and something of a celebrity in his own right. There were intermediate steps along the way, but the contrast between these relatively timid early drawings and his mature posters of the stars of Montmartre is remarkable. And he did not restrict himself to one medium: starting with posters, then capitalizing on his success by producing paintings and limited edition prints, Lautrec invented a new graphic language of promotion that survives to this day.

LAUTREC AND THE PUBLICITY POSTER

Toulouse-Lautrec's innovations in the realm of the publicity poster involve not just his masterful handling of lithography, his skillful integration of text and image, and his keen perception of celebrity and popular trends. If this were the case, then he might be remembered today only as a talented commercial artist who satisfied the demands of advertising. Instead, Lautrec went beyond the basic requirements of the entertainment poster to create what might be called a new conceptual style, a bold step in the marketing of individual personalities. He did so by focusing on the unique aspects of the performer he was depicting; he honed in on the essential elements that made a person recognizable, even if it meant emphasizing features that were less than becoming. Thus in Lautrec's depictions La Goulue's squinty eyes are as important as her sex appeal, and Aristide Bruant's scowl is as integral to the design as his trademark hat and scarf. In addition, Lautrec cleverly used a modernist visual vocabulary of cut-off angles and flat color as a means of commercial communication.

Lautrec's initial success in the intersecting domains of celebrity culture and avant-garde art was his poster for La Goulue performing at the Moulin Rouge. Although it is a cliché to speak of achieving fame overnight, in Toulouse-Lautrec's case, it appears to be true: one evening late in December 1891 around three thousand copies of his first poster, *Moulin Rouge: La Goulue* (fig. 51), were pasted on walls all across Paris. The reaction was immediate and overwhelming. Critics and contemporaries described the "shock," "surprise," and "emotion" they felt when seeing the work for the first time, and Lautrec's reputation was made.[15]

Yet despite its ubiquity and well-known reception, the genesis of *Moulin Rouge: La Goulue* is unclear. The poster was Lautrec's first foray into lithography, and although it is not known who introduced him to

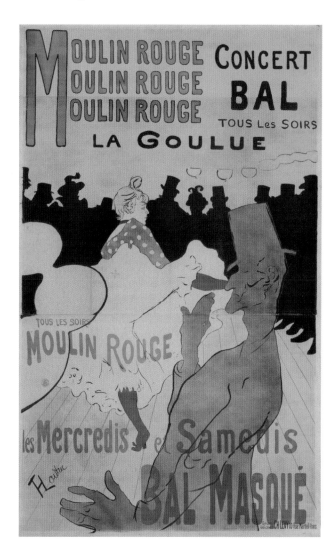

52

Pierre Bonnard, *Sketch for the Moulin Rouge Poster*, 1891, pastel and charcoal, 54.6 x 48.4 cm. The J. Paul Getty Museum, Los Angeles

53

Photograph of Toulouse-Lautrec and unidentified man (Zidler or Trémolada?) in front of a poster by Jules Chéret. Musée Toulouse-Lautrec, Albi; Gift of Maurice Joyant

54

Henri de Toulouse-Lautrec, *La Goulue and Valentin le Désossé*, 1891, charcoal and oil on canvas, 154 x 118 cm. Musée Toulouse-Lautrec, Albi; Gift of the Comtesse A. de Toulouse-Lautrec, 1922

Le Quadrille naturaliste aux Ambassadeurs.

55

Jean-François Raffaëlli, *The Naturalist Quadrille at the Ambassadeurs,* in *Paris illustré,* 1 August 1886, color photorelief. The Jane Voorhees Zimmerli Art Museum, Rutgers, The State University of New Jersey, Gift of Herbert D. and Ruth Schimmel

the medium, tradition has long held that it was Pierre Bonnard, whose own innovative poster of 1891, *France-Champagne,* had greatly impressed Lautrec.[16] The history of the commission itself is not well understood either. The director of the Moulin Rouge, Charles Zidler, may have given Lautrec the assignment outright, or he may have staged a competition for the design. The existence of a highly finished pastel and charcoal drawing by Bonnard for a Moulin Rouge poster supports the latter possibility (fig. 52).

A photograph of one of the proprietors of the Moulin Rouge with Lautrec, hat in hand before Jules Chéret's 1889 poster for the Moulin Rouge (fig. 53), makes clear that Lautrec was aware of the high standard in poster design he had to meet. In any event, once he had gained the prestigious commission, he painted oil sketches on cardboard of La Goulue in profile and a nearly full-size drawing of the entire composition (fig. 54). He then worked closely with the printers, a process he greatly enjoyed.[17] Although Lautrec probably supervised the transfer of the image rather than drawing directly on the stone himself, as he would for subsequent lithographs, his mature signature style was already evident. So too was his accomplished handling of *crachis,* or spatter, to create mists of color and atmosphere.

The poster astounded the public for several reasons. First of all, its massive size was unusual: almost two meters high and over a meter wide, it required three sheets of paper to accommodate the image, and

it dwarfed other posters placed near it. Lautrec's virtuoso handling of the technique of lithography added to the power of the design. Although he was new to this process, he showed a precocious ability to manipulate the medium to produce flat areas of pure color—as in the egg-yolk-yellow globe lights on the left—as well as carefully modulated applications of spatter that blend to form intermediate tones, as in the purplish form of La Goulue's dance partner Valentin le Désossé on the right. The composition is also novel. Although related to works by other artists, such as Raffaëlli (fig. 55) and Henri-Gabriel Ibels, as well as his own painting, *The Rehearsal of the New Girls* (see fig. 131), Lautrec's rendering goes beyond these precedents in its formal daring.[18] On the left side of the poster a string of yellow lamps is depicted as if seen from above, even though the perspective of the floorboards indicates a lower viewpoint; this destabilizing device sets up a shifting ground that evokes the frenetic motion of the dance and suggests multiple angles of viewing.

Lautrec seized on the most important lure of the Moulin Rouge: the sex appeal and star power of La Goulue. She dominates the center of the composition, one leg raised in the provocative high kick of the cancan. Lautrec makes her whirling petticoats (and specifically, her sex) the focus of attention, the locus of movement for the entire visual field.[19] This effect is even greater in the preparatory drawing (compare figs. 51 and 54). Lautrec extended the sexual and visual puns in his strategic deployment of Valentin le Désossé, who becomes both an obstacle to the viewer's access to La Goulue as well as a stand-in for the onlooker straining to look up her skirts. Although Valentin is clearly positioned in the foreground, Lautrec emphasizes the sway of his back as if he were leaning away from La Goulue's dangerous kick. Here Lautrec makes visual reference to his subject's renown for kicking the top hats off men in the audience, a maneuver made even more shocking as she was known occasionally to "forget" to wear underpants.[20] Valentin's closed eyes and impassive expression imply that he is indifferent to his partner, but his bony chin, nose, and thumb of his right hand all point to the nether regions of La Goulue's petticoats, and the thumb of his left hand, positioned near his groin, suggests physical arousal. When the poster was first mounted on the walls around Paris and seen from below, Valentin's obscene gesture and the effect of looking up La Goulue's skirt were

56

Jules Chéret, *Bal du Moulin Rouge*, 1889, reprinted in 1892, color lithograph, 120 x 87 cm (plate). Los Angeles County Museum of Art, Kurt J. Wagner, M.D., and C. Kathleen Wagner Collection

photographic realism, as some of his contemporaries had (see fig. 114), he synthesized the various elements into something timeless, iconic, and instantly recognizable. The critic Arthur Huc understood Lautrec's genius for reduction, noting: "When he created the magnificent poster for Bruant [see fig. 113], which is and remains the masterpiece of the genre, he first painted him in detail as Bonnat might have done. Then to his sitter's utter astonishment and dismay, he deleted and deleted again, retaining only the essential lines. The basic idea remained sincere. Lautrec's capacity for synthesis had reduced it to an epigram."[22] Huc incorrectly assumed Bruant's displeasure, but his description is apt. Lautrec had distilled Bruant's larger-than-life reputation into a simple logo: a hat, cape, and scarf stood in for all that the myth entailed.

In his posters for La Goulue and Aristide Bruant, Lautrec broke with tradition by focusing on the singular aspect of each star. Because this is the normative practice of advertising today, it is difficult to appreciate the innovation in his approach. Even Jules Chéret, who pioneered the entertainment poster, still employed generically attractive women to interest clients in a venue or product. His 1889 poster for the opening of the Moulin Rouge is a good example of his style at this time: it depicts a series of beautiful, but vapid women—a figural type of his own invention known as *chérettes*—riding frisky donkeys en route to the red windmill that gave the establishment its name (fig. 56). The *chérette* began to dominate Chéret's posters in the later 1880s, and by the 1890s she had become an emblem of the ideal *parisienne*, an embodiment of fin-de-siècle gaiety rendered in the visual vocabulary and pastel palette of the rococo.[23] The *chérette* represented amusement and joy in general, thus was equally at home advertising the Moulin Rouge or the Eldorado, without regard to the particular performers who played there. Even when Chéret did feature a known personage, such as Yvette Guilbert in 1891, he tended to strip away all that was individual about her appearance until she too bore an uncanny resemblance to a *chérette* (see fig. 179).

Toulouse-Lautrec, in contrast, focused on very real performers. There is no mistaking the gloriously vulgar La Goulue for a *chérette* or the imposing Aristide Bruant for any of his followers. Lautrec accomplished this in part by the unique visual language he used to depict the stars. A sort of journalistic

even more striking. The sexual overtones were not lost on Lautrec's contemporaries; in fact, one of them acted on the innuendo: in the Art Institute of Chicago's version of the poster, someone placed the Moulin Rouge stamp squarely on La Goulue's bottom, directing further attention to the real attraction of the dance hall.[21]

In his posters for Aristide Bruant, Lautrec likewise captured the most salient aspects of the chansonnier's marketed personality: his trademark wide-brimmed hat, cape, red scarf, walking stick, and ironic scowl. Yet instead of rendering these features with

shorthand had developed among poster artists and illustrators; relying heavily on the tropes of illustration or trying to recreate a photographic realism, they had yet to realize a new visual idiom to communicate the pleasures of Paris. Lautrec was the first major talent to bring a modern, avant-garde interpretation to entertainment posters.[24] Critics immediately noticed this, praising him as an artist "with more to say than the others and who says it unhesitatingly in a language all his own."[25] This new vocabulary had two immediate effects: it imparted the cachet of modernity to his subjects—singers, dancers, cabaret acts—and it brought the imprimatur of art to a commercial venture.

This second point is worth considering further. Poster apologists and supporters of the decorative arts reform sought to elevate the color poster to an art form. The first poster exhibition in France opened in 1884, and the Paris Exposition Universelle of 1889 included a major retrospective of French *affiches*. Also in 1889 Chéret held his first solo exhibition.[26] Thus when Toulouse-Lautrec designed his first poster, it was in the context of a groundswell of interest in "artistic" posters created by commercial artists, illustrators, and avant-garde painters such as the Nabis. But even as the *affiche artistique* was gaining recognition, it still occupied a contested position, teetering between applied and fine art and still deemed by most to be the former. Lautrec willingly blurred the distinctions between high and low, by using an avant-garde visual vocabulary for his publicity posters and by showing and selling them alongside oil paintings at exhibitions in France and across Europe. Moreover, Lautrec exploited the poster's indeterminate position, highlighting rather than glossing over the conflict between art—exemplified by the radical, avant-garde composition and skillful manipulation of lithography—and commerce, as represented in the highly packaged entertainments of the Moulin Rouge and the sexual commerce suggested by La Goulue herself.

THE PRINT AND THE PERFORMER

Lautrec parlayed his success with the Moulin Rouge poster of 1891 into deluxe editions of prints of Montmartre dancers and singers in smaller formats. *At the Moulin Rouge, La Goulue and Her Sister* (fig. 57), for example, was created as a luxury product aimed at print collectors and fans of the dancer. The six-color lithograph measures 65 by 49.8 centimeters, a size that would be easier for an individual to collect than a huge poster. It was available for purchase through the art dealers Boussod & Valadon in October 1892 for twenty francs, a price that was within reach of collectors but that elevated it above the cheap star paraphernalia and souvenirs hawked on the boulevards.

Fine prints were a way for Lautrec to capitalize on the burgeoning interest in collecting original prints as well as to display his bravura skills as a lithographer.[27] *La Goulue and Her Sister* required seven lithographic stones as well as applications of spatter to produce a richly textured surface full of evocative details: a waiter in a white apron, men in top hats and black or blue coats, women in clusters on the balcony wearing fanciful hats with green and red plumes, a glimpse of a soldier's red trousers, and thick smoke wafting throughout. La Goulue, the subject of the print, stands with her back to the viewer, yet her famous red topknot and insolent posture leave no question concerning her identity. Lautrec was so confident in his ability to synthesize the features and style of a performer into a recognizable emblem that he often deployed sight gags like this. Not only did this please his cocky sense of humor but it startled the public by shaking up the conventions of publicity.

These smaller prints served Lautrec well. They increased his exposure to the art-buying public, enhanced his association with the performers, and allowed him to straddle the worlds of commercial art (entertainment posters) and fine art (original prints). They also benefited the performers. Aristide Bruant, cognizant of the power of the images, commissioned smaller photomechanical reproductions of Lautrec's posters of him to give away or sell to the patrons of his cabaret. The prints were not signed and numbered by Toulouse-Lautrec, creator of the graphic image, but by Bruant, mastermind of the living image. This confusion of hierarchies and genres points to the increasingly intertwined circles of publicity, entertainment, and fine art that characterized fin-de-siècle Paris and that Lautrec advanced.

Lautrec also offered original prints of performers in album and book formats. The production of luxury images of lower-class entertainers indicates the power of the Montmartre limelight and the changing climate of celebrity culture: people not only went to see the the stars perform but also sought to collect their images and bring them into their private homes, whether it be in the form of an expensive oil painting, a poster, a print, or a cheap erotic photograph. This is especially surprising given the low social status of the subjects—and in the case of La Goulue, the dancer's association with prostitution. Although prostitution was legal, it had spawned an epidemic of syphilis that was ravaging all sectors of society, including bourgeois families. The prospect of bringing an image of the dancer into the sanctity of the home was therefore all the more transgressive. Yet as the decade wore on, these performers, especially Bruant and Guilbert, gained such popularity and acceptance by the upper classes (both entertained at high society functions), that owning deluxe images of them became a mark of one's fashionable tastes.

57

Henri de Toulouse-Lautrec, *At the Moulin Rouge, La Goulue and Her Sister*, 1892, color lithograph, 65 x 49.8 cm (sheet). The Art Institute of Chicago, Charles F. Glore Collection

Lautrec's massive poster of La Goulue (fig. 51) was a watershed in the history of entertainment advertising, and he further pushed the boundaries of high art and celebrity with his limited edition prints of performers. But in many ways his paintings of figures from the entertainment industry were an even greater departure from artistic norms. Although it may have been considered appropriate to depict louche performers such as La Goulue in lower art forms such as illustrated magazines or erotic photographs (figs. 58–61), Lautrec was the first vanguard artist to devote a large-scale oil painting to a Montmartre celebrity. His first major canvas, *La Goulue Entering the Moulin Rouge*, 1891–1892 (see fig. 22), was painted on the heels of his successful poster. In this intentionally garish work Lautrec captures his model's famed décolletage, defiant bearing, and slightly crossed eyes. He exhibited it immediately at the Salon des Indépendants in Paris and the Association pour l'Art in Antwerp, both in 1892, then at the 1893 exhibition of Les XX in Brussels. He offered the oil painting for sale at 600 francs, a considerable sum that not only indicated the value he placed on it but contrasted with the inexpensive poster of La Goulue that hung beside it at exhibitions. The painting was purchased by Charles Zidler, the proprietor of the Moulin Rouge, who surely appreciated the attention Lautrec had brought to his establishment with his daring images of La Goulue.

It is surprising that Lautrec made few other paintings of entertainers following this tour de force, although he did create a number of oil-on-cardboard studies. Perhaps, recognizing that canvases would never have the circulation that his printed images would, he lost interest in their publicity potential, or perhaps he felt that lithography—with its more ephemeral nature and its insistence on the surface—was a more appropriate medium to convey the message of celebrity. Two notable exceptions are Lautrec's paintings of Jane Avril. Significantly, she is depicted not in her role as the star of the dance hall and café-concert, but in her private life, or rather on the cusp between the two. In *Jane Avril in the Entrance to the Moulin Rouge, Putting on Her Gloves* (fig. 62) and *Jane Avril Leaving the Moulin Rouge* (fig. 63), both of 1892, the artist depicts the dancer in her street clothes, wearing a solemn expression and wrapped up in her own thoughts. Her conservative outfit gives no

58, 59–61

Anonymous, photographs of La
Goulue (from top left): c. 1890,
National Gallery of Art Library,
John Rewald Collection; 1891,
c. 1889, and c. 1889, The Jane
Voorhees Zimmerli Art Museum,
Rutgers, The State University of
New Jersey, Gift of Herbert D.
and Ruth Schimmel

hint of her stage life in the raucous dance hall; her downward glance and closed body language take us from the realm of public personality to private individual. Unlike Lautrec's publicity work for the dancer, such as his poster for her performance at the Jardin de Paris (see fig. 175)—where Avril is immediately identifiable by her signature bonnet, supple movements, and characteristic orange underskirts—the paintings present her as an anonymous woman on the streets of Paris, the person behind the celebrity.[28]

Lautrec contrasted the public and the private in his painted oil studies as well, where he seems to have been more interested in the psychology of his sitters. Compare his sensitive oil sketch of May Milton (fig. 64) with her appearance in his finished canvas, *At the Moulin Rouge* (fig. 66). In the study Milton is pensive, her eyes slightly unfocused, her thoughts turned inward. Lautrec notes the circles under her eyes, her chalky face powder, and thin, wan smile. In the final painting Milton wears the smooth mask of celebrity, her full

lips painted orange red, her chin raised in a confident, commanding pose. In this and other examples Toulouse-Lautrec contrasts the public face of stardom with the day-to-day weariness that performance entails; he understood that celebrity was a construction, a superficial masquerade.

At the Moulin Rouge is more than just a likeness of May Milton in her celebrity role; it is a monumental group portrait summing up Lautrec's life at the Moulin Rouge and his friendships with the performers there. The large canvas, probably painted between 1892 and 1895, is a sort of valediction of his life as the court artist to the superstars of Montmartre. It portrays a gathering of his friends at the cabaret, including Edouard Dujardin, Paul Sescau, and Maurice Guibert along with the dancers La Macarona, La Goulue, Jane Avril (fig. 65), and May Milton. Lautrec himself also makes an appearance in the background, his diminutive figure contrasting with his cousin Gabriel's lanky frame. Mixing the public and the private, Lautrec

effectively collapsed the distance between his professional work and his private life.[29]

At the Moulin Rouge was also a physical testament to his close ties to this important establishment. Lautrec loved the institution in all its gaudy splendor, and his friends recount the delight he took in the dancers, the chanteuses, the clientele, and the surcharged atmosphere of the café-concert. Beyond his personal predilections, however, it was an astute move for Lautrec to be so closely associated with the Moulin Rouge, which stood as a symbol of all things Parisian, "with everything that implies in terms of promising innuendo and cynical debauchery," in the words of his friend Francis Jourdain.[30] By branding himself as the official painter of the Moulin Rouge, first by his friendships with the celebrities, then with his poster and his subsequent prints and paintings of its stars, Lautrec capitalized on the institution's international reputation and secured a place for himself as one of the Montmartre immortals.

THE CELEBRITY OF TOULOUSE-LAUTREC

In many ways Lautrec's finest publicity work was for himself. He made his name by associating with the rising stars of the Montmartre entertainment industry and crafting innovative and memorable images of them. Moreover, his posters, which literally covered the walls of the city, physically staked out his presence in the metropolis. He actively promoted his art, calling on journalist friends to write articles about his posters, and exhibiting his posters, prints, and paintings at venues ranging from the conservative Cercle Volney to serious avant-garde exhibitions like Les XX in Brussels. His work was also on view at entertainment rather than artistic establishments in the very heart of Montmartre, including Aristide Bruant's cabaret and the Moulin Rouge, furthering his ties to specific stars and to Montmartre, the hub of up-to-date entertainment.

Toulouse-Lautrec clearly understood the nature of contemporary celebrity, which was based on equal parts myth, rumor, and performance. Although his letters reveal him to be a complex, sensitive, and contradictory person, the public persona he projected was extroverted and outrageous. Like the stars he depicted, Lautrec was known for outlandish behavior that kept him in the public eye. He attended the most scandalous cafés-concerts, balls, and brothels, threw strange dinner parties, mixed exotic cocktails, and had a lightning-fast wit that kept him at the center of attention in any social gathering.[31]

Lautrec's unusual appearance contributed to his notoriety. He had broken his left leg at the age of thirteen and his right leg the year later, at which point his legs stopped growing while the rest of his body developed at a normal rate, giving him the appearance of a full-grown man on a child's legs. He reached the height of four feet, eleven inches—he was not, he emphatically insisted, a dwarf—but experienced pain and difficulty walking and had to use a cane. To compound these health problems, he was also hampered by congenital deformities, perhaps owing to numerous consanguineous marriages in his family. Malformed sinuses caused him to sniffle constantly, drool, and speak with a lisp (complicating his strong southern accent).[32] As a result, he made a startling impression.

Even Lautrec's close friends had felt a certain shock when they first met the artist. Yvette Guilbert, the café-concert diva, described him as having "an enormous dark head, a red face, and very black beard; oily, greasy skin; a nose that could cover two faces; and a mouth! a mouth like a gash from ear to ear, looking almost like an open wound! The flesh of the lips thick and 'violet-pink,' flattened and loose, hanging like a hem round this gash, terrifying and obscene!"[33] Thadée Natanson, an influential publisher, art collector, and a loyal friend of Lautrec's, also noted his initial horror at the artist's appearance: "Henri de Toulouse-Lautrec was very small, very dark. He gave the impression of being a dwarf even more because his torso, which was that of a man, seemed, with his weight and his very large head, to have crushed the legs that emerged below. His hands and his head, at least in comparison to his torso, seemed all the more disproportionate, since that head, unstable, like everything heavy that is suspended, bobbed up and down."[34] Jean-Jacques Bernard, son of Lautrec's friend Tristan Bernard, even claimed that the artist's appearance had given him nightmares as a child.[35]

It is hard to reconcile photographs of Lautrec (fig. 67)—which show a short, somewhat curious figure with a large head, dark hair, and expressive eyes— with the disgust he aroused. Perhaps the combination of his peculiar looks, his disabilities, and his high-pitched voice made people uncomfortable. But it is

67

Paul Sescau, *Toulouse-Lautrec,*
c. 1892, photograph. Musée
Toulouse-Lautrec, Albi

68

Maurice Guibert, *Toulouse-
Lautrec Dressed in Japanese
Costume,* c. 1892, photograph.
The Museum of Modern Art,
New York, Anonymous Gift

69

Anonymous, *Toulouse-Lautrec
in Jane Avril's Hat and Scarf,*
c. 1892, photograph. Musée
Toulouse-Lautrec, Albi

also possible that his allegedly frightful appearance was another part of his reputation. Writers repeated and embellished it, exaggerating his ugliness to the point of caricature and legend.

Lautrec, self-conscious about his appearance, used humor as a defensive mechanism and enjoyed all forms of masquerade and parody. Photographs document him wearing both feminine and masculine costumes: as a geisha (fig. 68), choirboy, clown, muezzin, gypsy dancer, and as Jane Avril, dressed in the dancer's hat and feather boa (fig. 69), to name just a few of his identities.[36] Lautrec was not a passive participant in these ventures; he actively staged masquerades and demanded that friends, including Maurice Guilbert and Paul Sescau (a professional photographer), take his photograph in his chosen costumes and mise-en-scènes.[37] Some critics have taken this as confirmation of Lautrec's eccentricities, but the photographs,

I believe, point to his complicity in the mythmaking and his understanding of the mutable character of identity. Possessed of an unusual and memorable appearance, Lautrec grasped the importance of marketing a unique style for the stars he depicted.

So successful was Lautrec in his performance of celebrity that he became a symbol of Montmartre. His friend Thadée Natanson recounts that he was one of the attractions of the Moulin Rouge, a luminary alongside La Goulue and Valentin le Désossé.[38] Extending from his professional work to his private life, Lautrec enacted such a distinctive persona that he achieved both celebrity and infamy within his own short lifetime. Even today, Lautrec's art—and especially his posters of the stars of Paris—immediately call to mind the heady atmosphere of celebrity, decadence, and entertainment that marked the capital at the fin de siècle.

Parts of this essay and the following sections on "The Chat Noir and the Cabarets" and "Stars of the Café-Concert" are drawn from my Ph.D. dissertation: "Henri de Toulouse-Lautrec and the Café-Concert: Printmaking, Publicity, and Celebrity in Fin-de-Siècle Paris," New York University, 2002.

1. Abel Hamel, "Chronique parisienne" La Vie moderne (23 January 1886): 903.

2. For the population figures, see Pinkney 1958, 152.

3. On the complex intersection of fashion and prostitution, see Clayson 1991, chap. 3.

4. A. Delvau, Les Plaisirs de Paris. Guide practique, 64; quoted in Clark 1984, 207.

5. For the history of fame and its derivative, celebrity, see Leo Braudy, The Frenzy of Renown: Fame and Its History (New York, 1986); and P. David Marshall, Celebrity and Power: Fame in Contemporary Culture (Minneapolis and London, 1997). On the shift from character to personality, see Warren I. Susman, "'Personality' and the Making of Twentieth-Century Culture," in Culture as History (New York, 1984), 271–285.

6. On the role of photography in the cult of personality, see Elizabeth Anne McCauley, A.A.E. Disdéri and the Carte de Visite Portrait Photograph (New Haven, 1985), esp. chaps. 3 and 4; and Gordon Baldwin and Judith Keller, Nadar-Warhol, Paris–New York: Photography and Fame [ext. cat., The J. Paul Getty Museum] (Los Angeles, 1999).

7. Berlanstein 2001, 216–217.

8. Rigolboche addressed this issue directly, imagining a conversation in which someone expresses surprise that she is writing her memoires: "But yes, my dear," she answers, "does that bother you? Don't I have as much right as Mr. So-And-So and Miss What's-Her-Name? They are amused to make me a celebrity, but too bad for them, I am their equal now." See Rigolboche 1860, 5–6.

9. Thérésa's memoir was an overwhelming success, selling 60,000 copies in just a few months; it had at least six additional printings. For an analysis of the memoir, see Chapin 2002, 27–33; Jean-Claude Klein, La Chanson à l'affiche (Paris, 1991), 17–18; and Adrian Rifkin, "Cultural Movement and the Paris Commune," Art History 2 (June 1979): 209–213.

10. For the early history of the poster and Chéret's role in its development, see Bradford Ray Collins Jr., "Jules Chéret and the Nineteenth-Century French Poster" (Ph.D. diss., Yale University, 1980).

11. For Chéret's oeuvre, see Broido 1980.

12. On Le Courrier français and its importance in propagating the myth of Montmartre, see Jacques Lethève, Caricature et la presse sous la IIIe République (Paris, 1961), 68–69; Patricia Eckert Boyer, "The Artist as Illustrator," in New Brunswick 1988a, 117–123; and Michael Logan-John Wilson, "Le Commerce de la Bohème: Marginality and Mass Culture in Fin-de-Siècle Paris" (Ph.D. diss., Cornell University, 1993), 136–138, 177–187.

13. Roques 1892, 3.

14. Murray 1980, 69.

15. See Chapin 2002, 60–61.

16. Natanson 1951, 168–170. In London and Paris 1991, 250, Thomson notes that both Rupert Carabin and Ibels claimed to have taught Lautrec lithography, and he had several other printmaker friends who could have shown him the way.

17. See Lautrec's letter to his mother of November–December 1891, in Schimmel ed. 1991, no. 209.

18. On the comparison to Ibels, see Boyer in New Brunswick 1988a, 146–147; on Raffaëlli, see Murray 1980, 69.

19. Thomson 1977, 59. See also Howard Lay, "La Fête aux Boulevards Exterieurs: Art and Culture in Fin-de-Siècle Montmartre" (Ph.D. diss., Harvard University, 1991), 235.

20. Natanson 1951, 227.

21. Whoever was responsible for placing the Moulin Rouge stamp on Lautrec's poster apparently enjoyed this sexual pun: the stamp also appears on La Goulue's bottom in this poster in the collections of the Metropolitan Museum of Art and the Baltimore Museum of Art, among others.

22. Huc, quoted in London and Paris 1991, 286.

23. On the *cherétte*, see Collins 1980, 117–119, 123–127; and Marcus Verhagen, "The Poster in Fin-de-Siècle Paris: 'That Mobile and Degenerate Art,'" in *Cinema and the Invention of Modern Life*, ed. Leo Charney and Vanessa R. Schwartz (Berkeley, 1995), 103–129.

24. This is not to say that Lautrec was the only artist interested in breaking down the division between high and low in the graphic arts; the Nabis—Pierre Bonnard in particular—were also exploring this realm, but in respect to the theater, rather than the dance hall or café-concert. On the Nabis and the avant-garde theater, see Washington 1998.

25. See Arsène Alexandre, "Chronique d'aujourd'hui: Henri de Toulouse-Lautrec," *Paris* (8 January 1892): 2. Ernest Maindron, *Affiches illustrées* (Paris, 1896), 110, used a similar metaphor: "it is a new language that this philosopher [Lautrec] speaks, but he has studied well what he writes, and he writes it in a striking manner."

26. New Brunswick 1978, 10–12. For a full treatment of the decorative arts reform see Silverman 1989. For a recent discussion of the role of the poster, see Karen Lynn Carter, "L'Age de l'Affiche: The Reception, Display, and Collection of Posters in Fin-de-Siècle Paris" (Ph.D. diss., University of Chicago, 2001). For Lautrec's printmaking in the context of the decorative arts reform, see Druick 1986, 41–47.

27. The literature on the original print movement is extensive. For a recent discussion and bibliography, see Washington 2000.

28. Néret 1991, 104, notes that Jane Avril was the only dancer at the Moulin Rouge who wore colored petticoats.

29. There is a debate about both the date of this picture and the identities of the sitters. For two opposing views see Heller 1986, 51–80; and Thomson 1991, 266–268.

30. Jourdain and Adhémar 1952, 38.

31. On Lautrec as a cocktail maker, see Jourdain 1895, 213; and Leclercq 1954, 111–113. On Lautrec's penchant for showing off, see Frey 1994, 167, 241–242.

32. Many posthumous attempts have been made to diagnose Toulouse-Lautrec's malady. For the medical references, see the bibliography in Frey 1994.

33. Guilbert 1927, 207.

34. Natanson 1951, 286. Natanson became accustomed to Lautrec's appearance and eventually found that it took enormous effort to see the artist as he appeared to the rest of the world (p. 11).

35. Jarrassé 1991, 11.

36. For photographs of Lautrec, see Beauté 1988.

37. On Lautrec's collaborative photography, see Adhémar 1951, 229–234; and Sagne 1980, 48–67.

38. Natanson 1951, 11.

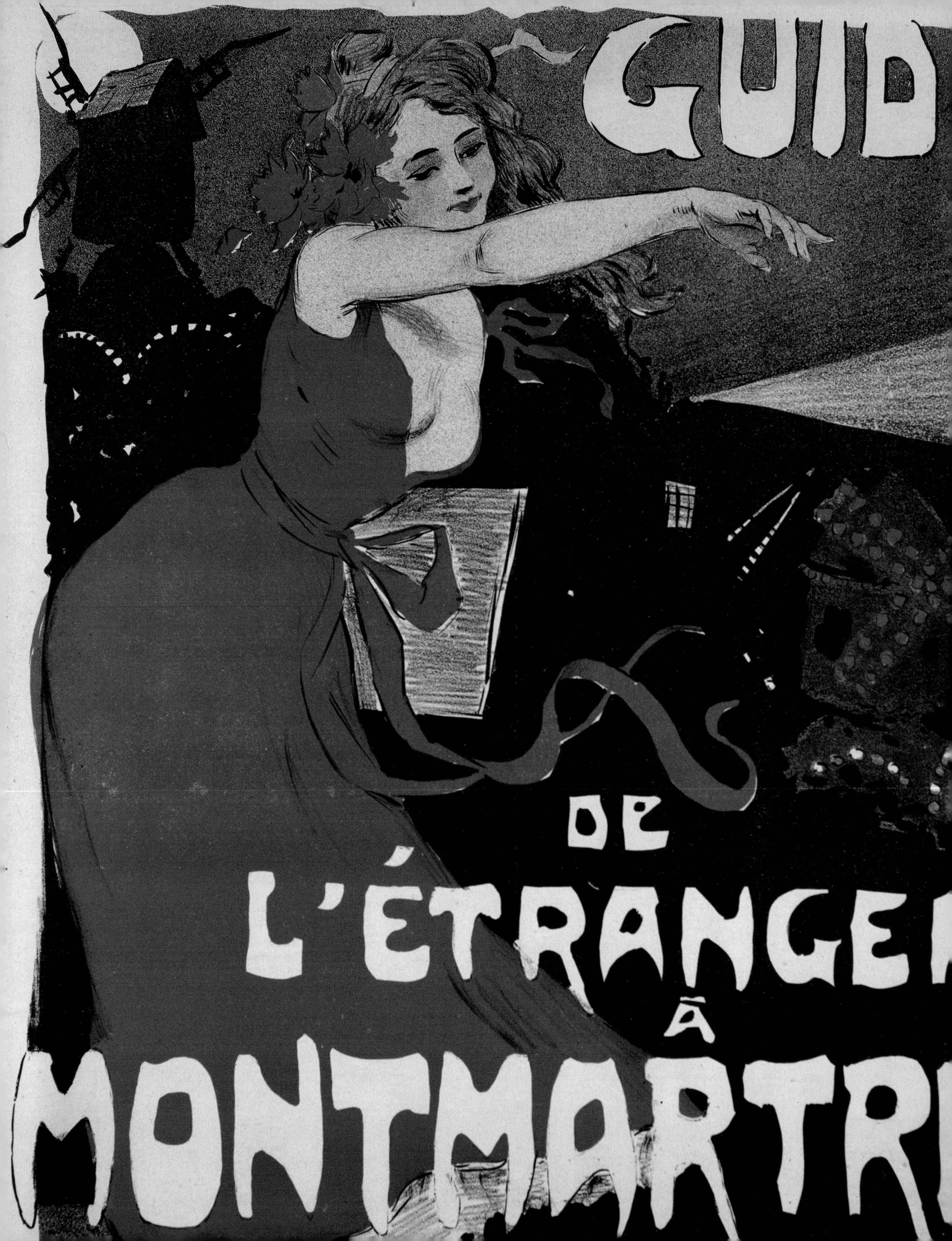
GUID
DE
L'ÉTRANGE
À
MONTMARTR

Richard Thomson

INTRODUCING MONTMARTRE

In Toulouse-Lautrec's time Montmartre had many dimensions, many meanings. It was a physical location, a part of Paris, a social environment with its own populations, class structure, and economy. It was also, as Mary Chapin's essay has shown, the hub of an entertainment industry. And it was the nerve center of an anti-establishment culture that, as Dennis Cate has demonstrated, not only was manifest in the activities of literature, performance, and shadow play but was also a frame of mind. Much of Montmartre's excitement at the end of the nineteenth century came from this diversity, and we should remain aware of it when we consider Lautrec in his different contexts. There was a binding element in this diversity, however. The crime, pimping, and prostitution of the backstreets; the profit-making of dance halls and cafés-concerts through performances that might infringe on the bounds of decency; the satire and irreverence of the cabarets may have been very diffuse activities. But they all cut across the values of the Third Republic, with its politics of egalitarianism and social control, its bourgeois family values, and its moralizing rhetoric of fraternity. Examined from most directions, Montmartre signified the truculent, things "outside the law."

The butte Montmartre had been populated since ancient times, a village outside the city, which itself stretched along the River Seine. Because it provided a view overlooking Paris and the sweep of the river, it had long been a place of excursion. In 1784 the construction of the Mur des Fermiers Généraux, a tax barrier around the city that made goods sold on the outside cheaper, had given Montmartre a separate identity.[1] But its physical enclosure by the ring of fortifications built around Paris in the 1840s and its inclusion within the capital's administrative structure in 1860 had gradually absorbed it into the metropolis. Even so, Montmartre retained its distinct character. In midcentury painters such as Camille Corot and Camille Pissarro had enjoyed its old buildings and steep, winding streets, for on the top of the hill Montmartre had very much the character of a rural village, its vineyards and windmills giving it an agricultural air that belied its proximity to the city.

By the end of the century, although it was still possible by judicious selection of site to maintain that fiction, view painters favored more naturalistic motifs. Maximilien Luce's view from the top of Montmartre, made in 1887 (fig. 70), represents in the foreground the upper story and roof of a seventeenth- or eighteenth-century house and a bank of trees, but between this ostensibly rural first plane and the distant Sannois ridge one sees the broad valley of the Seine filled with tenement blocks and factories. This is not a view south from Montmartre, with its panorama of Paris and the great city's monuments: Notre-Dame, the Louvre, the Opéra. It looks to the northwest, over industrial Clichy, Levallois-Peret, and Saint-Denis. It was in these poorer quarters, like those huddling up against the butte in Ramón Casas' view of the Sacré-Coeur (see fig. 4), that the proletariat that serviced the factories and workshops lived. These were the populations that, as the anarchist Luce well knew, strolled into Montmartre to take their cheap pleasures in the dance halls and cafés-concerts but also, from among their dispossessed and unemployed, furnished the prostitutes and muggers that made the working-class areas dangerous.

As a high point overlooking the city, Montmartre belonged to everyone. In early 1887, with the trees still not in leaf, Vincent van Gogh, who had then been in Paris a year, began to explore the butte. A painting like *A Corner of Montmartre: The Moulin à Poivre* (fig. 71) shows ordinary people, like the petit-bourgeois couple in the center, passing time under a dry chilly sky. Executed in thin paint and with spidery drawing that shows Van Gogh's admiration for Jean-François Raffaëlli, the picture also echoes the latter's egalitarianism. Under the *tricolore* of liberty, equality, and fraternity, the people of Paris enjoy themselves. This was what the republic wanted to see and hear about itself. In an account that coincidentally parallels another of Van Gogh's 1887 Montmartre cityscapes (fig. 72), Marcel Schwob, writing in the republican *Le Phare de la Loire* in 1889, described for his regional readers the platforms erected alongside the Blute-fin windmill. His tone was egalitarian, like Van Gogh's paintings. Between accounts of genial housing, good-natured workers, and cheap entertainment, he explained how the visitor can look from the platform over "the lake of fog in which swims the City of Light. Here and there, in the gaps, one vaguely sees Notre-Dame, the Panthéon, the Invalides, the Trocadéro."[2]

Schwob was not fooled by metropolitan grandeur. He went on to point out that if one looked in other directions one saw tenements and factories, as if he were describing Luce's vista. Even the view over Paris, if taken from lower down the southern slope of the butte, revealed a different Montmartre. The scene that Van Gogh painted from the apartment he shared with his brother Theo on the rue Lepic looks southeast over the city, toward the church of Saint-Vincent de Paul (fig. 73). In the foreground are tall tenements, dormitory accommodations for the city's workers, with the poorer housed on the higher floors. There is something unresolved and transitional about the irregular relationships of the buildings, their blank flanks awaiting the construction of an adjacent block. The painting's sense of confinement is shared by Pierre Bonnard's later view of the parallel rue Tholozé by night (fig. 74). Here the artist's gaze is both denied—by the buildings that shield points of interest, such as the courtyard to the left—and directed: toward the lights of the storefronts along the rue des Abbesses. This was a street of little shops and vegetable stalls, a center for the predominantly working-class and petit-bourgeois

community that lived in the steep streets rising up from the main thoroughfares lower down.

These ran roughly east-west, with the boulevard de Rochechouart becoming the boulevard de Clichy. That artery broadened at junctions, creating the place Pigalle with the Café de la Nouvelle-Athènes where the impressionists had met in the 1870s and the place Blanche where the Moulin Rouge was to be found. These boulevards were part of an outer ring of main traffic channels that encircled the capital. They were outside the *grands boulevards*—the boulevards des Capucines, des Italiens, and their like—which formed the chic city center around the Opéra, the Bourse, the big department stores, and the other major amenities of the metropolis. But if the boulevards de Rochechouart and de Clichy acted as a kind of porous frontier between two parts of Paris, divisions of class, wealth, and culture should not be oversimplified. Many of the important art dealers such as Georges Petit and Durand-Ruel, representing both major Salon artists and up-and-coming modern painters such as Edgar Degas and Claude Monet, were in the center. Van Gogh called this grouping the *grand boulevard* as opposed to the *petit boulevard*: the small dealers like Père Tanguy who served unknown avant-garde figures such as Lautrec, Emile Bernard, and himself.[3] But the main gallery of the major dealer Goupil was on the rue Chaptal, two blocks south of the boulevard de Clichy, and a large building in the place Pigalle housed the studios of leading painters such as Pierre Puvis de Chavannes, a number of whom lived on the neighboring streets in the southern flanks of Montmartre.[4]

The social geography thus offered a complex mixture. In many ways this was a microcosm of French life in the 1890s. There was a proletariat, geared to factory and manual work; a petite bourgeoisie of artisans and shopkeepers; more bourgeois accommodations within easy reach; and a shifting tide of tourists and consumers visiting the viewpoints and places of entertainment. These populations mutated, even during the course of a single day. One journalist described how on the rue Pigalle from seven in the morning to midday the vegetable stalls held sway, after which the prostitutes took over.[5] Montmartre supported the nationalist right, visible in the construction of the Sacré-Coeur, that emphatic architectural expression of Catholicism and patriotism, and in the anti-Semitic imagery of Adolphe Willette.[6] Equally it articulated the grievances of the left: for instance, in the performances of Aristide Bruant, Eugénie Buffet, and Mévisto. In its dance halls and cafés-concerts Montmartre encouraged the classes to mix, which the republic would have approved. Yet the mixture of proletarian prostitute and bourgeois male—the essential staffage of Lautrec's paintings of the Moulin Rouge—represented an insidious conjunction of crime and disease with prosperity and rectitude.

At the same time, we should beware of rigid judgments about class and morality. In fact, the Parisian working classes cast girls out of their communities if they lapsed into prostitution, and the ostensibly respectable bourgeois was the commercial motor of the Montmartre entertainment economy.[7] This, as evidenced by places such as the Moulin Rouge, balanced precariously between the licit and the illicit: on the one hand the staged spectacle, sometimes deliberately provocative, and on the other the unstaged parade of prostitutes available for off-site consumption. Both class, in its insidious comminglings and jarring conjunctions, and the hypocrisy that underlay much of the *quartier*'s social commerce, made Montmartre almost symptomatic of the divisions and decadence of contemporary France. It was an environment in which decadence could be observed, lived, condemned, or shared.

As such, it was an ideal environment for the modern artist. Having moved across Paris to the Marais in 1893, Félicien Rops missed the "democratico-artistic side of Montmartre."[8] Neither Rops nor Toulouse-Lautrec was interested in street scenes or vistas but in the populations of the *quartier*. Although Lautrec made no attempt to categorize the full gamut of the Montmartrois populus, he used the device of the type to focus on two broad groupings: the bourgeois man and the young working-class woman. The men were frequently his own friends, who, though not aristocratic and thus his social inferiors in old-fashioned terms, were relatively well-to-do (in an age of low taxation), sometimes property owners, often in the world of the arts and letters, or a professional like Dr. Bourges, with whom Lautrec shared an apartment. If this group was one with which Lautrec associated socially, the second was quite unlike it: the women were often of the working class and differed from him biologically, economically, and culturally. In some respects Lautrec used these women in the conventional

ways a man of his class might at this time: employing them as servants, paying them for sex. In other cases his use of them had a more "democratico-artistic" dimension. His observation of working-class women indulged the egalitarianism of republicanism and naturalism, while his manipulation of them as artist's models, his representation of them as alcoholic or promiscuous, played with the notion of female irregularity, which coincided with the irregularity of Lautrec's own bohemian lifestyle.[9]

For his portraits of men Lautrec adopted the full-length format that was common at the time, admiring Whistler's example.[10] It was a flexible idiom (figs. 75–78). For instance, in Jean-Louis Forain's portrait of the society painter Jacques-Emile Blanche the artist made subtle use of his caricaturist's skills (fig. 78). Stumpily confronting us, Blanche appears simultaneously blasé and alert; his shapeless body, planted on flat feet, seems poised in an unathletic readiness to move. Forain also made a more flattering full-length image of Lautrec's father at the races.[11] Casas also took up the formula for his portrait of the musician Erik Satie (fig. 75). Satie had been part of the Chat Noir circle but after a recent row with the proprietor Rodolphe Salis had become pianist at the Auberge du Clou on the avenue Trudaine.[12] Very much a Montmartre bohemian—his work experimental and subversive, his appearance and behavior eccentric—Satie appealed to the visiting Catalan. Casas took all the hallmarks of the self-satisfied bourgeois full-length—life-size scale, top hat and frock coat, proprietorial backdrop—and turned them upside down. The grandeur of scale is subverted by the scruffiness of the clothes; the gaze shows less hauteur than sarcasm; the setting is no sunlit estate but the proletarian Moulin de la Galette, in poor weather. In the spring of 1891 Casas exhibited the painting at the Salon National des Beaux-Arts. That in itself was something of a Montmartrois gesture, the image of the bohemian Satie infiltrating portraits in the same idiom of politicians and industrialists, just as Forain could give the formula a caricatural twist.

In February of the same year Toulouse-Lautrec was coincidentally at work on three full-length portraits of male friends, as he wrote to his mother.[13] One was of Gaston Bonnefoy, a family friend and son of a doctor from Bordeaux (fig. 76).[14] Lautrec was clearly fascinated by the deeply carved crescent cheekbones on Bonnefoy's aquiline face. But the portrait is not without humor. The head is balanced atop the almost conical form of the dark overcoat, rather like a sphere on top of a skittle, and it has been suggested that the protuberant cane makes a cheeky phallic allusion.[15] *Gaston Bonnefoy* was shown at the 1891 Salon des Indépendants with two other male portraits.[16] Another full-length made at the same time was not shown. Situated, like the others, within Lautrec's studio, this portrait shows the photographer Paul Sescau standing nonchalantly alongside a stack of canvases and an oriental hanging (fig. 77). Once again Lautrec gave scrupulous attention to the physiognomy, detailing the strong jaw fringed by a luxuriant moustache, the gaze both wistful and combative. These are portraits not only of friends and equals but of men seen on Lautrec's own terms.

On other occasions Lautrec added another allusive dimension by portraying the subjects alongside his own work. In 1897 he painted the Belgian Henri Nocq (fig. 79), who was active in the applied arts, had produced a ceramic plaque of Yvette Guilbert (see fig. 195), and had appeared the year before in Lautrec's poster *L'Artisan moderne*.[17] Nocq had published a book of interviews on the applied arts in 1896, to which Lautrec had contributed a letter admiring William Morris and Jules Chéret.[18] But the relationship seems to have cooled,[19] and in this portrait Lautrec showed Nocq leaning forward somewhat obsequiously, a pose that echoes that of a figure in Lautrec's large canvas of *Marcelle Lender Dancing the Bolero in "Chilpéric"* (see fig. 227) depicted on an easel behind him. As this character is the rather inappropriately lecherous Don Nervoso, the parallel was not exactly kind.[20] Also in 1897 Lautrec painted the poet Paul Leclercq, this time seated, in his new studio on the avenue Frochot (fig. 80). Leclercq recalled that it was executed quickly, with the sittings lasting a total of about three hours, and that Lautrec sang the obscene "Chanson du Forgeron" while working.[21] That bachelor bonhomie manifested itself within the portrait in the juxtaposition of the seated Leclercq, eyebrow raised and mouth tilted in a smirk, with a rendering of Lautrec's painting *Woman in a Corset (Conquête de Passage*, see fig. 257) in progress on the easel behind. Its scene of a man watching while a woman tackles the lacing of her corset underscores the heterosexual bond between artist and sitter.

In all these portraits Lautrec's friends read as individuals when one knows their names—and at the 1891 Indépendants Lautrec conventionally identified the men by their initials—and as types if not. Each one could stand for the boulevardier: masculine, prosperous, sexually independent, attuned to the modern world. With his paintings of women the relationships are usually different. Lautrec did paint portraits of specific individuals, such as the one of the pianist Marie Dihau that he exhibited at the 1890 Indépendants (Musée d'Orsay, Paris), but often the women he painted were models whom he manipulated in various ways. *Young Woman at a Table, "Poudre de riz" (Rice Powder)* (fig. 82), for example, seems to have been posed in his rue Caulaincourt studio, with its big studio windows in the background and a metal table and wicker chair that are familiar props in a number of paintings of the later 1880s and early 1890s. The painting functions both as a test-bed for the young painter—how to use a broken, tonal touch freed from exact description, how to paint pale flesh tones—and as a type of the young working woman. It also has accessories—the red tub of powder, the frilly shoulders of her chemise—that try to pull it into the category of a genre painting. The combination is uncomfortable, as if Lautrec could not resolve the painting's purpose.

A later painting, *Rousse (Redhead)*, also known as *La Toilette* (fig. 84), made in 1889 and exhibited in February 1890 at Les XX in Brussels, also suggests ambiguities.[22] Lautrec was evidently pleased enough with the painting to show it, and the figure's foreshortening is indeed a remarkable example of his draftsmanship. At the same time, given the debate that had circulated around the pastels of naked women Degas had exhibited at the eighth impressionist show in 1886, in which it was widely assumed that he had represented prostitutes in their rooms and at their ablutions, one might assume the same about *Rousse*, depicting a woman in a half-dressed state. But Degas' figures are equivocal. In one of his paintings from this period showing a seated, naked woman combing her hair (fig. 83), seen from above and behind, there is nothing to indicate whether she is a prostitute or not. The figure thus could operate either as a type (a prostitute) or as a model (an exercise in foreshortening). But when we return to *Rousse*, it appears less ambiguous. The zinc tub and the smart wicker chairs that surround the woman are

68

familiar studio props. We might wonder if the painting represents a prostitute, and Lautrec allows us to do so; but knowledge of his art reveals her as merely a model.

The portrait of Hélène Vary (fig. 87) is another case in which the relationship between portrait and type—as well as between the socially, even morally, equivocal—has a fluid character. Lautrec was struck by his lovely neighbor's "Grecian profile," and he painted her elegant features in profile against stacked canvases in his studio.[23] Precisely drawn and sober in mien, if loosely handled in the background, it was exhibited in 1891 at the conservative Cercle Volney. If we did not know the sitter's name, we would take it as a—literally—upright type of young woman. Yet in 1890 Louis Anquetin also used Hélène as a model. He too set her half-length and in profile, but this time stripped to the waist and seen against a lurid wallpaper. It is a frank image of sexual display, and critics at the 1891 Indépendants greeted it with pawing prose.[24] Anquetin's somewhat exploitative painting throws us back to Lautrec's, with its almost prim demeanor now besmirched. Between them, the two paintings play with that decadent cocktail of propriety, sexuality, and hypocrisy. Lautrec's *Woman Smoking a Cigarette* (fig. 86) may also have been exhibited at the Indépendants in 1891 and at Les XX in Brussels the following year.[25] The speckled blouse and quirky coiffure frame a slightly sad face, drawing one into the equivocal world of impoverished women living in "Furnished Rooms," as Lautrec called a group of such images. As a critic at Les XX wrote, the physiognomy is exquisite, "despite God knows what hidden vices."[26]

If Lautrec rarely represented portraits of Montmartre types on the street, he frequently painted them in appropriate public locales. His powerful portrait of Van Gogh is a rare pastel, showing the Dutchman seated at a café table (fig. 88). There is nothing to show that the sitter is an artist, though the thrusting diagonal of his back, his alert gaze (created with just a dab of olive green), and the revealing tension in his hands suggest a determined debater. Lautrec used his medium adeptly. The telling facial profile is delineated less by a contour than by the "negative" of the blue zinc bar behind. The graphic, gestural strokes and the rich greens, yellows, and blues also add to a mood of animated intensity.

Van Gogh's own contemporary image of Agostina Segatori (fig. 90) lacks Lautrec's psychological depth or draftsmanly confidence, being a more documentary account of a Montmartre personality. As a younger woman La Segatori had been a model for painters like Corot. In the later 1880s she ran the Café du Tambourin at 60 boulevard de Clichy, and Van Gogh recorded the tambourine theme in the table and stools, with Japanese prints on the wall behind. La Segatori and Van Gogh may briefly have been lovers. He depicted her with a tired, vacant stare, while the cigarette added to her hand was an improvised marker of the independent bohemian woman, scorning bourgeois etiquette and running her own business.

It was in cafés such as the Tambourin that the mixed populations of Montmartre relaxed, met, and drank. The café was a multivalent space. Each establishment had its own identity and contributed to the collective personality of the *quartier*. Lautrec depicted the pimp Alfred la Guigne going about his criminal activities in a crowded café (see fig. 19), whereas in a painting at the 1893 Indépendants (fig. 91) he showed the portly Monsieur Boileau sitting in a café where bourgeois businessmen gather to play dominoes and chat. For all the latter's smug male conviviality, Boileau's companion—given the spectator's place—has before him a glass of absinthe, a highly alcoholic, indeed poisonous drink, seen as a threat to the health of the Third Republic and regularly condemned by doctors for its damage to mental and physical health.[27]

Lautrec's *Gueule de Bois* (fig. 92), probably made in 1888, takes its title from the slang for hangover. A drawing after it appeared in *Le Courrier français* on 21 April the following year.[28] Argot and illustration gave this work the peculiarly Montmartrois identity Lautrec probably desired. As such, it occupied the equivocal terrain the artist enjoyed, for it combines simultaneously social observation (the type, the working woman drinker) and role-playing sitter (probably Suzanne Valadon, former circus rider, artist's model, single mother, aspiring artist, herself characterizing the shifting identities that the struggle for life in the city involved). It also played the decadent card, as an exposé of female alcoholism, what one doctor damned as "the greatest social peril of today."[29] Other artists worked in the same territory. Edouard Vuillard's *Paul's Sin (Le Péché de Paul)* (fig. 94) represents a grinning woman who leans enthusiastically across the table toward the spectator, a glass of wine before her. Her somewhat exaggerated expression combines with Vuillard's giddy loops of the brush to give the image a sense of inebriation, while the title—Paul's sin—suggests that wine or women, those staples of café life, were doing that man no good.

Lautrec was no moralizer, nor was he a rigid ethnographer of Montmartre. He chose to paint people who interested him, and he employed them in different ways: as straightforward portraits, as performers, or just as models posed to present a type. He put his picked staffage from the populus of Montmartre to painterly problems, to specific projects, such as the full-length male portrait or the café scene. Lautrec's procedure may have been ad hoc, but his shrewd psychological analyses of the denizens of Montmartre, and his intricate, humorous, and ambiguous ways of weaving them into the discourses of the day remain remarkable social and artistic documents.

---

1. Hewitt 2000, 454–455.

2. "Notes sur Paris. Les Bals publics," *Le Phare de la Loire*, 5 February 1889, quoted in Schwob 1981, 43; B. Thomson 2001, 38–40.

3. Richard Thomson, "The Cultural Geography of the Petit Boulevard," in St. Louis 2001, 65–108.

4. Milner 1988, 111–163.

5. Hoche 1883, 33–34.

6. For the Sacré-Coeur, see Raymond Jonas, "Sacred Tourism and Secular Pilgrimage: Montmartre and the Basilica of the Sacré-Coeur," in Weisberg 2001, 94–119.

7. Leyret 1895 (2000 ed.), 86.

8. Letter to Armand Rassenfosse, 15 March 1893, quoted in Hélène Védrine, "Les Ateliers de Rops à Paris," in Namur, Corbeil-Essonnes, Quebec 1998, 62.

9. On this point see Michael Wilson, "'Sans les femmes, qu'est-ce qui nous resterait?': Gender and Transgression in Bohemian Montmartre," in Epstein and Straub 1991, 195–122.

10. Joyant 1927, 63,

11. Joyant 1927, opp. p. 74.

12. Paris 1982, 23.

13. Schimmel ed. 1991, 140–141, nos. 186 and 187.

14. Frey 1994, 280.

15. Chicago 1979, 225–226.

16. Dortu 1971, P. 376, 467; Murray 1991, 213–214.

17. Wittrock 1985, P. 24.

18. Schimmel ed. 1991, 295, no. 463; Nocq 1896, n.p. I am grateful to Robert Herbert for bringing Nocq's book to my attention.

19. Lautrec rudely quipped that Nocq had a reversible name. Natanson 1951, 42.

20. Coman 1994, n.p.

21. Leclercq 1921 (1954 ed.), 114–115.

22. London and Paris 1991, 412.

23. Gauzi 1954, 160–161.

24. Retté 1891, 296; Gauthier-Villars 1891, 112; Thomson 2004, 42–43.

25. London and Paris 1991, 180.

26. Olin 1892, 343–344.

27. Richer 1885, 328–332.

28. Murray 1991, 163; Cambridge 2002.

29. Devoisins 1885, 69.

70

Maximilien Luce, *View from Montmartre*, 1887, oil on canvas, 54 x 63 cm. Petit Palais. Musée d'art moderne, Geneva

71

Vincent van Gogh, *A Corner of Montmartre: The Moulin à Poivre*, 1887, oil on canvas, 35 x 64.5 cm. Van Gogh Museum Amsterdam (Vincent van Gogh Foundation)

72
Vincent van Gogh, *Terrace and Observation Deck at the Moulin de Blute-Fin, Montmartre,* **1886, oil on canvas, mounted on pressboard, 43.6 x 33 cm. The Art Institute of Chicago, Helen Birch Bartlett Memorial Collection**

73
Vincent van Gogh, *The View from Vincent's Room, Rue Lepic,* **1887, oil on cardboard, 46 x 38 cm. Private collection**

74

Pierre Bonnard, *Montmartre in
the Rain*, c. 1897, oil on paper
laid down on panel, 70 x 95 cm.
Galerie Jan Krugier, Ditesheim &
Cie, Geneva

75

Ramón Casas, *Erik Satie
(El bohemio; Poet of
Montmartre)*, 1891, oil on
canvas, 198.8 x 99.7 cm.
Northwestern University
Library

76

Henri de Toulouse-Lautrec,
Gaston Bonnefoy, 1891,
oil on cardboard, 71 x 37 cm.
Museo Thyssen-Bornemisza,
Madrid

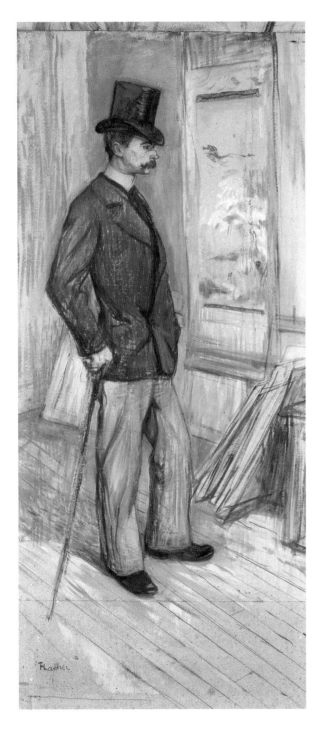

77

Henri de Toulouse-Lautrec,
Paul Sescau, 1891, oil on
cardboard, 82.5 x 35.6 cm.
Brooklyn Museum, Museum
Surplus Fund and purchased
with funds given by Dikran G.
Kelekian 22.66

78

Jean-Louis Forain, *Jacques–
Emile Blanche*, 1884, oil on
canvas mounted on cardboard,
64 x 40 cm. Musée des Beaux-
Arts de Rouen

Henri de Toulouse-Lautrec,
Young Woman at a Table,
"Poudre de riz" (Rice Powder),
1887, oil on canvas, 56 x 46 cm.
Van Gogh Museum Amsterdam
(Vincent van Gogh Foundation)

Edgar Degas, *Woman Brushing
Her Hair*, c. 1884, oil on canvas,
74.3 x 60.6 cm. The Kreeger
Museum, Washington, D.C.

84

Henri de Toulouse-Lautrec,
Rousse (Redhead), also
known as *La Toilette*, 1889,
oil on canvas, 67 x 54 cm.
Musée d'Orsay, Paris; bequest
of Pierre Goujon, 1914

85
———
Edouard Manet, *Plum Brandy*,
c. 1877, oil on canvas, 73.6 x
50.2 cm. National Gallery of
Art, Washington, Collection of
Mr. and Mrs. Paul Mellon

86
———
Henri de Toulouse-Lautrec,
Woman Smoking a Cigarette,
1890, oil on cardboard,
47 x 30 cm. Brooklyn Museum,
Museum Surplus Fund and
purchased with funds given
by Dikran G. Kelekian

87

Henri de Toulouse-Lautrec,
Hélène Vary, **1889,** oil
on cardboard, **74.5 x 49** cm.
Kunsthalle Bremen

Henri de Toulouse-Lautrec,
Vincent van Gogh, 1887, pastel
on board, 57 x 46.5 cm. Van
Gogh Museum Amsterdam
(Vincent van Gogh Foundation)

89

Vincent van Gogh, *Glass of Absinthe and a Carafe*, 1887, oil on canvas, 46.5 x 33 cm. Van Gogh Museum Amsterdam (Vincent van Gogh Foundation)

90

Vincent van Gogh, *Agostina Segatori at the Café du Tambourin*, 1887, oil on canvas, 55 x 46.5 cm. Van Gogh Museum Amsterdam (Vincent van Gogh Foundation)

Henri de Toulouse-Lautrec,
Monsieur Boileau, c. 1893,
gouache on cardboard, 80 x
65 cm. The Cleveland Museum
of Art, Hinman B. Hurlbut
Collection

92

———

Henri de Toulouse-Lautrec, *The Hangover (Gueule de Bois)*, probably 1888, oil on canvas, 45.1 x 53.3 cm. Fogg Art Museum, Harvard University Art Museums, Bequest from the Collection of Maurice Wertheim, Class of 1906

93

———

Henri de Toulouse-Lautrec, *At Grenelle*, c. 1888, oil on canvas, 55.9 x 46.8 cm. Sterling and Francine Clark Art Institute, Williamstown, Massachusetts

94

Edouard Vuillard, *Paul's Sin*
(*Le Péché de Paul*), 1895, oil on
canvas, 65.5 x 54 cm. Courtesy
of Galerie Schmit, Paris

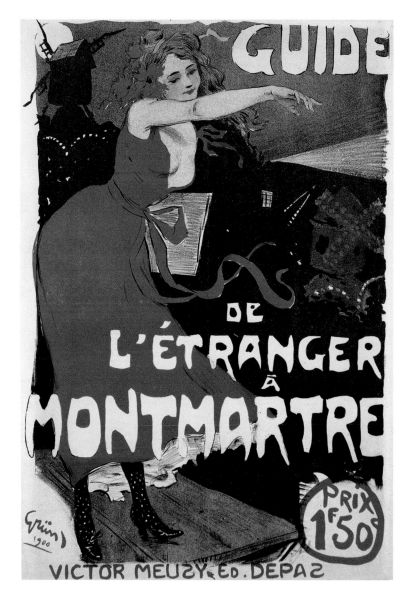

95

Jules Alexandre Grün, *"Guide de l'Etranger à Montmartre,"* 1900, color lithograph, 60 x 40.5 cm. The Jane Voorhees Zimmerli Art Museum, Rutgers, The State University of New Jersey, David A. and Mildred H. Morse Art Acquisition Fund

96

Maxime Dethomas, *"Montmartre,"* 1897, color lithograph, 80.5 x 61 cm. The Jane Voorhees Zimmerli Art Museum, Rutgers, The State University of New Jersey, Gift of Herbert D. and Ruth Schimmel

Mary Weaver Chapin

THE CHAT NOIR & THE CABARETS

———

When Rodolphe Salis died in 1897, the inscription on his tombstone read: "God created the world, Napoleon the Legion of Honor, and I, Montmartre."[1] And in truth, the neighborhood of Montmartre had undergone a profound transformation since the founding of his cabaret artistique, the Chat Noir, in 1881. In the intervening years this arrondissement had metamorphosed from a dangerous outlying quarter into the entertainment and pleasure center of Paris. Salis and his cadre of talented writers, poets, artists, and singers spawned a specifically Montmartrois performance and experience that drew audiences throughout Paris, the provinces, and Europe.[2] The adjective "Chatnoiresque" was coined to describe this unique blend of irreverence, humor, and art, which was a defining attribute of Montmartre culture. Moreover, Salis had a keen eye for talent and supported a remarkable group of artists and performers, some of whom, like the charismatic and influential Aristide Bruant, later opened competing cabarets. And although it would be some years before Toulouse-Lautrec became intimately involved in the production of this entertainment and designed his groundbreaking posters advertising Montmartre, the early days of the Chat Noir were essential to the artistic formation of Lautrec and his contemporaries. Thus, at the time of his death, Salis could rightly claim credit for creating, at least in part, the mythic Montmartre of fin-de-siècle Paris, an image that lingers even today.

THE FIRST CHAT NOIR

Salis, the son of a brewer in central France, came to Paris with artistic ambitions but modest talent. After a brief period at the Ecole des Beaux-Arts and rejection at the official French Salon, Salis took an entrepreneurial turn. With the blessing and financial backing of his father, he opened a small café in a former post office at 84 boulevard Rochechouart, a bustling street at the foot of the butte Montmartre.[3] His choice of location was astute: Montmartre was rapidly replacing the Latin Quarter as the locus for student activity. It was also close to artists' ateliers, including that of Fernand Cormon, where Toulouse-Lautrec enrolled late in 1882.[4] In addition, Salis' cabaret was situated near important entertainment centers such as the Elysée-Montmartre dance hall and the Grande Pinte, a popular café founded in 1878.

Salis opened the doors of his cabaret artistique in November 1881 under the name "Le Chat Noir" (The Black Cat). This appellation had a wide resonance, evoking the work of both Charles Baudelaire and Edgar Allan Poe, the latter author being widely admired by the artistic community in Paris at this time.[5] It also recalled traditional French auberges.[6] And the black cat was often a character in classic French folktales, "sometimes as a figure who punished disobedient children and sometimes as a seductive lover."[7] Moreover, the image and the term *chat noir* were double entendres and "could be simultaneously innocent and sexually provocative."[8] The mixture of history, art, literature, and sexual suggestion implied by the name suited Salis' intentions perfectly, and the black cat, with all its innuendo, became an enduring symbol of Montmartre.

Among the first patrons at the Chat Noir were the Hydropathes, the loose-knit group of students, artists, and writers gathered around the inventive poet Emile Goudeau (discussed more fully in Dennis Cate's essay). Forsaking their familiar café on the Left Bank, they found a home at Salis' eclectic establishment. Word of mouth, in addition to Salis' vigorous promotional activities, made the Chat Noir a favorite destination for writers, poets, musicians, and artists, including Toulouse-Lautrec. These talented young people were not only the clients but also the entertainment: poets recited their latest verses, up-and-coming songwriters penned witty and risqué chansons for singers like Aristide Bruant, and artists contributed to the lively bohemian atmosphere by donating paintings, drawings, and stained-glass windows for the décor and by producing illustrations for the journal published by Salis, *Le Chat Noir*. This paper was a brilliant publicity organ, advertising the venue's entertainment and publishing excerpts of songs heard in the cabaret. Just as important, it established the identity of the Chat Noir by the irreverent tone of the articles and the illustrations by Montmartrois artists. The journal disseminated Chatnoiresque art and humor throughout Paris and the provinces. By 1884 *Le Chat Noir* had a weekly circulation of 20,000, which testifies to the widespread celebrity the cabaret and its journal achieved in two short years.[9]

The Chat Noir was decorated in a pseudo-medieval style, bursting with Louis XIII furniture, heavy oak tables, and a playful assortment of accessories, including medieval armor, tapestries, pewter mugs, and stained glass. This was in sharp contrast to the more refined cafés on the *grands boulevards,* where tastefully decorated interiors featured chandeliers, mirrors, and harmonious furniture. Within this hodge-podge of decoration, the black cat was the unifying motif, both inside and out. Adolphe Willette designed three signs featuring the cat perched on a crescent moon, which hung outside the establishment. Once inside, patrons could find the feline in a large ironwork sculpture of a sunburst with a cat's head over the mantel of the fireplace and in paintings and stained glass. Soon after the opening of the cabaret, Willette created a stained-glass panel of a woman standing before a full moon, a black cat perched on her head; the preliminary canvas for this work survives

(fig. 97). The cat, a scraggly creature with a scruffy tail, holds its paws high in the air in a sign of aggression. The painting, known as *The Green Virgin* or *The Virgin with Cat,* is a compelling combination of innocence and sexuality. Georges Montorgeuil, a writer and Montmartre regular, noted this aspect, describing the figure as a "gracious sphinx with the eyes of a wild beast, innocent and cruel."[10] The blond, fresh-faced young woman in the painting lifts her large green eyes upward in a gaze of reverence; the lily tucked into her green cloak is both the attribute of the Virgin Mary and a symbol of purity. Yet the full moon and the domineering pose of the alley cat convey the uninhibited sexuality that characterized Montmartre as well as the double entendres and mixed messages that made Chatnoiresque humor so witty and sophisticated.

Nowhere is the black cat more insistently present than in the paintings that Théophile-Alexandre Steinlen prepared for the cabaret. In one canvas the imperious feline stands on its hind legs and holds a red flag bearing the word "Gaudeamus" (fig. 98), a reference to the Latin phrase "Gaudeamus igitur iuvenes dum sumas" (Be joyful while we are young), the opening line of a famous student song dating to the Middle Ages.[11] In *Apotheosis of Cats* (fig. 99), a massive mural three meters wide and over a meter and a half tall, cats of all colors perch on rooftops and turn toward a large black cat poised before a full moon. They appear to be worshiping the feline on the hill of Montmartre and all that it represents: freedom, sexuality, and an alternative to bourgeois Paris.

THE SECOND CHAT NOIR

So popular was Salis' amalgam of music, humor, and art that he sought larger quarters on the rue Laval (now called the rue Victor Massé) in May 1885. In a savvy promotional gesture he turned the move into a grand spectacle and parade, which he led himself. He was dressed in an embroidered suit and followed by a brass band, Swiss guards in uniform, and four men dressed as members of the Académie française carrying Willette's huge canvas *Parce Domine* (see fig. 6) with great pomp. This heterogeneous group processed through the boulevards attracting large crowds and arousing curiosity before rushing into the spacious headquarters of the new Chat Noir.[12]

Salis continued to promote his particular brand of entertainment—chansons, poetry, irreverent plays—in the second Chat Noir, but a new feature would make this cabaret artistique even more famous: a shadow theater (théâtre d'ombres). Shadow theaters were not new; they were common family entertainments in eighteenth- and nineteenth-century France and dated back to ancient times. They had a Japanese heritage as well, and the vogue for japonisme was widespread in artistic circles. But the productions at the Chat Noir brought this art form to a new level in fin-de-siècle Paris.[13] The shadow theater also inspired painters and graphic artists to experiment with new expressive means, using silhouettes and shadows to suggest mystery, or the essence of a figure, or simply to refer to the fashionable shadow plays of the Chat Noir.[14]

The artist Henri Rivière was the genius behind the shadow theater of the Chat Noir. The first presentations were fairly modest: a stretched canvas served as the screen, and a light source was projected from behind. Artists manipulated cardboard cutouts behind the screen to create silhouettes (fig. 100). Soon, however, the shadow theater grew more complex, and the improvised cardboard figures were replaced by durable zinc cutouts, both simple silhouettes as well as elaborate, multifigure groupings (figs. 101a–d). The performances became even more advanced after the summer of 1887 when the theater was enlarged. Sound effects, colored lights, painted backgrounds, and an orchestra or chorus made these productions highly sophisticated entertainments, often employing twenty or more artists to maneuver the silhouettes to great effect.[15]

The shadow plays were an overwhelming hit, not just with the locals of Montmartre but with the elite circles in Paris, and they were advertised with posters by Rivière, often adorned with the silhouette of the black cat (figs. 102 and 103). The success of these programs prompted Salis to take his theater on tour, boldly announced by Steinlen's now-famous poster (fig. 104). Salis' good fortune did not go unnoticed by Parisian entrepreneurs, and competing venues began their own shadow theaters.[16] Georges Redon's poster for the Boîte à Musique cabaret depicts the smartly dressed men and women who flocked to Montmartre to see the spectacle (fig. 105). As with other Montmartre entertainments, like Aristide Bruant's performances, discussed below, what began

as impromptu, irreverent, and anti-bourgeois events soon drew crowds from all classes of Paris.

The death of Rodophe Salis in 1897 spelled the end of the Chat Noir. In the fifteen years of its operation, this cabaret was fundamental in establishing the spirit of Montmartre, what Maurice Donnay, a regular participant and patron, described as "alternately and at the same time teasing, ironic, tender, naturalistic, realistic, idealistic, cynical, lyrical, fumiste, religious, mystical, Christian, pagan, anarchistic, chauvinistic, republican, reactionary—everything except, in my opinion, boring."[17] Yet even before Salis' death other cabaret owners and their patrons had taken up this esprit, and none was more successful than the former star of the Chat Noir, Aristide Bruant.

ARISTIDE BRUANT AND THE MIRLITON

Although the Chat Noir reflected the remarkable collaborative effort of artists, poets, writers, and singers, and Salis served as a flamboyant and creative impresario, it was generally the establishment rather than individuals that became famous. An exception was the talented singer, songwriter, and entrepreneur Aristide Bruant. It is unclear who first introduced Bruant to Salis around 1883 or 1884, but Bruant became one of the most popular performers at the Chat Noir. He had enjoyed a comfortable childhood and education in the village of Courtenay, roughly fifty miles southeast of Paris, but at some point his family fell on hard times and Bruant sought employment in Paris, where he worked as a clerk and as a functionary of the railroad.[18] By night, however, he immersed himself in the life of the street, studying the language, attitudes, and subculture of the rough outer boulevards and quartiers like Montmartre. He composed verses recounting tales of pimps, prostitutes, and others down on their luck. Written entirely in the argot of lower- and working-class Parisians, Bruant's songs chronicled their daily struggles for existence. "At Saint-Ouen" was the lament of an exhausted laborer, while "At Saint-Lazare" was narrated by a poor streetwalker writing to her lover from the syphilis hospital/prison (fig. 106). By adopting the slang and gestures of these characters, Bruant appeared to offer the authentic experience of the disinherited, performed for the increasingly bourgeois audiences of the Chat Noir.

When Salis moved the Chat Noir to its second location in 1885, Bruant took over the old space at 84 boulevard Rochechouart and renamed it the Mirliton. He immediately took steps to make his operation stand apart from his former employer's. Unlike the Chat Noir, with its claustrophobic interior crammed full of bric-a-brac, Bruant's cabaret was furnished with rough benches and tables. In direct contrast to Salis' ironically obsequious manner, Bruant harassed and insulted his clientele. Yet like his competitor and inspiration, Bruant also published an eponymous journal, *Le Mirliton*, featuring songs, interviews, and illustrations. Toulouse-Lautrec, who probably knew Bruant from the Chat Noir, quickly joined him at his new cabaret.[19] Steinlen, who had contributed such salient images to the Chat Noir, became the unofficial illustrator for Bruant's volumes of songs and monologues as well as for *Le Mirliton* (figs. 107–111).

ARISTIDE BRUANT AND TOULOUSE-LAUTREC

The trajectories of Toulouse-Lautrec's and Bruant's careers intersected with dramatic results in 1892. Both were gaining recognition in Montmartre and beyond, and both marketed a vision of life on the butte that appealed to bourgeois audiences. Soon Bruant was invited to leave his small cabaret to perform at the upscale cafés-concerts on the boulevards of central Paris, which could accommodate large crowds and would be more acceptable to the genteel audiences who were fascinated by him. When he secured a contract at the Ambassadeurs on the Champs-Elysées, Bruant immediately commissioned a poster from Lautrec to announce his arrival. Although Lautrec had created only one previous publicity poster—*Moulin Rouge: La Goulue* (see fig. 10)—Bruant appreciated the sensation it had caused and recognized it as a watershed in marketing a personality and the experience of Montmartre. Bruant's instincts were excellent: together he and Lautrec forged a relationship that skillfully promoted Bruant's act, enhanced Lautrec's art, and accelerated the celebrity status of both men. On a personal level, Bruant's association with Lautrec also helped him bridge the worlds of high society and déclassé Montmartre, for Lautrec, who was an aristocrat as well as an enthusiastic denizen of Montmartre, represented this paradox well.

Lautrec seized on the irony of marketing the outsider Bruant to the elite of Paris and created a poster that captured Bruant's Montmartrois persona with panache. *Ambassadeurs: Aristide Bruant* (fig. 113) was printed on two sheets of paper using five colors of ink. The massive figure of the entertainer, standing in three-quarter profile to the left, dominates the composition. He is instantly recognizable by his signature costume—a dark cloak, wide-brimmed hat, and red scarf—as well as by his characteristic expression: part scowl, part knowing smirk. A shadowy proletarian form looms in the background, suggesting the dangerous nights of Montmartre, even though Bruant was appearing at the luxurious Ambassadeurs café-concert, safe in the heart of bourgeois Paris.[20]

The flat colors, schematic design, and irregular, hand-lettered text evoke inexpensive chromolithographs and folk prints (*images d'Epinal*) and established an association between the rough, popular aspect of the poster and the reputation Bruant cultivated. The effect of unmediated spontaneity, however, is belied by the masterfully arranged composition, which integrates text and image, balances the dark exterior with the vibrant light of the café-concert, and uses flat color yet also gives an illusion of depth behind the performer. Pinning the entire composition in place is the red scarf, which forms a T-shape with its strong vertical down the center of the poster; the crossbar highlights Bruant's face and provides a connection between his dark cape and the figure of the hoodlum behind him. The placement on the page, too, is artful, producing an image that is both dynamic and iconic. Bruant seems to be striding in from the dark, and the diagonal of his walking stick generates the sensation of forward movement.

Bruant recognized the brilliance of Toulouse-Lautrec's achievement. One anecdote relates that when Bruant first saw the poster, he was overwhelmed by the powerful presence of his imposing figure. "Am I that grand?" he asked, to which the artist replied, "Even grander, that's what posterity will say."[21] Although most likely apocryphal, this exchange highlights the monumentality Lautrec was able to convey with only five colors on just under one and a half square meters of paper. The manager of the Ambassadeurs, Pierre Ducarre, was less pleased and initially refused to use the poster. Bruant insisted, adding,

"Well, old man, as a punishment you must cover the walls of Paris with it!"[22] Other accounts of this episode suggest that Ducarre did not capitulate immediately but hired the printshop of Charles Lévy to make a new poster. The resulting image privileges Bruant's features, producing a photographic likeness of the performer (fig. 114). This was obviously the intent, for the work boasts that it was created "after the photograph by Benque," but the vapid stare of Bruant does little to promote his specific act or the persona he had crafted.[23]

Lautrec's poster for Bruant provoked a tremendous stir. An article in *La Plume* praised the artist for rendering "the fierce, slightly wild and imposing side of the street singer. He certainly captures this fiercely bitter man with his harsh and poignant talent. . . . You can see in his face the daring of the gallant rebel and his hatred of the 'filthy rich' as well as the sadness born of pain and poverty."[24] The irony, of course, is that Bruant was performing for the "filthy rich" while becoming richer and richer himself. The commanding posters by Lautrec, which communicated Bruant's marketed personality while attracting a wealthy audience, fit the bill perfectly.

Bruant continued to commission posters from Lautrec to advertise his engagements at upscale Parisian cafés-concerts. For *Eldorado: Aristide Bruant*, 1892 (fig. 115), Lautrec used new lithographic stones but recycled the composition and dimensions of his poster for the Ambassadeurs while reversing the image. The following year Lautrec created his sparest design for Bruant (fig. 116), with the performer turning his back to the viewer and glancing over his left shoulder, to reveal his face in profile. Now reduced to a few elemental shapes, this forceful hieroglyph served as Bruant's logo in a variety of formats. Not only did the poster hang outside the Mirliton (in a slightly modified form), but Bruant also took the detail of his head and hat from Lautrec's rendering and had it printed on glass for use on all sides of a large lantern hanging on the second story of the building.[25] Once inside the cabaret, patrons could see Lautrec's posters hanging on the wall and could purchase reduced versions as keepsakes. In addition, Steinlen depicted this image in his illustration for the cover of the 9 June 1893 edition of *Le Mirliton,* in which a well-dressed man (representing the right-wing novelist Maurice Barrès) stands before a copy of the poster, carefully considering the work (see fig. 33). Behind him, several dogs sniff each other and urinate against a wall, illustrating the Bruant monologue printed beneath, "Les Quat'Pattes" (The Four Paws). Here Steinlen artfully suggests several confluent trends in the Bruant mythology. By placing the scene in Montmartre, he implies the dangerous, indeterminate *quartiers* about which Bruant sang; the gentleman's presence in this neighborhood suggests the appeal of Montmartre for the bourgeoisie; and Lautrec's iconic poster testifies to the success of the artist's and the chansonnier's packaging and promotion of the Bruant cult of personality.

When Bruant commissioned a fourth poster from Lautrec, his trademark costume and posture were so well known that the artist could depict the performer from behind and still count on the public to recognize him (fig. 117). This poster was printed with three different texts and also used on the cover of *Le Mirliton* (fig. 118). The version of the poster shown here announces the appearance of Bruant's second volume of songs and monologues, *Sur la Route.* Interestingly, Bruant chose Steinlen to illustrate both books but still turned to Lautrec for the poster to advertise it, astutely sensing the difference between Steinlen's more narrative, illustrative style and Lautrec's bold graphic language.

Bruant's performances, books, biographies (fig. 119), lithographs (fig. 120), and savvy promotional skills made him a wealthy man. In 1895 he sold his cabaret to his pianist but continued to compose songs and monologues, produced a two-volume dictionary of Parisian argot, and wrote a novel in five volumes that recounted tales of life in Montmartre, *Les BasFonds de Paris (The Seediest Parts of Paris).* It is remarkable that Bruant was able to maintain his outsider status even after retiring to a country estate in his native Courtenay. His personal charisma and business savvy certainly played a role. Yet Lautrec's contribution should not be overlooked. His posters, vigorously drawn and rigorously spare, encapsulated the rough, déclassé image that made Bruant a star of Montmartre. Meanwhile, Lautrec's association with the master entertainer burnished his own celebrity reputation as the official painter and poster maker of the pleasures and personalities of Montmartre.

1. Houchin 1984, 11.

2. For an analysis of Montmartre humor and style, see New Brunswick 1996.

3. Paris 1992, 4; Santa Barbara 1993, 11.

4. Lautrec entered Cormon's studio, which was about a dozen blocks from the Chat Noir, in late November or early December 1882 (Murray 1991, 40).

5. Catalogue of the Chat Noir auction, 1898, vii, preface by Georges Montorgueil.

6. Michael Logan-John Wilson, "Le Commerce de la Bohème: Marginality and Mass Culture in Fin-de-Siècle Paris" (Ph.D. diss., Cornell University, 1993), 91–92

7. Santa Barbara 1993, 11.

8. Phillip Dennis Cate in New Brunswick 1996, 37

9. Wilson 1993, 127.

10. Chat Noir auction catalogue, 1898, viii.

11. Entry for "Gaudéamus" in Pierre Larousse, *Grand Dictionnaire universel du XIXe siècle*, vol. 8, pt. 2 (Paris, 1866–1879; repr. Geneva and Paris, 1982), 1076.

12. For an account of this dramatic move, see, for example, Horace Valbel, *Les Chansonniers et les cabarets artistiques* (Paris, 1895), 67–68, quoted in New Brunswick 1996, 39.

13. Cate in New Brunswick 1996, 54–55; Elena Cueto-Asín, "The Chat Noir's Théâtre d'Ombres: Shadow Plays and the Recuperation of Public Space," in Weisberg 2001, 233; Paris 1992, 40–41; and Forgione 1999, 490–512.

14. See Forgione 1999 for a discussion of the multivalent meanings and uses of show and silhouette in fin-de-siècle art, theater, and illustration. On the Nabi artists and the aesthetics of the shadow, see New Brunswick 1988c, 53–75. See also New Brunswick 1996, 53–63.

15. For a description of the elaborate effects created at the Chat Noir shadow theater, see Donnay 1926, 38–40.

16. The Quat'z'Arts, the Boîte à Fursy, the Lune Rousse, and the Chaumière cabaret, for instance, all added shadow plays to their list of attractions (Renoy 1975, 178).

17. Donnay 1926, 46.

18. Bruant's biographies (and his autobiography) are full of contradictions, but most authors agree on these basic facts. See, for example, Méténier 1893; Zévaes 1943; Mouloudji 1972; and Marc 1989.

19. Lautrec continued to frequent the Chat Noir even after Bruant left, as his letter to his mother of July 1886 attests: "I've been having a very good time lately here at the Chat Noir. We organized an orchestra and got the people dancing. It was great fun, only we didn't get to bed until 5 in the morning, which made my work suffer a little that morning" (Schimmel ed. 1991, no. 129).

20. In this poster, Richard Thomson observes, Lautrec uses the silhouette, which the Chat Noir's shadow plays had trained the public's eye to "read" as a minimalist suggestion of a proletarian urban type—a worker, if not a mugger or thug. The figure does not threaten Bruant, reinforcing the sense that the singer moves freely through the backstreets where the bourgeois dare not go. In this way Lautrec uses a modish visual idiom to convey Bruant's "mean streets" credentials and his modernity. Louis Valtat's painting, *The Couple at the Lapin Agile Cabaret*, c. 1895 (fig. 112), uses a similar device and composition. The imagery of the shadow theater is thus translated for use in posters, then paintings.

21. Sauvage 1992, 7.

22. Joyant 1927, 106.

23. The Musée de Montmartre dates this poster to c. 1890. Sauvage 1992, 7–8, however, argues that it could not be anterior to Lautrec's poster, for this was Bruant's first appearance at the Ambassadeurs. It is not clear if or when Lévy's design was posted.

24. Jourdain 1893, 490. Murray 1992, 165, notes that this text was probably penned by Francis Jourdain, who signed it with the name of his father, the well-known architect Frantz Jourdain.

25. Chapin 2002, 112.

99

Théophile-Alexandre Steinlen,
Apotheosis of Cats, c. 1890,
oil on canvas, 164.5 x 300 cm.
Petit Palais, Musée d'art moderne,
Geneva

100

Louis Morin et al., *Théâtre
du Chat Noir*, n.d., album of
ink and crayon drawings for
plays and programs for plays,
32.5 x 25.5 x 2.5 cm. The Jane
Voorhees Zimmerli Art Museum,
Rutgers, The State University
of New Jersey, Joyce and Alvin
Glassgold Fund

I O I a

Henry Somm, *Five Female Figures with a Dog,* **silhouettes for the shadow play** *Le Fils de l'eunuque,* **1887, zinc, 49 x 55.6 cm. The Jane Voorhees Zimmerli Art Museum, Rutgers, The State University of New Jersey, Mindy and Ramon Tublitz Purchase Fund**

I O I b

Anonymous, *Old Lady,* **silhouette for an unidentified shadow play, c. 1890–1895, zinc, 44.5 x 24.4 cm. The Jane Voorhees Zimmerli Art Museum, Rutgers, The State University of New Jersey, Norma B. Bartman Purchase Fund**

I O I c

Anonymous, *Young Woman,* **silhouette for an unidentified shadow play, c. 1890–1895, zinc, 37 x 14 cm. The Jane Voorhees Zimmerli Art Museum, Rutgers, The State University of New Jersey, Mindy and Ramon Tublitz Purchase Fund**

I O I d

Henri Rivière, silhouette for the shadow play *La Tentation de Saint Antoine (The Temptation of Saint Anthony),* **1887, zinc, 75 x 42 cm. The Jane Voorhees Zimmerli Art Museum, Rutgers, The State University of New Jersey, Gift of University College Rutgers New Brunswick Alumni Association**

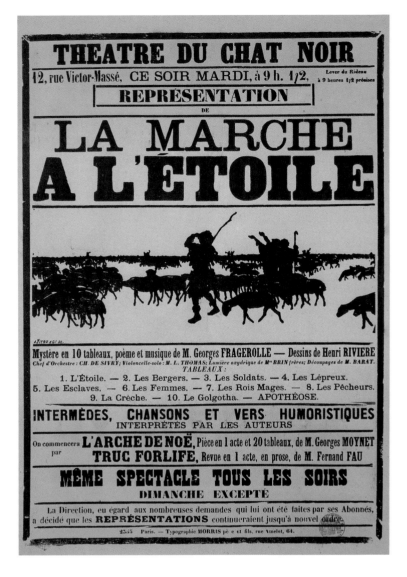

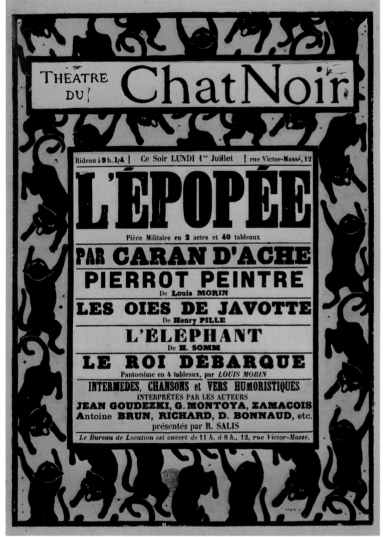

102

Henri Rivière, *Chat Noir:*
"La Marche à l'étoile," c. 1890,
stencil-colored photorelief,
58 x 41.5 cm. The Jane Voorhees
Zimmerli Art Museum, Rutgers,
The State University of New
Jersey, Herbert D. and Ruth
Schimmel Museum Library Fund

103

Henri Rivière, *Chat Noir:*
"L'Epopée," c. 1890, stencil-
colored photorelief, 58 x 41 cm.
The Jane Voorhees Zimmerli
Art Museum, Rutgers, The
State University of New Jersey,
Herbert D. and Ruth Schimmel
Museum Library Fund

104

Théophile-Alexandre Steinlen,
Tournée du Chat Noir, 1896,
color lithograph, 135.9 x 95.9
cm. The Jane Voorhees Zimmerli
Art Museum, Rutgers, The State
University of New Jersey,
Gift of Susan Schimmel Goldstein

105

Georges Redon, *La Boîte à
Musique*, 1897, color lithograph,
86.6 x 118.6 cm. Collection
Musée de Montmartre, Paris

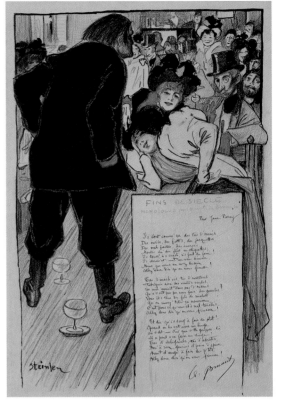

106

Henri de Toulouse-Lautrec
(signed Tréclau), *"A Saint-
Lazare,"* cover for *Le Mirliton*
(August 1887), color photorelief.
The Jane Voorhees Zimmerli Art
Museum, Rutgers, The State
University of New Jersey, Herbert
D. and Ruth Schimmel Museum
Library Fund

107

Théophile-Alexandre Steinlen,
*"Fins de siècle: Monologue par
Aristide Bruant,"* c. 1894–1895,
color lithograph, 46 x 30.5 cm.
Arthur E. Vershbow

108

Théophile-Alexandre Steinlen,
"Dans la rue," cover for *Le
Mirliton* (January–February
1891), color photorelief. The Jane
Voorhees Zimmerli Art Museum,
Rutgers, The State University of
New Jersey, Herbert D. and Ruth
Schimmel Museum Library Fund

109

Théophile-Alexandre Steinlen,
"La Vigne au vin," cover for
Le Mirliton (20 January 1893),
color photorelief. The Jane
Voorhees Zimmerli Art Museum,
Rutgers, The State University of
New Jersey, Herbert D. and Ruth
Schimmel Museum Library Fund

110

Théophile-Alexandre Steinlen,
"Tha-ma-ra-boum-de-hé,"
cover for *Le Mirliton* (17 Febru-
ary 1893), color photorelief.
The Jane Voorhees Zimmerli
Art Museum, Rutgers, The
State University of New Jersey,
Herbert D. and Ruth Schimmel
Museum Library Fund

111

Théophile-Alexandre Steinlen
(signed Jean Caillou), *Sainte
Marmite,* cover for *Le Mirliton*
(15 January 1886), color photo-
relief. The Jane Voorhees
Zimmerli Art Museum, Rutgers,
The State University of New
Jersey, Herbert D. and Ruth
Schimmel Museum Library Fund

Louis Valtat, *The Couple at the
Lapin Agile Cabaret*, c. 1895,
oil on paper, 79.9 x 62.1 cm.
Collection, Art Gallery of Ontario,
Toronto; Gift of Sam and Ayala
Zacks, 1970

113

Henri de Toulouse-Lautrec,
Ambassadeurs: Aristide Bruant,
1892, color lithograph, 147.2 x
99.9 cm (both sheets). The Art
Institute of Chicago, Mr. and
Mrs. Carter H. Harrison Collection

114

Anonymous, *Ambassadeurs:
Aristide Bruant in His Cabaret*,
c. 1890, color lithograph,
122.8 x 87 cm. Collection Musée
de Montmartre, Paris

Henri de Toulouse-Lautrec,
Eldorado: Aristide Bruant,
1892, color lithograph, 145.2 x
98.7 cm (sheet). The Art Institute
of Chicago, Mr. and Mrs. Carter
H. Harrison Collection

Henri de Toulouse-Lautrec,
Aristide Bruant in His Cabaret,
1893, color lithograph, 138 x
99.1 cm (sheet). The Art Institute
of Chicago, Mr. and Mrs. Carter
H. Harrison Collection

Henri de Toulouse-Lautrec, *Bruant at the Mirliton*, 1893, color lithograph, 82.3 x 60.9 cm (sheet). The Art Institute of Chicago, Mr. and Mrs. Carter H. Harrison Collection

118

Henri de Toulouse-Lautrec, *"Bruant au Mirliton,"* cover for *Le Mirliton* (15 November 1894), color photorelief. The Jane Voorhees Zimmerli Art Museum, Rutgers, The State University of New Jersey, Herbert D. and Ruth Schimmel Museum Library Fund

119

Oscar Méténier, *Aristide Bruant* (Paris 1893), book. The Jane Voorhees Zimmerli Art Museum, Rutgers, The State University of New Jersey, Gift of Norma D. Bartman

120

Anonymous, *Aristide Bruant,* c. 1892, color lithograph. The Jane Voorhees Zimmerli Art Museum, Rutgers, The State University of New Jersey, Gift of Herbert D. and Ruth Schimmel

Dimanches et Fêtes
à
2 heures

Matinées dansantes
Kermesse

Richard Thomson

DANCE HALLS

———

The paintings that Toulouse-Lautrec made of the dance halls of Montmartre are among his most complex works. They constitute the majority of his large, multifigure canvases, works challenging his compositional skill. With their subject drawn from a particular contemporary social phenomenon and their staffage of types taken from various strata of the Parisian population, they articulate his understanding of a specific subculture. Finally, Lautrec's ready use of this important group of paintings in his exhibiting strategy, as he sought to make a name for himself in the Salon des Indépendants and other avant-garde forums, suggests that he was satisfied with these pictures. The dance hall was a subject that suited his personal representation of modernity. Yet praised as these paintings were in Lautrec's lifetime and famous as they have become since, they are intricate works that raise tricky questions about how they should be read.

Dance halls had long existed in Paris as places of diversion for its working classes. They were not new to the 1880s and 1890s. The Elysée-Montmartre on the boulevard Rochechouart, between the city center and the butte Montmartre, had opened its doors in 1840.[1] A large number of places offered dancing, but many of these sites were very modest. *Paris qui danse*, a survey of the scene published about 1890, reckoned that there were about 250 *bals publics* operating in the city, but many of these were simply *bals musettes*, little more than cafés where dancing was permitted but the music was limited to a single instrument.[2] Several larger, more established venues, such as the Bal Bullier on the Left Bank, had enjoyed lively reputations since midcentury, mixing a student and laboring clientele. But the pressures of capitalism within the increasingly structured and competitive economy of the metropolis had its effect on the dance halls. Shifting patterns of consumption and the developing commodification of goods and services made their impact. The clientele even for a well-known establishment might decline. In 1882 the Château Rouge and the Bal Mabille closed, followed two years later by the Reine Blanche.[3] The public was there, however, with disposable income. In the quarter century between 1879 and 1913—into the middle of which fitted Lautrec's career—the population of Paris doubled, but the amount it spent on entertainment tripled.[4] Three factors led to a new burgeoning of the dance halls in the late 1880s and early 1890s.

First, the Third Republic had the broad ideological initiative to engender greater social harmony between the classes. Indeed, two of the republic's slogans were equality and fraternity. Progressive cultural genres such as the naturalist novels of Emile Zola encouraged a middle-class readership to learn about proletarian culture, not to fear it after the crisis of the Commune. Divisions between the classes ran too deep for the republic's ideal to be realized, but symptoms as diverse as the enormous sales of Zola's novels or the appearance of Aristide Bruant at his publisher Charpentier's elegant soirée indicate a new level of awareness, even of exchange, across social divides. Providing further evidence of change, a growing number of bourgeois made up the audiences of popular forms of entertainment such as the café-concert and the dance hall.

Second, the improved facilities, novelty, and chic of the dance halls attracted a smarter clientele. The *bal musette* had few amenities. But a new breed of entrepreneur, aware of potential profits, had begun to upgrade strategic outlets. Charles Zidler, who had already made a name for himself with his management of the Hippodrome, set up the Jardin de Paris in 1885. Centrally situated between the Champs-Elysées and the Seine, behind the Palais de l'Industrie, on what had been originally been the location of the Bal Musard in 1854, the Jardin de Paris offered a range of spectacles. As early as 1886 *Le Courrier français* extolled the new initiative of having a set piece presented by selected dancers several times a week.[5] In November 1887 Zidler petitioned the municipal council of Paris, arguing that he, unlike his predecessors on that site, who had gone bankrupt, could make a success of it by diversifying: might he supplement his orchestra and dance floor with a stage for performances? That year the city had received 52,554 francs from him in rent, while the Jardin de Paris employed two hundred people and accounted for a thousand cab fares every evening. The Jardin, he stressed, made a significant contribution to the Paris economy.[6] Three years later *Paris qui danse* itemized the Jardin's attractions: not only dancing but a diorama, a puppet theater, a stage for singers, acrobats, and tight-rope walkers, and distorting mirrors in the foyer.[7] Here was entrepreneurial capitalism at work in the entertainment sector.

The third factor in the new success of the dance halls was the rise of celebrity culture, as Mary Chapin discusses earlier in the present catalogue. Impresarios like Zidler took advantage of a new dance form, the *chahut*—its name being derived from the verb *chahuter*, to create a disturbance. The *chahut* was an exaggerated form of the long-established cancan. With two pairs of dancers, as in many of the staged performances, the dance was known as the *quadrille naturaliste*, an allusion to naturalism's willingness to represent even the grossest aspects of human behavior: the female dancers in particular went out of their way to eroticize their performances, by provocative body language, overexcited yelps, and high kicks that often exposed bare flesh to the point of indecency. Rather like new waves in rock music such as punk or grunge, what began as a localized, backstreet phenomenon was soon seized upon and packaged by the marketing men. Writing in 1892, the author of a book illustrated by Louis Legrand, which explained the basic movements of the *quadrille naturaliste*, insisted that this form had been generated at the Moulin de la Galette.[8] As this dance hall was located at the top of the butte Montmartre, it was implicit that the new dance came from

the working-class youth of that *quartier*. But Zidler was quick to advance the best of these, bringing dancers such as Louise Weber, "La Goulue," to the Jardin de Paris. There, her status as a star was puffed in periodicals like *Le Courrier français,* itself geared to the promotion of the entertainment economy.[9]

Lautrec's dance hall paintings thus belonged to a complex network of ideological, social, and commercial forces. The dance hall was not a set entity; it functioned in the flux of the modern city. And representations of the dance hall were themselves flexible; a writer or artist would produce a construction that articulated a particular notion—dance hall as honestly observed or exaggeratedly decadent, community entertainment or morally corrupt. Lautrec's first major painting on the theme was *Moulin de la Galette* of 1889 (fig. 126). The dance hall was within easy reach of Lautrec's studio in the rue Caulaincourt, and he prepared the substantial composition carefully, making a portrait study of the woman at the left (fig. 127) and an oil sketch of the whole.[10] He was evidently pleased with the result, for he exhibited the work at his first showing at the Salon des Indépendants in early 1889, at the Brussels avant-garde group Les XX the following year, and twice more during the 1890s. In addition, a line drawing after it appeared in *Le Courrier français* on 19 May 1889.[11] Lautrec designed his canvas in two sections. In the background he created a frieze of dancers and spectators—standing figures—using a thinly painted, linear touch, which imparts a fluid, mobile character to the group. The foreground space he organized around the receding diagonal of a bench, along which sit three women whose gazes reach in different directions around the room. Seated at a table behind them, a man in a bowler hat leans forward attentively. This division between lightly and more heavily painted areas also underscores different kinds of behavior: to the rear people are together, dancing or in conversation; in the foreground they are separate, watching and waiting.

One might parallel Lautrec's painting with an exactly contemporary description of the Moulin de la Galette by Marcel Schwob for the *Le Phare de la Loire:* "One dances in the middle of a large square room. The *chahut* is not danced. . . . Polishers, bookbinders, seamstresses come to amuse themselves without ceremony; the crowd circulates around the dance floor or sits at tables with a drink." This could almost be a direct representation of Lautrec's painting, with Schwob's observation that teenage girls dance together borne out by Lautrec's pair at the left.[12] Rodolphe Darzens also discussed the Moulin de la Galette in 1889, in a little book illustrated by Adolphe Willette, *Nuits à Paris*. He noted the dance floor surrounded by benches and tables, and he mentioned the balustrade. He said that the typical public comprised working-class families, painters, and prostitutes with their pimps, and that when they danced, even the younger girls kicked up their skirts so high they flashed their pubic hair.[13] The two texts are contradictory—in their denial or description of the *chahut,* for instance—but Schwob was writing for a republican provincial newspaper, which called for the language of placid egalitarianism, whereas Darzens was penning a racy account of metropolitan nightlife and eroticized his slant.

With both publications in mind, Lautrec's painting no longer seems so similar to Schwob's prose. Although the painter only showed genteel dancing, the types in the foreground cluster must be the tarts, supervised by their pimp, as Darzens described. Lautrec's pictorial construction of the Moulin de la Galette thus negotiated for itself a position that gave a strong suggestion of the underworld without abandoning a reassuring image of a good-humored proletariat.

The Moulin de la Galette attracted many painters and illustrators around 1890, notably two Catalan friends, Ramón Casas and Santiago Rusiñol. Between them they provided almost an inventory of the place, Rusiñol's work in particular offering views of the entrance, pleasure garden, and interior.[14] Naturalistically treated in subtle blonde and somber tones, their paintings are very evocative of the place. Rusiñol's canvas of the garden shows the café tables and roundabout seen from an upper floor in a dry, cold winter light, empty during the day (fig. 125). His most ambitious canvas of the Moulin de la Galette was painted from the kitchen, looking through a large open door into the garden (fig. 129). Although a very exact rendering of worn steps, steaming pots, and other details, its open spaces, amplified by the powerful diagonals of the design, suggest a mood of loneliness, reinforced by the solitary old woman seated in the doorway. Casas, who was a more confident draftsman than Rusiñol, tackled the dancers. His *Dance at the Moulin de la Galette* (fig. 130) was shown at the Indépendants in

1891. Like Rusiñol's view of the garden, Casas took a high vantage point, looking down on the dance floor. There a woman twirls her skirt, her partner standing nonchalantly beside her; other women hang around the edge, while a worker shuffles across the room in a light that, filtered through the green curtains, has the subaqueous quality that Lautrec also suggested. Yet for all the ostensible precision of the Catalans' paintings they represent the Moulin de la Galette at a distance. This distance is not merely physical—the view from above that both Casas and Rusiñol adopted—but also social. The artists seem, as foreigners perhaps, to prefer to operate from apart; they do not allow themselves or the spectator to engage too closely with the subjects they portray.

Lautrec achieved that in his next major painting. *The Rehearsal of the New Girls* of 1890 (fig. 131) depicts the dance floor of the Moulin Rouge and involves the viewer directly. Lautrec used the stock naturalist device of figures cut-off by the edge or the bottom of the frame to evoke a sense of their proximity to the spectator, implying a role for us in the fiction of his picture. At eye level we look into the *grande salle* of the Moulin Rouge, and Lautrec shows us in his fixed image what we might take in with a cursory scan of the room: the extraordinarily elastic figure of Valentin le Désossé rehearsing a dancer; an apparently prim but probably cruising woman in pink; a casual rank of mainly middle-class men lining the bar; and the foliage of the garden beyond.

The Moulin Rouge had been opened by Zidler and his partner Joseph Oller in October 1889 on the site of the former Reine Blanche. Like the Jardin de Paris, the Moulin Rouge put forward a range of attractions. The dance floor featured high-profile *chahuteuses* such as La Goulue and Môme Fromage; a stage accommodated café-concert performances by singers from the popular Yvette Guilbert to the famous Le Pétomane, who performed feats of controlled flatulence; the garden offered donkey rides and skittle alleys; and new entertainments such as processions and costume balls regularly appeared to catch the public's eye. That public varied over the course of the evening, with the café-concert enjoyed early by the local petite bourgeoisie, and the quadrilles beginning at 9:30 with the arrival of the smarter crowd that Lautrec depicted.[15] Oller and Zidler had craftily located their new pleasure facility on the boulevard de Clichy, one of the outer boulevards that separated stylish central Paris from lower-rent Montmartre. Placed on a porous class frontier, it encouraged the frisson of class mixture.

The painting, though, encapsulated only part of the Moulin Rouge's services. While it is a social picture—conveying an environment, drawing us in—it also threw the spotlight on commerce: the spectacle, the bar, the facilities of the chic venue. Above all, the composition focuses on sex: on sexual difference (the dark-coated, black-hatted men; the frilly, warm-toned women) and on sexual temptation (a grasped arm to the right, the spread legs in the center).

Sexual commerce was not what Oller and Zidler sold, at least on the surface. But the proprietors would have been well aware that their flashy commercial attractions thrived on the black economy of prostitution. Of course they did not profit from this directly, but the barely discreet presence of prostitutes on their premises served as a lure to their clientele. The dubious morality of the dance halls had long drawn notice—a police ordinance of 31 May 1833 had insisted on their supervision by gendarmes[16]—but these issues pressed to the fore with the Third Republic's anxieties about decadence.

Lautrec exhibited *The Rehearsal of the New Girls* at the 1890 Indépendants, where—coincidentally—Georges Seurat showed his own ambitious *Chahut* (fig. 7). The two paintings are quite different, Lautrec's closer to naturalist and illustrative idioms, Seurat's a sophisticated essay in neo-impressionist handling and new theories about "psychophysics."[17] But Seurat's composition, especially in its final preliminary study, more economically isolated the key elements of the dance hall. He juxtaposed a female dancer with raised petticoats and spread legs with a male onlooker. Everything is reduced to display and gaze. Much the same is true of Lautrec's poster advertising La Goulue's sensational performances at the Moulin Rouge (see fig. 10). First placarded on the Parisian walls in December 1891, it distilled elements from *The Rehearsal of the New Girls* and articulated the same telegraphic message as *Chahut*, though personalized to a specific performer. In their different ways both *Chahut*, with its neo-impressionist chromatics, and *Moulin Rouge: La Goulue*, with its silhouettes, used up-to-the-minute visual languages to convey the modernity of the dance hall's commercial cocktail of spectacle and sex.

Lautrec made clever insinuations regarding the interplay between performer and public in his images. To the left in the La Goulue poster one male silhouette is positively porcine. The association of the male spectator with the pig was common: in 1886 *Le Courrier français* had made the connection generically, and in 1892 Félix Fénéon wrote specifically of the "bons spectateurs porcins" in the poster.[18] Lautrec was playing with the metaphors of decadence: lechery degrades men to a bestial state, the opposite of Darwinian evolution. The discourse of decadence permeated the dance halls. Jane Avril recalled that when she performed at the Moulin Rouge rumors circulated that she was the black sheep of a distinguished English family, the kept "mistress" of a famous actress, or a morphine addict.[19] None of these assertions was true. But they were stock decadent tropes, easy enough to deploy, whatever their purpose: spicing up her allure or condemning her morality. For neoconservatives who warned about the lowering of the nation's moral threshold, the dance hall epitomized the danger. In an 1896 article damning the lubricity of contemporary posters, Maurice Talmeyr complained that they furnished the imagination of inhabitants of Paris with "a perpetual interior Moulin Rouge."[20]

The notion of corruption and contagion was central to the decadent reading of society. If Talmeyr, from his moralizing position, used the image of the Moulin Rouge to suggest the pollution of the imagination, Lautrec, with his libertine stance, gloried in that dangerous environment. Lautrec used his art to observe and offer commentary on behavior in Montmartrois habitats. For instance, he published the resonant color lithograph *The Englishman at the Moulin Rouge* in 1892 (fig. 142), combining areas of flat color and softer passages of *crachis*. Somewhat like the poster for La Goulue, silhouette indicated the consumer, and a more sensual surface the consumable. But Lautrec did not pitch this image as predator and prey. The model for the man was the young English painter William Warrener, and Lautrec's first portrait study shows him with a fresh-faced smile.[21] In the painted study for the overall composition and in the final lithograph, however, Warrener's features undergo a transformation that makes him appear more hard-bitten and lecherous. At the same time, the two women Lautrec introduced have slanted eyes and thin lips, appearing mercenary and ungenerous. Man and woman, buyer and seller, this image seems to say, are equalized by the corrupting conditions in which they meet.

Nowhere is this more ambitiously explored than in his major statement, *At the Moulin Rouge* of 1892–1893 (fig. 66). The core of the composition is the conventional arrangement of figures seated around a table. It is a generic image of sociability and concord. The men in their hats and dark overcoats make solid, warm forms, anchoring the seemingly dependable center of the design. Yet the closer we look, the less reliable such an initial reading seems to be. The cluster of five does not appear to speak or to catch each others' eyes. Each face is a mask. The two women are elaborately made up, coiffed, clothed, and bonneted. Surface appearance is everything. The men belie their outer appearance as stolid bourgeois by their facial expressions. To the left the monocled Edouard Dujardin takes on a new dimension when we notice the flash of his orange scarf and his blasé profile, while to the right Maurice Guibert's heavy-lidded eyes preside over an expectant smirk. The seated group forms a vortex of precarious stability around which flow different currents. Across the background plane cruise Lautrec himself and his cousin Gabriel Tapié de Céleyran, not as professionals in this context—artist and medical student—but as mismatched men, both oddly proportioned. They pass La Goulue arranging her hair in a mirror, watched by a woman friend: private feminine gestures, public female display. The foreground is animated and jarred by two different elements: the driving diagonal of the balustrade and the frontal presence of the sharply lit woman who seems to lurch toward us. These contrasting but insistent pictorial presences are compositional contrivances that increase the vertiginous impact of the painting. All is artifice in this quintessential image of decadence: the Moulin Rouge itself, with its mirrors repeating its own world; the establishment's patrons; the ersatz sociability based on display, lust, and money; the picture's push-and-pull of lurid likenesses and distancing diagonals.

Lautrec took different approaches in his dance hall pictures. Although the subject was a staple among his exhibited works at the Indépendants, Les XX, and elsewhere between 1890 and 1894, some resolved paintings, such as *At the Moulin de la Galette*, stayed in his studio.[22] In the early 1890s he painted scenes of both the Moulin de la Galette and the Moulin Rouge but

rarely represented other locales. Yet for all the specificity of his titles, the settings of his paintings are typically so generalized that they could have been invented. In the highly finished *A Corner of the Moulin de la Galette* (fig. 144) some figures—such as the seated woman in green or the standing central woman—might have been painted directly from the model, while others, notably the man on the right, appear concocted from memory. Imbalance in the making suggests imbalance in how the figures seem intended to be read. Some faces read as types and others as caricatures, resulting in a jarring quality. A painting like *Quadrille at the Moulin Rouge* (fig. 145) opens out into space, inviting the spectator to follow the forward progress of the couple to the left, whereas *At the Moulin de la Galette* contrives to block us out with the angled bench and crush of uninviting figures. In sum, Lautrec's cumulative vision of the dance halls is uneven, disconcerting, even unstable.

Lautrec toyed with themes of instability and control in the portraits of middle-class men he set in such equivocal surroundings. He exhibited the first of these paintings, inscribed "to my good friend Fourcade" (fig. 146), at the 1889 Indépendants, along with *Moulin de la Galette*. Lautrec represented the man, identified as the banker Henri Fourcade, strolling through the corridors of some dance hall or theater, oblivious to the other gentleman and costumed figures engaged in exchanges around him.[23] Although the leaning figures give Lautrec's composition a careening quality, Fourcade himself seems self-possessed and confident. The same applies to a later portrait, apparently of Léon Delaporte, manager of the advertising agency Delaporte and Chetard, at the Jardin de Paris (fig. 147).[24] Seated in a wicker chair, Delaporte genially surveys the ebb and flow of loosely painted figures circulating in the aqueous ambiance, one of whom accosts the gentleman behind him. If Fourcade and Delaporte appear in control, this is less the case with Lautrec's portrait of his good friend the artist Maxime Dethomas at the Opera Ball (fig. 148). Atop Dethomas' lumpen torso, the undulations of his profile echo the rippling flanks and haunches of the masked woman in pink who flaunts her charms at him. Lautrec thus subtly implicated gaze and object, vision and desire, for we do not see Dethomas' full face. But caught as is his gaze, his bodily mass seems paradoxically unmoved, inert. Nevertheless, Lautrec's observation of mood—whether Dethomas' equivocation or in the earlier picture Delaporte's placidity—is coupled with a suggestion of physical instincts in the way both men's canes are deployed.

The dance hall was a long-established topos for tourists, artists, and those seeking decadent thrills when Pablo Picasso arrived in Paris in 1900. Fitting all three categories, it was inevitable that Picasso should treat the subject. His most important canvas represents the Moulin de la Galette (fig. 151) and registers how quickly he had picked up the appropriate visual languages. The subaqueous greens and blues recall Lautrec's work, just as the sharp accent of scarlet and black brings to mind the posters of Jules Alexandre Grün and Maxime Dethomas (figs. 95 and 96). The composition, with its close-up and cut-off figures, adopts the naturalist conventions, while the staffage plays the decadent card, with excessive *maquillage*, suggested lesbian confidence on the left, and splendidly corvine whore to the right. But one suspects that this was decadence learned by rote. Not long afterward the English novelist Arnold Bennett was taken to the Moulin de la Galette by Schwob, being promised "plenty of scoundrels," but he was disappointed.[25] Decadent Montmartre had disappeared, and nowhere showed it more clearly than a dance hall.

---

1. Roques 1886, 4.

2. Bloch and Sagari c. 1890, 35, 39–40.

3. Rearick 1985, 183.

4. Rearick 1985, 29.

5. Patrick 1886, 6.

6. Bibliothèque Nationale de France, Paris, BN 40 Lk7 25839.

7. Bloch and Sagari c. 1890, 61–63.

8. Rodrigues 1892, 4.

9. For example, Patrick 1886, 6; Mermeix 1886, 2.

10. Dortu 1971, P. 334.

11. Dortu 1971, D. 3.091.

12. "Notes sur Paris. Les Bals publics," *Le Phare de la Loire,* 5 February 1899, in Schwob 1981 ed., 44.

13. Darzens 1889, 58–60.

14. Madrid and Barcelona 1997, nos. 17, 19, 24, 25, 27, 31.

15. Guilbert 1927, 76.

16. Bloch and Sagari c. 1890, 35.

17. For *Chahut* see *inter alia* Thomson 1985, 201–209; Smith 1997, 126–132; Herbert 2001, 155–163; Howard G. Lay, "Pictorial Acrobatics," in Weisberg 2001, 145–179.

18. Patrick 1886, 6; Félix Fénéon, "Au Pavillon de la Ville de Paris. Société des Artistes Indépendants," *Le Chat Noir* (2 April 1892) (in Fénéon 1970 ed., 1:213).

19. Avril 1933.

20. Talmeyr 1896, 214.

21. Dortu 1971, P. 426.

22. Dortu 1971, P. 388.

23. Jourdain and Adhémar 1952, 91.

24. Jourdain and Adhémar 1952, 89; Joyant 1926, 140.

25. Bennett 1971, 69–70: 4 October 1903.

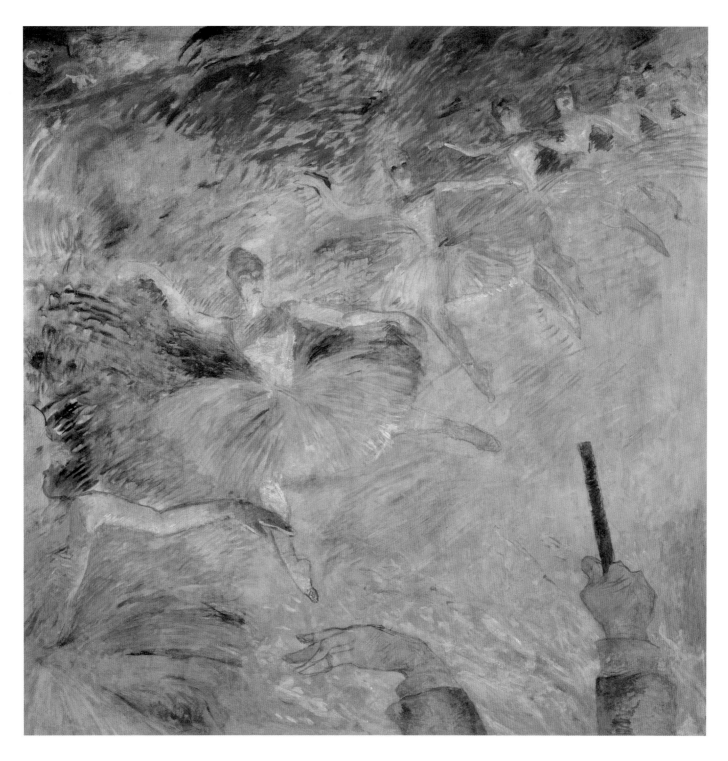

Henri de Toulouse-Lautrec,
Ballet Dancers, 1885/1886,
oil and charcoal (?) on plaster,
mounted on canvas, 153.5 x
152.5 cm. The Art Institute of
Chicago, Helen Birch Bartlett
Memorial Collection

122
Anonymous, *Jardin de Paris: Fête de Nuit — Bal*, invitation, n.d., color photorelief. The Jane Voorhees Zimmerli Art Museum, Rutgers, The State University of New Jersey, Gift of Herbert D. and Ruth Schimmel

123
Georges Redon, *Moulin de la Galette*, invitation, 1892, photorelief with pen and ink. The Jane Voorhees Zimmerli Art Museum, Rutgers, The State University of New Jersey, Gift of Herbert D. and Ruth Schimmel

124
Adolphe Léon Willette, *Bal des Femmes*, invitation, 1892, photorelief. The Jane Voorhees Zimmerli Art Museum, Rutgers, The State University of New Jersey, Gift of Herbert D. and Ruth Schimmel

116

Santiago Rusiñol, *The Garden
of the Moulin de la Galette*,
1891, oil on canvas, 61 x 50 cm.
Museo Cau Ferrat (Consorcio del
Patrimoni de Sitges)

126

Henri de Toulouse-Lautrec,
Moulin de la Galette, 1889,
oil on canvas, 88.5 x 101.3 cm.
The Art Institute of Chicago,
Mr. and Mrs. Lewis Larned
Coburn Memorial Collection

127

Henri de Toulouse-Lautrec,
*Study for "Moulin de la
Galette,"* c. 1889, oil on
cardboard, 71 x 47 cm. State
Pushkin Museum of Fine Arts,
Moscow

128

Henri de Toulouse-Lautrec,
*At the Moulin de la Galette:
La Goulue and Valentin le
Désossé*, 1887, oil on cardboard,
52 x 39.2 cm. Musée Toulouse-
Lautrec, Albi; Gift of the
Comtesse A. de Toulouse-Lautrec

129

Santiago Rusiñol, *The Kitchen*
of the Moulin de la Galette,
c. 1890–1891, oil on canvas,
97.5 x 131 cm. Museu Nacional
d'Art de Catalunya, Barcelona

Ramón Casas, *Dance at the Moulin de la Galette,* c. 1890–1891, oil on canvas, 98.5 x 80 cm. Museo Cau Ferrat (Consorcio del Patrimoni de Sitges)

131
—
Henri de Toulouse-Lautrec,
*The Rehearsal of the New Girls
at the Moulin Rouge*, 1890,
oil on canvas, 115 x 150 cm.
Philadelphia Museum of Art, The
Henry P. McIlhenny Collection in
memory of Frances P. McIlhenny

132
—
Ferdinand Misti-Mifliez, *Moulin
Rouge*, program, 1895, color
photorelief. The Jane Voorhees
Zimmerli Art Museum, Rutgers,
The State University of New
Jersey, Gift of Herbert D. and
Ruth Schimmel

133
Auguste Roedel, *Moulin Rouge: Noël à Montmartre*, **invitation**, 24 December 1897, color photorelief. The Jane Voorhees Zimmerli Art Museum, Rutgers, The State University of New Jersey, Gift of Herbert D. and Ruth Schimmel

134
Auguste Roedel, *Moulin Rouge: La Bohème Artistique*, invitation, 16 January 1897, color photorelief. The Jane Voorhees Zimmerli Art Museum, Rutgers, The State University of New Jersey, Gift of Herbert D. and Ruth Schimmel

135
Auguste Roedel, *Moulin Rouge: A qui la Pomme?* **10 March 1900**, color photorelief. The Jane Voorhees Zimmerli Art Museum, Rutgers, The State University of New Jersey, Gift of Herbert D. and Ruth Schimmel

136

Auguste Roedel, *Moulin Rouge: Reprise de la Fête du Printemps,* invitation, 13 June 1897, color photorelief. The Jane Voorhees Zimmerli Art Museum, Rutgers, The State University of New Jersey, Gift of Herbert D. and Ruth Schimmel

137

Henri-Patrice Dillon, *Moulin Rouge,* c. 1895, gouache, graphite, collage, and ink, 30 x 21.8 cm. The Jane Voorhees Zimmerli Art Museum, Rutgers, The State University of New Jersey, David A. and Mildred H. Morse Art Acquisition Fund

138

Faria, "Cha-u-ka-o," song
sheet, c. 1889–1890, color
lithograph. The Jane Voorhees
Zimmerli Art Museum, Rutgers,
The State University of New
Jersey, Gift of Herbert D. and
Ruth Schimmel

139

Anonymous, *The Dance Hall of
the Moulin Rouge*, illustration
in *Le Panorama: Paris La Nuit*,
c. 1898, photorelief. The Jane
Voorhees Zimmerli Art Museum,
Rutgers, The State University
of New Jersey, Anonymous
Donation

MOULIN-ROUGE. — Entrée du Hall.

140

L. Lagarte, *Moulin Rouge:*
The Entrance, illustration in
Maurice Delsol's *Paris–Cythère,*
n.d., photorelief. The Jane
Voorhees Zimmerli Art Museum,
Rutgers, The State University of
New Jersey, Herbert D. and Ruth
Schimmel Museum Library Fund

141

Henri de Toulouse-Lautrec,
The Englishman at the Moulin
Rouge, 1892, oil and gouache on
cardboard, 85.7 x 66 cm. Lent by
The Metropolitan Museum of Art,
Bequest of Miss Adelaide Milton
de Groot (1876–1967), 1967

142

Henri de Toulouse-Lautrec,
*The Englishman at the Moulin
Rouge*, 1892, color lithograph,
61.8 x 48.7 cm (sheet). The Art
Institute of Chicago, Gift of the
Print and Drawing Club

143

Louis Anquetin, *At the Bar*,
c. 1891, pastel on cardboard,
55 x 72 cm. Private collection,
Courtesy Brame & Lorenceau,
Paris

144

Henri de Toulouse-Lautrec,
*A Corner of the Moulin de la
Galette,* 1892, oil on cardboard,
100 x 89.2 cm. National Gallery
of Art, Washington, Chester Dale
Collection

Henri de Toulouse-Lautrec,
Quadrille at the Moulin Rouge,
1892, oil on cardboard, 80.1 x
60.5 cm. National Gallery of Art,
Washington, Chester Dale
Collection

146

Henri de Toulouse-Lautrec,
Monsieur Fourcade, 1889,
oil on cardboard, 77 x 63 cm.
Museu de Arte de São Paulo Assis
Chateaubriand, São Paulo, Brazil

147

Henri de Toulouse-Lautrec,
Monsieur Delaporte, 1893,
gouache on cardboard, glued on
wood, 76 x 70 cm. Ny Carlsberg
Glyptotek, Copenhagen

Henri de Toulouse-Lautrec,
Maxime Dethomas, 1896,
oil on cardboard, 67.5 x 50.9 cm.
National Gallery of Art,
Washington, Chester Dale
Collection

149 | 150

Henri de Toulouse-Lautrec, *The Clowness at the Moulin Rouge*, 1897, color lithograph, 41.1 x 32.3 cm (sheet). The Art Institute of Chicago, Mr. and Mrs. Carter H. Harrison Collection

Henri de Toulouse-Lautrec, *The Dance at the Moulin Rouge*, 1897, color lithograph, 48.4 x 35.5 cm. Francey and Dr. Martin L. Gecht

151

Pablo Picasso, *The Moulin de
la Galette*, 1900, oil on canvas,
88.2 x 115.5 cm. Solomon R.
Guggenheim Museum, New York,
Thannhauser Collection, Gift,
Justin K. Thannhauser, 1978

133 · *Dance Halls*

152
—
Pablo Picasso, *Divan Japonais,*
1901, oil on cardboard, mounted
on panel, 69.9 x 53 cm. Mugrabi
Collection

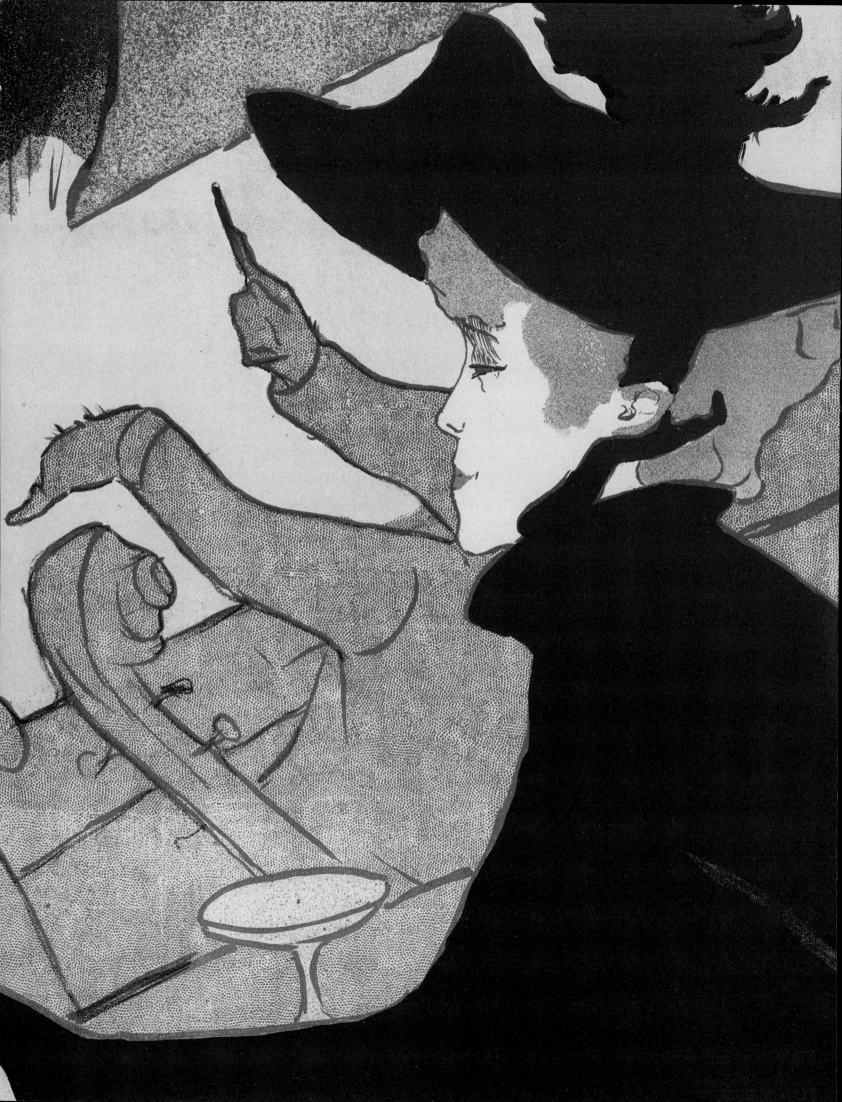

Mary Weaver Chapin

STARS OF THE CAFÉ-CONCERT

———

Of all the pleasures of Paris—the dance halls, circuses, cabarets, and brothels—it was the café-concert and its stars that cast the greatest spell on Toulouse-Lautrec. He developed what he called *furias*, intense obsessions, with certain performers who would enthrall him for a single season or several years. Lautrec would return night after night, recording the gestures, facial expressions, and postures that made each performer unique. His sketches, hastily scribbled in notebooks, on napkins, or even on tablecloths, served as the basis for a remarkable body of work.[1] From the most ephemeral drawings to innovative publicity posters, technically sophisticated prints, limited-edition lithographic albums, fully realized paintings, and a ceramic, Lautrec explored the construction of the café-concert star in a vast array of guises and media, creating some of the most memorable images of fin-de-siècle celebrity.

Although cafés-concerts could be found throughout Paris, Lautrec at first favored those in Montmartre, which offered more avant-garde, sardonic, and risqué programs than those found in central Paris. This particular Montmartrois style became so popular in the 1890s that its stars exported their acts to the posh cafés-concerts on the *grands boulevards*, and artists like Lautrec followed. As Montmartrois entertainment became more mainstream, however, artists had to compete in the increasingly commercial realm of entertainment that included posters, printed programs (figs. 156 and 157), illustrated journals, photographs (fig. 158), limited prints, statuettes, souvenirs (fig. 222), and celebrity endorsements. Thus the café-concert in the 1880s and 1890s was at the vortex of several trends that signaled modernity at the end of the century: art, publicity, and celebrity.

Toulouse-Lautrec was not alone in his love for the café-concert. Since its inception around the 1840s, this form of entertainment had been popular with Parisians as well as the provincials and tourists who flocked to the capital. Because of the relatively low admission prices, the café-concert appealed to a wide spectrum of people: not only aristocrats but also shopgirls, bourgeois gentlemen, artists, prostitutes, and soldiers. This mixture of classes was a topic of great interest and alarm, and the frisson created by rubbing elbows with members of different social groups formed part of the appeal.[2] Furthermore, unlike the traditional theater, where a certain level of decorum was expected, patrons of the café-concert could move freely around the establishments smoking, drinking, socializing, or cruising for prostitutes. Of course, they could also watch the entertainment, which initially consisted of individual singers (usually fetching young women from the lower classes) presenting sentimental or comic chansons. By the turn of the century, however, programs had expanded to include a great variety of singers and dancers, light opera, one-act plays, and novelty events like boxing kangaroos.[3]

Edgar Degas, Lautrec's artistic forebear and strongest influence, brilliantly conveyed the atmosphere of entertainment and casual sociability of the café-concert. In *Café-Concert* (fig. 159) he focused on a comely singer surrounded by a group of young women whose principal purpose was to attract male attention. The assortment of men in the foreground, from the stately orchestra conductor to the man in the petit-bourgeois melon hat, implies the range of patrons in attendance. Degas eschewed the audience entirely in *Café Singer* of 1879 (fig. 160), directing his eye instead to the emphatic gesture of the chanteuse. It has been suggested that the singer was Alice Desgrange, but Degas was interested less in capturing a specific likeness—which would become Lautrec's special trademark—than in depicting the general type of the café-concert performer.

Lautrec's first images of the café-concert borrowed much from Degas in terms of theme and composition. Nowhere is his debt more obvious than in the lithograph *At the Ambassadeurs: Singer at the Café-Concert* (fig. 161), but Lautrec soon found his own artistic voice. In *Fashionable People at the Ambassadeurs* (fig. 162) he, like Degas before him, focused on the people in attendance: in this case, a smartly dressed woman in a green dress and chic hat and a gentleman in evening clothes. This dashing couple dominates the composition, while the singer on stage is just a tiny figure in the left middle ground. Her long black gloves and outstretched neck identify her as the newly renowned performer Yvette Guilbert, but Lautrec toys with the juxtaposition of the celebrity of the singer and the stylishness of the clientele.

Lautrec also privileged the audience over the performer in his poster for the Divan Japonais, a café-concert that featured a pseudo-oriental décor (fig. 164). Jane Avril, the cancan dancer, occupies the center of the poster, accompanied by the critic and man-about-town, Edouard Dujardin. As in *Fashionable People*, the performer is secondary to the design. Not only is she reduced to a small figure at the upper left, but her head is cut off by the edge of the poster. Even so, she clearly stands for Yvette Guilbert. This sight gag is representative of Lautrec's humor, but it also testifies to his promotional sense: Lautrec misled viewers into thinking they would see the diva Guilbert at the Divan Japonais, although she had not performed there in over two years.[4] Still, Lautrec knew that Guilbert's star power, combined with the stylish figures of Avril and Dujardin, could serve as a lure. The selling power of personality—Guilbert, Avril, Dujardin—is even more obvious when we compare Lautrec's poster to Henry Somm's preparatory design for the same café-concert (fig. 163).[5]

After these witty manipulations of the elegant audience, Lautrec devoted himself almost exclusively to the stars of the stage. A series of lithographs he prepared for a portfolio in collaboration with Henri-Gabriel Ibels entitled *Le Café-Concert* of 1893 (figs. 165 a–v) marked this transition. Commissioned by the groundbreaking print publisher, André Marty, *Le Café-Concert* featured eleven monochromatic lithographs by each artist and a text by Georges Montorgueil, a frequent commentator on life in Montmartre. This exceptional publication was the first album of prints dedicated exclusively to the theme of the café-concert and its performers, and it operated at the intersection between fine art (as represented by the "original print" movement) and celebrity culture.

Lautrec had met Ibels around 1888 through mutual friends. They first exhibited together in 1891, when critics noted stylistic similarities and praised their sharp observations and caricatural vision.[6] Both had a strong interest in the amusements of Montmartre, and Ibels was closely tied to the world of the café-concert (figs. 166–170). They joined forces to convey the spirit of these establishments and to capture the stars in their characteristic poses. In Ibels' depiction of Jeanne Bloch, a heavy-set chanteuse known for belting out military songs, her face is hidden by the kepi pulled low over her eyes, but her swayed back and formidable figure instantly communicate her identity (fig. 165 b). Ibels created a simple outline of her dress using brush and ink and suggested the haze of darkness surrounding her on stage by his use of spatter or *crachis,* a fine "rain" of ink produced by running a finger or blade across a small brush dipped in ink. Lautrec also used spatter to great effect in his lithograph of the comic actor Caudieux, known as the "human cannonball" (fig. 165 s), who appears here to rocket across the page leaving a blank expanse of white paper in his wake. Lautrec cropped the composition just below the actor's knees, a device he had employed in a widely distributed poster for the performer earlier that year, thereby increasing the effect of movement.[7] In other cases Lautrec applied spatter more lightly, as in his elegant print of Jane Avril, where he emphasized the supple movement of the dancer by means of calligraphic line (fig. 165 l) and enhanced the sensation of weightlessness and flight by stopping out the *crachis* for the area under her dress, which highlighted the almost supernatural grace of Avril.

JANE AVRIL

Toulouse-Lautrec's lithograph of Avril for the café-concert portfolio was not his first image of the dancer. The artist had probably met the performer in the early 1890s when she could be seen at the Moulin Rouge. Among the many stars Lautrec portrayed, Avril was the one who most appreciated his artistic genius and remained a loyal friend and patron throughout his life. Unlike most cancan dancers, Avril was educated and refined; she kept company with many avant-garde writers of the day and visited the ateliers of leading artists. Paradoxically, she was known for her highly sensual dancing as well as for her ethereal detachment, giving her what decadent writer and dandy Arthur Symons called an "air of depraved virginity."[8]

Lautrec knew Avril both as a personal friend and a public celebrity, and he produced telling images of her in both roles. In 1892 he created several important paintings of her in private life: a quick study in oil on cardboard (fig. 172), a fully realized half-length portrait (fig. 173), and views of her entering or leaving the Moulin Rouge (figs. 62 and 63). In each of these Lautrec suggests the inner life of this notable woman, who was very intelligent yet was plagued by nervous complaints. In March of the next year Lautrec depicted her again, this time as a print connoisseur examining a freshly pulled proof at the Imprimerie Ancourt (fig. 177). This lithograph was used as the cover for the first installment of *L'Estampe originale,* an important series of original prints published by André Marty. According to its prospectus, the venture would feature "the elite of the art world and contemporary young artists." It turned out to be enormously influential, effectively launching the vogue for limited-edition color lithographs.[9]

Lautrec's use of Avril for the inaugural cover of *L'Estampe originale* points to his desire to position himself at the center of the increasingly intertwined worlds of original printmaking, decorative arts reform, and celebrity culture.[10] His work for Avril as a performer is equally compelling. Unlike his publicity images of Aristide Bruant or La Goulue, which present the packaged celebrity for public consumption, Lautrec allowed Avril greater emotional privacy. This is evident in the work she commissioned for her appearance at the Jardin de Paris (fig. 175). The poster offers a fascinating contrast of open and shut, public and private:

Avril wears an impassive expression, her eyes closed in concentration, giving the viewer no entrée into her private thoughts; yet she contorts her lower body to display her long, black-stockinged legs and colorful skirts. The looming presence of a musician at the lower right, his hairy hand gripping the neck of the contrabass, suggests the sexual nature of this dance, but Avril seems aloof from the licentious overtones. Lautrec also contrasted Avril's inner life with her exhibitionistic performance in his poster for a troupe in which she appeared in 1896 (fig. 176). The dancer is pictured at the far left and does not meet the viewer's gaze. Instead, all focus is on the lively rhythm of the frothy petticoats raised to reveal maroon stockings. It is possible that Pablo Picasso saw this poster by Lautrec when he first arrived in Paris, for his 1901 watercolor study for a poster advertising the Jardin de Paris (fig. 174) seems to owe much to Lautrec's innovative design.

Avril commissioned one final poster from Lautrec in 1899. Although he was suffering from advanced stages of alcoholism, his poster shows the creativity and wit that marked his best work (fig. 178). A large serpent, inked in several colors, appears to slither up Avril's dress, animating her wild dance. Arthur Symons described the poster as "simply magnificent," adding that Avril "is painted with his feverish colors; . . . her red mouth, fine nose and perverse eyes glitter before me . . . and—so like the depravity of Lautrec—a living cobra writhes around her body. . . . The more he coils around her, the more violent are his colors."[11] This charming poster was never distributed, but it remains a fitting valediction to Lautrec and Avril's collaboration in the construction of her celebrity.

YVETTE GUILBERT

The performer Yvette Guilbert achieved the greatest success and most lasting influence of all of Toulouse-Lautrec's celebrity subjects. Not only Lautrec, but countless other artists, illustrators, poster designers, photographers, sculptors, and enterprising advertisers sought to capture (and capitalize on) the fame of this talented woman. Guilbert began her career as an actress in the traditional theater in Paris in January 1887 but soon turned her attention to the café-concert. Her skyrocketing success was due to her unique style and her savvy for promotion. Unlike the buxom beauties of the café-concert stage, Guilbert was tall, unfashionably thin, and hampered by a poor singing voice. She made these traits her hallmark, highlighting rather than hiding them. Her costume—black gloves and a simple satin dress with a deep v-neck in front and back—made her stand out from her heavily corseted and bejeweled colleagues. Her repertoire and delivery also departed from the traditional. She favored the clever creations of Montmartre songwriters and poets such as Bruant, Maurice Donnay, and Léon Xanrof. Rather than singing her ditties, she half-spoke, half-sang them—hence the term, *diseuse*—in a highly witty and suggestive fashion. The result was spectacular. Audiences found something new and particularly Montmartrois about Guilbert, and as early as 1891 she was billed as the "*diseuse* fin de siècle."[12]

Guilbert commissioned the biggest names in design for her earliest posters. Jules Chéret produced one of the first publicity images for her in 1891 for her debut at the Concert Parisien (fig. 179). This was followed by posters by Ferdinand Bac for her engagement at the Scala around 1893 (fig. 180) and by Théophile-Alexandre Steinlen for her appearance at the Ambassadeurs in 1894 (fig. 182). All three flatter the performer, smoothing out her irregular features and presenting her as a respectable matron of the café-concert stage.

Although Guilbert rejected the poster design Lautrec made for her (Musée Toulouse-Lautrec, Albi), they did work together on several important projects that advanced both their careers. Images in illustrated journals of the *diseuse* in action kept both of their names in the spotlight (figs. 184 and 185). The most significant undertaking, however, was the *Album Yvette Guilbert* of 1894, which consisted of a cover, sixteen original lithographs, and a text by the critic Gustave Geffroy. Lautrec began by making preparatory sketches and watercolors (fig. 186). Two graphite drawings in Chicago provide insight into how the artist worked. *Yvette Guilbert Singing* and *Yvette Guilbert* (fig. 187 and 188) were originally executed on the same piece of paper. This sheet measured approximately 36 by 46 centimeters, and Lautrec made rapid sketches of the diva in action on both sides. He then folded it, perhaps to fit into his coat pocket, and subsequently used the drawings as the basis for finished lithographs. At some point in its history the sheet was cut in two. Perfectly matched creases as well as graphite offset pro-

duced by the folding confirms this relationship and supports the reading.[13] These sorts of rapid drawings, taken from life, animate the final lithographs in the album. For the cover Lautrec reduced all the celebrity and star power of Yvette Guilbert down to her trademark black gloves. In the study for this lithograph the gloves seem almost alive, slithering down the table (fig. 189). The sixteen portraits constituting the body of the book portray Guilbert in various poses and gestures, both on stage and off (figs. 190 a–q).

The *Album Yvette Guilbert* was a remarkable hybrid of fine art, original printing and bookmaking, and celebrity culture.[14] It is surprising that the vain and celebrated Guilbert endorsed the project, which showed her in less-than-flattering poses. According to her friends, she was shocked by Lautrec's acerbic draftsmanship, and they encouraged her to file suit for defamation of character. Despite Guilbert's misgivings, the album was an artistic and commercial success. An anonymous reviewer in *La Vie parisienne*, a popular illustrated journal, praised it as "the apotheosis of the diva" and hailed the brilliant collaboration between Lautrec and the *diseuse*.[15] It boosted Lautrec's career, fueled Guilbert's cult status, and inspired at least one imitation, Veber's unrealized album of 1895 (fig. 191). Other artists created paintings of the star; Joseph Granié's portrait of Guilbert (fig. 192) presents her in a humble dress with her hair askew, but against a gold background painted on panel that recalls a medieval altarpiece and suggests the secular and popular divinity of this star of the café-concert. Other pictures, such as Leonetto Cappiello's painting of 1899, capture her sinuous body language by economical means of flowing line (fig. 193).

Guilbert's success sparked a slew of marketing opportunities. Images of the diva flooded the market in both high and low art, printed, painted, and sculpted. One commentator noted sardonically that Guilbert "is the very latest thing up-to-date in Paris; we shall have the Christmas hawkers selling toy models of her soon on the boulevards."[16] He was not far from the truth. Sculptures did in fact follow her fame: in 1893 the artist Henri Nocq produced a polychrome medallion sculpture of Guilbert (fig. 195), and in 1895 Lautrec himself made a small number of ceramic tiles (fig. 196). Cappiello created a statuette of Guilbert for limited mass production that was heavily advertised in the journal *Le Rire* (fig. 194).

The artists who depicted Guilbert—Lautrec, Steinlen, Bac, and Cappiello among others—and the entertainer herself were astute at branding her particular identity. It is understandable, then, that advertisers leveraged her sensational reputation and immediately recognizable profile. A massive poster by Henri Gustave Jossot for Saupiguet Sardines (fig. 197), for instance, showed Yvette Guilbert with Sarah Bernhardt and Aristide Bruant happily consuming sardines alongside the legendary politician and journalist Henri Rochefort (center) and notorious politico Sidi-Ali Bey (at left).[17] Although celebrity endorsements were not new, it is hard to imagine Jossot's forceful poster without the precedents of Lautrec's gripping images of Guilbert and Bruant. Furthermore, it indicates the leveling power of celebrity culture, with a café-concert personality, a famed *tragedienne,* and a bawdy cabaret star pictured side by side with two infamous politicians, all eating sardines straight out of the can.

MAY BELFORT AND MAY MILTON

After Lautrec's fascination with the talented Guilbert, the artist came under the spell of two lesser performers from Great Britain, May Belfort and May Milton. Belfort's act, according to contemporary Gustave Coquiot, consisted merely of "a whole series of *tarrara-boomdyays* and pathetic nonsense anemically sung," yet Lautrec was entranced.[18] He produced many images of her, including painted portraits of her on stage, several lithographs, and a bold color poster (figs. 198, 200, and 201). The poster relates to one he did for the Englishwoman May Milton (fig. 202), who was said to be Belfort's lover. Although deceptively simple in design, the poster for Milton was complex in execution, calling for crayon, brush, spatter, and five lithographic stones. Without disguising her strong profile— what one critic called her "pale, almost clownish face ...reminiscent of a bulldog"—Lautrec created an elegant design that emphasized the grace of the dancer, her flowing skirts, and supple kick.[19] He seems to acknowledge the liaison between Milton and Belfort by conceiving of the lithographs as pendants, making the subjects a matching set in print as they were in life. Maurice Joyant, Lautrec's lifelong friend, art dealer, and biographer, picked up on their paired graphic quality, writing "In the posters of May Belfort and May

Milton, Lautrec took care to make thoroughly English posters, the gleaming red of the first vying with the blue of the second."[20] Testament to the appeal of Lautrec's image of May Milton can be found in the work of young Picasso: in *The Blue Room* (fig. 203), painted in the fall of 1901, Picasso represented the interior of his own studio, where Lautrec's poster of May Milton hung on the back wall. It seems fitting that Picasso would be drawn to Lautrec's publicity work, which embodied the elements of modernity of Parisian culture at this time: high art and low life, celebrity and self-promotion.

LOÏE FULLER

Toulouse-Lautrec had personal relationships with the aforementioned stars. Numerous anecdotes tell of his carousing with La Goulue and Aristide Bruant, his designing a greeting card for May Belfort, his professional connection with Yvette Guilbert, and his genuine friendship with Jane Avril, who often served as hostess for his outlandish dinner parties. A notable exception was the American dancer Loïe Fuller, whom he knew only from a distance. Perhaps because her act was more upmarket, closer to the theater than the raucous café-concert, Lautrec took only a short, yet very intense interest in this celebrity, and never made the personal connection that distinguished his work with the other stars of Montmartre.

Fuller's unique act involved manipulating voluminous translucent gowns with the aid of large poles held in each hand. She danced in a specially designed space featuring a glass floor illuminated from below and surrounded by mirrors. Electric lights of various colors projected onto the stage created an ethereal, swirling effect, which was heightened by the accompanying music.[21] All of Paris was captivated by Fuller's performances, and artists of many media attempted to convey the ephemeral mood of the shifting light, color, and music in a single image. Frustrated in their attempts, some responded in serial form.

The most dramatic use of seriality was Toulouse-Lautrec's limited-edition prints of the dancer at the Folies Bergère. These are among his most experimental lithographs—and also his most abstract (figs. 204–217). Lautrec depicted the dancer in midflight, the wings of her costume held high above her head, her tiny feet barely anchoring her to the stage. Although he used the same five lithographic stones for each of the sixty or so copies, every image is unique, for he altered the colors with each printing and lightly pounced the final stone with a bag full of powdered silver or gold, which added a metallic sheen to the top layer.[22] The results of Lautrec's efforts are as beautiful as they are varied; examples in rich browns and golds compete with impressions featuring curry yellows, rosy reds, aubergine, and periwinkle blue. Lautrec's manipulation of subtle changes in color implies sequential movement over time in an almost proto-cinematic fashion.

Artists working in different media also sought to portray Fuller's dance in serial form. Rupert Carabin's bronzes (figs. 218 a–f) explore her many poses and the motion of her skirts, while Charles Maurin's pastels, like Lautrec's lithographs, suggest the flickering quality of light and color moving across her veils (figs. 219–221). Poster designers too struggled to portray the magical effect of light and color. Chéret printed his 1893 poster of Fuller in four color variations; the example in the present exhibition employs vermilion, yellow, dark violet, and black (fig. 223), but other versions use orange, dark greens, and blues to hint at the play of light and color on her silk skirts.[23] The artist Pal's poster design of 1894 (fig. 224) used only four colors, but Georges de Feure used no fewer than eight stones to create the vividly colorful— some might even say gaudy—image in orange, yellow orange, sea green, dark green, Prussian blue, blue green, turquoise, and lilac brown (fig. 225).[24] In Manuel Orazi's poster for Fuller's appearance at the 1900 Paris World's Fair, the dancer's body and veils disappear almost entirely in a mist of nine carefully blended colors (fig. 226).

None of these artists paid much attention to Fuller's facial features or personality. She was said to be short, plump, and rather plain, yet Chéret makes her a sprightly *chérette*; Pal treats her as a semi-nude and shapely young woman; de Feure gives her a strong Grecian profile; and Orazi shows her with the sinuous flowing hair of an art nouveau goddess. Lautrec gives no clue to her physical appearance, concentrating instead on the veils that enveloped her. For artists depicting Loïe Fuller, the interest was clearly on her dazzling performance and not the individual behind it.

MARCELLE LENDER

By the mid-1890s Lautrec was beginning to lose interest in Montmartre, with its increasingly packaged and sanitized entertainments aimed at foreigners. One of his final *furias* was with the actress Marcelle Lender, who was featured in the operetta "Chilpéric" at the Théâtre des Variétés in central Paris in 1895.[25] He attended the performance more than twenty times, arriving just in time to see her dance the final bolero, and he captured this moment in his monumental painting of 1895–1896 (fig. 227).[26] Lender kicks her black-stockinged legs, so that her skirts explode in a froth of peony pink and deep green. The stagelights bleach out her ample décolletage and create a masklike effect around her eyes. The entire composition reveals Lautrec as a virtuoso with color: the pink flowers of Lender's headdress vie with her deep red hair; the olive green floorboards resonate against the orange red tent covering; while the blues, greens, and reds of the other costumes on stage produce a veritable riot of color. Despite the brilliance of the finished canvas, Lender never reciprocated Lautrec's admiration and reportedly refused the gift of this painting. Lautrec kept it in his studio for the remainder of his life, a magnificent testimony to his career of painting Parisian celebrities.

1. On Lautrec's *furias* and obsessive sketching, see Frey 1994, 243–244.

2. For contemporary fears about mixing social classes at the café-concert, see Louis Veuillot, *Les Odeurs de Paris* (Paris, 1867); and Talmeyr 1902, for example. For a recent analysis, see Clark 1984, chap. 4.

3. For an explanation of the range of performers found at the café-concert, see Vauclair 1886. See also Sallée and Chauveau 1985; and Dillaz 1991.

4. Frey 1994, 310–311.

5. For Lautrec's use of the celebrity audience as a marketing ploy, see Chapin 2002, 83–88.

6. New Brunswick 1985, 123.

7. Wittrock 1985, P 7.

8. Symons 1930, 22.

9. On *L'Estampe originale*, see New Brunswick 1991; and Bass 1982–1983, 12–27. For the prospectus, see Stein and Karshan 1970, 17.

10. Chapin 2002, 137–141.

11. Symons 1930, 22.

12. For Guilbert's rise to fame and a history of her career, see Albi 1994. A less reliable source is her autobiography of 1927.

13. Margo McFarland, paper conservator at the Art Institute of Chicago, made this discovery.

14. Chapin 2002, 164–179.

15. "X," "Les Livres de la semaine," *La Vie parisienne* (20 October 1894): 594.

16. Jean Lorrain, quoted in Knapp and Chipman 1964, 89.

17. Sidi-Ali Bey was the name adopted by Dr. Grenier when he converted to Islam.

18. Coquiot 1921, 149–150.

19. Joyant 1926, 198.

20. Joyant 1927, III.

21. For depictions of Loïe Fuller in art, see, among others, Richmond 1979; and Munich 1995.

22. Lautrec's exact printing process for this innovative print is not entirely clear. For three descriptions of the states and presumed process, see Wittrock 1985, 1:17; Adriani 1987, cat. 10; and Brisbane 1991, 52.

23. See Broido 1980, cat. 125, for a description of the four variations.

24. Los Angeles 1985, cat. 92.

25. For an excellent history of this painting and its context, see Coman 1994.

26. On Lautrec's passion for Lender in "Chilpéric," see Coolus 1931, 139.

153

Jules Chéret, *Musée Grévin*, 1900, color lithograph, 119.7 x 81.9 cm (sheet). Los Angeles County Museum of Art, Kurt J. Wagner, M.D., and C. Kathleen Wagner Collection

154

Jules Chéret, *Folies-Bergère: L'Arc-en-Ciel*, 1893, color lithograph, 117.2 x 81.9 cm (sheet). Los Angeles County Museum of Art, Kurt J. Wagner, M.D., and C. Kathleen Wagner Collection

155

Jules Chéret, *Olympia*, 1892, color lithograph, 117.2 x 81.9 cm (sheet). Los Angeles County Museum of Art, Kurt J. Wagner, M.D., and C. Kathleen Wagner Collection

Georges Meunier, *Eldorado*,
program, 1894, color photorelief.
The Jane Voorhees Zimmerli Art
Museum, Rutgers, The State
University of New Jersey, Gift of
Herbert D. and Ruth Schimmel

Ferdinand Misti-Mifliez,
Olympia: Music Hall, program,
1896, color photorelief. The Jane
Voorhees Zimmerli Art Museum,
Rutgers, The State University of
New Jersey, Gift of Herbert D.
and Ruth Schimmel

Anonymous, *Photographs of
Yvette Guilbert* from *La
Panorama*, 1897, photorelief.
The Jane Voorhees Zimmerli Art
Museum, Rutgers, The State
University of New Jersey, Herbert
D. and Ruth Schimmel Museum
Library Fund

159 160

Edgar Degas, *Café-Concert*, 1876/1877, pastel over monotype on paper and board, 23.5 x 43.2 cm. Corcoran Gallery of Art, Washington, D.C., William A. Clark Collection

Edgar Degas, *Café Singer*, 1879, oil on canvas, 53.5 x 41.8 cm. The Art Institute of Chicago, Bequest of Clara Margaret Lynch in memory of John A. Lynch

161

Henri de Toulouse-Lautrec,
*At the Ambassadeurs: Singer
at the Café-Concert*, **1894**,
color lithograph, **60.2 x 43.2 cm**
(sheet). The Art Institute of
Chicago, Mr. and Mrs. Carter H.
Harrison Collection

162

Henri de Toulouse-Lautrec,
*Fashionable People at the
Ambassadeurs*, **1893**, oil à
l'essence over black chalk on
paper, mounted on cardboard,
84.3 x 65.5 cm. National Gallery
of Art, Washington, Collection
of Mr. and Mrs. Paul Mellon

163

Henry Somm, *Divan Japonais*,
c. 1890, watercolor and gouache,
49 x 37.2 cm. The Jane Voorhees
Zimmerli Art Museum, Rutgers,
The State University of New
Jersey, Gift of Mr. and Mrs.
Herbert Littman

164

Henri de Toulouse-Lautrec,
Divan Japonais, 1893, color
lithograph, 80.2 x 61.8 cm
(sheet). The Art Institute of
Chicago, Mr. and Mrs. Carter H.
Harrison Collection

Henri-Gabriel Ibels, portfolio
cover for *Le Café–Concert*,
1893, lithograph, 44.3 x 33 cm
(approx.). The Art Institute of
Chicago, Gift of Horace M. Swope

165 b

Henri-Gabriel Ibels, *Jeanne
Bloch*, 1893, lithograph, 44.1 x
31.7 cm (sheet). The Art Institute
of Chicago, Gift of Horace M.
Swope

Henri-Gabriel Ibels, *Marcel Legay*, 1893, lithograph, 44.2 x 32 cm (sheet). The Art Institute of Chicago, Gift of Horace M. Swope

Henri-Gabriel Ibels, *Libert*, 1893, lithograph, 44.2 x 32 cm (sheet). The Art Institute of Chicago, Gift of Horace M. Swope

165 e

Henri-Gabriel Ibels, *Mévisto*,
1893, lithograph, 44.3 x 31.7 cm
(sheet). The Art Institute of
Chicago, Gift of Horace M. Swope

165 f

Henri-Gabriel Ibels, *Paulus*,
1893, lithograph, 43.7 x 31.9 cm
(sheet). The Art Institute of
Chicago, Gift of Horace M. Swope

165 g

Henri-Gabriel Ibels, *Anna Thibaud*, 1893, lithograph, 44 x 32.1 cm (sheet). The Art Institute of Chicago, Gift of Horace M. Swope

165 h

Henri-Gabriel Ibels, *Emilienne d'Alençon Rehearsing at the Folies-Bergère*, 1893, lithograph, 42.8 x 31.9 cm (sheet). The Art Institute of Chicago, Gift of Horace M. Swope

165i

Henri-Gabriel Ibels, *Polin,*
1893, lithograph, 43.7 x 31.8 cm
(sheet). The Art Institute of
Chicago, Gift of Horace M. Swope

165j

Henri-Gabriel Ibels, *Kam-Hill,*
1893, lithograph, 43.5 x 32 cm
(sheet). The Art Institute of
Chicago, Gift of Horace M. Swope

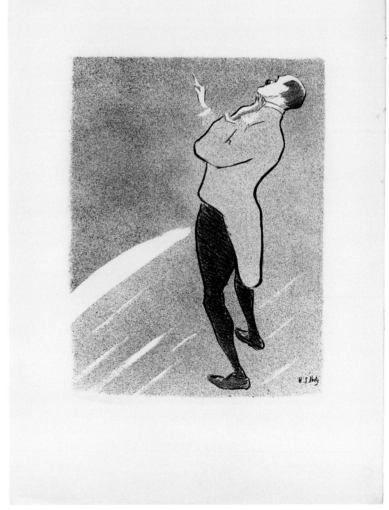

165 k

Henri-Gabriel Ibels, *Ouvrard*, 1893, lithograph, 43.4 x 31.9 cm (sheet). The Art Institute of Chicago, Gift of Horace M. Swope

165 l

Henri de Toulouse-Lautrec, *Jane Avril*, 1893, lithograph, 43.5 x 31.8 cm (sheet). The Art Institute of Chicago, Albert H. Wolf Memorial Collection

165 m

Henri de Toulouse-Lautrec,
Yvette Guilbert, 1893,
lithograph, 44 x 32.3 cm (sheet).
The Art Institute of Chicago,
Charles F. Glore Collection

165 n

Henri de Toulouse-Lautrec,
Paula Brébion, 1893, lithograph,
44.2 x 32 cm (sheet). The Art
Institute of Chicago, Joseph
Brooks Fair Collection

165 o

Henri de Toulouse-Lautrec, *Mary Hamilton*, 1893, lithograph, 44.1 x 31.9 cm (sheet). The Art Institute of Chicago, Joseph Brooks Fair Collection

165 p

Henri de Toulouse-Lautrec, *Edmée Lescot*, 1893, lithograph, 43.8 x 32.3 cm (sheet). The Art Institute of Chicago, William McCallin McKee Memorial Collection

165 q

Henri de Toulouse-Lautrec,
Madame Abdala, 1893,
lithograph, 43.5 x 32.3 cm
(sheet). The Art Institute of
Chicago, Mr. and Mrs. Carter H.
Harrison Collection

165 r

Henri de Toulouse-Lautrec,
Aristide Bruant, 1893,
lithograph, 44 x 32.3 cm (sheet).
The Art Institute of Chicago,
Gift of Mr. Frank B. Hubachek

158

Henri de Toulouse-Lautrec,
Caudieux at the Petit Casino,
**1893, lithograph, 42.6 x 32 cm
(sheet). The Art Institute of
Chicago, Gift of Horace M. Swope**

Henri de Toulouse-Lautrec,
Ducarre at the Ambassadeurs,
**1893, lithograph, 44.2 x 31.8 cm
(sheet). The Art Institute of
Chicago, Mr. and Mrs. Carter H.
Harrison Collection**

165 u

Henri de Toulouse-Lautrec,
A Spectator, 1893, lithograph,
43.6 x 32 cm (sheet). The Art
Institute of Chicago, Charles F.
Glore Collection

165 v

Henri de Toulouse-Lautrec,
American Singer, 1893,
lithograph, 44.3 x 32.5 cm
(sheet). The Art Institute of
Chicago, Mr. and Mrs. Carter H.
Harrison Collection

166

Henri-Gabriel Ibels, *Le Café-Concert*, 1892, pastel, 48.7 x 31 cm. The Jane Voorhees Zimmerli Art Museum, Rutgers, The State University of New Jersey, Norma B. Bartman Purchase Fund

167

Henri-Gabriel Ibels, *Le Café-Concert*, 1893, lithograph, 35.5 x 27.4 cm. The Jane Voorhees Zimmerli Art Museum, Rutgers, The State University of New Jersey, Herbert Littman Purchase Fund

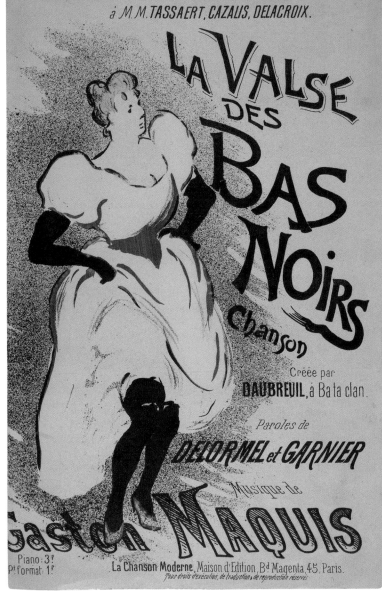

168

Henri-Gabriel Ibels, *Study for "Les Bas Noirs,"* c. 1895, pastel, 23.5 x 15 cm. The Jane Voorhees Zimmerli Art Museum, Rutgers, The State University of New Jersey, Lillian Lilien Memorial Art Acquisition Fund

169

Henri-Gabriel Ibels, *"Des Bas Noirs,"* song sheet, c. 1895, color lithograph, 27 x 17.7 cm. Private collection

170

Henri-Gabriel Ibels, "Coeur
Meurtri," song sheet,
c. 1892–1895, color lithograph,
27 x 35 cm. The Jane Voorhees
Zimmerli Art Museum, Rutgers,
The State University of New
Jersey, Herbert D. and Ruth
Schimmel Art Purchase Fund

171

Henri-Gabriel Ibels, Mévisto:
Concert la Gaïété, 1892, color
lithograph, 168.8 x 118.5 cm.
The Jane Voorhees Zimmerli Art
Museum, Rutgers, The State
University of New Jersey, Friends
Purchase Fund

172

Henri de Toulouse-Lautrec,
Jane Avril, 1892, oil on
cardboard, mounted on wood,
67.8 x 52.9 cm. National Gallery
of Art, Washington, Chester Dale
Collection

Henri de Toulouse-Lautrec, *Jane Avril*, c. 1891–1892, oil on cardboard, mounted on panel, 63.2 x 42.2 cm. Sterling and Francine Clark Art Institute, Williamstown, Massachusetts

174

Pablo Picasso, *Jardin de Paris*,
1901, brush and ink and
watercolor, 64.8 x 49.5 cm.
Lent by The Metropolitan
Museum of Art, Gift of Raymonde Paul, in memory of her
Brother, C. Michael Paul, 1982

175

Henri de Toulouse-Lautrec,
Jane Avril, 1893, color
lithograph, 129 x 94 cm (sheet).
The Art Institute of Chicago,
Mr. and Mrs. Carter H. Harrison
Collection

176

Henri de Toulouse-Lautrec,
*Mademoiselle Eglantine's
Troupe,* 1896, color lithograph,
62 x 79.9 cm (sheet). The Art
Institute of Chicago, Mr. and
Mrs. Carter H. Harrison Collection

177

Henri de Toulouse-Lautrec,
Cover for *"L'Estampe originale,"*
1893, color lithograph, 57.6 x
83 cm. Phyllis Rothschild

178

Henri de Toulouse-Lautrec,
Jane Avril, 1899, color
lithograph, 55.6 x 37.6 cm
(sheet). The Art Institute of
Chicago, Mr. and Mrs. Carter H.
Harrison Collection

179
—
Jules Chéret, *Yvette Guilbert au Concert Parisien*, 1891, color lithograph, 118.1 x 84.1 cm (sheet). Los Angeles County Museum of Art, Kurt J. Wagner, M.D., and C. Kathleen Wagner Collection

180
—
Ferdinand Bac, *Scala: Yvette Guilbert*, 1893, color lithograph, 213 x 88 cm. The Jane Voorhees Zimmerli Art Museum, New Brunswick, Rutgers, The State University of New Jersey, Gift of Herbert D. and Ruth Schimmel

181

Charles-Lucien Léandre, *Yvette
Guilbert*, c. 1892–1894,
graphite, 20.3 x 15.2 cm.
The Jane Voorhees Zimmerli
Art Museum, Rutgers, The
State University of New Jersey,
Anonymous Donation

182

Théophile-Alexandre Steinlen,
Yvette Guilbert, 1894, color
lithograph, 179.4 x 75.9 cm.
Los Angeles County Museum of
Art, Kurt J. Wagner, M.D., and
C. Kathleen Wagner Collection

183

Théophile-Alexandre Steinlen,
Yvette Guilbert, 1896, blue
and black chalk with gray wash,
36.1 x 27.5 cm. Sterling and
Francine Clark Art Institute,
Williamstown, Massachusetts

184

Henri de Toulouse-Lautrec,
Yvette Guilbert, illustration
in *Figaro illustré*, July 1893,
chromotypograph. The Jane
Voorhees Zimmerli Art Museum,
Rutgers, The State University
of New Jersey, Anonymous
Donation

185

Henri de Toulouse-Lautrec,
*Yvette Guilbert: "Linger,
longer, loo,"* c. 1894, oil on
cardboard, 58 x 44 cm. State
Pushkin Museum of Fine Arts,
Moscow

Henri de Toulouse–Lautrec,
Yvette Guilbert Taking a Bow,
1894, mixed media drawing,
41.8 x 24.1 cm. Museum of Art,
Rhode Island School of Design,
Providence, Gift of Mrs. Murray
S. Danforth

Drawings of Yvette Guilbert by
Henri de Toulouse-Lautrec that
were originally executed in
graphite on one sheet of ivory
wove paper, c. 1894, but were
later separated.

187
—
Recto: left, *Yvette Guilbert
Singing,* 33.4 x 20.5 cm. The Art
Institute of Chicago, Promised
gift of Francey and Dr. Martin L.
Gecht; right, *Yvette Guilbert,*
23.1 x 35.6 cm. The Art Institute
of Chicago, Albert H. Wolf
Memorial Collection

188
—
Verso: left, *Three-Quarter-
Length Study of Yvette Guilbert.*
The Art Institute of Chicago,
Albert H. Wolf Memorial
Collection; right, *Yvette
Guilbert.* The Art Institute of
Chicago, Promised gift of Francey
and Dr. Martin L. Gecht

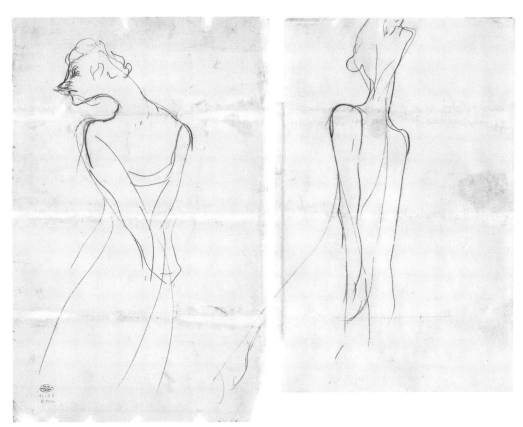

Henri de Toulouse-Lautrec, *The Black Gloves of Yvette Guilbert*, 1894, oil on cardboard, 62.8 x 37 cm. Musée Toulouse-Lautrec, Albi; Gift of Dr. Bourges

190 a

Henri de Toulouse-Lautrec,
Yvette Guilbert, 1894, cover for
album of sixteen lithographs,
41 x 39 cm. National Gallery
of Art, Washington, New Century
Fund, Gift of Edwin L. Cox –
Ed Cox Foundation, 2000.1.1 – 17

Yvette Guilbert

Avant de savoir ce qu'elle chante, on entend qu'elle chante bien, et qu'elle dit bien. Son premier secret est là : elle prononce, elle articule, elle expédie les mots dans toute la salle, où à travers le jardin des Champs-Élysées, elle perce le brouillard de fumée de tabac, la vapeur d'alcool, la buée des haleines. Chaque syllabe arrive en flèche, décochée par le gosier, par les dents, par la langue, portée sur la claire onde sonore, transparente, à la fois ferme et frêle comme un cristal vibrant. Son second secret, c'est son flair de chanteuse, son sûr odorat qui a subodoré l'arôme de la pourriture dite fin-de-siècle, — l'odieux mot sans signification et qui en acquiert une, et qu'il faut bien se résigner à écrire. Elle s'est trouvée là tout exprès pour dresser une statue gaie et macabre, en chair, en robe claire et en gants noirs, pour faire entendre une voix ennuyée et mordante, qui chante la noce sur des airs d'enterrement. La bouche est ironique, le nez a le comique français, à l'évent, et la face blanche apparaît tout à coup funèbre, les paupières mortes. D'autres secrets, elle en a sans doute, mais qui sont les siens, des secrets d'instinct et de volonté. Et puis, elle a sa personne, qu'elle plie à toutes les gymnastiques, à toutes les contorsions, mais qui n'en reste pas moins une personne ondulante et gracieuse, d'une apparition inattendue lorsqu'elle jaillit des coulisses d'un pas délibéré, et qui se brise et s'évapore en lignes fuyantes lorsqu'elle disparaît dans un salut.

Telle quelle, arabesque vivante, froide ironiste, précise diseuse, rieuse en dedans, sensuelle et acerbe, nerveuse comédienne, muse d'une atmosphère de mort, cette Yvette Guilbert adoptée par ceux qu'elle raille, mise en vedette sur l'affiche de Paris, représente à l'heure actuelle le mélange du café-concert, et par cela même une des manières d'être de la foule d'aujourd'hui. Elle a la signification, l'importance de Théréa à la fin du Second Empire. C'est donc son image qui devait être évoquée au début de ces pages, et son nom qui pouvait être mis en enseigne logique à cette suite de réflexions sur le café-concert et l'esprit de la foule.

Yvette Guilbert a apporté sur la scène du café-concert de l'originalité, de la voix, de l'ironie, mais le café-concert vivrait, et il vit souvent ainsi, sans talents, sans poésie, sans musique, sans rien. Il vivait avec les apparences, avec le seul décor de la chanson. Le flamboiement du gaz à la porte, ou la nappe lunaire de la lumière électrique, des affiches grimaçantes, des noms en vedette, des visages glabres d'hommes, des visages plâtrés de femmes. A l'intérieur, l'odeur de la bière et du tabac, des rangs serrés de fauteuils, l'orchestre tapageur et gai, un rideau qui se lève, quelqu'un qui apparaît et qui chante selon l'un des genres admis. Il n'en faut pas davantage pour que la foule vienne, compacte et bruyante, au rendez-vous.

Quel attrait mystérieux l'attire donc ? Quelle odeur lui indique la piste ? Quelle lumière voit-elle briller ? Entrez avec elle.

Quoi que l'on chante, et chanté par n'importe qui, si les couplets ressortent du patriotisme, de l'obscénité, de la scatologie, la joie sera unanime, vous assisterez au rire brutal, à la pâmoison naïve, aux bravos d'enthousiasme.

C'est affreux, blessant, et vous, Monsieur, ou Madame, vous vous levérez, quitterez votre siège, fuirez ce lieu empesté, déclarerez sur le seuil que jamais plus vous ne reviendrez respirer cette atmosphère, entendre ces cris, assister à ce scandale.

Il est certain que la répulsion peut être vive, que l'esprit peut gagner là un malaise, un effroi, un dégoût, une sorte de courbature morale dont il sera quelque temps à se défaire. Et même, il se peut concevoir un sentiment moins vif, moins horrifié, moins agressif, qui rejette néanmoins ceux qui auraient tenté la fâcheuse expérience à leurs passe-temps acceptés, musiquettes convenues, plates comédies, ordinaires vaudevilles, tels que l'on peut en trouver dans les théâtres les mieux tenus. Au moins, un décorum est conservé, les femmes rient derrière l'éventail et les hommes ne fument pas à l'orchestre. Mais avouez que l'intellectualité du plaisir admis n'est pas toujours sensiblement supérieure. Et avouez aussi que la déclaration contre le café-concert, si elle est quelquefois, chez quelques-uns, sincère, peut se trouver aussi, chez un grand nombre, hypocrite. Il y a des faits et il y a des présomptions.

Les faits, c'est que le public des cafés-concerts, de certains tout au moins, varie avec les jours, et finit par résumer assez bien les différents états des couches sociales. Il y a même une saison de l'année, de Juillet à Septembre, où le public habituel est presque totalement remplacé. C'est l'époque des concerts en plein air, dans les verdures, sous les astres. La scène est installée, cette fois, assez loin des faubourgs, et si quelques fidèles émigrent, si les étrangers affluent, il n'est pas interdit de croire que nombre de spectateurs des théâtres d'hiver changent de distraction avec l'été. Comme on chante les mêmes choses sous le ciel étoilé que sous les quinquets, c'est donc l'atmosphère matérielle qui était, pour beaucoup, l'objection, et non l'atmosphère morale.

La vérité, c'est qu'il n'y a pas, dans une grande ville telle que Paris, de si grandes différences de public. Ou plutôt, la grande différence crée une infime minorité et une immense majorité. Et il y a ceux qui restent chez eux, qui

choisissent les pièces dont ils veulent se donner les représentations de lecture à eux-mêmes, sans décors et sans acteurs, sur la scène de l'imagination.

Pour les autres, l'important, qu'ils l'avouent donc, est de sortir de chez eux où ils s'ennuient, et de s'en aller n'importe où chercher la lumière, le bruit, et la complicité tacite de la foule, des êtres semblables à eux, de la cohue des ennuyés.

En venir, à cette constatation, c'est en venir, non à la défense du café-concert, — le monstre est vivace, et nul ne défendrait son insolente santé, — mais à la défense, ou plutôt, à l'explication du public du café-concert.

On n'a pas tout dit quand on a dit l'abjection du spectacle, le bas-fond remué, la montée de ruisseau, la débâcle de fange. Le réquisitoire a souvent été fait, et il est facilement fait, il se formule de lui-même.

Mais cette masse riante, qui applaudit les niaiseries et les cochonneries, pourquoi est-elle là ? Tous ces gens qui pourraient donner leurs cinquante sous au Drame, à la Comédie, ou à l'Opéra...

Comment dites-vous cela ?

Quelle erreur est la vôtre ! Ces cinquante sous, ils pourraient les porter ailleurs, mais savez-vous bien à quelles conditions ? Avez-vous réfléchi aux misères et aux vexations de la vie, à tout ce qui poursuit le misérable homme, la pauvre unité sociale, jusque dans ses plaisirs ? Ces cinquante sous, pris sur le nécessaire, sur la paie de la semaine, sur les appointements du mois, sur les bénéfices de la boutique, on n'est pas

190 b–e

(from top left)

admis à les donner aussi facilement, sur la simple inspection de l'affiche. La journée finie, le dîner vite pris, la course faite, il est bien temps de se présenter au guichet d'un théâtre ! Les quelques places du parterre au Théâtre-Français ou à l'Opéra-Comique sont vite prises par ceux qui ont pu attendre l'ouverture des portes entre les balustrades. Il reste les étages supérieurs, d'où l'on entend et l'on voit comme on peut. Et encore ne faut-il pas compter sur le premier rang.

Le plaisir, ainsi, devient vite une fatigue et une peine, une humiliation pour les plus humbles. Pour être assis, pour voir et pour entendre, ce n'est pas cinquante sous qu'il faut donner, c'est cinq francs, ou sept francs, et plus, en s'y prenant d'avance. Le populo estime qu'il vaut mieux entrer tout de go, à l'heure que l'on veut, au café-concert, s'installer devant un verre, sortir son tabac et bourrer sa pipe.

Nous sommes en mil huit cent quatre-vingt-quatorze, et il va y avoir bientôt vingt-quatre ans que la troisième République existe. Depuis ce temps-là, et même depuis un peu plus longtemps, les plus retentissants orateurs de la démocratie n'ont cessé de réclamer la mise enfin à l'ordre du jour de l'éducation du peuple. Ils ont affirmé en discours et en écrits la nécessité de faire et de parfaire la mentalité et la moralité de l'homme nouveau. Mais en pratique, et même dans la plus simple pratique, ils se sont montrés plus timides. Nombre d'efforts, et des plus sincères, des mieux persistants, des plus tenaces, ont porté sur l'Ecole. Qui oserait en contester ici l'utilité et la justice ? Seuls quelques personnages, parfois instruits et gradés, proclament le mal fondé de ce budget d'instruction. Ils diraient volontiers, et ils disent, qu'il faut l'ignorance pour le peuple, comme il lui faut la religion. Eux peuvent se passer de l'une et de l'autre, et s'en passent, à l'aide de quelques consolations matérielles extraites des biens de ce monde. Aussi ont-ils inventé les Ecoles fondées sur l'esprit de caste, celles qui

préparent à l'autorité, et ils les ont installées, monumentales et luxueuses, faites pour recevoir les fils de la bourgeoisie, en face l'Hôtel-Dieu primaire du pauvre, ou le triste chalet de planches de la municipalité. Nulle enquête sur les goûts et les facultés, nulle possibilité pour certains de continuer les études commencées. Les uns doivent sortir de l'école à douze ans pour entrer à l'atelier et à l'usine. Les autres continuent leurs monômes jusqu'à l'âge d'homme en les entremêlant des expériences de la galanterie dans les brasseries du Boul'Mich. On constitue ainsi, partout et en tout, les directions nécessaires.

Croit-on, en regardant ainsi le début de l'existence de l'homme des villes s'écarter du sujet mis en question, de ce café-concert où défilent les silhouettes pittoresques d'Yvette Guilbert ? Nullement. L'éternel sujet, le drame partout présent, c'est l'homme. C'est le même être que vous rencontrerez sans cesse, cherchant à résoudre l'énigme de sa vie, sciemment ou inconsciemment, par toutes ses pensées, par tous ses actes, par toutes les manifestations de son instinct.

Cet homme, le premier venu, celui de la foule, vous venez de le voir à ses commencements pourvu d'un moyen insuffisant. Il est né, et le voilà parti pour la tombe. Il va vivre un au-jour-le-jour laborieux pendant quelques brèves années, on lui prendra une partie de sa jeunesse pour la caserne, une partie de son gain pour l'impôt, il connaîtra tant bien que mal l'amour, la paternité, pour continuer les destinées de la terre, il sera l'engrais social avant d'être l'engrais naturel.

Véritablement, pourquoi voulez-vous que cet homme là n'aille pas au café-concert ? C'est la seule porte qui lui soit ouverte, la seule maison qui lui soit hospitalière. Pour un prix infime en proportion, il est placé comme un abonné des mardis de la Comédie-Française ; pour presque rien, il peut entrer et se trouver avec ses semblables. Il faut bien, tout de même, qu'il emploie d'une

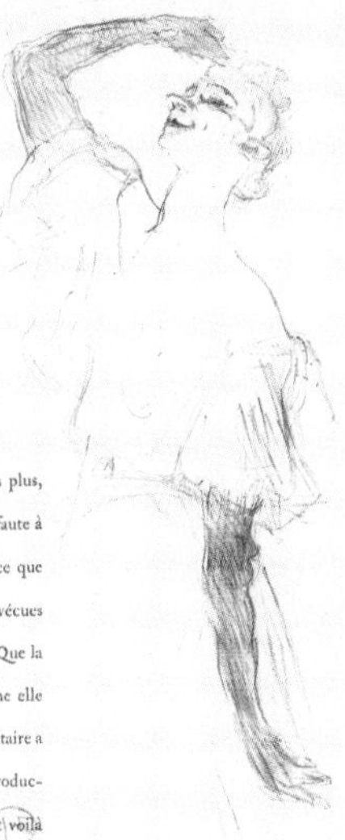

manière quelconque le temps laissé libre par le travail. Que lui offre-t-on d'autre comme organisation de repos et de plaisir ?

L'Eglise ? Oui, c'est là la pensée secrète, la même chez la bourgeoisie d'aujourd'hui que chez l'aristocratie d'autrefois. C'est à l'Eglise que l'on voudrait bien envoyer le peuple, et même en ce moment un suprême effort est tenté, nos bourgeois sont prêts à toutes les simagrées, se trémoussent odieusement pour singer la foi qu'ils n'ont plus, avec l'espoir de la communiquer, de rendre la torpeur à la masse menaçante. C'était si commode, un remède si endormeur du présent, si bon préparateur de l'avenir. Sottise que d'y avoir renoncé ! Comment persuader de nouveau à ce troupeau humain qu'il lui faut accepter toutes les charges, tous les renoncements, toutes les misères, avec la seule compensation d'un paradis chimérique ? Peine perdue ! On ne redonne pas la foi à volonté, pas plus, d'ailleurs, qu'on ne l'ôte. On aura beau dire, répéter sur tous les tons que c'est la faute à Voltaire, crier haro sur le positivisme, sur le matérialisme, sur le savoir, sur tout ce que l'on voudra, — ces clameurs ne donneront pas le change, et les périodes nouvelles vécues par l'humanité sont des ensembles auxquels les individus ne peuvent rien changer. Que la haute bourgeoisie effarée invoque la mule du Pape ou la botte de Napoléon, comme elle nous en donne le spectacle assez répugnant depuis quelque temps, rien n'y fera. Voltaire a de l'action, certes, et heureusement, mais il est encore bien plus un produit qu'un producteur d'action. Le populaire ne va plus à l'Eglise parce qu'il ne veut plus y aller, et voilà tout. Il s'est aperçu de la mystification sociale et il est devenu méfiant. Autrefois il y avait trône et l'autel, aujourd'hui, c'est la caisse et l'autel. Flair de payant, payant de toutes les le manières ! Voilà pourquoi on aperçoit les bons types en redingote obstinés à rester à la porte des églises, lors des cérémonies tarifées. Le croyant apôtre disparait en même temps que s'affirme le prêtre fonctionnaire.

Même au fond des provinces, dans les bourgs perdus, des hommes en habit de drap, endimanchés, mais abstentionnistes, resteront au cabaret pendant messe et vêpres.

Le cabaret ? C'est encore un lieu d'asile offert à l'homme de travail. Le marchand de vin sévit partout, débite, avec son vin frelaté, l'absinthe empoisonnée, l'eau-de-vie incendiaire. Hélas ! l'homme de travail en use, pas autant qu'on le dit, mais trop, beaucoup trop, autant que l'oisif use du café et du restaurant, et certains apportent là une frénésie de malades, un désespoir de miséreux. Ils donnent leurs forces à ces fées dorées, vertes et rouges, du comptoir, à ces naïades de feu qui gazouillent dans les alambics et appellent les passants. C'est un mal universel, la recherche du stupéfiant, le laisser-aller dans l'oubli, et ceux qui vont à l'église se saoûlent comme ceux qui n'y vont pas.

Quoi encore ? Qu'est-il offert au peuple ?

Les cours du soir ? Ils sont suivis par un petit nombre, de ceux qui savent surmonter leur fatigue. La lecture dans les bibliothèques publiques ? La lecture à domicile ? Il faut être préparé, entraîné à la lecture, pour trouver le charme à ces voyages de l'esprit. Les travailleurs manuels sont peu enclins, forcément, aux longues et fortes méditations après dix, douze heures de métier. Réduisez d'abord la journée de travail. Des employés lisent, collectionnent des livraisons.

Et encore ?

Le musée ? Il est fermé à cinq heures en été, à quatre en hiver. Il n'y a de South Kensington ouvert jusqu'à dix heures,

190 f–i

(from top left)

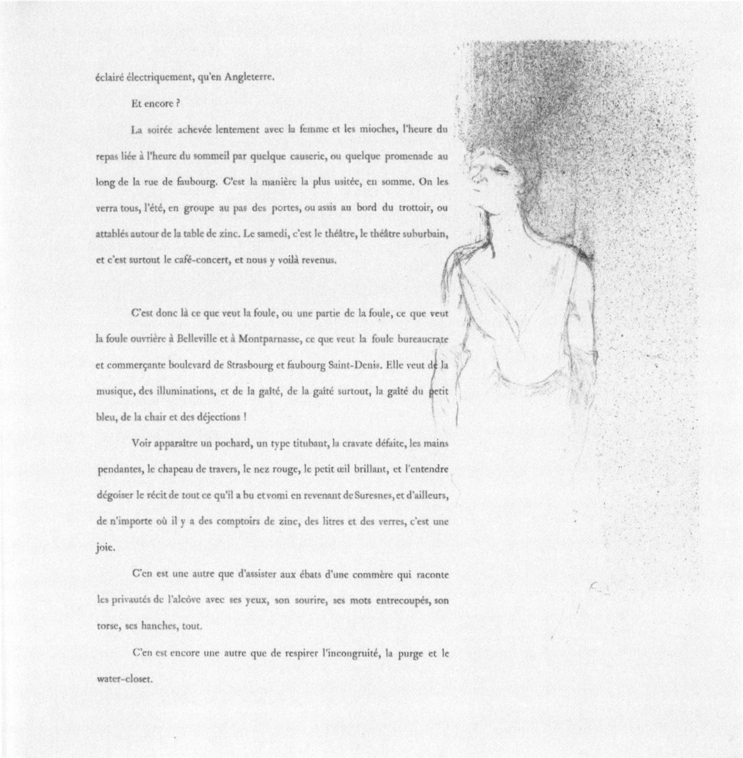

éclairé électriquement, qu'en Angleterre.

Et encore ?

La soirée achevée lentement avec la femme et les mioches, l'heure du repas liée à l'heure du sommeil par quelque causerie, ou quelque promenade au long de la rue de faubourg. C'est la manière la plus usitée, en somme. On les verra tous, l'été, en groupe au pas des portes, ou assis au bord du trottoir, ou attablés autour de la table de zinc. Le samedi, c'est le théâtre, le théâtre suburbain, et c'est surtout le café-concert, et nous y voilà revenus.

C'est donc là ce que veut la foule, ou une partie de la foule, ce que veut la foule ouvrière à Belleville et à Montparnasse, ce que veut la foule bureaucrate et commerçante boulevard de Strasbourg et faubourg Saint-Denis. Elle veut de la musique, des illuminations, et de la gaîté, de la gaîté surtout, la gaîté du petit bleu, de la chair et des déjections !

Voir apparaître un pochard, un type titubant, la cravate défaite, les mains pendantes, le chapeau de travers, le nez rouge, le petit œil brillant, et l'entendre dégoiser le récit de tout ce qu'il a bu et vomi en revenant de Suresnes, et d'ailleurs, de n'importe où il y a des comptoirs de zinc, des litres et des verres, c'est une joie.

C'en est une autre que d'assister aux ébats d'une commère qui raconte les privautés de l'alcôve avec ses yeux, son sourire, ses mots entrecoupés, son torse, ses hanches, tout.

C'en est encore une autre que de respirer l'incongruité, la purge et le water-closet.

L'estomac, la tripe et le reste ont ainsi leur fête. Les nécessaires fonctions humaines ont leur apothéose.

C'est désolant, répugnant, mais que l'on ne se hâte pas tout de même de jeter une défaveur spéciale sur ceux qui vont se réjouir de ces rappels des conditions de la vie. Ils font partie d'une lignée, ils sont dans une tradition qui n'est pas moins que l'une des traditions classiques françaises.

Il n'est peut-être pas nécessaire d'ouvrir les bibliothèques, de rechercher toutes les pièces justificatives. Il suffit d'éveiller le souvenir, de montrer l'âme d'un pays flottante au-dessus de l'Histoire. La France n'est-elle pas une terre de vignes, de la Bourgogne au Bordelais, du Jura à la Touraine, de la Champagne au Roussillon ? Il est difficile, à ceux qui sont nés de cette race, d'échapper aux antécédents séculaires, à cette vapeur de terroir. La France ne fut-elle pas aussi un séjour d'amour vif et de galants propos ? Et son réalisme aussi s'embarrassa-t-il des basses fonctions, contrepoids nécessaires d'une cérébralité alerte, rétablissement d'équilibre utile à la spéculation de la pensée ? N'en a-t-il pas été fait un élément de comique et de force ?

En plein moyen-âge, aux pierres même des cathédrales, ce réalisme de la race s'affirme et triomphe, nargue le destin, se réjouit de la minute concédée à l'être. La nationalité française n'a pas attendu le grand docteur François Rabelais, le bon docteur qui décrète la Renaissance, qui rassure définitivement l'humanité, qui lui enjoint d'accepter son sort et de vivre sa vie.

Hélas ! sans doute, le rabelaisisme est à bon marché, et ceux qui se payent de mots et détournent les ordures en affirmant continuer l'ancêtre, n'ont rien recueilli de la haute philosophie du vaste esprit, de son mystérieux savoir, de sa prévoyante et bienveillante conscience. Ils pataugent dans le marécage d'une manière, ne s'en iront jamais, comme l'autre, sur le libre océan de la pensée.

Mais ceux-là qui viennent du fin fond des foules pour assister à quelque spectacle, entendre quelque parole, ceux-là

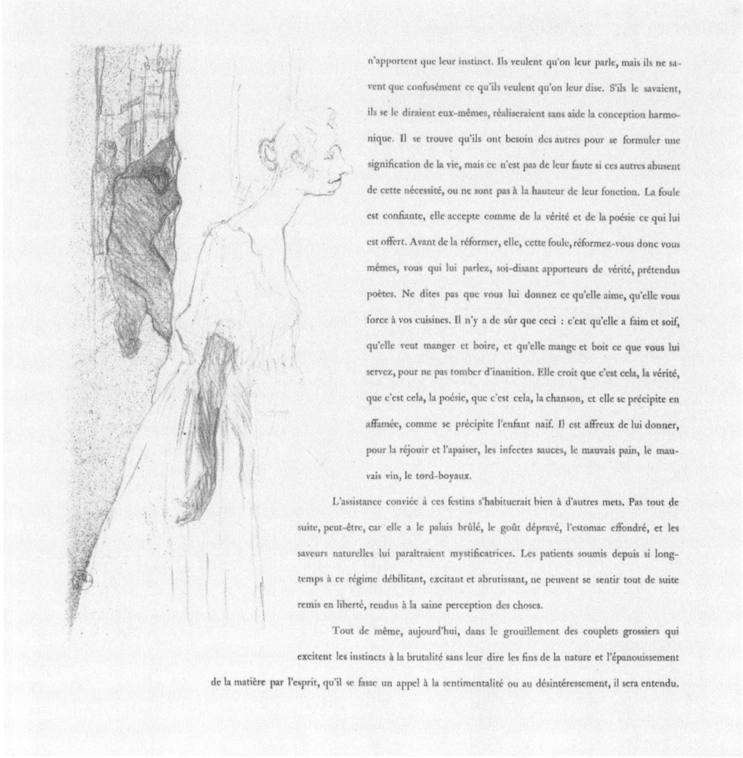

n'apportent que leur instinct. Ils veulent qu'on leur parle, mais ils ne savent que confusément ce qu'ils veulent qu'on leur dise. S'ils le savaient, ils se le diraient eux-mêmes, réaliseraient sans aide la conception harmonique. Il se trouve qu'ils ont besoin des autres pour se formuler une signification de la vie, mais ce n'est pas de leur faute si ces autres abusent de cette nécessité, ou ne sont pas à la hauteur de leur fonction. La foule est confiante, elle accepte comme de la vérité et de la poésie ce qui lui est offert. Avant de la réformer, elle, cette foule, réformez-vous donc vous mêmes, vous qui lui parlez, soi-disant apporteurs de vérité, prétendus poètes. Ne dites pas que vous lui donnez ce qu'elle aime, qu'elle vous force à vos cuisines. Il n'y a de sûr que ceci : c'est qu'elle a faim et soif, qu'elle veut manger et boire, et qu'elle mange et boit ce que vous lui servez, pour ne pas tomber d'inanition. Elle croit que c'est cela, la vérité, que c'est cela, la poésie, que c'est cela, la chanson, et elle se précipite en affamée, comme se précipite l'enfant naïf. Il est affreux de lui donner, pour la réjouir et l'apaiser, les infectes sauces, le mauvais pain, le mauvais vin, le tord-boyaux.

L'assistance conviée à ces festins s'habituerait bien à d'autres mets. Pas tout de suite, peut-être, car elle a le palais brûlé, le goût dépravé, l'estomac effondré, et les saveurs naturelles lui paraîtraient mystificatrices. Les patients soumis depuis si longtemps à ce régime débilitant, excitant et abrutissant, ne peuvent se sentir tout de suite remis en liberté, rendus à la saine perception des choses.

Tout de même, aujourd'hui, dans le grouillement des couplets grossiers qui excitent les instincts à la brutalité sans leur dire les fins de la nature et l'épanouissement de la matière par l'esprit, qu'il se fasse un appel à la sentimentalité ou au désintéressement, il sera entendu.

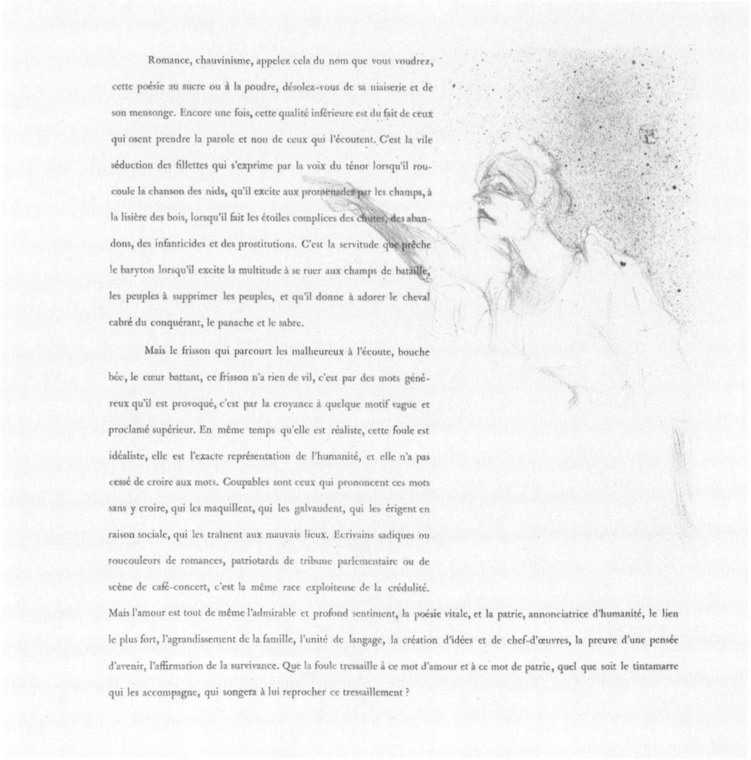

Romance, chauvinisme, appelez cela du nom que vous voudrez, cette poésie au sucre ou à la poudre, désolez-vous de sa niaiserie et de son mensonge. Encore une fois, cette qualité inférieure est du fait de ceux qui osent prendre la parole et non de ceux qui l'écoutent. C'est la vile séduction des fillettes qui s'exprime par la voix du ténor lorsqu'il roucoule la chanson des nids, qu'il excite aux promenades par les champs, à la lisière des bois, lorsqu'il fait les étoiles complices des chutes, des abandons, des infanticides et des prostitutions. C'est la servitude que prêche le baryton lorsqu'il excite la multitude à se ruer aux champs de bataille, les peuples à supprimer les peuples, et qu'il donne à adorer le cheval cabré du conquérant, le panache et le sabre.

Mais le frisson qui parcourt les malheureux à l'écoute, bouche bée, le cœur battant, ce frisson n'a rien de vil, c'est par des mots généreux qu'il est provoqué, c'est par la croyance à quelque motif vague et proclamé supérieur. En même temps qu'elle est réaliste, cette foule est idéaliste, elle est l'exacte représentation de l'humanité, et elle n'a pas cessé de croire aux mots. Coupables sont ceux qui prononcent ces mots sans y croire, qui les maquillent, qui les galvaudent, qui les érigent en raison sociale, qui les traînent aux mauvais lieux. Ecrivains sadiques ou roucouleurs de romances, patriotards de tribune parlementaire ou de scène de café-concert, c'est la même race exploiteuse de la crédulité. Mais l'amour est tout de même l'admirable et profond sentiment, la poésie vitale, et la patrie, annonciatrice d'humanité, le lien le plus fort, l'agrandissement de la famille, l'unité de langage, la création d'idées et de chef-d'œuvres, la preuve d'une pensée d'avenir, l'affirmation de la survivance. Que la foule tressaille à ce mot d'amour et à ce mot de patrie, quel que soit le tintamarre qui les accompagne, qui songera à lui reprocher ce tressaillement ?

190j–m

(from top left)

Aussi, dit-on, ce n'est pas ce reproche qui est formulé, ce tressaillement est trouvé bon. Chaque fois que la foule est ingénue et croyante, elle plaît à ses maîtres.

Quoi donc ?

Le reproche, c'est que le frisson ne soit pas assez prolongé, c'est que tout de suite le feu d'artifice s'éteigne dans les eaux croupissantes, que tous quittent le Drapeau pour aller au Plaisir, et au plaisir proclamé défendu, à la corruption, à la luxure, à l'ivresse.

Plaisant et funèbre réquisitoire ! Ceux qui le rédigent avec indignation ne s'aperçoivent-ils pas du singulier état d'esprit qu'ils révèlent ? C'est la corruption d'en bas qui les choque, non celle d'en haut. Or, celle d'en bas est une suite, un aboutissement fatal. La corruption gagne de proche en proche, se propage comme une inondation, se répand partout, dans les coins reculés que l'on aurait pu croire hors de ses atteintes. Pendant longtemps, les intéressés ont pu croire qu'elle serait un monopole, qu'ils la garderaient pour eux seuls et leurs intimes, que la masse des hommes trouverait une compensation suffisante dans les phrases héroïques, bénisseuses et endormeuses. De même que l'on trouvait la religion bonne pour le peuple, pour des raisons identiques le plaisir était proclamé bon pour quelques-uns. Les dirigeants oublient vraiment par trop de se réserver une part de ce gâteau de l'idéal affirmé par eux si délicieux. Ils se nourrissent d'autres festins. Quoi d'étonnant si le désir et la faim sont venus à ceux qui les regardaient manger d'un air si heureux, si supérieur, si au-dessus de la commune misère. Les dirigeants n'ont pas dirigé, ils ont dépravé. L'histoire de la Monarchie française avorte et crève comme un abcès sous Louis XV. On y a mis le fer sous Louis XVI, mais la contagion s'était répandue, et le Tiers-État puritain, vêtu de drap noir, qui prit la place de la noblesse en faillite, se pervertit bien vite à la possession du pouvoir et des écus. Depuis cent ans, les dirigeants laissent leurs devoirs d'éducateurs pour jouir de la minute qui passe, et en jouir mal. Tous les petits fragments de souveraineté disent le même « Après moi le déluge » que disait l'autre. Ils sont les privilégiés de la possession et du savoir, ils doivent l'exemple et celui qu'ils donneront sera imité.

Ils en donnent un, il est suivi, et ils s'étonnent, ils geignent que le peuple ait perdu l'idéal. C'est le contraire qui serait étonnant. Si l'esprit jouisseur et gouailleur s'installe dans une partie de la population, c'est qu'il a été fait pour cela tout ce qu'il fallait. Tout est à la rigolade dans ce que l'on appelle la société. Des hommes s'occupent de leur toilette autant que les femmes, vivent pour leurs organes, fêtent leur ventre comme un dieu. Pourquoi les passants ne s'attrouperaient-ils pas au défilé des voitures, aux vitres des restaurants chics, et ne finiraient-ils pas par apprendre qu'il y a des dessous aux déclarations morales, et des dessous vite aperçus, une débauche à peine secrète, un éreintement génésiaque d'une quinzaine ou d'une vingtaine d'années avant le mariage d'argent. Et pourquoi ces passants qui peinent pour gagner leur vie et qui ne connaissent que les logis hasardeux, les nourritures insuffisantes, le vin corrosif, plus rien de naturel, rien que du falsifié, du gâté, du pourri, pourquoi ne s'aviseraient-ils pas d'être hommes comme tant d'autres hommes, c'est-à-dire envieux, malfaisants, et tout au moins curieux de ce qui s'affiche avec tranquillité. Pourquoi ne s'en iraient-ils pas à la dérive comme la belle jeunesse et la respectable vieillesse qui défilent devant eux, ramollies et joyeuses.

Ne cherchez pas ailleurs que dans l'homme semblable à l'homme les raisons du dévergondage qui vous offusque, du cynisme qui vous effraie. Ceux qui ne peuvent pas avoir la réalité des choses veulent au moins en avoir les apparences, le spectacle. Ils s'en vont donc là où le fumet cherché affectera leurs narines, ils iront se récréer de la niaiserie et de la crapule, ils deman-

deront à voir le personnel du brillant lupanar, les couchers, les levers et les lavages de ces dames. Qu'en pensez-vous, n'est-ce pas de la révolte qui finit en envie et en bassesse ?

On trouve cela, à l'analyse, dans les éléments confondus au café-concert, comme on y trouve l'instinct de nature exprimé par Rabelais, et le moyen sentiment de gaudriole des chansonniers du Caveau et des romanciers grivois, Désaugiers et Béranger, Pigault-Lebrun et Paul de Kock. Comment faire le tri dans tout cela, parmi ces ingénuités et ces ordures, comment garder le sentiment de nature et proscrire l'obscénité, comment sauver le rire et défalquer la goujaterie, comment vouloir la seule vérité et la mettre à la place de tout faux idéal ? L'exemple seul, et le temps, peuvent accomplir l'œuvre. C'est toujours et partout que dix justes et même un seul juste peuvent sauver une ville. Il y a de bons ferments dans la bourgeoisie et dans le peuple. Qu'ils se joignent donc et fassent un nouveau monde, ou tout s'en va. Agissez, cadets de la bourgeoisie, intermédiaires attendus, comme ont agi les cadets de la noblesse aux premiers jours révolutionnaires, renoncez et affirmez à la fois, agissez, il est temps !

Bientôt, en bas, dans la région de travail et de misère, on ne croira plus à rien. Le désagrégement va s'achever, les liens avec le passé se rompent un à un. La romance est en baisse, et le drapeau aussi. A quoi sert de se dissimuler ce qui est, de ne pas vouloir voir. Ce jeu n'empêche pas les choses d'être. La période est difficile à passer dans le présent, et sera encore plus difficile à passer dans l'avenir, cela est certain. Il faut pourtant marcher quand même, continuer la vie. L'idée de justice veut sa solution, et elle l'aura, à travers tout. Pour cela, bien des décors qui sont encore debout s'effondreront, tout ce qui constitue la civilisation

héritée, l'Église et la Bourse, le Palais et la Caserne. Mais qui ne consentira, dans l'avenir, à l'effritement et à l'écroulement des monuments, si chacun peut enfin jouir de sa maison et de son jardin, de ses fleurs, de sa ruche et de son arbre ? Le fameux idéal invoqué comporte trop de truffes et de champagne pour les uns, et pas assez même de pain sec pour les autres. Ce sera tout bénéfice pour l'humanité si elle entend et comprend d'une certaine façon ce qui lui sera crié : « Il n'y a pas d'idéal, il y a la soupe et le bœuf, il faut vivre d'abord, créer de la vie, posséder la Terre, lui faire donner son maximum de bonheur. » Ce sera là le commencement de l'action.

Ce sera la conclusion de ces feuilles, si vous le voulez bien. La chanteuse Yvette Guilbert, lorsqu'elle a fini sa chanson, et qu'elle se sauve, la gorge âcre de la fumée respirée, toute sa personne imprégnée de l'atmosphère chaude, où va-t-elle ? Elle saute dans un train, quitte Paris, se rafraîchit à l'air sain de l'espace, retrouve son jardin et sa rivière de Vaux. Humanité tombée au café-concert, fais comme ta chanteuse, aussitôt que tu le pourras, quitte les grandes villes, retourne à la nature avec ce que tu as appris d'histoire et de civilisation, cherche l'ombre de l'arbre, le chant de la branche et du sillon, contente-toi du petit jardin autour duquel il y a l'espace, vis ta propre existence, unis-toi à la Terre enfin dominée par la Pensée.

GUSTAVE GEFFROY.

193
—
Leonetto Cappiello, *Yvette Guilbert*, 1899, oil on canvas, 116 x 90 cm. Musée d'Orsay, Paris; don du Mme Monique Cappiello, belle-fille de l'artiste, 1979

194
—
Leonetto Cappiello, *Yvette Guilbert*, 1899, polychrome plaster, 34 x 23.5 x 17.4 cm. The Jane Voorhees Zimmerli Art Museum, Rutgers, The State University of New Jersey, Garleton A. Holstrom and Mary Beth Kineke Purchase Fund

195

Henri Nocq, *Yvette Guilbert*,
1893, ceramic plaque (tondo),
54.4 cm (diameter with original
frame). Musée d'Orsay, Paris

196

Henri de Toulouse-Lautrec,
Yvette Guilbert, 1895, ceramic
plaque, 26.7 x 28.3 cm. San
Diego Museum of Art, Gift of
Mrs. Robert Smart

197

Henri Gustave Jossot, *Jockey-Club Sardines*, 1897, color lithograph, 125.5 x 201 cm (sheet). The Art Institute of Chicago, Gift of Peter Kort Zegers In memory of his brother Hans Zegers (1943–2000)

198

Henri de Toulouse-Lautrec,
May Belfort, 1895, oil on
cardboard, 63 x 48 cm.
The Cleveland Museum of Art.
Bequest of Leonard C. Hanna Jr.

199

Edouard Vuillard, *At the Café–
Concert, May Belfort*, c. 1895,
oil on cardboard, 32 x 51 cm.
A. Carter Pottash

200

Henri de Toulouse-Lautrec,
Miss May Belfort (large plate),
1895, color lithograph, 69.2 x
52.3 cm (sheet). The Art Institute
of Chicago, John H. Wrenn
Memorial Collection

201

Henri de Toulouse-Lautrec,
May Belfort, 1895, color
lithograph, 79.8 x 61.4 cm
(sheet). The Art Institute of
Chicago, Mr. and Mrs. Carter H.
Harrison Collection

202

Henri de Toulouse-Lautrec,
May Milton, 1895, color
lithograph, 80.4 x 61.9 cm
(primary support). The Art
Institute of Chicago, Mr. and
Mrs. Carter H. Harrison Collection

203

Pablo Picasso, *The Blue Room*,
1901, oil on canvas, 50.4 x
61.5 cm. The Phillips Collection,
Washington, D.C.

Henri de Toulouse-Lautrec,
Miss Loïe Fuller, 1893, color
lithograph, 38.4 x 28.1 (sheet)
cm. National Gallery of Art,
Washington, Rosenwald
Collection

205

Henri de Toulouse-Lautrec,
Miss Loïe Fuller, 1893, color
lithograph, 38.1 x 28.1 cm
(sheet). National Gallery of Art,
Washington, Rosenwald
Collection

206

Henri de Toulouse-Lautrec,
Miss Loïe Fuller, 1893, color
lithograph, 38.1 x 28.2 cm
(sheet); The Art Institute of
Chicago, Joseph Brooks Fair
Collection

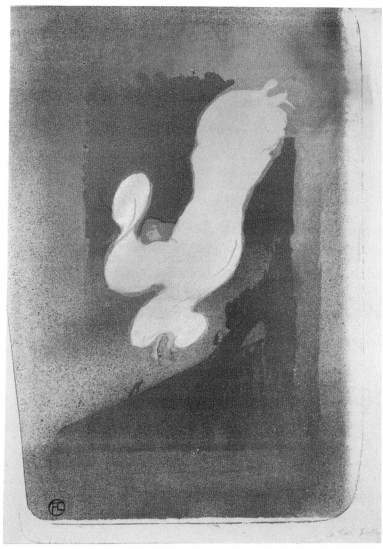

207

Henri de Toulouse-Lautrec,
Miss Loïe Fuller, 1893, color
lithograph, 36.8 x 26.8 cm.
The Baltimore Museum of Art:
Gift of Mrs. Nelson Gutman,
in Memory of her late Husband's
Birthday, June 21, 1956

208

Henri de Toulouse-Lautrec,
Miss Loïe Fuller, 1893, color
lithograph, 36.8 x 26.8 cm.
Museum of Fine Arts, Boston.
Bequest of W. G. Russell Allen

209

Henri de Toulouse-Lautrec,
Miss Loïe Fuller, 1893, color
lithograph, 36.8 x 26.8 cm.
Courtesy Boston Public Library,
Print Department, Collection of
Albert H. Wiggin

210

Henri de Toulouse-Lautrec,
Miss Loïe Fuller, 1893, color
lithograph, 36.8 x 26.8 cm.
Francey and Dr. Martin L. Gecht

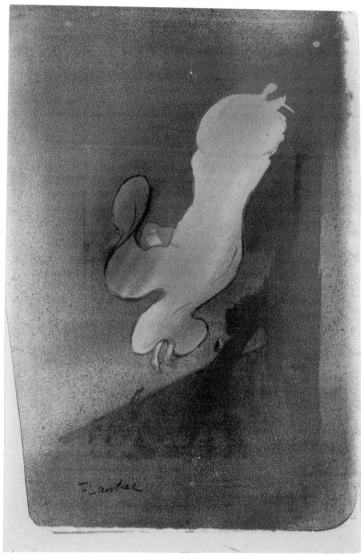

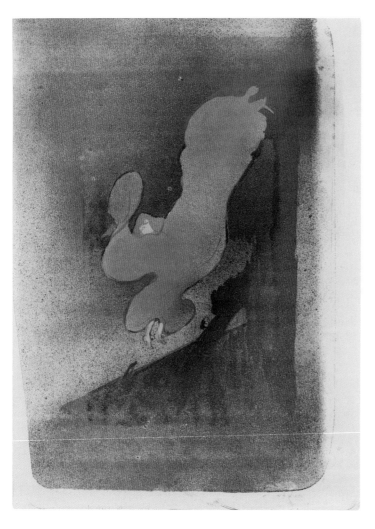

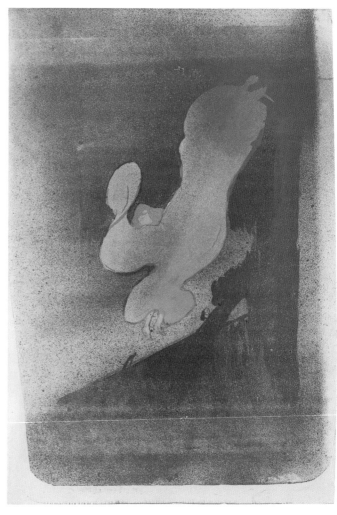

Henri de Toulouse-Lautrec,
Miss Loïe Fuller, 1893, color
lithograph, 38 x 27.9 cm (sheet).
The Art Institute of Chicago,
Joseph Brooks Fair Collection

Henri de Toulouse-Lautrec,
Miss Loïe Fuller, 1893, color
lithograph, 37.9 x 25.9 cm.
The Metropolitan Museum of Art,
Rogers Fund, 1970

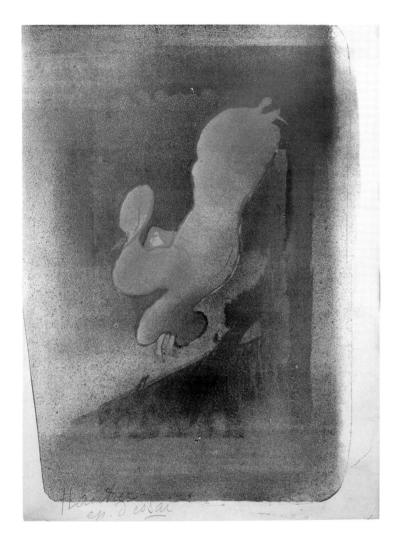

217

Henri de Toulouse-Lautrec,
Miss Loïe Fuller, 1893, color
lithograph, 36.8 x 26.8 cm.
Phyllis Rothschild

218 a – f

François Rupert Carabin,
Miss Loïe Fuller, c. 1896–1897,
bronze, height (clockwise from
top left): 19 cm, 18.5 cm, 19.5 cm,
22 cm, 20.3 cm, 22.5 cm. The Jane
Voorhees Zimmerli Art Museum,
Rutgers, The State University
of New Jersey, Gift of Herbert D.
and Ruth Schimmel

219
—
Charles Maurin, *Loïe Fuller*,
c. 1895, pastel, 63 x 47 cm.
The Jane Voorhees Zimmerli Art
Museum, Rutgers, The State
University of New Jersey, Regina
Best Heldrich Art Acquisition Fund

220
—
Charles Maurin, *Loïe Fuller*,
c. 1895, pastel, 63 x 47 cm.
The Jane Voorhees Zimmerli Art
Museum, Rutgers, The State
University of New Jersey, Regina
Best Heldrich Art Acquisition Fund

221

Charles Maurin, *Loïe Fuller*,
c. 1895, pastel and charcoal,
65.8 x 53.2 cm. The Jane Voorhees Zimmerli Art Museum,
Rutgers, The State University of
New Jersey, Regina Best Heldrich
Art Acquisition Fund

222

Lucien Lemariey, *La Loïe Fuller*,
1893, printed paper fan. Musée
Carnavalet – Histoire de Paris

223

Jules Chéret, *Folies-Bergère:*
La Loïe Fuller, 1893, color
lithograph, 110.2 x 81.9 cm
(sheet). Los Angeles County
Museum of Art, Kurt J. Wagner,
M.D., and C. Kathleen Wagner
Collection

224

Pal [Jean de Paléologue], *Loïe*
Fuller, c. 1894, color lithograph,
121.9 x 83.8 cm. Los Angeles
County Museum of Art, Kurt J.
Wagner, M.D., and C. Kathleen
Wagner Collection

227

Henri de Toulouse-Lautrec,
*Marcelle Lender Dancing the
Bolero in "Chilpéric,"* **1895–
1896, oil on canvas, 145 x 149 cm.
National Gallery of Art, Washington, Collection of Mr.
and Mrs. John Hay Whitney**

Richard Thomson

MAISONS CLOSES

Toulouse-Lautrec's paintings of the world of prostitution are difficult to analyze. The subject—women hiring their bodies for sex—is unpleasant; it shows neither women nor men in a good light. Yet prostitution seems always to have been a part of ordered societies, and as such, it has frequently been a subject for art. The prostitute takes her turn in great art from Titian through Goya to Manet. Lautrec would have been aware of this. Indeed, in 1889 he contributed to the subscription to buy Edouard Manet's infamous *Olympia* of 1863 (Musée d'Orsay, Paris) for the French state collections.[1] Perhaps even more than his predecessors, Lautrec was prepared to take on prostitution as a major theme in his work and produced some fifty paintings on the theme between the mid-1880s and mid-1890s.[2] This willingness to tackle such a morally dubious and socially disputed topic leads us to question Lautrec's motives. Was he attracted to the theme because it was "outside the law," and so placed him too beyond the constraints of the bourgeois morality of the Third Republic? Was he driven by personal pressures such as his own sexual appetites, or by a desire to observe this shadowy world? As an observer, was his gaze objective, critical, or sympathetic?

These paintings are not easy to read. Take *In the Salon: The Sofa* (fig. 228). It shows women sitting and waiting for clients in a *maison close,* the official French euphemism for a brothel. It is a frank scene of sexual commerce. Yet it is not a grim one. The women appear contented, well fed and groomed; the room is plushly furnished. It may be a comfortable establishment. At the same time, the women do not appear particularly appealing, with their modest peignoirs and neighborhood faces. Finally, the relationship of the viewer to the women is ambiguous. We look at them from the same level, as the artist might study a sitter for a portrait. The women ignore us entirely, and there is nothing that suggests the gaze of a client, even though the artist himself was male and an aficionado of brothels. Indeed, the spectator's position might almost be that of a waiting prostitute. These paintings resonate with ambiguities and uncertainties.

But perhaps that was deliberate, for the world of prostitution itself was surreptitious, shifting, and difficult to grasp. This was a problem for the authorities in Paris during the 1880s and 1890s, and it was a matter of debate among various groups such as politicians, the police, and those interested in public health and social reform.[3] Like those of the many artists whose work touched on prostitution at this period, Lautrec's images formed part of the fabric of this debate. It had long been accepted that prostitution was a necessary, if undesirable, element in the modern city. Men's lusts need to be serviced, not least to protect respectable women, whose purity as a bride was seen as an essential guarantee of the family, which was the basic social unit and mechanism for the transmission of wealth. To safeguard the bourgeois social order from potentially disruptive male urges, a distinct cadre of women was necessary to divert them. However expedient such a solution, prostitution was also immoral, so it needed to be disguised and monitored. Hence the establishment of licensed *maisons closes,* which could be discreetly housed, regulated by the police, and their personnel subject to regular medical inspection. This was a system of control allied with a moral vision that had underpinned the world of Parisian prostitution since midcentury, enshrined in Dr. Parent-Duchatelet's two-volume study of 1836.[4]

The brothel system was centered on the registered prostitute (*fille soumise*), who was tied to her establishment, worked under the supervision of a madam, and was given routine medical checks. By the end of the nineteenth century, however, this mechanism was under threat from *filles insoumises,* women working unregulated on the streets. Their number was on the rise for a variety of reasons. Independence, even if supervised by a pimp, gave women a degree of choice of client impossible to the *fille soumise.* In addition, prostitution was an option few women adopted except from necessity. It was an expedient to which women might be reduced by unemployment or the vagaries of seasonal work such as the floristry trade; in other words, it was often a temporary, sporadic means of earning a living.[5] As a result, prostitutes were to be found beyond the confines of the *maison close,* infiltrating the public spaces of the city. These are the women to be seen cruising the dance halls Lautrec painted. This fluid state created worrying ambiguities for the bourgeoisie. How could a prostitute be differentiated from a respectable woman? Where did prostitution begin and end? As so often, Lautrec's work operated within social patterns that engaged contemporary France.

They engaged other artists too. During the later 1870s Edgar Degas had made about fifty monotypes of brothel scenes (figs. 229–232).[6] Created by applying ink with brush, rag, or even finger to a metal plate and then printing it, with one or at most two impressions possible, the monotype is a hybrid between drawing and print. It is an improvisatory medium, having to be made in the studio, and the consistent sizes of Degas' plates suggest that he made them in rapid sequences. A letter from Degas to his fellow artist Giovanni Boldini indicates that Degas was familiar with brothels, then an habitual matter of convenience for the bachelor.[7] Yet the casual drawing of the bodies and the approximated settings imply that he produced the monotypes from memory or his imagination rather than from direct observation. This is supported by Degas' usual depiction of the prostitutes naked, whereas in practice they were generally clad, however skimpily.[8] The monotypes capture a variety of scenes: women alone or in groups, washing or waiting, sometimes with male clients. Some represent explicit sexual encounters: for example, a lesbian couple or a bawdy dinner in which a *fille* standing on the table bares her backside. Others are more prosaic, such as the trio seated on divan, a monotype touched

with pastel that passed through a Paris auction house in 1891, where Lautrec could conceivably have seen it. Usually matter-of-fact and occasionally obscene, Degas' brothel subjects often have a comic quality. In some the client is caricatured, at sea in this enclosed world of female flesh. In many the women are portrayed with flabby bodies and bland faces, their simian features and sometimes frankly coarse behavior apparent. This kind of characterization conforms to the Darwinism that dominated much thinking about social organization in late nineteenth-century France.

Emile Bernard, closer in age to Lautrec than the cynical, middle-aged Degas, also produced a number of watercolors and pen-and-ink drawings on brothel subjects, sending a clutch of them to Vincent van Gogh in Arles in the spring of 1888.[9] As Lautrec would later do, Bernard showed the women involved in ordinary activities such as waiting for clients and playing cards (figs. 233–237). To some he added captions, and this, combined with his simple graphic style, gives the works their caricatural quality. Bernard also sent Van Gogh poems on brothel subjects. Their tone mixes youthful lust and desire to shock with Catholic disgust and self-reproach. Bernard's entire fascination with the brothel may have been the young man's posturing; after all, the idea that one needed to sink into sin the better to find redemption was a decadent topos in the neo-Catholic novels of contemporaries such as Joséphin Péladan.

Around 1886–1887, while still a pupil at Cormon's studio, Bernard had drawn a large and elaborate composition of a lower-class brothel, mercantile and sinister in its bottle greens and livid yellows (fig. 238). Probably stimulated by the common subject matter of Aristide Bruant's songs, which the artist would have heard at Le Mirliton, *The Hour of the Flesh* was never worked into a finished painting, just as Louis Anquetin's project for a major picture of the singer's cabaret was never realized. Perhaps it was Bernard's feelings of guilt, allied to his conversion to rustic Breton subjects, that aborted a scheme that, had it been resolved, could have matched Lautrec's ambitious dance hall paintings of 1889 and 1890. When Bernard returned to the brothel theme around 1890, once again the caricatural idiom came to the fore. *Le Salon* represents a sparsely furnished room, the prostitutes' faces and bodies reduced to schematic simplicity, a pictorial metaphor for a featureless existence (fig. 239).

Lautrec seems to have initiated himself into the theme in an ad hoc manner. His first painting with a whiff of the subject is *La Grosse Maria* (fig. 242). It was made about 1886, a transitional phase when the twenty-two-year-old Lautrec was finding his independence from Cormon's studio. The dark-toned, carefully worked canvas has much of the character of a student's painting from life, a test of the ability to paint flesh tints and foreshorten limbs. But something brazen and hard-bitten about the model, as well as the rather seedy intrusion of the mask that seems to peer from the wall, gives this canvas an equivocal quality between the conventional *académie* and the prostitute type.

For Lautrec, as for his fellow student Bernard, it was the cabaret culture of Montmartre that led him to the subject and the *quartier*'s sexual mores that took him to the prostitutes. By 1886 Lautrec was a regular at the Mirliton. One of Bruant's songs, "A Grenelle," described a prostitute who serviced soldiers, and it was undoubtedly this that Lautrec had in mind as he worked on his first explicitly meretricious picture, *Artilleryman and Whore*.[10] Lautrec never completed the composition, but the studies abruptly juxtapose the blank profile of the woman and the soldier's leer as he adjusts his trousers. The artist's conception is as cruel and uncompromising as Bruant's slang verses:

J'en ai t'i' connu des lanciers,	I've known lancers,
Des dragons et des cuirassiers,	Dragoons and cuirassiers,
I's m'montainet à m'tenir	They mounted me and kept me
en selle,	in hand,
A Grenelle.	At Grenelle.[11]

Lautrec's cocktail of uncompromising bluntness, smutty humor, and willingness to try to read the woman's role was the refreshing mixture with which Lautrec revitalized this much-used subject in art.

Between about 1893 and 1896 Lautrec produced a substantial group of paintings of *maisons closes*. These are now among his most famous works, and much of Lautrec's celebrity as an artist has rested on this aspect of his oeuvre. But they are complex pictures and should not be attributed to simplistic strategies: an expression of his own sexuality or the desire to shock. Indeed, they should not be considered as a unified group, because Lautrec viewed this sexual underworld from a variety of angles and depicted it with different brushes. Just as there were distinct levels

of prostitution, from the elegant courtesan—via the kept woman or the denizen of a smart *maison close*— to the meanest streetwalker and inmate of a soldiers' brothel, so Lautrec's images ran the gamut of pictorial possibilities. Some paintings were overtly smutty. This is the case with *The Laundryman* (fig. 240). To the left a battered-looking *insoumise* scrutinizes the laundry list, while the deliveryman facing her clasps his bundle to his groin, his ogling leer suggesting that she has absent-mindedly left open her peignoir. The anecdote is curtly insinuated. What counts are the faces: ugly, brutish, exaggerated.

In works such as these Lautrec reached for the caricatural idiom that was so instinctive to men's representations of brothel life. Laughter, we might say, was a defensive, distancing mechanism. Jean-Louis Forain, a friend of Degas and of Lautrec's father, had made an elaborate watercolor of a brothel scene (fig. 241), which he exhibited at the 1880 impressionist exhibition. Its gross subject of sexual commerce is masked behind the ridiculousness of the client's ruminative connoisseurship, the posturings of the knock-kneed, pot-bellied prostitutes, and Forain's teasing use of the compositional convention for the Judgment of Paris theme.

Another category of Lautrec's brothel pictures is portraits of prostitutes. Some of these, such as *Lucie Bellanger* (fig. 243), have come down to us with names, in contradiction to the anonymous function of the woman in the *maison close*. Although rapidly painted, with the medium densest on face and bust and tailing off below the waist, this portrait has a massive, sculptural presence. Lautrec did not neglect Lucie Bellanger's physicality, her tousled blonde chignon, ample breast, and thrusting neck. But he also picked out her personality in *profil perdu*. We are invited to discover her small, heavy-lidded eyes, purplish and fatigued; her small nose, hooked and flared; her jutting lower lip; and her jowled jaw with pointed chin. In portraits such as this Lautrec evinced a social tolerance rare for his period and class that enabled him to see such women as individuals. If most artists escaped caricaturing the prostitute, they rarely got further than depicting her as a type. Picasso's *Nude with Stockings* (fig. 244) may have portrayed a particular person, but the way the artist displayed the woman's naked body framed by fetishistic materials, the soft play of color and texture amplifying a sensual reading of the picture, sacrificed the individual for the stock image.

In other pictures Lautrec did use types. They appear in a number of scenes that operate as very low-key anecdotes describing how the women pass their time before clients arrive. This is a world of women, sitting around a table chatting, using cards to tell their fortunes, making beds. Lautrec's use of medium is significant here. For his *maison close* images he chiefly employed his favored *peinture à l'essence,* but he also used pastel. Both allow for rapid, graphic application of color, and they give a sense of something seen on the spot, thus adding to the apparent authenticity of the scenes. Lautrec's brothel interiors, like his dance hall subjects, concentrate on the figures and give only schematic backgrounds. The upright piano, potted plant, and stuccoed columns in *In the Salon* suggest an upmarket *maison* (fig. 245), maybe the rue des Moulins establishment with fifteen women, not in Montmartre but off the avenue de l'Opéra.[12] But these backdrops are little more than visual props for generic locales in which prostitute types follow their typical business. The women wait in *In the Salon,* the attention of the two on the left possibly drawn by an open door that illuminates their faces, while another lounges to the right. *Monsieur, Madame, and the Dog* offers a contrasting use of types: a caricatural treatment of the elderly *patronne* of an establishment, her yapping lapdog, and a man who—whether her husband or perhaps a client—sits fecklessly smoking (fig. 246).

Lautrec also painted some eroticized brothel motifs. These constitute a third category, along with portraits and interiors. But they are rare, most likely because the artist's family destroyed the evidence.[13]

If the larger and more resolved of Lautrec's brothel pictures, in particular the major composition *Salon of the Rue des Moulins* (fig. 248), are essentially domestic interiors, it remains a question how to read them. We might perceive them simply as genre paintings, representations of likely everyday activities. Yet the paintings do not add up to a systematic charting of the different aspects of brothel life—clients, for example, only very occasionally appear—and they do not function like the almost sociological account of brothel life delineated in novels such as Paul Adam's *Chair molle (Soft Flesh)* of 1886 or in the many "scientific" texts on prostitution that contributed to the contemporary debate. The paintings' very placidity, their reduction of anecdote or pastime to the most tedious, seems almost to disqualify them from the status of narrative pictures.

Paradoxically, then, it may be that dullness that counts. In the *Salon of the Rue des Moulins* very little happens. Five women sit. They do not converse. They do not look at each other or even look in the same direction. The right side of the picture cuts off the figure of a sixth woman, chemise hitched up over her haunch. This ambiguous presence is the only irregular element. But perhaps our interest should be aroused not by what we see but from where we see it. Lautrec took a viewpoint that is at the eye-level of the prostitutes, as if artist and viewer are seated on another red plush divan. We are thus made to join the world of this image, to share its tedium.

The irregular figure in the *Salon of the Rue des Moulins* may represent the practice of the regular medical inspection, which Lautrec depicted in the most moving of his brothel paintings (fig. 249). Here two women queue up, like a fragment of a degraded secular procession, while the madam goes about her business in the background. These inspections were intended to curb the spread of venereal disease, another threat to the family, but the unhygienic procedures often had the opposite effect.[14] The soft warm colors of the crimson and pink fabrics and buttery flesh in Albi's *Salon* picture (fig. 248), set off by the dull greens of the stuccowork, give the room a stifling temperature, even a fragrance. But in the *Medical Inspection* the strident reds and insidiously livid violets create an edgy atmosphere in which two women of real individuality follow deadened lives, like two mute sleepwalkers. The way these women are physically differentiated—the older woman with the creamier complexion but slack buttocks; the redhead more rubicund, youthful, and sinuous—again involves the gaze. The way we look at these women is both the medical gaze, assessing the body's health, and the client's gaze, gauging its desirability.

Lautrec's sympathy toward such women, it is often said, also manifested itself in his paintings of lesbians. Prostitutes in the *maisons closes* sometimes turned to one another for affection. But once more the situation is more complicated. Whereas *The Two Friends* (fig. 250) shows an embrace in what appears to be a brothel setting, other situations are by no means so explicit. *In Bed: The Kiss* (fig. 251), an image of a lustful clinch apparently exhibited at Le Barc de Boutteville's gallery in November 1892, defines its environment no further than the sheets between which the couple lies.[15] Again, the spectator's viewpoint is crucial, because we are placed so close to this moment of passion. In a group of later paintings (see figs. 252 and 253) Lautrec also kept the viewer close, posing the women at different psychological moments in their lovemaking, at certain times tentative and tender, at other times sundered and disgruntled. As so often, reading these images is difficult. We are reminded of Lautrec's fascination with Krafft-Ebbing's *Psychopathia Sexualis,* first published in 1886, in which case studies are presented as narratives. Lautrec's lesbian paintings, we might say, are like vignettes to such texts. Brothels did stage lesbian encounters, and Lautrec may have had such commercial voyeurism in mind.[16] Lesbians were also a topos in decadent critiques of society, taking their turn in the imagery of Félicien Rops and Georges de Feure and the novels of Catulle Mendès and Jean Lorrain.[17] They seemed a decadent symptom, perversely denying the norms of fertility and family. Whatever Lautrec's motives in representing lesbians, his images were a combination of scrupulous observation of the interaction of body language and sexual psychology with the artful contrivance of staged compositions.

In 1896 Lautrec published *Elles,* an album of eleven remarkable color lithographs. These prints too deal with the world of prostitution. Some derive from oil paintings that may have originated as brothel scenes; this may be true of *Conquête de Passage,* unusual for its inclusion of a man (fig. 257). In the main, the *Elles* prints represent an interior, women's world (figs. 259 a–l). Their subjects typically focus on the boudoir: the toilette, breakfast in bed, conversation between friends. Once again, however, whether they have a precise collective identity is unclear. It has been suggested that they depict different stages in

the prostitute's day, a paradigm in the Japanese color woodcuts Lautrec so admired.[18] Perhaps more likely they show an aspect of prostitution different from that of the *maisons closes* of the paintings: in *Elles'* case, the world of the kept mistress in her comfortable apartment.[19] Demonstrating the whole range of Lautrec's skills as a printmaker, *Elles* is also lightly spiced with the comic, manifested in Lautrec's repertoire of smug faces and bulging bodies.

Lautrec may have painted dozens of images of the brothel world, but he was discreet about exhibiting them. They were not shown at the Indépendants; some lesbian paintings were displayed privately with dealers; and his 1896 one-man show kept the *maison close* pictures in a back room, available only to privileged clients. *Elles* alone was public. Why? It is possible that Lautrec was anxious about censorship. The police had required one of his lesbian pictures to be removed from Le Barc's window in 1892, and Arthur Huc remembered the artist's telling him that he would try to avoid scandal by not exhibiting the *Salon of the Rue des Moulins.*[20] The surreptitious nature of these images—from Lautrec's extraordinarily intimate, almost participatory viewpoints to their quasi-clandestine display—implies that they functioned as a private frisson for gentlemen. Certainly paintings disappeared into the private collections of Gustave Pellet, Paul Gallimard, and Roger Marx. There they might have been treated as Huysmans did his Forain *Le Client,* kept in a private room and shown to other men with a conspiratorial: "You certainly don't know this. . . ."[21] In the final account, Lautrec's representations of the world of prostitution evince a real sympathy for the women, but they are dominated by a matter-of-factness common to the period; they say that this is how the world is, this is what men need.

---

1. Duret 1919, 218–219.

2. London and Paris 1991, 406–461.

3. See *inter alia* Guyot 1882; Berck 1885; Corlieu 1887; Carlier 1887; Virmaître 1889; Richard 1890, Taxil 1891, and more recently Bernheimer 1989; Corbin 1990; Clayson 1991.

4. Dr. Alex Parent-Duchatelet, *De La Prostitution dans la ville de Paris* (Paris, 1836; rev. ed., 1857); see Corbin 1990, 3–18.

5. E.g. Berck 1885, 12, 15, 24–25; Richard 1890, 44.

6. Thomson 1988, 97–117; Clayson 1991, 27–55; Callen 1995, 71–104.

7. Letter of August 1889, in Loyrette 1989, 418.

8. Carlier 1887, 63.

9. New Brunswick 1988b.

10. Murray 1991, 118–122; Dortu 1971, P. 268–272.

11. Murray 1991, 118–119. The translation is Gale Murray's.

12. Virmaître 1889, 40.

13. See Dortu 1971, P. 495; Leclercq 1921 (1954 ed.), 53–54.

14. Taxil 1891, 20–21.

15. See the caricature in *Le Journal,* 26 November 1892.

16. Taxil 1891, 229.

17. Casselaer 1986, 10–23.

18. Saint-Germier 1992, 74–83.

19. London and Paris 1991, 436–437; Thomson in Washington 2000, 51, 55.

20. Jourdain and Adhémar 1952, 38; Huc 1922.

21. Huret 1891 (1999 ed.), 201.

228

Henri de Toulouse-Lautrec,
In the Salon: The Sofa,
c. 1892–1893, oil on cardboard,
60 x 80 cm. Museu de Arte de
São Paulo Assis Chateaubriand,
São Paulo, Brazil

229
Edgar Degas, *Two Women*,
c. 1876–1877, monotype, 24.9 x
28.3 cm. Museum of Fine Arts,
Boston. Katherine E. Bullard
Fund in memory of Francis
Bullard

230
Edgar Degas, *The Supper
Party (The Connoisseur)*,
c. 1876–1877, monotype,
22 x 16.3 cm (sheet). Francey
and Dr. Martin L. Gecht

231

Edgar Degas, *Three Seated Prostitutes,* c. 1876–1877, pastel over monotype, 23 x 31 cm. Rijksmuseum, Amsterdam

232

Edgar Degas, *The Reluctant Client,* c. 1876–1877, monotype, 21 x 15.9 cm (plate). National Gallery of Canada, Ottawa. Purchased 1977

233

Emile Bernard, *The Daily Grind*, c. 1888, pen, ink, and watercolor, 19 x 12.6 cm. The Jane Voorhees Zimmerli Art Museum, New Brunswick, Rutgers, The State University of New Jersey, Edward and Lois Grayson Purchase Fund

234

Emile Bernard, *Le Café*, c. 1888, pen and ink, 23 x 19 cm. The Jane Voorhees Zimmerli Art Museum, New Brunswick, Rutgers, The State University of New Jersey, Edward and Lois Grayson Purchase Fund

235

Emile Bernard, *Brothel Scene*
(dedicated to Vincent van Gogh),
1888, watercolor, 30.8 x 20 cm.
Van Gogh Museum Amsterdam
(Vincent van Gogh Foundation)

236

Emile Bernard, *Three Prostitutes
Seated*, 1888, watercolor,
40.5 x 26.2 cm. Van Gogh
Museum Amsterdam (Vincent
van Gogh Foundation)

237

Emile Bernard, *Three Prostitutes
around a Table*, 1888, watercolor, 40.4 x 28.3 cm. Van Gogh
Museum Amsterdam (Vincent
van Gogh Foundation)

238

Emile Bernard, *The Hour of
the Flesh*, c. 1886–1887, pastel
and gouache on wrapping paper
mounted on canvas, 125 x
170 cm. Private collection

239

Emile Bernard, *Le Salon,*
1890, oil on canvas, 81 x 116 cm.
Private collection

240

Henri de Toulouse-Lautrec,
The Laundryman, c. 1894,
oil on cardboard, 57.8 x 46.2 cm.
Musée Toulouse-Lautrec, Albi;
Gift of the Comtesse A. de
Toulouse-Lautrec

241

Jean-Louis Forain, *The Client*,
1878, pencil, watercolor, and
gouache, 24.7 x 32.8 cm.
Collection of The Dixon Gallery
and Gardens, Memphis,
Tennessee; Museum purchase

Henri de Toulouse-Lautrec,
La Grosse Maria, c. 1886, oil
on canvas, 79 x 64 cm. Von der
Heydt-Museum, Wuppertal

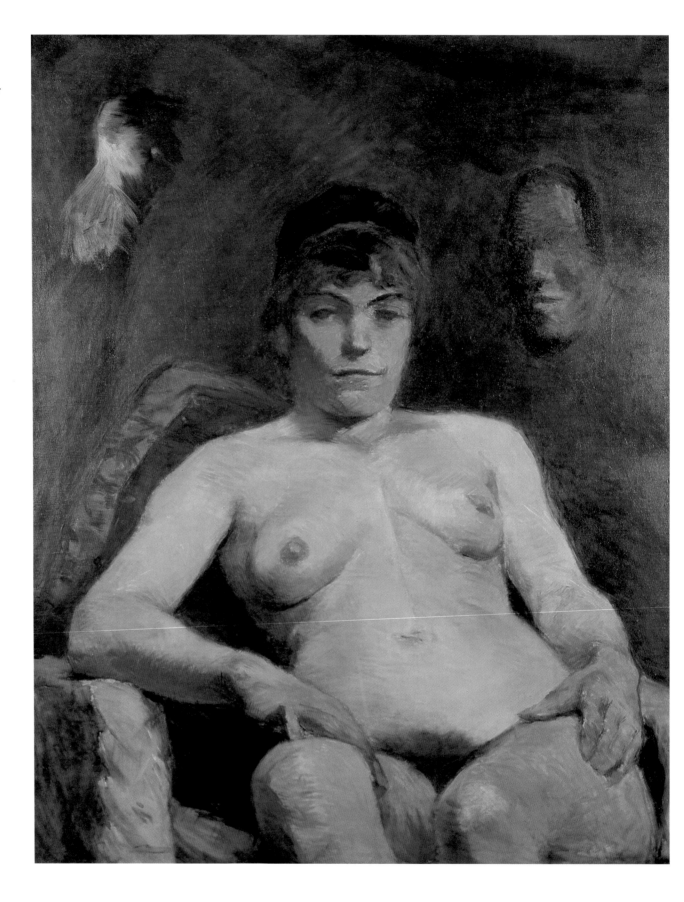

Henri de Toulouse-Lautrec,
Lucie Bellanger, c. 1895,
oil on cardboard, 80.7 x 60 cm.
Musée Toulouse-Lautrec, Albi;
Gift of the Comtesse A. de
Toulouse-Lautrec

246

Henri de Toulouse-Lautrec,
*Monsieur, Madame, and the
Dog*, 1893, oil on canvas, 48 x
60 cm. Musée Toulouse-Lautrec,
Albi; Gift of the Comtesse A. de
Toulouse-Lautrec

247

Henri de Toulouse-Lautrec,
Woman Seated on a Couch,
1894, oil on cardboard, 58 x
46 cm. Anonymous lender

248

Henri de Toulouse-Lautrec,
Salon of the Rue des Moulins,
1894, charcoal and oil on canvas,
111.5 x 132.5 cm. Musée Toulouse-
Lautrec, Albi

Henri de Toulouse-Lautrec,
*Medical Inspection (Rue des
Moulins)*, c. 1894, oil on
cardboard on wood, 83.5 x
61.4 cm. National Gallery of Art,
Washington, Chester Dale
Collection

252

Henri de Toulouse-Lautrec,
The Two Friends, 1895,
oil on cardboard, 45 x 67 cm.
Private collection, Courtesy
of Sotheby's, New York

253

Henri de Toulouse-Lautrec,
Women Resting, c. 1894 – 1895,
oil on cardboard, 59.5 x 81 cm.
Galerie Neue Meister, Staatliche
Kunstsammlungen Dresden

254

Henri de Toulouse-Lautrec, *Red-Headed Nude Crouching,* 1897, oil on cardboard, 46.4 x 60 cm. San Diego Museum of Art, Gift of the Baldwin M. Baldwin Foundation

255

Henri de Toulouse-Lautrec, *Woman with Mirror,* study for *Elles,* 1896, oil on cardboard, 60 x 36.5 cm. Gail and Richard Elden

(See also fig. 259 h)

256

Henri de Toulouse-Lautrec,
Woman Brushing Her Hair,
study for *Elles,* 1896, oil on
cardboard, 55.4 x 41 cm.
Musée Toulouse-Lautrec, Albi;
Gift of the Comtesse A. de
Toulouse-Lautrec

(See also fig. 259 i)

257

Henri de Toulouse-Lautrec,
*Woman in a Corset (Conquête
de Passage),* **study for** *Elles,*
c. 1894–1896, black and blue
chalk and oil à l'essence, on
paper, laid down on canvas,
103 x 65 cm. Musée des Augustins,
Toulouse

(See also fig. 259 k)

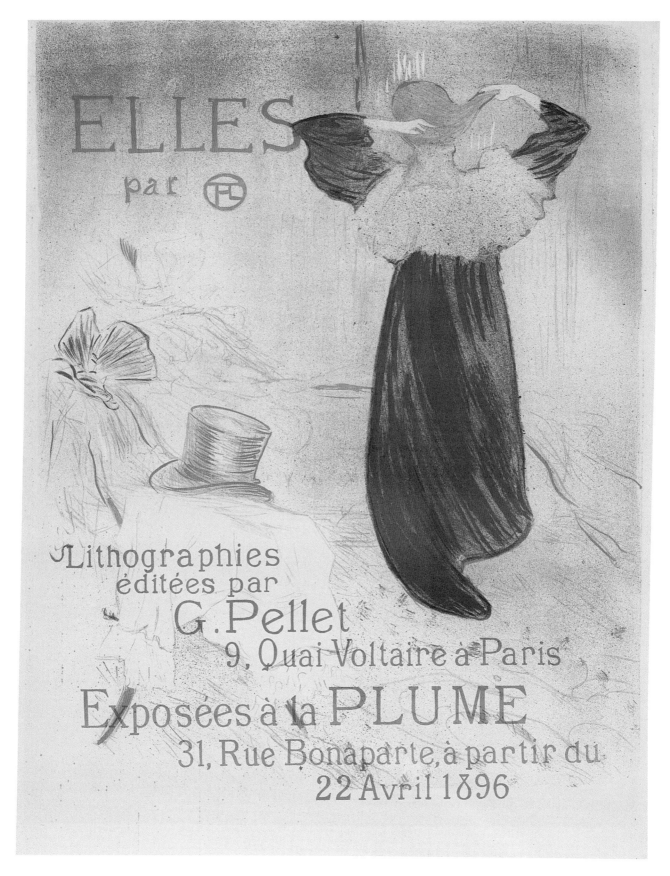

259 a

Henri de Toulouse-Lautrec, cover
for *Elles*, 1896, color lithograph,
57.1 x 47.2 cm (sheet, folded).
The Art Institute of Chicago,
Charles F. Glore Collection

259 b

Henri de Toulouse-Lautrec,
frontispiece for *Elles*, 1896,
color lithograph, 52.6 x 40.3 cm
(sheet). The Art Institute
of Chicago, Charles F. Glore
Collection

259 e

Henri de Toulouse-Lautrec,
Woman Reclining — Waking Up,
1896, color lithograph,
40.5 x 52.7 cm (sheet). The
Art Institute of Chicago,
Charles F. Glore Collection

259 f

Henri de Toulouse-Lautrec,
Woman at the Tub — The Tub,
1896, color lithograph,
40.4 x 52.3 cm (sheet).
The Art Institute of Chicago,
Charles F. Glore Collection

259 i

Henri de Toulouse-Lautrec,
*Woman Brushing Her Hair —
The Coiffure*, 1896, color
lithograph, 52.8 x 40.3 cm
(sheet). The Art Institute
of Chicago, Charles F. Glore
Collection

259 j

Henri de Toulouse-Lautrec,
*Profile of a Woman in Bed —
Getting Up*, 1896, color
lithograph, 40.1 x 52.1 cm
(sheet). The Art Institute
of Chicago, Charles F. Glore
Collection

Richard Thomson

THE CIRCUS

One of the great spectacles of the nineteenth century, the circus combined extraordinary gymnastic and acrobatic feats, animals trained to obey and amuse, crazy clowns, breath-taking daring and slapstick comedy, control and chaos. It drew excited crowds, whether to the grand performances in the big cities or to the little shows that traveled the countryside. The circus was deeply ingrained in Toulouse-Lautrec's imagination. He knew the world of horses from his childhood. No doubt as a boy he had been taken to the circus. And in the early 1880s, while in his teens and taking his first steps as a painter under the informal tutelage of the deaf-mute painter René Princeteau, he became fascinated by the ring, often visiting the Cirque Fernando in Montmartre.[1] Years later, in 1899, images of circus performers resurfaced in Lautrec's creative imagination at a time of great personal diffi-culty, when he was forcibly hospitalized, his alcoholism having grown dangerous and his behavior spinning out of control. In the unpromising surroundings of a clinic for the mentally disturbed, memories of the circus nurtured a great cycle of drawings, one of Lautrec's last major groups of work.

France did not have a native circus tradition but derived the idiom of traveling players during the late eighteenth century from the Italian commedia dell'arte. Astley's circus from Britain made a great impact in 1780s, while a century later came American extravaganzas: the grandiose Barnum and Bailey phenomenon in the 1870s, and later, in 1889, Buffalo Bill's show based on the taming of the American West. The circus world was fluid, fueled by an international circuit of performers, its rival companies vying with each other to produce more and more exciting entertainment for the growing audi-ences in the major cities. Gradually circuses acquired permanent facilities, but whether tented or housed in buildings, the ring always conformed to the regulation thirteen-meter radius essential for acts that traveled from venue to venue. In Paris the Cirque d'Eté was constructed on the Champs-Elysées in 1848, and the Cirque d'Hiver on the boulevard Beaumarchais four years later. These were custom-built, eliminating the mirrors and chandeliers typical of theaters so that spectators would focus their attention on and above the ring.

Such capitalization demanded new attractions. It was at the Cirque d'Hiver in 1859, for instance, that Jules Léotard introduced the flying trapeze.[2] The circuses engaged in rivalry with the even larger hippodromes, where huge events were staged. But these were in decline in Lautrec's day, whereas he was fortunate enough to work when the circus was thriving. A hierarchy existed among circuses, of course, extending from grand permanent structures such as the Cirques d'Eté and d'Hiver, both designed by the distinguished architect Ignace Hittorff; through newer, less capitalized operations such as the Cirque Fernando, which Lautrec favored; to the *fêtes foraines*, or traveling circuses, such as the Cirque Corvi, which Seurat represented in his *Parade du cirque* of 1887–1888 (The Metro-politan Museum of Art, New York).

As an important part of the entertainment industry, the circus relied on both tra-dition and expectation, on innovation and novelty, as did the dance halls. In 1888 Joseph Oller was planning not just the Moulin Rouge but also the Nouveau Cirque, outfitted with the most advanced machinery and even a pool for aquatic routines.[3] Circus directors had to compete for the best acts. According to Hugues Le Roux, who published an exhaustive account of the contemporary circus in 1889, there were only about thirty top-class clowns in the world, as much in demand as the greatest operatic tenors.[4] In Le Roux's view, many of the best clowns were British, because the necessary combination of the gross, anarchic, and violent was not a Latin trait but Shakespearean.[5] In the 1880s one of the premier clowns was the Birmingham-born Billy Hayden, who performed with a black pig.[6] About 1887 Lautrec painted a lively little picture of a clown cavorting with a scampering piglet (fig. 260). This probably does not represent Billy Hayden but Médrano, the leading clown at the Cirque Fernando, who is shown in a contemporary drawing by Jules Faverot as performing with pigs.[7] Success, as ever, spawned imitation.

The circus won wide admiration as a creative medium in the Paris of the 1880s and 1890s. The conservative theater critic Jules Lemaître enjoyed its defiance of nature, and thus its repudiation of real life; he preferred the circus to opera or melodrama.[8] From the opposite end of the ideological spectrum, the anarchist Félix Fénéon took a similar view, arguing in 1888 that, with the theater then in an abysmal state, the circus offered the best performances in Paris.[9] Its visual and physical spectacle attracted the attention of many artists as well. Lautrec would not have seen *Miss Lala at the Circus Fernando* (National Gallery, London), a vertiginous composition that his artistic hero Degas had shown at the 1879 impressionist exhibition, but he would have been well aware of the currency of the circus theme among painters. In 1888, for example, Lautrec had his first major public exhibition with the enterprising Belgian modernist group Les XX in Brussels, at which he showed his own large *At the Circus Fernando,* while Seurat exhibited *Parade du cirque* at the Indépendants, and the Salon included Fernand Pelez's vast *Grimaces et misères* (Petit Palais, Paris), a moving scene of scruffy and impoverished performers outside their tatty tent.

Lautrec favored the Cirque Fernando, under the direction of Ferdinand Beert (famed for his harsh but effective training of horses), which originally consisted of tents pitched at the corner of the rue des Martyrs and the boulevard de Rochechouart, not far from Aristide Bruant's Mirliton. Gradually it acquired greater permanence, first with wooden walls raised around the big top, then in 1878 reopening in an actual building. One of the performers whom Lautrec would have seen, Jérôme Médrano (the clown Médrano), took over the circus in 1912, and it was finally demolished in 1972.[10] Fernando offered the usual circus repertoire—clowns, acrobats, trained horses—but also presented novelties to keep the enterprise in the public eye. In early 1889, for instance, he staged a revue that included La Goulue, a venture that drew criticism from some who considered the dancer's lewd reputation inappropriate for the circus' local petit-bourgeois patrons and their families.[11] This pattern of change, involving modernization, hyped-up spectacle, and even a degree of shock, was typical of the rhythms of the Montmartre entertainment economy.

Lautrec's treatment of circus subjects falls into two concentrated phases, with a third, more fluid cluster of works in between. He produced the first of these main groups over a relatively short period from 1886 to 1888. Thus along with images of dance halls and proletarian types related to Bruant's songs, the circus ranks among the earliest motifs that Lautrec explored as he expressed his growing independence as an artist by choosing themes from the contemporary city. A painting of behind-the-scenes at the circus, in which a clown pats a horse while a female performer and a lugubrious man look on, was one of his first resolved compositions (fig. 261). Executed in grisaille, it marks Lautrec's transition from the more conventional execution he had learned in Cormon's studio to the modern, dynamic, and improvised manner he would develop in the later 1880s. We might even argue that the circus, which demanded from the artist a style that echoed its own perpetual movement, vulgar color, and wicked sense of fun, helped Lautrec formulate the very mobile and graphic handling that was the hallmark of his mature work.

Indeed, the circus provided the subject for what seems to have been Lautrec's largest painting.[12] Now lost (perhaps cut up after having been rolled and poorly stored in Lautrec's studio), this vast canvas is known from photographs of Lautrec's studio about 1890, in which it filled the rear space.[13] François Gauzi, a close friend of Lautrec at the time, described how the artist worked from a stepladder to create the composition, which depicted a clown holding a paper disc through which a bareback rider standing on a horse was about to leap.[14] With its larger-than-life-size figures, the painting was exceptionally ambitious for a young painter. It seems probable that a canvas on this scale was intended as a decorative painting, a genre for which another close friend Maurice Joyant recalled that Lautrec always nursed ambitions.[15] But we know nothing definite about its putative patron or destination, however unlikely it is that Lautrec would undertake such a major project without a commission. The artist did write to his mother in June 1887 that he was "busy doing a large panel for the circus," a tantalizing suggestion that he made this monumental painting to serve as a backdrop at the Cirque Fernando.[16]

Lautrec partly fulfilled his desire to create a work that would function as decoration when his painting *Equestrienne (At the Circus Fernando)* (fig. 266) was purchased to hang in the Moulin Rouge after its return from exhibition in Brussels. Although smaller than the lost canvas, this painting, measuring a meter and a half across, has a substantial presence, its steep perspective even suggesting that it was painted to be seen from slightly below.[17] The composition is dominated by the interplay between the authoritarian figure of Fernando, smartly clad in tails and clasping a whip, and a bareback rider—possibly portrayed by the aspiring artist Suzanne Valadon, herself formerly a circus performer—atop a large stallion.[18] The horse canters into the ring, a red arc that imparts a sense of dynamism. Subsidiary characters cut off at the edges of the design include sundry spectators, a clown on a stool holding a paper hoop, and to the left another clown—an Auguste recognizable by his white gloves and tails—whose careening waddle seems to parody the virile swagger of Fernando.

The painting carries a strong sexual charge. The heavily made-up bareback rider perches on the saddle, her skirt flipped up to reveal her legs up to her buttocks. Not only are the spectators almost exclusively male, and Fernando rather aggressively dominant, but the horse's powerful haunches flank its very evident testicles. Contemporary literature on the circus dwelt on the erotic nature of the relationship between the bareback rider and her horse. As Le Roux explained: "It's through love of those little hands that pat their necks that the stallions put all their energy into leaps that wear them out; it's because of love that they debase themselves, that they kneel."[19] In addition, the riders themselves—necessarily scantily clad because of their acrobatics—provided an attraction to male audiences. As one authority wrote in 1888: "Is it the horse or is it the woman that their opera-glasses ogle? Both, for goodness sake!"[20]

The pictorial character of *Equestrienne* is as interesting for what Lautrec rejected as for what he adopted. The dominant voice in circus imagery at the time belonged to Jules Chéret, whose posters of gyrating figures in primary colors had advertised so many events. In visual terms, his brand of good humor, arresting chromatics, and gymnastic brio was the lingua franca of the circus. Seurat amalgamated Chéret's visual language with his own neo-impressionist touch in his large painting *Cirque* of 1891 (Musée d'Orsay, Paris), apparently attempting to elide the popular and the avant-garde.[21] But Lautrec eschewed Chéret's example. His painting is horizontal rather than vertical like the poster; his colors are strong but somber reds and greens; and, above all, the mood is far from gay. Lautrec's disposition of figures is similar to contemporary illustrations in periodicals such as *Le Courrier français*.[22] Yet despite adopting an arrangement suitable for inventorying the delights of the circus, Lautrec's picture seems to militate against conventional notions of fun and fantasy that surround the spectacle. His circus image both offers and denies. He shows us fragments of the audience, but no excited crowd. He gives us half of one clown and the back view of another. And for all the claims by Antoine-Jean Dalsème and others about the titillation of the bareback riders, Lautrec's handling of her heavily made-up features and long legs is perfunctory, both inviting and rebuffing the male gaze. Of all the men in the image, in fact, only the ringmaster, the Monsieur Loyal, actually looks at her. And he is a bulging-eyed, boat-jawed figure, less a master of revels than an intimidating bully.

Other artists also articulated that aspect of the circus in which figures with exaggerated, caricatural features bring out the sinister side of the spectacle. In 1887, as Lautrec was working on *Equestrienne*, his friend Louis Anquetin produced a large pastel with a green-faced clown gesturing across the mustard-colored ring toward an Auguste juggling in the distance, while a portly Monsieur Loyal looks on from the shadows (fig. 264). Squared up and carefully crafted, unlike Lautrec's more spontaneous painting, Anquetin's pastel is an image of menace rather than jollity.[23] About the same time Théo Wagner, who had trained as a painter with Seurat in the late 1870s before becoming a circus performer, also made a pastel of a circus scene (fig. 265).[24] Aptly but strangely framed with whips and tambourines painted in white and gold, Wagner's image pivots on a smiling clown, the fabric of his pantaloons stretched across his legs so that they distort his body shape. Behind, only two on-lookers watch Monsieur Loyal oversee a bareback rider, the whole image wrapped in a miasma of red, white, and blue, perhaps an ironic comment on the Third Republic or on notions of *patrie*. Both pastels exhibit a threatening, even grotesque, quality. In his book on the circus Le Roux had emphasized that the clown's English heritage had produced not only Shakespeare but Darwin, and that the cruelty and aggression often manifested in the clown's performance also character-ized the Darwinian struggle for life.[25] Darwinian ideas were becoming newly current in French discourse during the 1880s, and Le Roux's adoption of them to analyze the nature of the clown had a scientific and up-to-the-minute charge. Lautrec, Anquetin, and Wagner seem to have intuited in their works that the clown also personified caricature, fantasy, and violence —and hence, brimmed with modernity.

Not all of the imagery in Lautrec's first circus pictures had that caricatural edge. A sketch of a trapeze artist seen from below, for instance, is a study in fore-shortening (fig. 262). And of course it is naturalistic, for we expect to look up at the acrobat on her trapeze, high above the ring. Whether made as an independent work or as a study for a composition such as the large, lost canvas, this lively painting has the flavor of some-thing observed rather than wittily improvised.

During the 1890s the circus played a subsidi-ary, sporadic part in Lautrec's work. In the middle of the decade, for instance, the female clown Cha-u-kao cropped up in a number of disparate images (fig. 259c), though she was never represented actually performing.[26] When Lautrec received a commission from Siegfried Bing, the Art Nouveau entrepreneur, to provide a design for Louis Comfort Tiffany to realize in stained glass, Lautrec chose a scene from the Nouveau Cirque (Musée d'Orsay, Paris). And in 1895, when La Goulue, with her glory days in the dance halls over and forced to earn a living dancing in the traveling fairs, asked him to paint large canvases (Musée d'Orsay, Paris) to animate her booth, Lautrec generously com-plied. Painting ad hoc on a number of pieces of coarse canvas, which would be open to the elements, Lautrec met his goal—perhaps for the first time—to create large-scale decorations. He undertook all of these projects on the wing, as a typical passing obsession with an unusual character or as responses to commissions

both chic and dutiful. They register Lautrec's continu-ing fascination with the circus, but not the concen-tration of the late 1880s, fueled by the experience of the Cirque Fernando and focused on the idiom of caricature.

Toulouse-Lautrec made his final, major group of circus pictures in 1899. Having lost control of his drinking to such a degree that both his health and behavior had broken down, he was interned against his will at Dr. Sémelaigne's clinic on the avenue Madrid at Neuilly, a smart suburb in the west of Paris. Desperate to demonstrate his improvement and speed his release, he produced a substantial series of crayon drawings on circus subjects. These images—created in the elegant institution to which Lautrec's social status and family means gave him entry, not in Montmartre, among the populations of the outer boulevards— nevertheless recall the Cirque Fernando and the work he had done a dozen years earlier. Indeed, memory plays a crucial part in these drawings. The very fact that Lautrec had no models at the clinic and had to rely on his memory allowed him to prove to his doctors that he had control of his mental functions. At the same time, these pictures evoke not nostalgic memories but a mood less warm and more tense. The circus had a dimension in Lautrec's creative imagination that differed from the dance halls and the *maisons closes,* with their lubricious adult pleasures. It had roots in child-hood, as Jules Lemaître explained in 1889; the circus conjured up a world like that of fairy tales or *Gulliver's Travels* in which nothing resembled ordinary life.[27]

Memory and fantasy mingle in Lautrec's late suite of circus drawings. Using sheets of paper, many from the same block, the artist manipulated the crayons with extraordinary virtuosity considering his fragile physical condition. He returned to chiaroscuro, as in his recent paintings, using light and shade to model strong, sometimes sculptural forms. But if that aspect of the drawings signaled a return to the conven-tional draftsmanship he had learned as a student, other characteristics reflected the liberating developments of the avant-garde: perspective is tilted; scale and propor-tions arbitrary (thus figures may have tiny heads); and color applied sparingly for expressive effect.

Given their serial quality, seeming to result from a bout of intense and troubled work, the draw-ings collectively amount to something of an inventory of circus types and repertoires—not in a programmatic way, but in the sense that Lautrec's imagination and memory latched onto a range of possibilities. He represented ringmasters and clowns, dancers and riders, horses, dogs, and monkeys, scenes of comedy and of skill. Erotic overtones appear in, for example, the image of the petite bareback rider in blue sidesaddle on a massively proportioned stallion (fig. 267) or the sketch of a yellow-clad clown who kneels imploringly before a pin-headed ballerina, her arms crossed implacably across her décolletage (fig. 268). So too the sinister asserts itself. In several drawings the horses look like draft animals such as Percherons rather than svelte circus mounts. They have a dark, grim, brooding presence, their massive weight overpowering the slight, skirted figure of their rider (fig. 269). This group of drawings, especially when seen collectively as they were made, quickly dispenses with any impression of gaiety their subjects might superficially suggest, prompting instead a mood of threat and even foreboding.

Many of the late drawings represent animals that have been, or are being, trained. At first sight, this seems typical enough of the circus. Lautrec's contemporary Pierre Bonnard also created a lively painting of a circus rider, with the horse and its perilously balanced rider performing what they have trained to do together. But Bonnard presents the figures in a fluid composition, light of touch and harmonious in color (fig. 282). By contrast, Lautrec's animals can have an almost nightmare character (figs. 267 and 269). In sum, these drawings appear to have a subtext. They concern human control of bestial forces: by training, by rules and repetition, and if necessary by force, for the whip is a common element in the images. They project an artificial playfulness, which only thinly masks an atmosphere of restraint of the improper.

Lautrec drew massively muscled stallions, their tails cropped and bound in ribbons, a decorative emasculation. He drew a top-hatted clown with a trained pony and baboon in which the voluminous costume and pancake makeup essentially dehumanize the clown (fig. 281); he—like the animals—has become a creature of the circus, trained to perform, acting alongside animals that have themselves been trained to do tricks outside their natural condition. Returning to Le Roux's Darwinian account of the circus, we might say that the animals have been trained to a higher level of evolution.

Finally, Lautrec represented sparse audiences in his circus drawings. There are, however, professional onlookers checking progress, upholding standards. In this, the idea of control surfaces once again. If Lautrec's great 1899 circus series is about training and discipline, about forcing animals to act against their nature to suit their human masters, to sublimate their physical instincts to his or her command, then it is also about the artist's own plight. Having been photographed as a clown some years earlier—playfully, we assume—Lautrec may well have seen his own situation at the clinic in this light.[28] He too was being forced to control his urges, to obey the rules, to conform to a certain code of conduct. Indeed, the whole process of making the drawings was a performance calculated to win his release, as a horse's well-drilled paces might win it a lump of sugar. In the end, the series is about order—at one level the discipline of circus performances, and at another the artist's psychological order. Both involve restraint and a degree of pain; both require mastering nature. The circus served as an ideal metaphor for the disordered Lautrec to articulate pictorially his inner struggles and traumas.

1. Joyant 1926, 55.

2. Giret 2001, 12.

3. Dalsème 1888, 100–101.

4. Le Roux 1889, 205.

5. Le Roux 1889, 206, 214.

6. Giret 2001, 18.

7. Reproduced in *Le Courrier français* (2 January 1887), 12.

8. Jules Lemaître, *Impressions de théâtre* (Paris, 1889); quoted in Giret 2001, 42.

9. "Cirques, théâtres, politique (calendrier de Décembre 1887)," *Revue indépendante* (January 1888), in Fénéon 1970 ed., 2:720.

10. Valter 1874, 1–2; Anonymous 1878, 581; Giret 2001, 12–13.

11. Roques 1889, 4.

12. Murray 1991, 131–133.

13. Murray 1991, 132, fig. 80.

14. Gauzi 1954, 119.

15. Joyant 1926, 77, 86.

16. Schimmel ed. 1991, 113, no. 142 (mid-June 1887).

17. Thomson in London and Paris 1991, 236.

18. According to Verhagen 1997, 128, Gauzi 1954, 119, did not identify Valadon in the Chicago painting but in the huge, lost canvas.

19. Le Roux 1889, 126–127.

20. Dalsème 1888, 277.

21. For the most recent discussion of this issue see Le Men 2002 and 2003.

22. For example, Faverot, *Le Courrier français* (12 December 1886), 3.

23. I am grateful to François Lorençeau for information about the squaring.

24. Thomson 1985, 18, 155.

25. Le Roux 1889, 214–215.

26. Dortu 1971, P. 580–583.

27. Lemaître 1889; quoted in Giret 2001, 42.

28. Reproduced in London and Paris 1991, 535.

260

Henri de Toulouse-Lautrec,
At the Circus Fernando:
Medrano with a Piglet, c. 1887,
oil on paper laid down on
board, 55.9 x 36.8 cm. Private
collection, Chicago

261

Henri de Toulouse-Lautrec,
At the Circus: In the Wings,
c. 1886–1887, oil on canvas,
67 x 60 cm. Private collection,
Courtesy of Wildenstein & Co.

262

Henri de Toulouse-Lautrec,
At the Circus: Trapeze Artist,
1887–1888, gouache on gray
cardboard, 79.5 x 60.2 cm. Fogg
Art Museum, Harvard University
Art Museums, bequest of Annie
Swan Coburn

263

Henri-Gabriel Ibels, *Study
for "L'Eventail du cirque,"*
1896, ink and graphite on paper,
43 x 68.6 cm. Collection of
Carleton A. Holstrom and Mary
Beth Kineke

264

Louis Anquetin, *At the Circus*,
1887, pastel, 46.5 x 61.7 cm.
Private collection

265

Théophile Pierre Wagner,
Circus Scene, c. 1886–1888,
pastel on canvas, 66 x 78.7 cm
(with original frame). The Jane
Voorhees Zimmerli Art Museum,
Rutgers, The State University of
New Jersey, David A. and Mildred
H. Morse Art Acquisition Fund

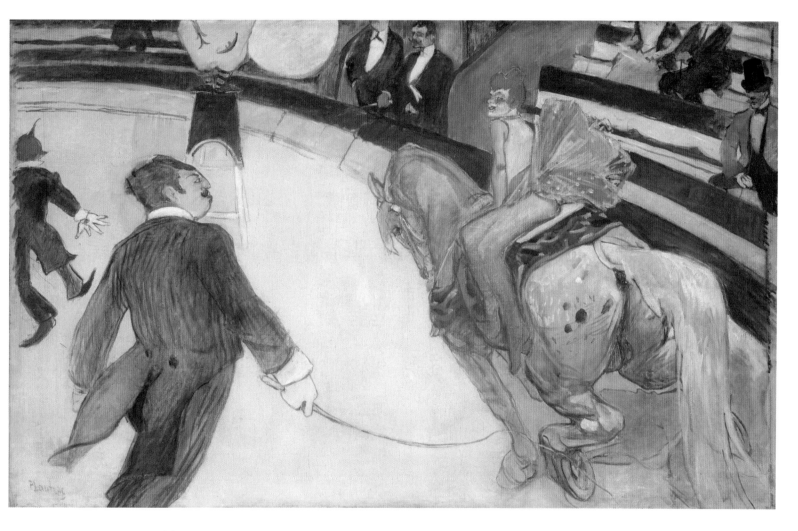

266

Henri de Toulouse-Lautrec,
*Equestrienne (At the Circus
Fernando)*, 1887–1888, oil on
canvas, 100.3 x 161.3 cm. The Art
Institute of Chicago, Joseph
Winterbotham Collection

267

Henri de Toulouse-Lautrec,
At the Circus: Bareback, 1899,
colored pencil, 49.7 x 32.4 cm.
Museum of Art, Rhode Island
School of Design, Providence,
Gift of Mrs. Murray S. Danforth

268

Henri de Toulouse-Lautrec,
At the Circus: The Encore,
1899, black and colored pencil,
35.9 x 24.9 cm. Collection
Michael and Judy Steinhardt,
New York

269
———
Henri de Toulouse-Lautrec,
At the Circus: Work in the Ring,
1899, charcoal, pastel, and black
chalk with stumping and colored
pencil, 21.7 x 31.6 cm. The Art
Institute of Chicago, Gift of
Mr. and Mrs. B. E. Bensinger

270
———
Henri de Toulouse-Lautrec,
*At the Circus: The Entry into the
Ring,* 1899, black and colored
pencil, 31 x 20 cm. The J. Paul
Getty Museum, Los Angeles

271

Henri de Toulouse-Lautrec,
At the Circus: Horse Rearing,
1899, black chalk with orange
and yellow crayon additions
by the artist, 35.7 x 25.4 cm.
Fine Arts Museums of San
Francisco, Achenbach Foundation
for Graphic Arts, Museum
Purchase, Elizabeth Ebert and
Arthur W. Barney Fund

272

Henri de Toulouse-Lautrec,
*At the Circus: The Spanish
Walk,* 1899, colored pencil,
35 x 25 cm. Lent by The Metro-
politan Museum of Art, Robert
Lehman Collection, 1975

273
Henri de Toulouse-Lautrec,
*At the Circus: Dressage Rider,
the Bow*, 1899, black chalk,
35.7 x 25.4 cm. Fine Arts
Museums of San Francisco,
Achenbach Foundation for
Graphic Arts, Memorial Gift from
Dr. T. Edward and Tullah Hanley,
Bradford, Pennsylvania

274
Henri de Toulouse-Lautrec,
At the Circus: The Dog Trainer,
1899, black and colored chalks,
35.5 x 25.3 cm. Sterling and
Francine Clark Art Institute,
Williamstown, Massachusetts

275

Henri de Toulouse-Lautrec,
At the Circus: Acrobats,
1899, black and colored
chalks, touches of gouache,
25.3 x 35.5 cm. Sterling and
Francine Clark Art Institute,
Williamstown, Massachusetts

276

Henri de Toulouse-Lautrec,
At the Circus: Chocolat, 1899,
black and colored chalk, touches
of gouache, 25.3 x 35.5 cm.
Sterling and Francine Clark
Art Institute, Williamstown,
Massachusetts

277

Henri de Toulouse-Lautrec,
At the Circus: The Rehearsal,
1899, black and colored pencil,
35.5 x 25 cm. Private collection,
New York

278

Henri de Toulouse-Lautrec,
At the Circus: The Pas de Deux,
1899, black pencil, 35.6 x 25 cm.
Private collection

279

Henri de Toulouse-Lautrec,
At the Circus: Clowness (Le Salut), 1899, graphite, black chalk, colored chalk, and colored crayon, 35.6 x 25.4 cm. Fogg Art Museum, Harvard University Art Museums, Bequest of Frances L. Hofer

280

Henri de Toulouse-Lautrec,
At the Circus: Training, 1899, colored pencil, pencil, and conté crayon, 34.9 x 25.4 cm. Courtesy of The Metropolitan Museum of Art, Lent by The Alex Hillman Family Foundation

Henri de Toulouse-Lautrec,
*At the Circus: Trained Pony and
Baboon*, c. 1899, black pastel
with stumping, colored pencil,
and graphite, 43.9 x 26.7 cm.
The Art Institute of Chicago,
Margaret Day Blake Collection

Pierre Bonnard, *Circus Rider*,
1894, oil on cardboard, on
panel, 27 x 34.9 cm. The Phillips
Collection, Washington, D.C.

ARTISTS' BIOGRAPHIES AND CHECKLIST OF THE EXHIBITION

---

detail

Henri de Toulouse-Lautrec,
The Englishman at the Moulin Rouge, **1892 (fig. 142)**

Henri de Toulouse-Lautrec

French; Albi 1864—Château de Malromé, near Langon, Gironde, 1901

Toulouse-Lautrec was the only surviving son of closely related families from the provincial aristocracy of southwestern France. His father and his uncles were tal-ented amateur artists, and Lautrec showed a keen interest and natural ability in draw-ing from childhood. At age thirteen he fell while getting up from a chair and broke his left femur. The following year he broke his right leg. Although it was not properly diagnosed during his lifetime, it is likely that Lautrec suffered from a bone disease (perhaps owing to the numerous consan-guineous marriages in the family), and his legs stopped growing after the accidents. During his long convalescence Lautrec filled notebooks with his drawings and watercolors. His first art teacher, René Princeteau, encouraged his efforts, and Lautrec persuaded his parents to allow him to pursue further training in Paris. In 1882 he entered the atelier of Léon Bon-nat, then transferred to Fernand Cormon's studio that autumn. He studied with Cor-mon until 1886, where he met his lifelong friends Louis Anquetin, Emile Bernard, and Vincent van Gogh.

Lautrec's work was intimately con-nected to the life of Montmartre from the start of his professional career. His first illustrations were published in the Mont-martrois journals *Le Courrier français* and *Le Mirliton* in 1886, the same year that the Mirliton cabaret began displaying Lautrec's paintings. His work focused on the life of the butte, featuring the dance halls, cir-cuses, cafés-concerts, and brothels that dotted the slopes of the hillside. An out-going and social person, Lautrec befriended a heterogeneous group of Montmartre denizens, including aristocrats, streetwalk-ers, artists, writers, models, and cancan dancers. His portraits of his companions—often set in his studio (fig. 87, 84, 77, 80, 79, 82), in neighborhood cafés (fig. 92, 18, 91), at dance halls (fig. 148), or at the café-concert (fig. 147)—present a cross section of the population of Montmartre.

In the later 1880s Lautrec began to exhibit widely, at venues ranging from the avant-garde Les XX in Brussels to the Ex-position Universelle des Arts Incohérents, the Salon des Indépendants in Paris, and the Exposition du Petit Boulevard orga-nized by Vincent van Gogh in 1887. Vin-cent's brother, Theo van Gogh, began to support Lautrec's art at the gallery Boussod and Valadon in 1888, a policy continued more actively when Lautrec's childhood friend Maurice Joyant became manager following Theo's death in 1891. Lautrec created his first lithograph—the poster *Moulin Rouge: La Goulue* (fig. 10)—in Decem-ber 1891 and went on to design another twenty-nine posters and hundreds of prints, drawings, and paintings in the re-maining ten years of his life.

In 1899, his health failing from the effects of alcoholism and syphilis, Lautrec was institutionalized for several months at an asylum near Paris, where he produced a remarkable group of drawings of the circus, drawn from memory (fig. 271, 272, 274, 275, 269, 273, 270, 277, 276, 281, 267, 268, 278, 279, 280). Soon after his release he returned to drinking, and his artistic production dropped significantly. In 1901 he suffered a stroke and died two months before his thirty-seventh birthday at his mother's estate, the Château de Malromé.

PAINTINGS

3

"A la Bastille" (Jeanne Wenz),
1888, oil on canvas, 72.5 x 49.5 cm
(28 9/16 x 19 9/16). National Gallery of Art,
Washington, Collection of Mr. and
Mrs. Paul Mellon, 1985.64.39
Dortu P. 307

16

The Laundress, c. 1886, oil on canvas, 91.4 x
72.4 cm (36 x 28 1/2). Private collection
Dortu P. 346
(Chicago only)

18

A la Mie, c. 1891, watercolor and gouache
on paper mounted on millboard, mounted
on panel, 53 x 67.9 cm (20 7/8 x 26 3/4).
Museum of Fine Arts, Boston, S. A. Denio
Collection, and General Income, 40.748
Dortu P. 386

19

Alfred la Guigne, 1894, oil on cardboard,
65.6 x 50.4 cm (25 3/4 x 19 3/4). National
Gallery of Art, Washington, Chester Dale
Collection, 1963.10.220
Dortu P. 516
(Washington only)

21

Parody of "The Sacred Grove" by Puvis de Chavannes,
1884, oil on canvas, 172 x 380 cm
(67 11/16 x 149 5/8). The Henry and Rose
Pearlman Foundation, Inc., L.1988.62.13
Dortu P. 232
(Chicago only)

27

At the Rat Mort, 1899, oil on canvas,
55 x 46 cm (21 5/8 x 18 1/8). The Samuel
Courtauld Trust, Courtauld Institute of
Art Gallery, London, P.1948.SC.466
Dortu P. 677

63

Jane Avril Leaving the Moulin Rouge, 1892,
essence on board, 84.3 x 63.4 cm
(33 3/16 x 24 15/16). Wadsworth Atheneum
Museum of Art, Hartford, Connecticut,
Bequest of George A. Gay, 1941.163
Dortu P. 414

64

May Milton, c. 1895, oil and pastel on
cardboard, 66.1 x 49.4 cm (26 x 19 7/16).
The Art Institute of Chicago, Bequest
of Kate L. Brewster, 1949.263
Dortu P. 572

65

Seated Woman from Behind: Study for "At the Moulin Rouge," 1892/1895, oil on cardboard, 59.7 x 39.4 cm (23 ½ x 15 ½). National Gallery of Art, Washington, Collection of Mr. and Mrs. Paul Mellon, 1994.59.12
Dortu P. 458

66

At the Moulin Rouge, 1892/1895, oil on canvas, 123 x 141 cm (48 ⁷/₁₆ x 55 ½). The Art Institute of Chicago, Helen Birch Bartlett Memorial Collection, 1928.610
Dortu P. 427

77

Paul Sescau, 1891, oil on cardboard, 82.5 x 35.6 cm (32 ½ x 14). Brooklyn Museum, Museum Surplus Fund and purchased with funds given by Dikran G. Kelekian, 22.66
Dortu P. 383

79

Henri Nocq, 1897, oil on cardboard, 64.1 x 48.9 cm (25 ¼ x 19 ¼). Courtesy of The Metropolitan Museum of Art, Lent by The Alex Hillman Family Foundation, L.1988.92.21
Dortu P. 639

80

Paul Leclercq, 1897, oil on cardboard, 64.6 x 81 cm (25 ⁷/₁₆ x 31 ⅞). Musée d'Orsay, Paris; Gift of the Sitter, 1920, RF2281
Dortu P. 645

81

Carmen Gaudin, 1885, oil on wood, 23.8 x 14.9 cm (9 ⅜ x 5 ⅞). National Gallery of Art, Washington, Ailsa Mellon Bruce Collection, 1970.17.85
Dortu P. 244

82

Young Woman at a Table, "Poudre de riz" (Rice Powder), 1887, oil on canvas, 56 x 46 cm (22 ¹/₁₆ x 18 ⅛). Van Gogh Museum Amsterdam (Vincent van Gogh Foundation), s 274 V/1962
Dortu P. 348

84

Rousse (Redhead), also known as *La Toilette,* 1889, oil on canvas, 67 x 54 cm (26 ⅜ x 21 ¼). Musée d'Orsay, Paris; bequest of Pierre Goujon, 1914, RF2242
Dortu P. 610

86

Woman Smoking a Cigarette, 1890, oil on cardboard, 47 x 30 cm (18 ½ x 11 ¹³/₁₆). Brooklyn Museum, Museum Surplus Fund and purchased with funds given by Dikran G. Kelekian, 22.67
Dortu P. 362

87

Hélène Vary, 1889, oil on cardboard, 74.5 x 49 cm (29 ⁵/₁₆ x 19 ⁵/₁₆). Kunsthalle Bremen, 188-1914/2
Dortu P. 320

88

Vincent van Gogh, 1887, pastel on board, 57 x 46.5 cm (22 ⁷/₁₆ x 18 ⁵/₁₆). Van Gogh Museum Amsterdam (Vincent van Gogh Foundation), d 693 V/1962
Dortu P. 278

91

Monsieur Boileau, c. 1893, gouache on cardboard, 80 x 65 cm (31 ½ x 25 ⁹/₁₆). The Cleveland Museum of Art, Hinman B. Hurlbut Collection, CMA 394.1925
Dortu P. 465
(Chicago only)

92

The Hangover (Gueule de Bois), probably 1888, oil on canvas, 45.1 x 53.3 cm (17 ¾ x 21). Fogg Art Museum, Harvard University Art Museums, Bequest from the Collection of Maurice Wertheim, Class of 1906, 1951.63
Dortu P. 340

93

At Grenelle, c. 1888, oil on canvas, 55.9 x 46.8 cm (22 x 18 ⁷/₁₆). Sterling and Francine Clark Art Institute, Williamstown, Massachusetts, 1955.564
Dortu P. 328

121

Ballet Dancers, 1885/1886, oil and charcoal(?) on plaster, mounted on canvas, 153.5 x 152.5 cm (60 ⅜ x 60). The Art Institute of Chicago, Helen Birch Bartlett Memorial Collection, 1931.571
Dortu P. 241
(Chicago only)

126

Moulin de la Galette, 1889, oil on canvas, 88.5 x 101.3 cm (35 ⅞ x 39 ⅝). The Art Institute of Chicago, Mr. and Mrs. Lewis Larned Coburn Memorial Collection, 1933.458
Dortu P. 335

127

Study for "Moulin de la Galette," c. 1889, oil on cardboard, 71 x 47 cm (27 ¹⁵/₁₆ x 18 ½). State Pushkin Museum of Fine Arts, Moscow, 3288
Dortu P. 351

128

At the Moulin de la Galette: La Goulue and Valentin le Désossé, 1887, oil on cardboard, 52 x 39.2 cm (20 ½ x 15 ⁷/₁₆). Musée Toulouse-Lautrec, Albi; Gift of the Comtesse A. de Toulouse-Lautrec, MTL 123
Dortu P. 282

141

The Englishman at the Moulin Rouge, 1892, oil and gouache on cardboard, 85.7 x 66 cm (33 ¾ x 26). Lent by The Metropolitan Museum of Art, Bequest of Miss Adelaide Milton de Groot (1876–1967), 1967, 67.187.108
Dortu P. 425

144

A Corner of the Moulin de la Galette, 1892, oil on cardboard, 100 x 89.2 cm (39 ⅜ x 35 ⅛). National Gallery of Art, Washington, Chester Dale Collection, 1963.10.67
Dortu P. 429
(Washington only)

145

Quadrille at the Moulin Rouge, 1892, oil on cardboard, 80.1 x 60.5 cm (31 ½ x 23 ¾). National Gallery of Art, Washington, Chester Dale Collection, 1963.10.221
Dortu P. 424
(Washington only)

146

Monsieur Fourcade, 1889, oil on cardboard, 77 x 63 cm (30 ⁵⁄₁₆ x 24 ¹³⁄₁₆). Museu de Arte de São Paulo Assis Chateaubriand, São Paulo, Brazil
Dortu P. 331

147

Monsieur Delaporte, 1893, gouache on cardboard, glued on wood, 76 x 70 cm (29 ¹⁵⁄₁₆ x 27 ⁹⁄₁₆). Ny Carlsberg Glyptotek, Copenhagen, MIN. 1911
Dortu P. 464

148

Maxime Dethomas, 1896, oil on cardboard, 67.5 x 50.9 cm (26 ⁹⁄₁₆ x 20 ⅞). National Gallery of Art, Washington, Chester Dale Collection, 1963.10.219
Dortu P. 628
(Washington only)

162

Fashionable People at the Ambassadeurs, 1893, oil à l'essence over black chalk on wove paper, mounted on cardboard, 84.3 x 65.5 cm (33 ³⁄₁₆ x 25 ¹³⁄₁₆). National Gallery of Art, Washington, Collection of Mr. and Mrs. Paul Mellon, 1995.47.67
Dortu P. 477

172

Jane Avril, 1892, oil on cardboard, mounted on wood, 67.8 x 52.9 cm (26 ¾ x 20 ⅞). National Gallery of Art, Washington, Chester Dale Collection, 1963.10.66
Dortu P. 419
(Washington only)

173

Jane Avril, c. 1891–1892, oil on cardboard, mounted on panel, 63.2 x 42.2 cm (24 ⅞ x 16 ⅝). Sterling and Francine Clark Art Institute, Williamstown, Massachusetts, 1955.566
Dortu P. 418

185

Yvette Guilbert: "Linger, longer, loo," c. 1894, oil on cardboard, 58 x 44 cm (22 ¹³⁄₁₆ x 17 ⁵⁄₁₆). State Pushkin Museum of Fine Arts, Moscow, 3446
Dortu P. 522

189

The Black Gloves of Yvette Guilbert, 1894, oil on cardboard, 62.8 x 37 cm (24 ¾ x 14 ⁹⁄₁₆). Musée Toulouse-Lautrec, Albi; Gift of Dr. Bourges, MLT 161
Dortu P. 520

198

May Belfort, 1895, oil on cardboard, 63 x 48 cm (24 ¹³⁄₁₆ x 18 ⅞). The Cleveland Museum of Art, Bequest of Leonard C. Hanna, Jr., CMA 1958.54
Dortu P. 588
(Washington only)

227

Marcelle Lender Dancing the Bolero in "Chilpéric," 1895–1896, oil on canvas, 145 x 149 cm (57 ⅛ x 59). National Gallery of Art, Washington, Collection of Mr. and Mrs. John Hay Whitney, 1990.127.1
Dortu P. 627

228

In the Salon: The Sofa, c. 1892–1893, oil on cardboard, 60 x 80 cm (23 ⅝ x 31 ½). Museu de Arte de São Paulo Assis Chateaubriand, São Paulo, Brazil
Dortu P. 502

240

The Laundryman, c. 1894, oil on cardboard, 57.8 x 46.2 cm (22 ¾ x 18 ³⁄₁₆). Musée Toulouse-Lautrec, Albi; Gift of the Comtesse A. de Toulouse-Lautrec, MLT 173
Dortu P. 544

242

La Grosse Maria, c. 1886, oil on canvas, 79 x 64 cm (31 ⅛ x 25 ³⁄₁₆). Von der Heydt-Museum, Wuppertal, G 1085
Dortu P. 229

243

Lucie Bellanger, c. 1895, oil on cardboard, 80.7 x 60 cm (31 ¾ x 23 ⅝). Musée Toulouse-Lautrec, Albi; Gift of the Comtesse A. de Toulouse-Lautrec, MLT 194
Dortu P. 621

245

In the Salon, 1893, pastel, gouache, oil, pencil, and watercolor on cardboard, 53 x 79.7 cm (20 ⅞ x 31 ⅜). Solomon R. Guggenheim Museum, New York, Thannhauser Collection, Gift, Justin K. Thannhauser, 1978, 78.2514.73
Dortu P. 500
(Washington only)

246

Monsieur, Madame, and the Dog, 1893, oil on canvas, 48 x 60 cm (18 ⅞ x 23 ⅝). Musée Toulouse-Lautrec, Albi; Gift of the Comtesse A. de Toulouse-Lautrec, MTL 158
Dortu P. 494

247

Woman Seated on a Couch, 1894, oil on cardboard, 58 x 46 cm (22 ¹³⁄₁₆ x 18 ⅛). Anonymous lender
Unknown to Dortu

249

Medical Inspection (Rue des Moulins), c. 1894, oil on cardboard on wood, 83.5 x 61.4 cm (32 ⅞ x 24 ⅛). National Gallery of Art, Washington, Chester Dale Collection, 1963.10.69
Dortu P. 557
(Washington only)

250

The Two Friends, c. 1894, oil on cardboard, 47.9 x 34 cm (18 ⅞ x 13 ⅜). Tate. Bequeathed by Montague Shearman through the Contemporary Art Society 1940, N05142
Dortu P. 549

251

In Bed: The Kiss, 1892, oil on cardboard, 42 x 56 cm (16 ⁹⁄₁₆ x 22 ¹⁄₁₆). Private collection, courtesy of G.P.S.
Dortu P. 438

253

Women Resting, c. 1894–1895, oil on cardboard, 59.5 x 81 cm (23 7/16 x 31 7/8). Galerie Neue Meister, Staatliche Kunstsammlungen Dresden, 2603
Dortu P. 597

254

Red-Headed Nude Crouching, 1897, oil on board, 46.4 x 60 cm (18 1/4 x 23 5/8). San Diego Museum of Art, Gift of the Baldwin M. Baldwin Foundation, 1987:115
Dortu P.649

255

Woman with Mirror, study for *Elles,* 1896, oil on cardboard, 60 x 36.5 cm (23 5/8 x 14 3/8). Gail and Richard Elden
Dortu P. 632

256

Woman Brushing Her Hair, study for *Elles,* 1896, oil on cardboard, 55.4 x 41 cm (21 13/16 x 16 1/8). Musée Toulouse-Lautrec, Albi; Gift of the Comtesse A. de Toulouse-Lautrec, MTL 191
Dortu P. 622

257

Woman in a Corset (Conquête de Passage), study for *Elles,* c. 1894–1896, black and blue chalk and oil à l'essence on paper, laid down on canvas, 103 x 65 cm (40 9/16 x 25 9/16). Musée des Augustins, Toulouse, Ro 618
Dortu P. 617

260

At the Circus Fernando: Medrano with a Piglet, c. 1887, oil on paper laid down on board, 55.9 x 36.8 cm (22 x 14 1/2). Private Collection, Chicago
Dortu P. 488

261

At the Circus: In the Wings, c. 1886–1887, oil on canvas, 67 x 60 cm (26 3/8 x 23 5/8). Private collection. Courtesy of Wildenstein & Co.
Dortu P. 321

262

At the Circus: Trapeze Artist, 1887–1888, gouache on gray cardboard, 79.5 x 60.2 cm (31 5/16 x 23 11/16). Fogg Art Museum, Harvard University Art Museums, Bequest of Annie Swan Coburn, 1934.34
Dortu P. 489

266

Equestrienne (At the Circus Fernando), 1887–1888, oil on canvas, 100.3 x 161.3 cm (39 1/2 x 63 1/2). The Art Institute of Chicago, Joseph Winterbotham Collection, 1925.523
Dortu P. 312

DRAWINGS AND WATERCOLORS

186

Yvette Guilbert Taking a Bow, 1894, black crayon, watercolor, and oil with white heightening on tracing paper, mounted on cardboard, 41.8 x 24.1 cm (16 7/16 x 9 1/2). Museum of Art, Rhode Island School of Design, Providence, Gift of Mrs. Murray S. Danforth, 35.540
Dortu A. 214
(Washington only)

187a/188b

Yvette Guilbert Singing (recto), c. 1894, graphite with smudging on ivory wove paper, *Yvette Guilbert* (verso), c. 1894, graphite on ivory wove paper, 33.4 x 20.5 cm (13 1/8 x 8 1/16). The Art Institute of Chicago, Promised gift of Francey and Dr. Martin L. Gecht
Dortu D. 3640 (recto); verso unknown to Dortu

187b/188a

Yvette Guilbert (recto), c. 1894, graphite on ivory wove paper, *Three-Quarter Length Study of Yvette Guilbert* (verso), c. 1894, graphite on ivory wove paper, 23.1 x 35.6 cm (9 1/8 x 14). The Art Institute of Chicago, Albert H. Wolf Memorial Collection, 1941.132R/V
Dortu D. 3637 (recto) and D. 3637 (verso)

267

At the Circus: Bareback, 1899, colored pencil on paper, 49.7 x 32.4 cm (19 9/16 x 12 3/4) image; 50.8 x 31.4 cm (20 x 12 3/8) sheet. Museum of Art, Rhode Island School of Design, Providence; Gift of Mrs. Murray S. Danforth, 34.003
Dortu D. 4541
(Washington only)

268

At the Circus: The Encore, 1899, black and colored pencil on paper, 35.9 x 24.9 cm (14 1/8 x 9 13/16). Collection Michael and Judy Steinhardt, New York, M1993.05
Dortu D. 4543

269

At the Circus: Work in the Ring, 1899, charcoal, pastel, and black chalk, with stumping, touches of colored pencil, and incising, on off-white wove paper, 21.7 x 31.6 cm (8 3/4 x 12 1/2). The Art Institute of Chicago, Gift of Mr. and Mrs. B. E. Bensinger, 1972.1167
Dortu D. 4554

270

At the Circus: The Entry into the Ring, 1899, black and colored pencil on paper, 31 x 20 cm (12 3/16 x 7 7/8). The J. Paul Getty Museum, Los Angeles, 2001.19
Dortu D. 4530

271

At the Circus: Horse Rearing, 1899, black chalk with orange and yellow crayon additions by the artist on paper, 35.7 x 25.4 cm (14 1/16 x 10). Fine Arts Museums of San Francisco, Achenbach Foundation for Graphic Arts, Museum Purchase, Elizabeth Ebert and Arthur W. Barney Fund, 1977.2.5 (A000240)
Dortu D. 4533

272

At the Circus: The Spanish Walk, 1899, colored pencil on paper, 35 x 25 cm (13 3/4 x 9 13/16), Lent by The Metropolitan Museum of Art, Robert Lehman Collection, 1975, 1975.1.731
Dortu D. 4536

273

At the Circus: Dressage Rider, the Bow, 1899, black chalk on white wove paper, 35.7 x 25.4 cm (14 1/16 x 10). Fine Arts Museums of San Francisco, Achenbach Foundation for Graphic Arts, Memorial Gift from Dr. T. Edward and Tullah Hanley, Bradford, Pennsylvania, 69.30.118 (A000241)
Dortu D. 4538

274

At the Circus: The Dog Trainer, 1899, black and colored chalks on paper, 35.5 x 25.3 cm (14 x 9 15/16). Sterling and Francine Clark Art Institute, Williamstown, Massachusetts, 1955.1427
Dortu D. 4553

275

At the Circus: Acrobats, 1899, black and colored chalk, touches of gouache on paper, 25.3 x 35.5 cm (9 ¹⁵⁄₁₆ x 14). Sterling and Francine Clark Art Institute, Williamstown, Massachusetts, 1955.1429
Dortu D. 4540

276

At the Circus: Chocolat, 1899, black and colored chalk, touches of gouache on paper, 25.3 x 35.5 cm (9 ¹⁵⁄₁₆ x 14). Sterling and Francine Clark Art Institute, Williamstown, Massachusetts, 1955.1428
Dortu D. 4558

277

At the Circus: The Rehearsal, 1899, black and colored pencil on paper, 35.5 x 25 cm (14 x 9 ¹³⁄₁₆). Private Collection, New York
Dortu D. 4555

278

At the Circus: The Pas de Deux, 1899, black pencil on paper, 35.6 x 25 cm (14 x 9 ¹³⁄₁₆). Private collection
Dortu D. 4535

279

At the Circus: Clowness (Le Salut), 1899, graphite, black chalk, colored chalk, and colored crayon on white wove paper, 35.6 x 25.4 cm (14 x 10). Fogg Art Museum, Harvard University Art Museums, Bequest of Frances L. Hofer, 1979.56
Dortu D. 4528

280

At the Circus: Training, 1899, colored pencil, pencil, and conté crayon on paper, 34.9 x 25.4 cm (13 ¾ x 10). Courtesy of The Metropolitan Museum of Art, Lent by The Alex Hillman Family Foundation, L.1988.92.22
Dortu D. 4550

281

At the Circus: Trained Pony and Baboon, 1899, black pastel with stumping, colored pencil, and graphite on cream wove paper, 43.9 x 26.7 cm (17 ⁵⁄₁₆ x 10 ½). The Art Institute of Chicago, Margaret Day Blake Collection, 1944.581
Dortu D. 4525

57

At the Moulin Rouge, La Goulue and Her Sister, 1892, brush and spatter lithograph, key stone in olive-green, color stones in blue, light green, red, yellow, and salmon-beige on wove paper
Wittrock 1

45.8 x 34.4 cm (18 ¹⁄₁₆ x 13 ⁹⁄₁₆) image; 49.7 x 37.4 cm (19 ⁹⁄₁₆ x 14 ¾) sheet. National Gallery of Art, Washington, Rosenwald Collection, 1952.8.312
(Washington only)

45.7 x 34.7 cm (18 x 13 ¹¹⁄₁₆) image; 65 x 49.8 cm (25 ⁹⁄₁₆ x 19 ⅝) sheet. The Art Institute of Chicago, Charles F. Glore Collection, 1946.449
(Chicago only)

106

"A Saint-Lazare," (signed Tréclau), cover for *Le Mirliton,* August 1887, color photorelief, 29.2 x 20 cm (11 ½ x 7 ⅞). The Jane Voorhees Zimmerli Art Museum, Rutgers, The State University of New Jersey, Herbert D. and Ruth Schimmel Museum Library Fund, 1990.0736.001

142

The Englishman at the Moulin Rouge, 1892, lithograph in aubergine, green, yellow, blue, orange, and black on ivory laid paper, 52.7 x 37.3 cm (20 ¾ x 14 ¹¹⁄₁₆) image; 61.8 x 48.7 cm (24 ⁵⁄₁₆ x 19 ³⁄₁₆) sheet. The Art Institute of Chicago, Gift of the Print and Drawing Club, 1931.67
Wittrock 2, state 2

149

The Clowness at the Moulin Rouge, 1897, lithograph from six stones in black, yellow, gold, blue, red, and gray-brown on ivory wove paper, 41 x 32 cm (16 ⅛ x 12 ⅝) image; 41.1 x 32.3 cm (16 ³⁄₁₆ x 12 ¹¹⁄₁₆) sheet. The Art Institute of Chicago, Mr. and Mrs. Carter H. Harrison Collection, 1949.938
Wittrock 178

150

The Dance at the Moulin Rouge, 1897, brush and spatter lithograph with scraper, printed in black and four colors, heightened with white ink, on off-white wove paper, 48.4 x 35.5 cm (19 ¹⁄₁₆ x 14). Francey and Dr. Martin L. Gecht
Wittrock 181

161

At the Ambassadeurs: Singer at the Café-Concert, 1894, crayon, brush and spatter lithograph, key stone in olive-green, color stones in yellow, beige-grey, salmon-pink, black, and blue on wove paper
Wittrock 58

30.3 x 24.1 cm (11 ¹⁵⁄₁₆ x 9 ½). National Gallery of Art, Washington, Collection of Mr. and Mrs. Paul Mellon, 1985.64.176
(Washington only)

31.1 x 24.5 cm (12 ¼ x 9 ⅝) image, including stray marks; 60.2 x 43.2 cm (23 ¹¹⁄₁₆ x 17) sheet. The Art Institute of Chicago, Mr. and Mrs. Carter H. Harrison Collection, 1951.7
(Chicago only)

165

Le Café-Concert, 1893, portfolio of twenty-two lithographs by Henri-Gabriel Ibels and Henri de Toulouse-Lautrec, with text by Georges Montorgueil, published by *L'Estampe originale,* Paris, lithographs on wove paper, various sizes up to 44.0 x 32.0 cm, in a cover, 44.2 x 32.5 cm, illustrated with a lithograph by Ibels with text in red.

165 l

Jane Avril, 1893, brush and spatter lithograph in black on wove paper
Wittrock 18

26.2 x 20.4 cm (10 ⁵⁄₁₆ x 8 ¹⁄₁₆) image; 43.4 x 31.8 cm (17 ¹⁄₁₆ x 12 ½) sheet. National Gallery of Art, Washington, Rosenwald Collection, 1947.7.163
(Washington only)

26.5 x 21 cm (10 ⁷⁄₁₆ x 8 ¼) image; 43.5 x 31.8 cm (17 ⅛ x 12 ½) sheet. The Art Institute of Chicago, Albert H. Wolf Memorial Collection, 1935.49
(Chicago only)

165 m

Yvette Guilbert, 1893, brush and crayon lithograph in brownish-black on wove paper
Wittrock 19

20.5 x 23.5 cm (8 ¹⁄₁₆ x 9 ¼) image; 43.7 x 31.8 cm (17 ³⁄₁₆ x 12 ½) sheet. National Gallery of Art, Washington, Rosenwald Collection, 1947.7.166
(Washington only)

25.5 x 21.9 cm (10 ¹⁄₁₆ x 8 ⅝) image;
44 x 32.3 cm (17 ⁵⁄₁₆ x 12 ¹¹⁄₁₆) sheet.
The Art Institute of Chicago, Charles F.
Glore Collection, 1935.50
(Chicago only)

165 n

Paula Brébion, 1893, brush lithograph
in light olive-green on wove paper
Wittrock 20

26 x 20 cm (10 ¼ x 7 ⅞) image; 44.2 x
32.1 cm (17 ⅜ x 12 ⅝) sheet. National
Gallery of Art, Washington, Rosenwald
Collection, 1947.7.171
(Washington only)

26.1 x 19.7 cm (10 ¼ x 7 ¾) image;
44.2 x 32 cm (17 ⅜ x 12 ⅝) sheet. The
Art Institute of Chicago, Joseph Brooks
Fair Collection, 1931.449
(Chicago only)

165 o

Mary Hamilton, 1893, brush and crayon lithograph in light olive-green on wove paper
Wittrock 21

27 x 16.6 cm (10 ⅝ x 6 ⁹⁄₁₆) image;
44.2 x 31.8 cm (17 ⅜ x 12 ½) sheet.
National Gallery of Art, Washington,
Rosenwald Collection, 1947.7.164
(Washington only)

26.6 x 16 cm (10 ½ x 6 ⁵⁄₁₆) image;
44.1 x 31.9 cm (17 ⅜ x 12 ⁹⁄₁₆) sheet. The
Art Institute of Chicago, Joseph Brooks
Fair Collection, 1931.450
(Chicago only)

165 p

Edmée Lescot, 1893, brush, crayon and
spatter lithograph in black on wove paper
Wittrock 22

26.7 x 18.6 cm (10 ½ x 7 ⁵⁄₁₆) image;
43.4 x 32.2 cm (17 ¹⁄₁₆ x 12 ¹¹⁄₁₆) sheet.
National Gallery of Art, Washington,
Rosenwald Collection, 1947.7.165
(Washington only)

26.9 x 19 cm (10 ⁹⁄₁₆ x 7 ½) image; 43.8 x
32.3 cm (17 ¼ x 12 ¹¹⁄₁₆) sheet. The Art
Institute of Chicago, William McCallin
McKee Memorial Collection, 1930.133
(Chicago only)

165 q

Madame Abdala, 1893, brush and spatter lithograph with scraper in black on wove paper
Wittrock 23

27.2 x 20.2 cm (10 ¹¹⁄₁₆ x 7 ¹⁵⁄₁₆) image;
44.1 x 31.8 cm (17 ⅜ x 12 ½) sheet.
National Gallery of Art, Washington,
Rosenwald Collection, 1947.7.167
(Washington only)

27.3 x 20 cm (10 ¾ x 7 ⅞) image;
43.5 x 32.3 cm (17 ⅛ x 12 ¹¹⁄₁₆) sheet. The
Art Institute of Chicago, Mr. and Mrs.
Carter H. Harrison Collection, 1931.32
(Chicago only)

165 r

Aristide Bruant, 1893, brush, crayon and
spatter lithograph in black on wove paper
Wittrock 24

26.6 x 21 cm (10 ½ x 8 ¼) image;
44.2 x 32.2 cm (17 ⅜ x 12 ¹¹⁄₁₆) sheet.
National Gallery of Art, Washington,
Rosenwald Collection, 1947.7.169
(Washington only)

26.7 x 21.6 cm (10 ½ x 8 ½) image;
44 x 32.3 cm (17 ⁵⁄₁₆ x 12 ¹¹⁄₁₆) sheet.
The Art Institute of Chicago, Gift of
Mr. Frank B. Hubachek, 1946.37
(Chicago only)

165 s

Caudieux at the Petit Casino, 1893, crayon and
spatter lithograph with scraper in black
on wove paper
Wittrock 25

27.2 x 21.3 cm (10 ¹¹⁄₁₆ x 8 ⅜) image;
44.1 x 32 cm (17 ⅜ x 12 ⅝) sheet. National
Gallery of Art, Washington, Rosenwald
Collection, 1947.7.161
(Washington only)

27.4 x 21.6 cm (10 ¹³⁄₁₆ x 8 ½) image;
42.6 x 32 cm (16 ¾ x 12 ⅝) sheet. The
Art Institute of Chicago, Gift of Horace
M. Swope, 1931.20
(Chicago only)

165 t

Ducarre at the Ambassadeurs, 1893, brush and
spatter lithograph in black on wove paper
Wittrock 26

25.8 x 19.4 cm (10 ³⁄₁₆ x 7 ⅝) image;
44.5 x 31.6 cm (17 ½ x 12 ⁷⁄₁₆) sheet.
National Gallery of Art, Washington,
Rosenwald Collection, 1947.7.170
(Washington only)

26.2 x 19.8 cm (10 ⁵⁄₁₆ x 7 ¹³⁄₁₆) image;
44.2 x 31.8 cm (17 ⅜ x 12 ½) sheet. The
Art Institute of Chicago, Mr. and Mrs.
Carter H. Harrison Collection, 1931.33
(Chicago only)

165 u

A Spectator, 1893, brush and spatter lithograph with scraper in black on wove paper
Wittrock 27

26.3 x 18.2 cm (10 ⅜ x 7 ³⁄₁₆) image;
44 x 32 cm (17 ⁵⁄₁₆ x 12 ⅝) sheet. National
Gallery of Art, Washington, Rosenwald
Collection, 1947.7.168
(Washington only)

26.2 x 18.5 cm (10 ⁵⁄₁₆ x 7 ⁵⁄₁₆) image;
43.6 x 32 cm (17 ³⁄₁₆ x 12 ⅝) sheet. The
Art Institute of Chicago, Charles F.
Glore Collection, 1927.987
(Chicago only)

165 v

American Singer, 1893, brush and spatter
lithograph in black on wove paper
Wittrock 28

27.4 x 17 cm (10 ¹³⁄₁₆ x 6 ¹¹⁄₁₆) image;
44.1 x 31.8 cm (17 ⅜ x 12 ½) sheet.
National Gallery of Art, Washington,
Rosenwald Collection, 1947.7.162
(Washington only)

28 x 20.4 cm (11 x 8 ¹⁄₁₆) image; 44.3 x
32.5 cm (17 ⁷⁄₁₆ x 12 ¹³⁄₁₆) sheet. The Art
Institute of Chicago, Mr. and Mrs. Carter
H. Harrison Collection, 1931.34
(Chicago only)

177

Cover for *"L'Estampe Originale,"* 1893,
brush and spatter lithograph, key stone
in olive-green, color stones in beige,
salmon-red, red, yellow, and black
on folded wove paper, 57.6 x 83 cm
(22 ¹¹⁄₁₆ x 32 ¹¹⁄₁₆). Phyllis Rothschild
Wittrock 3

184

Yvette Guilbert, illustration in *"Figaro illustré,"*
July 1893, chromotypograph, 41.2 x
32 x 2 cm (16 ¼ x 12 ⅝ x ¹³⁄₁₆). The Jane
Voorhees Zimmerli Art Museum, Rutgers,
The State University of New Jersey,
Anonymous Donation, 1991.0178

190a–q

Yvette Guilbert, 1894, an album of sixteen lithographs in a lithographic cover, with text by Gustave Geffroy, published by *L'Estampe originale,* Paris, 1894, each copy signed by Yvette Guilbert in green crayon on inside of cover, lithographs and text printed in olive-green on *Arches* laid paper, 38.0 x 76.0 cm, each sheet printed with an image on both sides, the sheet folded, resulting size 38.0 x 38.0 cm, published in a cover illustrated with an original lithograph printed in olive-black, 41.0 x 39.0 cm when folded.
Wittrock 69-85

40.5 x 38.6 cm (15 15/16 x 15 3/16) image; 40.4 x 80 cm (15 7/8 x 31 1/2) sheet. National Gallery of Art, Washington, New Century Fund, Gift of Edwin L. Cox—Ed Cox Foundation, 2000.1.1–17 *(Washington only)*

38.4 x 40.5 cm (15 1/8 x 15 15/16) image; 40.8 x 39.4 cm (16 1/16 x 15 1/2) sheet, folded; 40.8 x 78.7 cm (16 1/16 x 31) sheet, unfolded. The Art Institute of Chicago, Mr. and Mrs. Carter H. Harrison Collection, 1931.49-65 *(Chicago only)*

200

Miss May Belfort (large plate), 1895, lithograph, with scraping on stone, in black, dark olive-green, and grayish-tan on cream wove paper, with stray marks in blue pencil and graphite, 54.1 x 42.6 cm (21 5/16 x 16 3/4) image; 69.2 x 52.3 cm (27 1/4 x 20 9/16) sheet. The Art Institute of Chicago, John H. Wrenn Memorial Collection, 1941.37 Wittrock 114

204–217

Miss Loïe Fuller, 1893, brush and spatter lithograph, each printed in a unique color combination consisting of the following: i) key stone in blue-grey, green, green-blue, or blue; ii) tint stone in brown-aubergine-grey; iii) stone for face and legs in curry-yellow; iv) stone for dress in red, brown, violet, blue, yellow, green, or a combination thereof; and v) stone for dress and upper margins around the figure in white-blue, bronze, or without pigment, touched with a cotton sack containing gold or silver powder, the excess powder then wiped away with a brush or cotton, on wove paper Wittrock 17

204

38.4 x 28.1 cm (15 1/8 x 11 1/16) sheet. National Gallery of Art, Washington, Rosenwald Collection, 1947.7.185

205

36.4 x 26.2 cm (14 5/16 x 10 5/16) plate, cut within platemark; 38.1 x 28.1 cm (15 x 11 1/16) sheet. National Gallery of Art, Washington, Rosenwald Collection, 1952.8.338

206

38.1 x 27.8 cm (15 x 10 15/16) image; 38.1 x 28.2 cm (15 x 11 1/16) sheet. The Art Institute of Chicago, Joseph Brooks Fair Collection, 1931.451

207

36.8 x 26.8 cm (14 1/2 x 10 9/16). The Baltimore Museum of Art; Gift of Mrs. Nelson Gutman, in Memory of her late Husband's Birthday, June 21, 1956, BMA 1956.89

208

36.8 x 26.8 cm (14 1/2 x 10 9/16) image; 38 x 28.2 cm (14 15/16 x 11 1/8) sheet. Museum of Fine Arts, Boston, Bequest of W. G. Russell Allen, 60.761

209

36.8 x 26.8 cm (14 1/2 x 10 9/16). Courtesy Boston Public Library, Print Department, Collection of Albert H. Wiggin, inscribed "à Stern"

210

36.8 x 26.8 cm (14 1/2 x 10 9/16). Francey and Dr. Martin L. Gecht, 18

211

36.8 x 26.8 cm (14 1/2 x 10 9/16). Courtesy Boston Public Library, Print Department, Collection of Albert H. Wiggin

212

36.8 x 26.8 cm (14 1/2 x 10 9/16). Courtesy Boston Public Library, Print Department, Collection of Albert H. Wiggin

213

36.8 x 26.8 cm (14 1/2 x 10 9/16). Smith College Museum of Art, Northampton, Massachusetts. Gift of Selma Erving, class of 1927, 1978:1–45 *(Chicago only)*

214

37.9 x 25.7 cm (14 15/16 x 10 1/8). The Cleveland Museum of Art. Gift of Ralph King, CMA 1925.1202

215

38.1 x 26.5 cm (15 x 10 7/16) image; 38 x 27.9 cm (14 15/16 x 11) sheet. The Art Institute of Chicago, Joseph Brooks Fair Collection, 1942.20

216

37.9 x 25.9 cm (14 15/16 x 10 3/16). Lent by The Metropolitan Museum of Art, Rogers Fund, 1970.534

217

36.8 x 26.8 cm (14 1/2 x 10 9/16). Phyllis Rothschild, inscribed "HT Lautrec / ep. d'essai"

258

Poster for *Elles,* 1896, crayon, brush and spatter lithograph, key stone in olive-green, color stones in blue and orange, text stone in orange-red on beige wove paper Wittrock 155, state 3

62.5 x 46.2 cm (24 5/8 x 18 13/16) image; 65.1 x 50 cm (25 5/8 x 19 11/16) sheet. National Gallery of Art, Washington, Rosenwald Collection, 1952.8.433 *(Washington only)*

58.3 x 47.5 cm (22 15/16 x 18 11/16) image; 62.8 x 48.7 cm (24 3/4 x 19 3/16) primary support; 67.8 x 53.8 cm (26 11/16 x 21 3/16) secondary support. The Art Institute of Chicago, Mr. and Mrs. Carter H. Harrison Collection, 1948.442 *(Chicago only)*

259a–l

Elles, album of color lithographs, 1896, A lithographic cover, frontispiece, and ten color lithographs published by Gustave Pellet in Paris in April 1896 in an edition of 100, the cover in olive-green black or brown-black on laid Japan paper and signed by the artist. Although there are minimal differences in the paper sizes among the various lithographs in the series, the image and sheet size are identical for each lithograph; the large image size of some of the proof indicates that the drawing on the stone was larger than the paper used for the edition.
Wittrock 155 to 165

259a

Cover for *Elles*, 1896, lithograph in dark olive-green on thick cream Japan paper folded to make cover
Wittrock 155, state 1

57.1 x 46.2 cm (22 ½ x 18 ³/₁₆) image, to fold; 57.1 x 47.2 cm (22 ½ x 18 ⁹/₁₆) sheet, folded. The Art Institute of Chicago, Charles F. Glore Collection, 1927.969
(Chicago only)

259b

Frontispiece for *Elles*, 1896, crayon, brush and spatter lithograph, key stone in olive-green, color stones in blue and orange on wove paper
Wittrock 155, state 2

52.8 x 40.2 cm (20 ¹³/₁₆ x 15 ¹³/₁₆). National Gallery of Art, Washington, Rosenwald Collection, 1952.8.434
(Washington only)

52.6 x 40.3 cm (20 ¹¹/₁₆ x 15 ⅞) image/sheet. The Art Institute of Chicago, Charles F. Glore Collection, 1927.972
(Chicago only)

259c

The Seated Clowness (Mademoiselle Cha-u-ka-o), 1896, crayon, brush and spatter lithograph with scraper, key stone in green-black, color stones in black-brown, yellow, red, and blue on wove paper

51.8 x 40 cm (20 ⁷/₁₆ x 15 ¾). National Gallery of Art, Washington, Gift of Mr. and Mrs. Robert L. Rosenwald, in Honor of the 50th Anniversary of the National Gallery of Art, 1991.30.1
Wittrock 156, bon à tirer proof
(Washington only)

52.6 x 40.3 cm (20 ¹¹/₁₆ x 15 ⅞) image/sheet. The Art Institute of Chicago, Charles F. Glore Collection, 1927.970
Wittrock 156, only edition
(Chicago only)

259d

Woman with a Tray—Breakfast, 1896, crayon lithograph with scraper in sanguine on wove paper
Wittrock 157, only edition

40.5 x 52.6 (15 ¹⁵/₁₆ x 20 ¹¹/₁₆) image/sheet. National Gallery of Art, Washington, Rosenwald Collection, 1964.8.1889
(Washington only)

39.7 x 50.4 cm (15 ⅝ x 19 ¹³/₁₆) image; 40.2 x 50.7 cm (15 ¹³/₁₆ x 19 ¹⁵/₁₆) sheet. The Art Institute of Chicago, Charles F. Glore Collection, 1927.977
(Chicago only)

259e

Woman Reclining—Waking Up, 1896, crayon lithograph with scraper in olive-grey on wove paper
Wittrock 158, only edition

40.5 x 52.1 cm (15 ¹⁵/₁₆ x 20 ½) image/sheet. National Gallery of Art, Washington, Rosenwald Collection, 1964.8.1890
(Washington only)

40.5 x 52.7 cm (15 ¹⁵/₁₆ x 20 ¾) image/sheet. The Art Institute of Chicago, Charles F. Glore Collection, 1927.973
(Chicago only)

259f

Woman at the Tub—The Tub, 1896, crayon, brush and spatter lithograph, key stone in olive-green, color stones in blue-grey, salmon-red, yellow, and pale curry-brown on wove paper
Wittrock 159, only edition

39.6 x 51.2 cm (15 ⁹/₁₆ x 20 ³/₁₆) image/sheet. National Gallery of Art, Washington, Rosenwald Collection, 1946.21.339
(Washington only)

40.4 x 52.3 cm (15 ⅞ x 20 ⁹/₁₆) image/sheet. The Art Institute of Chicago, Charles F. Glore Collection, 1927.978
(Chicago only)

259g

Woman Washing Herself—The Toilette, 1896, crayon lithograph, key stone in olive-brown, color stone in blue on wove paper
Wittrock 160

52 x 40.1 cm (20 ½ x 15 ¹³/₁₆). National Gallery of Art, Washington, Rosenwald Collection, 1964.8.1891
(Washington only)

52.5 x 40.5 cm (20 ¹¹/₁₆ x 15 ¹⁵/₁₆) image/sheet. The Art Institute of Chicago, Charles F. Glore Collection, 1927.975
(Chicago only)

259h

Woman with Mirror—Mirror in Hand, 1896, crayon, brush and spatter lithograph, key stone in grey, color stones in yellow and brown-beige on wove paper
Wittrock 161, only edition

52.3 x 39.9 cm (20 ⁹/₁₆ x 15 ¹¹/₁₆) image/sheet. National Gallery of Art, Washington, Rosenwald Collection, 1964.8.1892
(Washington only)

52.3 x 40 cm (20 ⁹/₁₆ x 15 ¾) image/sheet. The Art Institute of Chicago, Charles F. Glore Collection, 1927.979
(Chicago only)

259i

Woman Brushing Her Hair—The Coiffure, 1896, crayon, brush and spatter lithograph, key stone in mauve-brown, color stone in pale olive-brown on wove paper
Wittrock 162, only edition

52 x 38.3 cm (20 ½ x 15 ¹/₁₆) image/sheet. National Gallery of Art, Washington, Rosenwald Collection, 1947.7.153
(Washington only)

52.8 x 40.3 cm (20 ¹³/₁₆ x 15 ⅞) image/sheet. The Art Institute of Chicago, Charles F. Glore Collection, 1927.976
(Chicago only)

259j

Profile of a Woman in Bed—Getting Up, 1896, crayon, brush and spatter lithograph with scraper, key stone in olive-green, color stones in grey, yellow, and red on wove paper
Wittrock 163, only edition

40.5 x 52.5 cm (15 ¹⁵/₁₆ x 20 ¹¹/₁₆). National Gallery of Art, Washington, Rosenwald Collection, 1964.8.1893
(Washington only)

40.1 x 52.1 cm (15 ¹³/₁₆ x 20 ½) image/sheet. The Art Institute of Chicago, Charles F. Glore Collection, 1927.971
(Chicago only)

259k

Woman in a Corset—Conquête de Passage, 1896, crayon, brush and spatter lithograph with scraper, key stone in olive-green, color stones in curry-yellow, grey-blue, pale orange-brown, and orange-sanguine on wove paper

52.4 x 40.3 cm (20 5/8 x 15 7/8) image/sheet. National Gallery of Art, Washington, Rosenwald Collection, 1947.7.152
Wittrock 164, only edition
(Washington only)

52.4 x 40.2 cm (20 5/8 x 15 13/16) image/sheet. The Art Institute of Chicago, Charles F. Glore Collection, 1927.974
Wittrock 164
(Chicago only)

259l

Woman Lying on Her Back—Lassitude, 1896, crayon lithograph, key stone in sanguine, tint stone in olive-green (not covering 1.0 cm of lower edge of image) on wove paper
Wittrock 165, only edition

40 x 52.2 cm (15 3/4 x 20 9/16) image/sheet. National Gallery of Art, Washington, Rosenwald Collection, 1947.7.154
(Washington only)

40.4 x 52.5 cm (15 7/8 x 20 11/16) image/sheet. The Art Institute of Chicago, Charles F. Glore Collection, 1927.980
(Chicago only)

POSTERS

10/51

Moulin Rouge: La Goulue, 1891, lithograph (poster) in black, yellow, red, and blue on three sheets of tan wove paper, 189 x 115.7 cm (74 7/16 x 45 9/16) image; 191 x 117 cm (75 3/16 x 46 1/16) sheet. The Art Institute of Chicago, Mr. and Mrs. Carter H. Harrison Collection, 1954.1193
Wittrock P. 1, edition B

113

Ambassadeurs: Aristide Bruant, 1892, lithograph (poster) in olive-green, orange, blue, red, and black on two sheets of tan wove paper, 139 x 95.2 cm (54 3/4 x 37 1/2) image, including stray marks; 147.2 x 99.9 cm (57 15/16 x 39 5/16) both sheets. The Art Institute of Chicago, Mr. and Mrs. Carter H. Harrison Collection, 1948.450
Wittrock P. 4

115

Eldorado: Aristide Bruant, 1892, lithograph (poster) in olive-green, yellow, red, blue, and black on two sheets of tan wove paper, 137.5 x 96.4 cm (54 1/8 x 37 15/16) image; 145.2 x 98.7 cm (57 3/16 x 38 7/8) sheet. The Art Institute of Chicago, Mr. and Mrs. Carter H. Harrison Collection, 1949.1024
Wittrock P. 5

116

Aristide Bruant in His Cabaret, 1893, lithograph (poster) in black, olive-green, red, and brown on buff wove paper, 127.3 x 94 cm (50 1/8 x 37) image; 138 x 99.1 cm (54 5/16 x 39) sheet. The Art Institute of Chicago, Mr. and Mrs. Carter H. Harrison Collection, 1949.1005
Wittrock P. 9, state C

117

Bruant at the Mirliton, 1893, lithograph (poster), with scraping on stone, in black, olive green, and red, with text added in another hand and printed in olive green, on tan wove paper, 82.1 x 58.7 cm (32 5/16 x 23 1/8) image; 82.3 x 60.9 cm (32 3/8 x 24) sheet. The Art Institute of Chicago, Mr. and Mrs. Carter H. Harrison Collection, 1949.1101
Wittrock P. 10, state C

164

Divan Japonais, 1893, lithograph (poster), with transferred screen, in black, olive-green-gray, yellow, and red on cream wove paper laid down on linen, 80.1 x 60.1 cm (31 9/16 x 23 11/16) image; 80.2 x 61.8 cm (31 9/16 x 24 5/16) sheet. The Art Institute of Chicago, Mr. and Mrs. Carter H. Harrison Collection, 1949.1002
Wittrock P. 11

175

Jane Avril, 1893, lithograph (poster) in olive-green, yellow, orange, red, and black on cream wove paper, 124 x 91.5 cm (48 13/16 x 36) image; 129 x 94 cm (50 13/16 x 37) sheet. The Art Institute of Chicago, Mr. and Mrs. Carter H. Harrison Collection, 1949.1004
Wittrock P. 6

176

Mademoiselle Eglantine's Troupe, 1896, lithograph (poster) in yellow, turquoise, and red on tan wove paper laid down on fabric, 61.4 x 79.5 cm (24 3/16 x 31 5/16) image; 62 x 79.9 cm (24 7/16 x 31 7/16) sheet. The Art Institute of Chicago, Mr. and Mrs. Carter H. Harrison Collection, 1936.220
Wittrock P. 21

178

Jane Avril, 1899, brush lithograph, key stone in black, one color stone in red, one in yellow and blue (the snake on dress printed from one stone) on one sheet of white wove paper
Wittrock P. 29

56 x 38 cm (22 1/16 x 14 15/16) image/sheet. National Gallery of Art, Washington, Rosenwald Collection, 1953.6.137
(Washington only)

55.6 x 30.9 cm (21 7/8 x 12 3/16) image; 55.6 x 37.6 cm (21 7/8 x 14 13/16) sheet. The Art Institute of Chicago, Mr. and Mrs. Carter H. Harrison Collection, 1949.1009
(Chicago only)

201

May Belfort, 1895, lithograph (poster), with scraping on stone, in red, black, olive-green, and yellow on tan wove paper, 79.8 x 60 cm (31 7/16 x 23 5/8) image; 79.8 x 61.4 cm (31 7/16 x 24 3/16) sheet. The Art Institute of Chicago, Mr. and Mrs. Carter H. Harrison Collection, 1949.1007
Wittrock P. 14

202

May Milton, 1895, lithograph (poster), with transferred screen, in blue, olive-green, yellow, red, and black on tan wove paper laid down on cream wove paper, 80.3 x 60.1 cm (31 5/8 x 23 11/16) image, including registration marks; 80.4 x 61.9 cm (31 5/8 x 24 3/8) sheet, primary support; 85.6 x 67.3 cm (33 11/16 x 26 1/2) sheet, secondary support. The Art Institute of Chicago, Mr. and Mrs. Carter H. Harrison Collection, 1948.451
Wittrock P. 17

196

Yvette Guilbert, 1895, ceramic plaque, 26.7 x 28.3 cm (10 ½ x 11 ⅛). San Diego Museum of Art, Gift of Mrs. Robert Smart, 1931:39 Dortu C. I, no. 3 in edition of about 10

Louis Anquetin

French; Etrépagny 1861 – Paris 1932

Born and raised in Normandy, Anquetin moved to Paris in 1882 and enrolled at the studio of Léon Bonnat, where he met Toulouse-Lautrec. The two men formed a lifelong friendship, and both transferred late that autumn to the atelier of Fernand Cormon, where they befriended Emile Bernard and Vincent van Gogh.

Anquetin and Lautrec could often be found together at the Moulin Rouge and other Montmartre haunts. They traveled to Normandy to visit Anquetin's parents in 1885 and toured museums in Holland in 1894 prior to attending the opening of the exhibition of Les XX in Brussels. Evidence of their friendship is also found in their art: Anquetin painted Lautrec's portrait around 1886 (fig. 283); and Lautrec appears to have depicted Anquetin (the figure in checked overalls) as a rabble-rouser in his *Parody of "The Sacred Grove" by Puvis de Chavannes* of 1884 (fig. 21), while Anquetin, in a similar spirit, included Lautrec in his *Meeting of Friends at Bourgueil* (fig. 32), with contemporary figures in a group gently mocking the eighteenth-century paintings of *fêtes champêtres.*

Anquetin worked in several styles during the 1880s, exploring impressionism and pointillism, then developing a new style called "cloisonisme" around 1888 influenced by stained glass and Japanese prints (see fig. 9). He exhibited widely at venues such as Les XX in Brussels, the Salon des Indépendants in Paris, and the Volpini show in Paris in 1889, along with Emile Bernard and Paul Gauguin. Anquetin received favorable reviews in the press and was an accomplished pastelist as well as painter. In the mid-1890s, however, he abandoned avant-garde styles and scenes of daily life in favor of the old masters and began to create murals and tapestry designs in the style of Titian and Rubens.

32

Meeting of Friends at Bourgueil, 1893, gouache on paper, 38 x 50 cm (14 ¹⁵⁄₁₆ x 19 ¹¹⁄₁₆). The Jane Voorhees Zimmerli Art Museum, Rutgers, The State University of New Jersey, Gift of Carleton A. Holstrom, 1986.0711.001

143

At the Bar, c. 1891, pastel on cardboard, 55 x 72 cm (21 ⅝ x 28 ⅜). Private collection, Courtesy Brame & Lorenceau, Paris

264

At the Circus, 1887, pastel, 46.5 x 61.7 cm (18 ⁵⁄₁₆ x 24 ⁵⁄₁₆); 61 x 76.2 cm (24 x 30). Private collection

Emile Bernard

French; Lille 1868 – Paris 1941

Bernard enrolled in the Cormon atelier in 1884 at the age of sixteen, where he befriended Louis Anquetin and Toulouse-Lautrec. His strong personality and outspoken ideas about art led to his expulsion from Cormon's studio in 1886, but he remained close to both Anquetin and Lautrec, frequenting the cabarets of Montmartre with them. In the spring of 1886 Bernard traveled on foot through Normandy and Brittany, where he met Gauguin. Together with Lautrec, Anquetin, and Van Gogh, Bernard participated in the Petit Boulevard exhibition at the Grand Bouillon-Restaurant du Chalet in Paris. When Van Gogh moved to Arles in February 1888, Bernard kept up a lively correspondence with him, sending drawings and watercolors of brothels. *Brothel Scene* of late June 1888 (fig. 235) is inscribed "to my friend Vincent, this silly sketch," and bears a poem about prostitution on the reverse. Van Gogh greatly admired the watercolor, forwarding it to his brother Theo, the art dealer. Bernard sent him more drawings throughout the summer, including an album of eleven sketches entitled *Au bordel* (fig. 236, 237).

At the end of the decade Bernard focused on Breton subjects, but in 1890 he returned to the theme of prostitution in the canvas *Le Salon* (fig. 239). He continued to exhibit with Lautrec and other Montmartre artists at the Salon des Indépendents and at the gallery of Louis Le Barc de Boutteville in 1891. He organized the first

large retrospective of Van Gogh's work in 1892. And the following year he traveled to Egypt, where he lived until 1903 and adopted a more traditional painting style, abandoning his avant-garde roots.

235

Brothel Scene, 1888, watercolor, 30.8 x 20 cm (12 ⅛ x 7 ⅞). Van Gogh Museum Amsterdam (Vincent van Gogh Foundation), d 636 V/1962

236

Three Prostitutes Seated, 1888, watercolor, 40.5 x 26.2 cm (15 ¹⁵⁄₁₆ x 10 ⁵⁄₁₆). Van Gogh Museum Amsterdam (Vincent van Gogh Foundation), d 629 V/1962

237

Three Prostitutes around a Table, 1888, watercolor, 40.4 x 28.3 cm (15 ⅞ x 11 ⅛). Van Gogh Museum Amsterdam (Vincent van Gogh Foundation), d 626 V/1962

239

Le Salon, 1890, oil on canvas, 81 x 116 cm (31 ⅞ x 45 ¹¹⁄₁₆). Private collection

Pierre Bonnard

French; Fontenay-aux-Roses 1867 – Le Cannet 1947

Although Bonnard won renown as a painter, printmaker, and photographer, he trained as a lawyer, even as he was enrolled as a student at the Ecole des Beaux-Arts and the Académie Julian. It was at the Académie Julian in 1888 that Paul Sérusier formed the group known as the Nabis, with Bonnard as a founding member. Bonnard exhibited regularly with the Nabis, though he, like his friend Edouard Vuillard, was more interested in the depiction of everyday life than in the symbolism that dominated the art of his fellow Nabis.

In addition to easel paintings, Bonnard turned his talents toward decorative works such as folding screens, fans, and posters. The success of his poster *France-Champagne* in 1891 encouraged him to abandon law in favor of a career as an artist. But he deferred to Toulouse-Lautrec's greater mastery of that format when the latter won a competition to design a poster for the Moulin Rouge that Bonnard had also entered.

Bonnard, along with Lautrec, Anquetin, and others, participated in the first Exposition des Peintres Impressionnistes et Symbolistes held at Louis Le Barc de Boutteville's gallery in 1891, exhibiting there throughout the 1890s. He became part of the circle of artists associated with *La Revue blanche*, contributing prints and posters to promote the journal; at the same time he became a regular guest of the publication's coeditor Thadée Natanson and his wife Misia.

After 1900 Bonnard's art moved in a more personal direction, marked by a union of expressive color and rigorous composition that distinguished him from both his fauve and cubist contemporaries. Admired by Henri Matisse and Georges Rouault among others, Bonnard became one of the most acclaimed artists of his generation.

282

Circus Rider, 1894, oil on cardboard on panel, 27 x 34.9 cm (10 ⅝ x 13 ¾). The Phillips Collection, Washington, D.C., 1554

Leonetto Cappiello

naturalized French; Livorno 1875 — Cannes 1942

Of Italian birth, Cappiello moved to Paris in 1898 and became known for his caricatures of celebrities of the theater and cabaret. His fluid, almost calligraphic drawings and paintings (see fig. 193) caught the essence of the performer, but Cappiello preferred to call them "portraits de caractère" (character portraits), believing that caricature was intended to ridicule, whereas he sought to highlight the performers' unique appearance without malice. Cappiello's first prints were published in the satirical journal *Le Rire*, an influential periodical that featured cartoons, lithographs, and drawings by other Montmartre artists, including Lautrec, Jean-Louis Forain, Henri Gustave Jossot, and Adolphe Willette. His work caught the attention of Alexandre Natanson, copublisher of *La Revue blanche*, who commissioned Cappiello to produce a portfolio of eighteen color lithographs devoted to actresses of the opera and theater in 1899. That same year Cappiello created a limited-edition statuette of the café-concert star Yvette Guilbert (fig. 194); he also painted portraits and created decorative projects; but he was best known for his

posters. His first, for the new humor magazine *Le Frou-Frou*, launched his career as a poster artist in 1899; and he went on to produce more than three thousand posters during the course of his life. Although just eleven years younger than Lautrec, Cappiello was essentially part of the next generation of poster artists, picking up where Lautrec, Jules Chéret, and Théophile-Alexandre Steinlen left off and carrying their innovations into the twentieth century.

193

Yvette Guilbert, 1899, oil on canvas, 116 x 90 cm (45 ¹¹⁄₁₆ x 35 ⁷⁄₁₆). Musée d'Orsay, Paris; Gift of Mme Monique Cappiello, granddaughter of the artist, 1979, RF1980-196

194

Yvette Guilbert, 1899, polychrome plaster, 34 x 23.5 x 17.4 cm (13 ⅜ x 9 ¼ x 6 ⅞). The Jane Voorhees Zimmerli Art Museum, Rutgers, The State University of New Jersey, Carleton A. Holstrom and Mary Beth Kineke Purchase Fund, 2001.0976

François Rupert Carabin

French; Saverne 1862 — Strasbourg 1932

In 1870 the defeated French armies passed through eight-year-old François Carabin's rural Alsatian village, followed by the conquering Prussian army. With Alsace annexed by Prussia by terms of the treaty that ended the Franco-Prussian War, the Carabin family moved to Paris in 1872, to an apartment above the café-concert Le Grand Turc in Montmartre. In his teens Carabin worked by day as an engraver of cameos (in 1878 he participated in a demonstration at the Exposition Universelle), then as a sculptor of architectural ornament, while studying art at night.

Frequenting cafés and cabarets of Montmartre, including the Nouvelle-Athènes (better known for its association with the impressionists), Carabin became acquainted with author Gustave Geffroy (1855–1926), who introduced him to avant-garde literary and artistic circles. With Lautrec, Anquetin, Steinlen, and Willette as well as Charles-Lucien Léandre, Maximilien Luce, Edouard Manet, Charles Maurin, Claude Monet, Camille Pissarro, Pierre Puvis de Chavannes, and Henri Rivière, Carabin became an habitué of the Chat Noir soon after it opened in 1881. Like Lautrec, he frequented the *maisons closes* in the 1890s, and the women

became his models. A sly allusion to Carabin's brothel patronage can be seen in a large allegorical painting by Maurin. The Strasbourg museum has a small wax figure he made, *Jeune Fille relevant sa chemise*, a woman with her shift raised that appears to be related to the subject of Lautrec's painting *Medical Inspection (Rue des Moulins)* (fig. 249). Carabin admired Loïe Fuller's performances as well, which he depicted in a suite of six bronzes (fig. 218a–f).

Carabin was a founding member of the Société des Artistes Indépendants and exhibited with the Société Nationale des Beaux-Arts starting in 1891. He had a long and successful career and is now best known for his work in wood, chiefly female nudes, both in sculpture and in finely crafted furniture.

218a

Miss Loïe Fuller, 1896–1897, bronze, 19 cm (7 ½) height. The Jane Voorhees Zimmerli Art Museum, Rutgers, The State University of New Jersey, Gift of Herbert D. and Ruth Schimmel, 2000.0644.006

218b

Miss Loïe Fuller, 1896–1897, bronze, 18.5 cm (7 ⁵⁄₁₆) height. The Jane Voorhees Zimmerli Art Museum, Rutgers, The State University of New Jersey, Gift of Herbert D. and Ruth Schimmel, 2000.0644.003

218c

Miss Loïe Fuller, 1896–1897, bronze, 19.5 cm (7 ¹¹⁄₁₆) height. The Jane Voorhees Zimmerli Art Museum, Rutgers, The State University of New Jersey, Gift of Herbert D. and Ruth Schimmel, 2000.0644.004

218d

Miss Loïe Fuller, 1896–1897, bronze, 22 cm (8 ¹¹⁄₁₆) height. The Jane Voorhees Zimmerli Art Museum, Rutgers, The State University of New Jersey, Gift of Herbert D. and Ruth Schimmel, 2000.0644.002

218e

Miss Loïe Fuller, 1896–1897, bronze, 20.3 cm (8) height. The Jane Voorhees Zimmerli Art Museum, Rutgers, The State University of New Jersey, Gift of Herbert D. and Ruth Schimmel, 2000.0644.001

218 f

Miss Loïe Fuller, 1896–1897, bronze, 22.5 cm
(8 ⅞) height. The Jane Voorhees Zimmerli
Art Museum, Rutgers, The State University
of New Jersey, Gift of Herbert D. and
Ruth Schimmel, 2000.0644.005

Ramón Casas

Spanish; Barcelona 1866–Barcelona 1932

Casas was a prodigy whose artistic training
began in Barcelona when he was eleven.
At fifteen he entered the Paris studio of
Carolus-Duran (Charles-Emile Auguste
Durand), a distinguished academician
whose portraits were admired for a pol-
ished technique and suave paint handling.
The precocious youth made a successful
debut at the Paris Salon of 1883 with a
Self-Portrait painted under the aegis of
Carolus-Duran, then embarked on an
independent artistic career.

Casas was alert as well to the avant-
garde currents in Paris; and the influence
of the impressionists—whose group exhibitions from 1874 to 1886 revolutionized
the contemporary art scene—is evident in
his work. He gravitated to modern, urban
subjects, such as the newly constructed
landmark of Sacré-Coeur in Montmartre,
which he depicted in a naturalist style. His
1892 painting *Au Moulin de la Galette (Madeleine.
L'Absinthe)* (Museu de Montserrat) is the-
matically related to Manet's *Plum Brandy*
(fig. 85) and resonates with contempora-
neous work by Lautrec (fig. 92, 3, 82, 93),
Van Gogh (fig. 90), and Vuillard (fig. 94)
in the Montmartre dance halls.

Casas's close friendship with fellow
Catalan artist Santiago Rusiñol (fig. 125,
129) began in Paris, and in 1897 the two
helped found Els Quatre Gats in Barcelona, an influential establishment that they
modeled on the Chat Noir; Quatre Gats
featured modernist literary and artistic
events and performances, including
a shadow theater. Casas's portrait of Pablo
Picasso in Montmartre, published in the
journal *Pèl y Plona* in 1901, echoes his 1891
portrait of composer Erik Satie (fig. 75).

4

The Sacré-Coeur, Montmartre, c. 1890,
oil on canvas, 67 x 55.5 cm (26 ⅜ x 21 ⅞).
Museu Nacional d'Art de Catalunya,
Barcelona, MNAC/MAM 4040

75

Erik Satie (El bohemio; Poet of Montmartre), 1891,
oil on canvas, 198.8 x 99.7 cm (78 ¼ x
39 ¼). Northwestern University Library

130

Dance at the Moulin de la Galette, c. 1890–1891,
oil on canvas, 98.5 x 80 cm (38 ¾ x 31 ½).
Museo Cau Ferrat (Consorcio del Patrimoni
de Sitges), 32.032

Jules Chéret

(French; Paris 1836–Nice 1932)

Jules Chéret is widely viewed as "the father
of the color poster." Apprenticed to a lithographer at the age of thirteen, he worked
for various printers in Paris as a young
man. In 1858 he sold his first poster design—*Orpheus in the Underworld*—to the composer Jacques Offenbach. Although it was a
success, Chéret could not find further
work in Paris as a poster designer.
He moved to London, where he worked
for Cramer publishers and designed several posters for local entertainments: the
circus, music hall, and opera. A turning
point in his career came when he was
introduced to the perfume manufacturer
Eugène Rimmel, who gave him the financial support to open his own printing shop
in Paris in 1866.

Chéret was both a master technician
and a talented artist. His innovations in
the lithographic printing process allowed
for a greater range of color and introduced
an artistic element to what had once been
a purely commercial realm. Throughout
the 1870s and 1880s the color poster grew
in popularity and ubiquity. In 1889 Chéret
won a gold medal at the Exposition Universelle, the same year that a large retrospective exhibition of his work was held.
The next year he was awarded the Chevalier
of the Legion of Honor in recognition for
his contributions to poster design.

Despite belonging to an older generation, Chéret was friendly with the younger
artists whom he had inspired to take up
poster design, including Toulouse-Lautrec,
Bonnard, Steinlen, Willette, and Jules
Alexandre Grün. A photograph from December 1891 or early 1892 shows Toulouse-
Lautrec posed in front of Chéret's poster
for the Moulin Rouge (fig. 56), his hat
removed in deference to the master's work
(fig. 52).

56

Bal du Moulin Rouge, 1889, reprinted in 1892,
lithograph in vermilion, yellow, blue
violet, gray green, and black, 120 x 87 cm
(47 ¼ x 34 ¼) plate; 124.1 x 88 cm (48 ⅞ x
34 ⅝) sheet. Los Angeles County Museum
of Art, Kurt J. Wagner, M.D., and C.
Kathleen Wagner Collection, M.87.294.7
Broido 316

153

Musée Grévin, 1900, lithograph in vermilion,
yellow, sea green, Prussian blue, and light
blue green, sheet: 119.7 x 81.9 cm (47 ⅛ x
32 ¼). Los Angeles County Museum
of Art, Kurt J. Wagner, M.D., and C.
Kathleen Wagner Collection, M.87.294.15
Broido 471, proof before letters

154

Folies-Bergère: L'Arc-en-Ciel, 1893, lithograph
in vermilion, yellow, dark green, Prussian
blue, and grey green, 117.2 x 81.9 cm
(46 ⅛ x 32 ¼) sheet. Los Angeles County
Museum of Art, Kurt J. Wagner, M.D.,
and C. Kathleen Wagner Collection,
M.87.294.11
Broido 123

155

Olympia, 1892, lithograph in pink,
vermilion, yellow, Prussian blue, and grey
green, 117.2 x 81.9 cm (46 ⅛ x 32 ¼)
sheet. Los Angeles County Museum of Art,
Kurt J. Wagner, M.D., and C. Kathleen
Wagner Collection, M.87.294.16
Broido 345

179

Yvette Guilbert au Concert Parisien, 1891, lithograph in vermilion, yellow, Prussian blue,
and gray green, 118.1 x 84.1 cm (46 ½ x
33 ⅛) sheet. Los Angeles County Museum
of Art, Kurt J. Wagner, M.D., and C.
Kathleen Wagner Collection, M.87.294.24
Broido 215

223

Folies-Bergère: La Loïe Fuller, 1893, lithograph
in vermilion, yellow, dark violet, and
black, 110.2 x 81.9 cm (43 ⅜ x 32 ¼)
sheet. Los Angeles County Museum of Art,
Kurt J. Wagner, M.D., and C. Kathleen
Wagner Collection, M.87.294.12
Broido 125 (first edition of four)

Edgar Degas

French; Paris 1834–Paris 1917

The eldest son of a Paris banking family, Degas originally intended to study law but entered the studio of Louis Lamothe in 1854. The classical training he received there, along with a formative period spent studying and copying the Italian masters in Italy, provided the foundation of Degas' art.

Although he was an original member of the impressionist group and participated in all but one of their exhibitions held between 1874 and 1886, Degas saw himself as a "realist" or "naturalist" painter and disliked the term "impressionist." In contrast to many others in the group, Degas displayed a marked preference for urban subjects and artificial light with an emphasis on drawing. A keen, often uncompromising observer of everyday scenes, he attempted to capture the unvarnished reality of the world around him.

In the mid-1870s Degas began to produce monotypes. Such prints, often heightened with pastel, appealed to Degas' experimental nature, while the speed with which they were created and the number produced made them marketable commodities. Among the most exceptional and disconcerting of these were fifty or so monotypes depicting brothel scenes.

By the late 1880s Degas led a rather reclusive existence. His reputation allowed him to exhibit only when he wished and to sell his art to discerning buyers. In his later years his style moved closer to symbolism, winning him the admiration of a new generation of painters, including Paul Gauguin and Odilon Redon. Toulouse-Lautrec, who openly acknowledged Degas as a cardinal influence, met the older artist through Mademoiselle Dihau, a distant relation of the former and a friend of the latter.

83

Woman Brushing Her Hair, c. 1884, oil on canvas, 74.3 x 60.6 cm (29 ¼ x 23 ⅞). The Kreeger Museum, Washington, D.C. Lemoisne 642

159

Café-Concert, 1876/1877, pastel over monotype on paper and board, 23.5 x 43.2 cm (9 ¼ x 17). Corcoran Gallery of Art, Washington, D.C., William A. Clark Collection, 26.72 Lemoisne 404 *(Washington only)*

160

Café Singer, 1879, oil on canvas, 53.5 x 41.8 cm (21 ¹/₁₆ x 16 ⁷/₁₆). The Art Institute of Chicago, Bequest of Clara Margaret Lynch in memory of John A. Lynch, 1955.738 *(Chicago only)*

229

Two Women, c. 1876–1877, monotype in black ink on light tan laid paper, 24.9 x 28.3 cm (9 ¹³/₁₆ x 11 ⅛) image; 21.5 x 16 cm (8 ⁷/₁₆ x 6 ⁵/₁₆) sheet. Museum of Fine Arts, Boston, Katherine E. Bullard Fund in memory of Francis Bullard, 61.1214 Janis 117

230

The Supper Party (The Connoisseur), c. 1876–1877, monotype on ivory laid paper, 22 x 16.3 cm (8 ¹¹/₁₆ x 6 ⁷/₁₆) sheet; 21.4 x 15.9 cm (8 ⁷/₁₆ x 6 ¼) plate. Francey and Dr. Martin L. Gecht Janis 115

231

Three Seated Prostitutes, c. 1876–1877, pastel over monotype in black ink on cream-colored paper, 23 x 31 cm (9 ¹/₁₆ x 12 ³/₁₆). Rijksmuseum, Amsterdam, RP-P-1967-88 Janis checklist no. 62

232

The Reluctant Client, c. 1876–1877, monotype in black ink on wove paper, 21 x 15.9 cm (8 ¼ x 6 ¼) plate. National Gallery of Canada, Ottawa, Purchased 1977, 18814 Janis 86

Maxime Dethomas

French; Garges-les-Gonesse 1867–Paris 1929

A student of Eugène Carrière at the Ecole des Arts Décoratifs in Paris, Dethomas became a painter, pastelist, lithographer, and illustrator but was best known for designing stage sets for the theater and the Opéra in the first years of the twentieth century. In the 1880s and 1890s he was part of the active Montmartre circle of artists and bohemians. He and Lautrec probably met in the late 1880s, attending Montmartre brothels, dance halls, and cafés-concerts together. Lautrec described his friend as "a charming lad and a painter who does not talk about his own painting, which is greatly to be admired" (Frey 1994, 411). Dethomas traveled to Spain with Lautrec in the mid-1890s and to Holland in 1898. Lautrec painted his portrait in 1896 (fig. 148). The poster that Dethomas published in *Montmartre* in 1897 shows the influence of Lautrec's graphic work (fig. 96).

96

"Montmartre," 1897, color lithograph, 80.5 x 61 cm (31 ¹¹/₁₆ x 24). The Jane Voorhees Zimmerli Art Museum, Rutgers, The State University of New Jersey, Gift of Herbert D. and Ruth Schimmel, 1994.0382

Henri-Patrice Dillon

French; San Francisco 1851–Paris 1909

Painter, lithographer, poster designer, and illustrator, Henri-Patrice Dillon was born in San Francisco to French parents. He was an attaché at the French consulate in New York prior to enrolling at the Ecole des Beaux-Arts in Paris. There he studied under Henri Lehmann, Carolus-Duran, and José Frappa, who steered him toward illustration. Dillon exhibited at the French Salon beginning in 1876 and was a member of the Société des Peintres-Graveurs and vice president of the Société des Lithographes. His early work consisted mostly of history painting. Then in the 1890s he turned his attention to drawings and small paintings of the circus, theater, and dancers (see fig. 137). As an active illustrator, he also created designs for books, posters, almanacs, and menus.

137

Moulin Rouge, c. 1895, gouache, graphite, collage, and ink, 30 x 21.8 cm (11 ¹³/₁₆ x 8 ⁹/₁₆). The Jane Voorhees Zimmerli Art Museum, Rutgers, The State University of New Jersey, David A. and Mildred H. Morse Art Acquisition Fund, 1998.1159

Faria

An illustrator and poster maker, Faria created a cover design for the sheet music for "Cha-u-ka-o" at the Moulin Rouge that probably dates to 1889–1890 (fig. 139).

138

"Cha-u-ka-o" (song sheet), c. 1889–1890, color lithograph, 26.5 x 34 cm (10 ⁷/₁₆ x 13 ³/₈). The Jane Voorhees Zimmerli Art Museum, Rutgers, The State University of New Jersey, Gift of Herbert D. and Ruth Schimmel, 1990.0052

Georges de Feure

French; Paris 1868–Paris 1928

Born to Dutch and Belgian parents, Georges de Feure (the pseudonym of Georges Joseph van Sluijters) was a poster designer, painter, lithographer, and illustrator as well as an important designer of furniture and porcelains. He spent his early years in the French capital as well as in Holland and Belgium, moving as his family's financial health waxed and waned. By 1889 de Feure, now twenty-one, settled in Montmartre. He attended the cafés-concerts and cabarets on the butte, including the Rat Mort and the Chat Noir, where he met other Montmartre artists such as Henri-Gabriel Ibels and Adolphe Willette.

His first published drawing appeared in *Le Courrier français* in 1890, and in 1892 he turned his attention to color lithography. De Feure created thirty-one posters during his career. Although it has been reported that he was a student of Jules Chéret, contemporary sources suggest that he learned the technique of color lithography before settling in Paris. Nonetheless, many of his early works show the influence of Chéret in his use of multiple tertiary colors: see, for instance, his poster for Loïe Fuller of 1895 (fig. 225), a complex design printed in eight colors.

After about 1893 de Feure began to explore symbolist style and content and to exhibit with artists such as Lautrec, Gauguin, and the Nabis at the Expositions des Peintres Impressionnistes et Symbolistes as well as the Salon de La Rose+Croix and the Salon des Cent. Toward the end of the decade de Feure became closely involved with the art nouveau movement centered around the decorative arts collector, dealer, and exhibitor Siegfried Bing. He contributed stained-glass windows, furniture, textiles, and decorative arts to the Pavillon de L'Art Nouveau Bing at the Exposition Universelle of 1900 in Paris. For the remainder of his career de Feure focused on furniture design, interiors, painting, and applied arts. He died during the German occupation of Paris in 1943.

225

Loïe Fuller, 1895, lithograph in orange, yellow orange, sea green, dark green, Prussian blue, blue green, turquoise, and lilac brown, 124.1 x 88.6 cm (48 ⅞ x 34 ⅞) sheet. Los Angeles County Museum of Art, Kurt J. Wagner, M.D., and C. Kathleen Wagner Collection, M.87.294.25

Jean-Louis Forain

French; Reims 1852–Paris 1931

Forain belonged to the generation of artists that followed Degas and Manet but was older than Lautrec and Anquetin; he was friendly with both groups. He exhibited with the impressionists beginning in 1879 and returned in 1880, 1881, and 1886. He was greatly influenced by Degas, and the two shared many of the same themes: the racetrack, opera, theater, ballet, and brothel (fig. 241). He began to make prints and illustrations in the 1870s, an activity that earned him wide renown. He contributed to periodicals such as *Le Courrier français, La Vie parisienne,* and *Le Rire* as well as political journals like *L'Echo de Paris, Le Journal,* and *Le Figaro.* His biting satire on the decadent exploits of the bourgeoisie earned him the sobriquet "the Juvenal of the *Figaro.*"

Toulouse-Lautrec probably met Forain shortly after settling in Paris in 1882. Forain had a studio in the same building as one of Lautrec's early art teachers, René Princeteau, and Lautrec's father, Alphonse, was friendly with Forain, who had painted his portrait in watercolor

around 1885. Lautrec would also have encountered Forain at the Chat Noir and the offices of *Le Courrier français,* and they had many Montmartre friends in common. Lautrec admired Forain, and his early work shows much of older artist's influence in both style and content.

Forain was an ardent anti-Semite and published caustic caricatures during the Dreyfus Affair in the journal *Psst!* that he cofounded with Caran d'Ache. Henri-Gabriel Ibels, in a remarkable journalistic dialogue, countered Forain's anti-Semitic drawings with illustrations of his own in *Le Sifflet.* After 1900 Forain concentrated on paintings of the legal courts. He served as the president of the Société Nationale des Beaux-Arts and was a member of the Académie Française.

241

The Client, 1878, pencil, watercolor, and gouache on paper, 24.7 x 32.8 cm (9 ¾ x 12 ¹⁵/₁₆). Collection of The Dixon Gallery and Gardens, Memphis, Tennessee; Museum purchase, 1993.7.1

Vincent van Gogh

Dutch; Zundert 1853–Auvers-sur-Oise 1890

The legendary painter Vincent van Gogh came to art late in life after a series of failed careers. It was not until he was twenty-seven years old that he committed himself fully to his calling as an artist. After living in remote areas of Holland and Belgium and studying art on his own, he arrived in Paris at the beginning of March 1886 to live with his brother, Theo van Gogh, an art dealer in Montmartre. In Paris he encountered the work of the impressionists for the first time and rapidly incorporated their chromatic lessons, creating scenes of Montmartre using their lighter palette and broken brushstroke (fig. 72).

Van Gogh enrolled at the atelier of Fernand Cormon in March, where he met Lautrec, Anquetin, and Bernard. Despite their different temperaments, Van Gogh and Lautrec forged an unlikely friendship. The irreverent Frenchman would invite the intense Dutchman to his studio for informal gatherings, where Van Gogh's shyness was noted by a contemporary: "He would arrive carrying a heavy canvas under this arm, which he would place in a well-lighted corner, and wait for someone to take notice of him. No one was the least concerned. He would sit down opposite his work, surveying the others' glances and sharing little in the conversation. Finally wearying, he would depart, carrying this latest example of his work. Nevertheless, the following week he would return and commence the same stratagem yet again" (Frey 1994, 232).

In 1886 Lautrec invited Van Gogh to Aristide Bruant's cabaret, the Mirliton, to see the unveiling of *The Quadrille of the Louis XIII Chair at the Elysée-Montmartre* (fig. 49). The following year Lautrec created a sensitive pastel portrait of Van Gogh (fig. 88), which he exchanged for the latter's view of rue Lépic (fig. 73). During these Paris years the two artists also painted similar themes, including women at café tables: Van Gogh's *Agostina Segatori at the Café du Tambourin* (fig. 90) has much in common with Lautrec's *Young Woman at a Table, "Poudre de riz" (Rice Powder)* (fig. 82) of the same year, which Theo van Gogh purchased for his own collection.

Van Gogh left the capital for Arles in the south of France in February 1888, but he stayed in touch with the Paris art world through correspondence with his brother, asking about the work of Lautrec. After a short but very intense and productive partnership with Gauguin in the autumn of that year, Van Gogh's health failed, and he voluntarily entered an asylum in St-Rémy in the spring of 1889. In January 1890 he sent six paintings to the seventh annual exhibition of Les xx in Brussels. At the opening (which Van Gogh did not attend) the Belgian artist Henry de Groux called him "an ignoramus and a charlatan," but Lautrec leapt to his friend's defense and challenged de Groux to a duel. Eventually de Groux backed down and resigned from Les xx.

His health waning, Van Gogh moved to Auvers-sur-Oise, twenty miles northwest of Paris in May 1890. Lautrec saw him for the last time in Paris on 6 July, just three weeks before Van Gogh took his own life. Lautrec, unable to attend the funeral, sent his condolences to Theo, writing, "You know what a friend [your brother] was to me and how anxious he was to prove it. Unfortunately, I can acknowledge all this only by shaking your hand cordially in front of a coffin. . . ." (Schimmel ed. 1991, no. 176).

71

A Corner of Montmartre: The Moulin à Poivre, 1887, oil on canvas, 35 x 64.5 cm (13 ¾ x 25 ⅜). Van Gogh Museum Amsterdam (Vincent van Gogh Foundation), s 14 V/1962 Faille 347

72

Terrace and Observation Deck at the Moulin de Blute-Fin, Montmartre, 1886, oil on canvas, mounted on pressboard, 43.6 x 33 cm (17 ⅛ x 13). The Art Institute of Chicago, Helen Birch Bartlett Memorial Collection, 1926.202 Faille 347

89

Glass of Absinthe and a Carafe, 1887, oil on canvas, 46.5 x 33 cm (18 ⁵⁄₁₆ x 13). Van Gogh Museum Amsterdam (Vincent van Gogh Foundation), s 186 V/1962 Faille 339

90

Agostina Segatori at the Café du Tambourin, 1887, oil on canvas, 55 x 46.5 cm (21 ⅝ x 18 ⁵⁄₁₆). Van Gogh Museum Amsterdam (Vincent van Gogh Foundation), s 17 V/1962 Faille 370

Joseph Granié

French; Toulouse 1866–1915

A student of Jean-Léon Gérôme at the Ecole des Beaux-Arts de Paris, Granié was a painter who specialized in religious subjects, interiors, and portraits. Some of his portraits, including that of Yvette Guilbert, feature gold backgrounds (fig. 192). He was renowned for his exquisite draftsmanship.

192

Yvette Guilbert, 1895, oil on panel, 41 x 31 cm (16 ⅛ x 12 ³⁄₁₆). Musée d'Orsay, Paris; gift of Max Schiller, 1947, RF. 1977-187

Gravelle

Almost nothing is known about the artist whose caricature of Aristide Bruant adorns the cover of the June 1903 issue of *Le Mirliton* (fig. 48).

48

"Tous les Clients sont des Cochons!" ("All the Clients Are Pigs!"), cover for *Le Mirliton*, June 1903, color photorelief, 29.2 x 20 x 4.2 cm (11 ½ x 7 ⅞ x 1 ⅝). The Jane Voorhees Zimmerli Art Museum, Rutgers, The State University of New Jersey, Herbert D. and Ruth Schimmel Museum Library Fund, 1990.0736.001

Jules Alexandre Grün

French; Paris 1868–Paris 1934

A painter, pastelist, illustrator, and poster designer, Grün was a member of the Chat Noir circle. He made silhouettes for the shadow theater and took part in many productions. He contributed illustrations to Montmartre publications such as *La Caricature, Fin de siècle,* and *Le Courrier français.* His posters are characterized by bold use of black and white, often with red as the secondary color, as seen in his poster advertising a guidebook to Montmartre (fig. 95).

95

"Guide de l'Etranger à Montmartre," 1900, color lithograph, 60 x 40.5 cm (23 ⅝ x 15 ¹⁵⁄₁₆). The Jane Voorhees Zimmerli Art Museum, Rutgers, The State University of New Jersey, David A. and Mildred H. Morse Art Acquisition Fund, 1995.0127

Henri-Gabriel Ibels

French; Paris 1867–Paris 1936

Ibels studied at the Académie Julian in Paris, where he met Pierre Bonnard and Edouard Vuillard and helped found the artistic group the Nabis in 1889. Unlike his fellow Nabis, who were interested in the symbolic representation of nature, Ibels focused on the everyday life of Paris and Montmartre, depicting bars, cafés-concerts, circuses, and the boxing ring. He first exhibited with Toulouse-Lautrec in 1891, when critics noticed affinities between their work. In 1893 André Marty commissioned Ibels and Lautrec to create a lithographic album portraying the life of the café-concert (fig. 165a–k).

A prolific illustrator, Ibels contributed to numerous Montmartre journals, including *Le Mirliton, L'Escarmouche, La Revue blanche,* and *La Plume,* as well as designing song sheets and theater programs. Like many other Montmartre artists, Ibels was also a poster designer. His first major color poster, for the café-concert singer Mévisto (fig. 171), appeared in 1892 and was followed by a poster advertising the first exhibition of the Salon des Cent in 1894. Ibels was awarded the Legion of Honor in 1913 in recognition of his successful career as an illustrator and lithographer.

165

Le Café-Concert, 1893, portfolio of twenty-two lithographs, lithographs by Henri-Gabriel Ibels and Henri de Toulouse-Lautrec, text by Georges Montorgueil, published by *L'Estampe originale,* Paris. Lithographs on wove paper, various sizes up to 44.0 x 32.0 cm, in a cover, 44.2 x 32.5 cm, illustrated with a lithograph by Ibels with text in red.

165a

Portfolio Cover for *Le Café-Concert,* 1893, bifold portfolio cover with black lithographic image and red letterpress text on heavy cream wove paper

37.8 x 26.7 cm (14 ⅞ x 10 ½) image; 44.5 x 33.5 cm (17 ½ x 13 ³⁄₁₆) sheet. National Gallery of Art, Washington, Rosenwald Collection, 1947.7.160
(Washington only)

44.3 x 33 cm (17 ⁷⁄₁₆ x 13) approximately. The Art Institute of Chicago, Gift of Horace M. Swope, 1938.1140
(Chicago only)

165b

Jeanne Bloch, 1893, lithograph in black on ivory wove paper

28.5 x 22.6 cm (11 ¼ x 8 ⅞) image; 44.3 x 31.8 cm (17 ⁷⁄₁₆ x 12 ½) sheet. National Gallery of Art, Washington, Rosenwald Collection, 1947.7.172
(Washington only)

29 x 22.4 cm (11 ⁷⁄₁₆ x 8 ¹³⁄₁₆) image, approximately; 44.1 x 31.7 cm (17 ⅜ x 12 ½) sheet. The Art Institute of Chicago, Gift of Horace M. Swope, 1938.1147
(Chicago only)

165c

Marcel Legay, 1893, lithograph in black on ivory wove paper

36.1 x 23.7 cm (14 ³⁄₁₆ x 9 ⁵⁄₁₆) image; 43 x 32 cm (16 ¹⁵⁄₁₆ x 12 ⅝) sheet. National Gallery of Art, Washington, Rosenwald Collection, 1947.7.173
(Washington only)

36 x 23.7 cm (14 ³⁄₁₆ x 9 ⁵⁄₁₆) image, approximately; 44.2 x 32 cm (17 ⅜ x 12 ⅝) sheet. The Art Institute of Chicago, Gift of Horace M. Swope, 1938.1149
(Chicago only)

165d

Libert, 1893, lithograph in black on ivory wove paper

35 x 24.7 cm (13 ¾ x 9 ¾) image; 44.1 x 31.6 cm (17 ⅜ x 12 ⁷⁄₁₆) sheet. National Gallery of Art, Washington, Rosenwald Collection, 1947.7.174
(Washington only)

36 x 25.2 cm (14 ³⁄₁₆ x 9 ¹⁵⁄₁₆) image, approximately; 44.2 x 32 cm (17 ⅜ x 12 ⅝) sheet. The Art Institute of Chicago, Gift of Horace M. Swope, 1938.1144
(Chicago only)

165e

Mévisto, 1893, lithograph in dark green on ivory wove paper

35.5 x 19.5 cm (14 x 7 ¹¹⁄₁₆) image; 44.1 x 31.8 cm (17 ⅜ x 12 ½) sheet. National Gallery of Art, Washington, Rosenwald Collection, 1947.7.175
(Washington only)

35 x 20.3 cm (13 ¾ x 8) image, approximately; 44.3 x 31.7 cm (17 ⁷⁄₁₆ x 12 ½) sheet. The Art Institute of Chicago, Gift of Horace M. Swope, 1938.1148
(Chicago only)

165f

Paulus, 1893, lithograph in black on ivory wove paper

22.8 x 15 cm (9 x 5 ⅞) image; 43.8 x 32 cm (17 ¼ x 12 ⅝) sheet. National Gallery of Art, Washington, Rosenwald Collection, 1947.7.176
(Washington only)

22.8 x 14.3 cm (9 x 5 ⅝) image, approximately; 43.7 x 31.9 cm (17 ³⁄₁₆ x 12 ⁹⁄₁₆) sheet. The Art Institute of Chicago, Gift of Horace M. Swope, 1938.1150
(Chicago only)

165g

Anna Thibaud, 1893, lithograph in black on ivory wove paper

20 x 9.6 cm (7 ⅞ x 3 ¾) image; 44 x 32.1 cm (17 ⁵⁄₁₆ x 12 ⅝) sheet. National Gallery of Art, Washington, Rosenwald Collection, 1947.7.177
(Washington only)

19.3 x 94 cm (7 ⅝ x 37) image, approximately; 44 x 32.1 cm (17 ⁵⁄₁₆ x 12 ⅝) sheet. The Art Institute of Chicago, Gift of Horace M. Swope, 1938.1146
(Chicago only)

165h

Emilienne d'Alençon Rehearsing at the Folies-Bergère, 1893, lithograph in black on ivory wove paper

30.8 x 23 cm (12 ⅛ x 9 ¹⁄₁₆) image; 43.8 x 31.8 cm (17 ¼ x 12 ½) sheet. National Gallery of Art, Washington, Rosenwald Collection, 1947.7.178
(Washington only)

30.8 x 22.7 cm (12 ⅛ x 8 ¹⁵⁄₁₆) image, approximately; 42.8 x 31.9 cm (16 ⅞ x 12 ⁹⁄₁₆) sheet. The Art Institute of Chicago, Gift of Horace M. Swope, 1938.1145
(Chicago only)

165i

Polin, 1893, lithograph in black on ivory wove paper

23.3 x 11.3 cm (9 ³⁄₁₆ x 4 ⁷⁄₁₆) image; 44.1 x 31.8 cm (17 ⅜ x 12 ½) sheet. National Gallery of Art, Washington, Rosenwald Collection, 1947.7.179
(Washington only)

23.2 x 11.1 cm (9 ⅛ x 4 ⅜) image, approximately; 43.7 x 31.8 cm (17 ³⁄₁₆ x 12 ½) sheet. The Art Institute of Chicago, Gift of Horace M. Swope, 1938.1141
(Chicago only)

165j

Kam-Hill, 1893, lithograph in black on ivory wove paper

27.7 x 21.3 cm (10 ⅞ x 8 ⅜) image; 43.5 x 32 cm (17 ⅛ x 12 ⅝) sheet. National Gallery of Art, Washington, Rosenwald Collection, 1947.7.180
(Washington only)

28.2 x 22 cm (11 ⅛ x 8 ¹¹⁄₁₆) image, approximately; 43.5 x 32 cm (17 ⅛ x 12 ⅝) sheet. The Art Institute of Chicago, Gift of Horace M. Swope, 1938.1142
(Chicago only)

165k

Ouvrard, 1893, lithograph in black on ivory wove paper

34.3 x 24 cm (13 ½ x 9 ⁷/₁₆) image; 43 x 32.2 cm (16 ¹⁵/₁₆ x 12 ¹¹/₁₆) sheet. National Gallery of Art, Washington, Rosenwald Collection, 1947.7.181 *(Washington only)*

34.3 x 23.9 cm (13 ½ x 9 ⁷/₁₆) image, approximately; 43.4 x 31.9 cm (17 ¹/₁₆ x 12 ⁹/₁₆) sheet. The Art Institute of Chicago, Gift of Horace M. Swope, 1938.1143 *(Chicago only)*

166

Le Café-Concert, 1892, pastel, 48.7 x 31 cm (19 ³/₁₆ x 12 ³/₁₆). The Jane Voorhees Zimmerli Art Museum, Rutgers, The State University of New Jersey, Norma B. Bartman Purchase Fund, 1987.0347

167

Le Café-Concert, 1893, lithograph, 35.5 x 27.4 cm (14 x 10 ¹³/₁₆). The Jane Voorhees Zimmerli Art Museum, Rutgers, The State University of New Jersey, Herbert Littman Purchase Fund, 1986.0886

168

Study for *"Les Bas noirs,"* c. 1895, pastel, 23.5 x 15 cm (9 ¼ x 5 ⅞). The Jane Voorhees Zimmerli Art Museum, Rutgers, The State University of New Jersey, Lillian Lilien Memorial Art Acquisition Fund, 1984.023.002

169

"Des Bas noirs" (song sheet), c. 1895, color lithograph, 27 x 17.7 cm (10 ⅝ x 6 ¹⁵/₁₆). Private collection

170

"Coeur meurtri" (song sheet), c. 1892–1895, color lithograph, 27 x 35 cm (10 ⅝ x 13 ¾). The Jane Voorhees Zimmerli Art Museum, Rutgers, The State University of New Jersey, Herbert D. and Ruth Schimmel Art Purchase Fund, 1991.0061

171

Mévisto: Concert la Gaïété, 1892, color lithograph, 168.8 x 118.5 cm (66 ⁷/₁₆ x 46 ⅝). The Jane Voorhees Zimmerli Art Museum, Rutgers, The State University of New Jersey, Friends Purchase Fund, 1976.031.006

263

Study for "L'Eventail du cirque," 1896, ink and graphite on paper, 43 x 68.6 cm (17 ¹/₁₆ x 27). Collection of Carleton A. Holstrom and Mary Beth Kineke

Eero Järnefelt

Finnish; Vyborg 1863–Helsinki 1937

Järnefelt's training took him from Helsinki to St. Petersburg and eventually to Paris. In Paris he and other younger painters in the colony of Scandinavian artists studied at the Académie Julian in the mid-1880s, where they studied with Jules Bastien-Lepage, whose realism they admired. *Le Franc, Wine Merchant, Boulevard de Clichy* (fig. 17) is a pivotal work in Järnefelt's oeuvre, the first he painted in his modern style. Its lower-class urban subject and uncompromising presentation are allied to contemporary work by Lautrec (fig. 18, 19), Van Gogh (fig. 90), Vuillard (fig. 94), and Louis Valtat (fig. 112).

17

Le Franc, Wine Merchant, Boulevard de Clichy, 1888, oil on canvas, 61 x 74 cm (24 x 29 ⅛). Ateneum Art Museum, Collection Antell, Finnish National Gallery, Helsinki, A II 1278

Henri Gustave Jossot

French; Dijon 1866–Sidi Bou Saïd, Tunisia 1951

The anarchist Jossot exhibited widely in Paris in the 1890s and the first decade of the twentieth century as a painter, draftsman, caricaturist, and printmaker. During this period he collaborated with many Paris journals, including *L'Epreuve, La Plume, Le Rire,* and *L'Estampe originale.* About the poster in this exhibition (fig. 197) he wrote, "The poster on the wall must howl, it has to force itself on the glance of the passerby.
I have to say without self-conceit that I have done an immense advertisement for the house of Saupiquet, doing as much with my noisy colors as with my grotesque drawing pushed almost to the monstrous" (Lelieur and Bachollet 1989, 124). Jossot settled in Tunisia in 1910 and converted to Islam three years later, taking the name Abdul Karim Jossot. Thereafter, he turned his attention to orientalist drawings in graphite and ink wash.

197

Jockey-Club Sardines, 1897, lithograph in orange-red, black, yellow, blue, and green on tan wove paper, 125.5 x 201 cm (49 ⁷/₁₆ x 79 ⅛) sheet. The Art Institute of Chicago, Gift of Peter Kort Zegers in memory of his brother Hans Zegers (1943–2000), 2000.448

L. Lagarte

Lagarte was the illustrator of *Paris-Cythère: Etude des moeurs parisiennes* by Maurice Delsol.

140

Moulin Rouge: The Entrance, and other illustrations of the Moulin Rouge in Maurice Delsol's *Paris-Cythère,* n.d., photorelief, 18.5 x 12.3 x 1.5 cm (7 ⁵/₁₆ x 4 ¹³/₁₆ x ⁹/₁₆) closed. The Jane Voorhees Zimmerli Art Museum, Rutgers, The State University of New Jersey, Herbert D. and Ruth Schimmel Museum Library Fund, 1993.0379

Charles-Lucien Léandre

French; Champsecret 1862–Paris 1930 or 1934

A student of Alexandre Cabanel, Léandre was a painter, illustrator, lithographer, and portraitist in the circle of the Chat Noir. He contributed to many Montmartre journals, including *Le Chat Noir* and *Le Rire.* Together with Louis Morin, he founded the Société des Humoristes. He was best known for his illustrations and cartoons in the popular press as well as for caricatures of artists and stars like Lautrec and Yvette Guilbert (fig. 181).

44

Henri de Toulouse-Lautrec, c. 1896–1897, graphite, 47.3 x 31.4 cm (18 ⅝ x 12 ⅜). The Jane Voorhees Zimmerli Art Museum, Rutgers, The State University of New Jersey, Acquired with the Herbert D. and Ruth Schimmel Museum Library Fund, 1992.1367

181

Yvette Guilbert, c. 1892–1894, graphite, 20.3 x 15.2 cm (8 x 6). The Jane Voorhees Zimmerli Art Museum, Rutgers, The State University of New Jersey, Anonymous Donation, 2001.1491

Lucien Lemariey

French; active late nineteenth century

Lemariey was apparently a commercial artist whose production is unknown except for the design of a fan advertising Loïe Fuller's 150th performance at the Folies-Bergère (fig. 222). His work was commissioned by the Maison Duvelleroy, a firm that specialized in the manufacture of fans. Lemariey based the central motif, Loïe Fuller dancing, on an 1893 *carte-de-visite* photograph by Leopold Reutlinger.

222

La Loïe Fuller, 1893, printed paper fan, 32.3 x 60 cm (12 ^{11}⁄$_{16}$ x 23 ^{5}⁄$_{8}$). Musée Carnavalet—Histoire de Paris, Ev. 720

Maximilien Luce

French; Paris 1858—Rolleboise 1941

Studies at the Académie Suisse and in the studio of Carolus-Duran brought Luce into impressionist circles in the early 1880s, and by 1885 he had become an adherent of the neo-impressionist style originated by Georges Seurat. Luce exhibited regularly at the Salon des Indépendants beginning in 1887, the year he painted *View from Montmartre* (fig. 70). A resident of Montmartre until 1904, Luce was acutely sympathetic to the plight of the urban poor and shared the anarchist politics of Camille Pissarro.

70

View from Montmartre, 1887, oil on canvas, 54 x 63 cm (21 ¼ x 24 ^{13}⁄$_{16}$). Petit Palais, Musée d'art moderne, Geneva, 16

Edouard Manet

French; Paris 1832—Paris 1882

Edouard Manet is perhaps most notable for introducing a new era of urban subject matter into modern art. In 1850 Manet enrolled in the atelier of Thomas Couture, where he remained for six years. During this time he visited museums throughout Europe, studying the works of the old masters. His early paintings are dark in tone and indebted notably to Velázquez, Rubens, and the Italian Renaissance masters.

Although viewed as the leader of a "school" that included Edgar Degas and the younger impressionists whom he saw regularly at the Café Guerbois, and later at the Café de la Nouvelle-Athènes in the place Pigalle, Manet never exhibited with them. In his paintings of the early 1870s he did begin to adopt a lighter palette and more fluid brushwork, due in no small part to his association with these younger painters.

85

Plum Brandy, c. 1877, oil on canvas, 73.6 x 50.2 cm (29 x 19 ¾). National Gallery of Art, Washington, Collection of Mr. and Mrs. Paul Mellon, 1971.85.1 Rouart and Wildenstein 282

Charles Maurin

French; Puy-en-Velay 1856—Grasse 1914

Maurin was classically trained at the Académie Julian, exhibited at the official Salon in the early 1880s, and began to teach at the Académie Julian in 1885. There he is reported to have met Lautrec, who often visited the studio, and the two became boon companions who together regularly patronized the Moulin Rouge and other Montmartre cafés, bars, and dance halls. As Lautrec planned an exhibition of his work in 1893, he invited Maurin to join him. That show, which garnered considerable attention for the uncompromising realism of Lautrec's work, is chiefly remembered anecdotally: Lautrec idolized Degas and invited him to attend the opening. Although Degas came, he remarked to his companion, a patron, that Lautrec was merely "the Gavarni of his time" and advised him to collect the work of Maurin.

A dedicated and innovative printmaker, Maurin's experiments in the application of color in lithography and etching were important for Lautrec's own, particularly for the *Elles* series (fig. 259b–l, 258, 259b–l, 259a). Maurin also created a group of ten or so pastels depicting Loïe Fuller's glamorous performances, three of which are included in this exhibition (fig. 219–221).

219

Loïe Fuller, c. 1895, pastel, 63 x 47 cm (24 ^{13}⁄$_{16}$ x 18 ½). The Jane Voorhees Zimmerli Art Museum, Rutgers, The State University of New Jersey, Regina Best Heldrich Art Acquisition Fund, 2001.0218

220

Loïe Fuller, c. 1895, pastel, 63 x 47 cm (24 ^{13}⁄$_{16}$ x 18 ½). The Jane Voorhees Zimmerli Art Museum, Rutgers, The State University of New Jersey, Regina Best Heldrich Art Acquisition Fund, 2001.0219

221

Loïe Fuller, c. 1895, pastel and charcoal, 65.8 x 53.2 cm (25 ⅞ x 20 ^{15}⁄$_{16}$). The Jane Voorhees Zimmerli Art Museum, Rutgers, The State University of New Jersey, Regina Best Heldrich Art Acquisition Fund, 2001.0220

Georges Meunier

French; Paris 1869—Saint-Cloud 1934

A painter, printmaker, and illustrator, Meunier contributed to the Montmartre journals *Le Rire* and *L'Assiette au Beurre*. He also created programs for cafés-concerts like the Eldorado.

156

Eldorado (program), 1894, color photorelief, 27 x 36.5 cm (10 ⅝ x 14 ⅜). The Jane Voorhees Zimmerli Art Museum, Rutgers, The State University of New Jersey, Gift of Herbert D. and Ruth Schimmel, 1990.0140

Ferdinand Misti-Mifliez

French; Paris 1865—Neuilly 1923

French illustrator and poster maker Ferdinand Mifliez was a student of Edmond Lechevallier-Chevignard at the Ecole des Arts Décoratifs in Paris. He exhibited under the pseudonym "Ferdinand Misti-Mifliez" at the Salon des Artistes Français as well as the Salon des Humoristes. In addition to posters, he produced color lithographic programs for dance halls and cafés-concerts (fig. 132, 157).

132

Moulin Rouge (program), 1895, color photorelief, 27 x 36.7 cm (10 ⅝ x 14 ⁷⁄₁₆). The Jane Voorhees Zimmerli Art Museum, Rutgers, The State University of New Jersey, Gift of Herbert D. and Ruth Schimmel, 1987.0461

157

Olympia: Music Hall (program), 1896, color photorelief, 23.9 x 36.4 cm (9 ⁷⁄₁₆ x 14 ⁵⁄₁₆). The Jane Voorhees Zimmerli Art Museum, Rutgers, The State University of New Jersey, Gift of Herbert D. and Ruth Schimmel, 1987.0460

Louis Morin

French; Paris 1855 – Migennes 1938

A talented illustrator, painter, and designer, Morin founded the Salon des Humoristes together with Charles Léandre. He contributed to journals and was known for his scenes of lusty Montmartre. He was an active member of the Chat Noir circle and designed zinc silhouettes for the shadow theater. His book *Théâtre du Chat Noir* is an album of ink and crayon drawings for plays (fig. 100).

100

Théâtre du Chat Noir, n.d., album of ink and crayon drawings for plays and programs for plays, 32.5 x 25.5 x 2.5 cm (12 ¹³⁄₁₆ x 10 ¹⁄₁₆ x 1). The Jane Voorhees Zimmerli Art Museum, Rutgers, The State University of New Jersey, Joyce and Alvin Glassgold Fund, 2001.0494

Henri Eugène Nocq

French; born Paris 1868

Nocq was a painter, sculptor, jeweler, and engraver of medals, who designed a ceramic tondo of Yvette Guilbert in 1893 (fig. 195). He and Lautrec were acquainted by 1896, when Lautrec wrote to him about his theories on art: "We could summarize the following *desideratum:* Fewer artists and more *good workers.* In a word: more craft" (Schimmel 1991, no. 463). Lautrec's portrait of Nocq (fig. 79) shows the artist posed in Lautrec's studio before the unfinished canvas of *Marcelle Lender Dancing the Bolero in "Chilpéric"* (fig. 227).

195

Yvette Guilbert, 1893, ceramic plaque (tondo), in original oak frame, 40 cm (15 ¾) diameter; 54.4 cm (21 ⁷⁄₁₆) diameter; depth: 2.7 cm (1 ¹⁄₁₆) with frame. Musée d'Orsay, Paris, OAO 1371

Manuel Orazi

Italian, active in France; Rome 1860 – Paris 1934

A painter, illustrator, and poster designer, Orazi contributed to many illustrated journals in Paris, including *Le Figaro illustré, L'Assiette au beurre,* and *Je sais tout.* His posters show the influence of the art nouveau movement, as seen in his poster for Loïe Fuller's theater at the 1900 Exposition Universelle in Paris (fig. 226).

226

Théâtre de Loïe Fuller, 1900, color lithograph, 202 x 63.5 cm (79 ½ x 25). The Jane Voorhees Zimmerli Art Museum, Rutgers, The State University of New Jersey, Acquired with the Brother International Corporation, 1997.0199

Pal [Jean de Paléologue]

Romanian; born in Bucharest 1855 or 1860, active in France

Pal, a painter and poster artist, lived in London before settling in Paris in 1893. His illustrations appeared in such Paris journals as *La Plume, Le Rire, Cocorico,* and *Le Frou-Frou* as well as foreign publications like *Vanity Fair, New York Herald Tribune,* and *Strand Magazine.* He designed many posters for the cycling industry as well as for cafés-concerts such as the Olympia and the Folies-Bergère, where Loïe Fuller appeared in 1894 (fig. 224).

224

Loïe Fuller, c. 1894, lithograph in red, yellow, blue, and light green, 121.9 x 83.8 cm (48 x 33). Los Angeles County Museum of Art, Kurt J. Wagner, M.D., and C. Kathleen Wagner Collection, M.87.294.47

Pablo Picasso

Spanish; Málaga 1881 – Mougins 1973

This protean artist received his first lessons in 1888 from his father, José Ruiz Blasco, a painter and teacher at the Escuela Provincial de Bellas Artes in Málaga and later in La Coruña. In 1895 the family moved to Barcelona, and Picasso entered the Escuela de Bellas Artes there, though he attended sporadically. After a period in Madrid and Horta de Ebro, he returned to Barcelona in February 1899 and began to frequent Els Quatre Gats, a café that served as a meeting place for the Catalan modernist movement. In his early art Picasso embraced a range of influences, from French art nouveau to the work of modern artists such as Steinlen, Degas, and particularly Toulouse-Lautrec, with whom he shared a sardonic vision.

Picasso made his first trip to Paris in October 1900 when his painting *Last Moments* (destroyed) was selected for the Exposition Universelle. He remained there through December, then made a second visit from May 1901 to January 1902, and a third from October 1902 to January 1903. Although Picasso benefited greatly from the artistic atmosphere in Paris and his circle of friends, he felt a degree of isolation that is reflected in his depiction of the Paris demimonde and his sympathetic portrayal of social outcasts. The garish colors and strident tone of many of these early works eventually gave way to the cool palette and melancholy mood of his "Blue period," which lasted from 1901 to 1904.

In 1904 Picasso settled in Paris permanently, taking up residence in Montmartre. Following his Blue period he began to explore primitivism, and from 1906 on, he and Georges Braque jointly developed the radical new style of cubism. Extremely prolific, Picasso left behind a rich and varied oeuvre and stands as one of the dominant artistic figures of the twentieth century.

151

The Moulin de la Galette, 1900, oil on canvas, 88.2 x 115.5 cm (34 ¾ x 45 ½). Solomon R. Guggenheim Museum, New York, Thannhauser Collection, Gift, Justin K. Thannhauser, 1978
(Washington only)

152

Divan Japonais, 1901, oil on cardboard, mounted on panel, 69.9 x 53 cm (27 ½ x 21). Mugrabi Collection, 1218 P24

174

Jardin de Paris, 1901, brush and ink and watercolor on paper, 64.8 x 49.5 cm (25 ½ x 19 ½). Lent by The Metropolitan Museum of Art, Gift of Raymonde Paul, in memory of her Brother, C. Michael Paul, 1982.179.17

203

The Blue Room, 1901, oil on canvas, 50.4 x 61.5 cm (19 ⅞ x 24 ¼). The Phillips Collection, Washington, D.C., 1554

244

Nude with Stockings, 1901, oil on cardboard, 66.5 x 52 cm (26 ³⁄₁₆ x 20 ½). Musée des Beaux-Arts de Lyon, 1997.44

Pierre Puvis de Chavannes

French; Lyon 1824 – Paris 1898

Born to a wealthy bourgeois family, Puvis de Chavannes was a painter known primarily for his large decorative projects. He decided to become an artist following an extended trip to Italy in 1846. Although he passed through several artists' studios, including those of Henry Scheffer and Thomas Couture, Puvis was largely self-taught. His earliest works are history paintings executed in a somber style, but he eventually turned to the creation of large-scale murals.

Puvis exhibited regularly at the Paris Salon, showing both decorative works and easel paintings. His mature style was distinctive, marked by a simplification of form and a delicate palette that owed much to the Italian muralists of the fifteenth and sixteenth centuries, most notably Piero della Francesco; his subject matter often veered into the allegorical. Critics were divided between ardent admirers and those who decried the lack of realism. When Puvis exhibited his painting *The Sacred Grove* in 1884 (a smaller version of this painting is included in the present exhibition; fig. 20), it was avidly discussed in Fernand Cormon's studio. Toulouse-Lautrec painted a parody of the work in response (fig. 21).

Despite his detractors, Puvis became one of the most celebrated artists of his day. Along with Ernest Meissonier and Auguste Rodin, he founded the Société Nationale des Beaux-Arts in 1890, and he received every official honor that could be granted to an artist. Generally considered a precursor of symbolism, Puvis was independent of any contemporary movement, and his works were admired by not only academic but avant-garde artists. His influence both during and after his lifetime was considerable in France as well as abroad.

20

The Sacred Grove, Beloved of the Arts and Muses, 1884–1889, oil on canvas, 93 x 231 cm (36 ⁷⁄₁₆ x 90 ¹⁵⁄₁₆). The Art Institute of Chicago, Potter Palmer Collection, 1922.445 *(Chicago only)*

Jean-François Raffaëlli

French; Lyon 1850 – Paris 1924

After a brief stint as an actor, Raffaëlli studied art in Jean-Léon Gérôme's studio and debuted at the Salon of 1870. A genre painter, Raffaëlli became interested in naturalist themes and exhibited with the impressionists in 1880 and 1881 at the invitation of Degas, whose preference for subjects of modern life Raffaëlli shared. Lautrec reportedly admired the graphic quality of the paintings Raffaëlli showed, works such as *Absinthe Drinkers* (private collection), as well as the gritty realism of his depiction of urban and suburban poverty. Raffaëlli's album *Les Types de Paris* was published in 1889, and his 1890 one-man exhibition at Boussod and Valadon opened with paintings of the lower classes, images that the artist identified as "types." *The Naturalist Quadrille at the Ambassadeurs* (fig. 55) is one of his illustrations for "Les Cafés Concerts" by Maurice Vaucaire, published in *Paris illustré* in August 1886.

55

The Naturalist Quadrille at the Ambassadeurs, illustration in *Paris illustré*, 1 August 1886, color photorelief, 45 x 32 cm (17 ¹¹⁄₁₆ x 12 ⅝). The Jane Voorhees Zimmerli Art Museum, Rutgers, The State University of New Jersey, Gift of Herbert D. and Ruth Schimmel, 1994.0380

Georges Redon

French; Paris 1869 – Paris 1943

Georges Redon was a painter, engraver, and lithographer who specialized in genre subjects. He began to exhibit with the Salon des Artistes Français in 1903, and in 1904 he was awarded an honorable mention. His later work includes illustrations of children in humorous situations, decorated menus, and advertising posters.

105

La Boîte à Musique, 1897, color lithograph, 86.6 x 118.6 cm (34 ⅛ x 46 ¹¹⁄₁₆); 92 x 125 cm (36 ¼ x 49 ³⁄₁₆) with mount. Collection Musée de Montmartre, Paris, A/3776.AF

123

Moulin de la Galette (invitation), 1892, photorelief with pen and ink, 12 x 21 cm (4 ¾ x 8 ¼). The Jane Voorhees Zimmerli Art Museum, Rutgers, The State University of New Jersey, Gift of Herbert D. and Ruth Schimmel, 1987.0383

Henri Rivière

French; Paris 1864 – Paris 1951

A Montmartre native, Henri Rivière was a printmaker, illustrator, photographer, theater designer, and director of shadow plays at the Chat Noir. He studied with the academic painter Emile Bin for a short time but received no formal training after Bin's death. Rivière was an active member of the Chat Noir cabaret from its inception in November 1881 and acted as secretary and as one of the illustrators for the journal *Le Chat Noir*. Perhaps more important, he perfected many of the sophisticated techniques of the Chat Noir shadow theater, employing sound, colored lights and paper, and a two-story stage. Rivière's plays *La Tentation de Saint Antoine* (*The Temptation of Saint Anthony*) of 1887 (fig. 38) and *Chat Noir: "La Marche à l'étoile"* (*Journey Following the Star*) of 1890 (fig. 102) were among the most successful productions of the Chat Noir.

Rivière was an active member of the original print movement of the 1890s. He is represented with the color lithograph *The Wave* in *L'Estampe originale*, and he produced several series of prints in color woodcut and color lithography, inspired by Japanese *ukiyo-e* woodcut prints. Incorporating lessons of Japanese prints, he created in 1902 the album of color lithographs entitled *Thirty-six Views of the Eiffel Tower*, inspired by Hokusai's woodblock print album *Thirty-six Views of Mount Fuji*.

38

The Sky, illustration in *La Tentation de Saint Antoine,* 1888, stencil-colored photorelief, 24 x 32 cm (9 7/16 x 12 5/8). The Jane Voorhees Zimmerli Art Museum, Rutgers, The State University of New Jersey, Norma B. Bartman Purchase Fund, 1986.1670.0001-045

101d

The Temptation of Saint Anthony, silhouette for the shadow play *La Tentation de Saint Antoine,* 1887, zinc, 75 x 42 cm (29 1/2 x 16 9/16). The Jane Voorhees Zimmerli Art Museum, Rutgers, The State University of New Jersey, Gift of University College Rutgers New Brunswick Alumni Association, 1986.0081

102

Chat Noir: "La Marche à l'étoile," c. 1890, stencil-colored photorelief, 58 x 41.5 cm (22 13/16 x 16 5/16). The Jane Voorhees Zimmerli Art Museum, Rutgers, The State University of New Jersey, Herbert D. and Ruth Schimmel Museum Library Fund, 1995.0078

103

Chat Noir: "L'Epopée," c. 1890, stencil-colored photorelief, 58 x 41 cm (22 13/16 x 16 1/8). The Jane Voorhees Zimmerli Art Museum, Rutgers, The State University of New Jersey, Herbert D. and Ruth Schimmel Museum Library Fund, 1995.0059

Auguste Roedel

(French; Paris 1859 – Paris 1900)

A friend of Adolphe Willette, Roedel was active as an illustrator, lithographer, and poster artist in the Montmartre circles. He contributed drawings to *Le Courrier français, Le Chat Noir,* and the *Quat'z'Arts* journals and was known for his illustrations and caricatures of Montmartre life. He made many invitations for local dance halls and cafés-concerts of Montmartre (fig. 133, 135, 134, 136).

133

Moulin Rouge: Noël à Montmartre (invitation), 24 December 1897, color photorelief, 16 x 24.6 cm (6 5/16 x 9 11/16). The Jane Voorhees Zimmerli Art Museum, Rutgers, The State University of New Jersey, Gift of Herbert D. and Ruth Schimmel, 1987.0398

134

Moulin Rouge: La Bohème Artistique (invitation), 16 January 1897, color photorelief, 11 x 13.6 cm (4 5/16 x 5 3/8). The Jane Voorhees Zimmerli Art Museum, Rutgers, The State University of New Jersey, Gift of Herbert D. and Ruth Schimmel, 1987.0388

135

Moulin Rouge: A qui la Pomme? (invitation), 10 March 1900, color photorelief, 10.8 x 14 cm (4 1/4 x 5 1/2). The Jane Voorhees Zimmerli Art Museum, Rutgers, The State University of New Jersey, Gift of Herbert D. and Ruth Schimmel, 1987.0396

136

Moulin Rouge: Reprise de la Fête du Printemps (invitation), 13 June 1897, color photorelief, 12.2 x 21 cm (4 13/16 x 8 1/4). The Jane Voorhees Zimmerli Art Museum, Rutgers, The State University of New Jersey, Gift of Herbert D. and Ruth Schimmel, 1987.0399

Santiago Rusiñol i Prats

Spanish; Barcelona 1861 – Aranjuez 1931

Barcelona native Rusiñol went to Paris to finish his art studies. There he roomed with Spanish painter Ignacio Zuloaga and fellow Catalan artist Ramon Casas. Through them he became connected with the avant-garde and began to paint landscapes and scenes of modern urban life in a naturalist or impressionist vein. Starting in 1891 he exhibited at the Salon des Indépendants.

Friendship with Toulouse-Lautrec and Maxime Dethomas introduced Rusiñol into progressive circles of the artistic, musical, and literary world. He described his experiences in correspondence to Spain: writing informally at first, he became a regular columnist in the Barcelona journal *La Vanguardia,* beginning with articles titled "Cartas desde el Molino" (Letters from the Mill) of 1890–1892, in which he wrote of bohemian Paris, particularly in Montmartre and more specifically at the Moulin de la Galette. Rusiñol divided his time between Paris and Barcelona, where, with his lifelong friend Casas, he helped found Els Quatre Gats in 1897 as a café and meeting place for modernist artists and writers, among them Pablo Picasso.

In 1891 Rusiñol visited Sitges, a small Catalan town on the coast south of Barcelona; there, in 1894, he opened El Cau Ferrat to house both his studio and his collection of Spanish art. In later years he specialized in landscapes, giving special emphasis to the gardens and scenery of Spain. He continued to write for journals such as *Els Quatre Gats* and *Pèl y Ploma,* translated Baudelaire, wrote symbolist fiction, and became a dramatist.

125

The Garden of the Moulin de la Galette, 1891, oil on canvas, 61 x 50 cm (24 x 19 11/16). Museo Cau Ferrat (Consorcio del Patrimoni de Sitges), 30.808

129

The Kitchen of the Moulin de la Galette, c. 1890–1891, oil on canvas, 97.5 x 131 cm (38 3/8 x 51 9/16). Museu Nacional d'Art de Catalunya, Barcelona, MNAC/MAM 10897

Henry Somm

French; Rouen 1844 – Paris 1907

François Clement Sommier, known as "Henry Somm," arrived in Paris in 1870 and exhibited two prints and several drawings with the impressionists in 1879. A good friend of Lautrec's, he was also actively involved with the illustrated press, supplying drawings to *Le Chat Noir, Chronique parisienne,* and *Le Rire,* among others. He was best known for his comical illustrations and his drawings and watercolors of fashionable Parisians. His watercolor and gouache of 1892, *Divan Japonais,* was a design for a poster for the orientalist café-concert (fig. 163).

101a

Five Female Figures with a Dog, silhouettes for the shadow play *Le Fils de l'eunuque,* 1887, zinc, 49.5 x 55.6 cm (19 ½ x 21 ⅞). The Jane Voorhees Zimmerli Art Museum, Rutgers, The State University of New Jersey, Mindy and Ramon Tublitz Purchase Fund, 1990.0715

163

Divan Japonais, c. 1890, watercolor and gouache, 49 x 37.2 cm (19 ⁵/₁₆ x 14 ⅝). The Jane Voorhees Zimmerli Art Museum, Rutgers, The State University of New Jersey, Gift of Mr. and Mrs. Herbert Littman, 1983.055.008

Théophile-Alexandre Steinlen

naturalized French; Lausanne 1859 – Paris 1923

A painter, printmaker, poster designer, and illustrator, Steinlen studied at the University of Lausanne and moved to Paris in 1881. He quickly immersed himself in the life of Montmartre, frequenting the Chat Noir where he met such artists as Toulouse-Lautrec, Henri Rivière, Henry Somm, and Adolphe Willette. Steinlen painted two large canvases for the interior of the Chat Noir (fig. 99, 98) and designed a memorable poster for the cabaret in 1896 (fig. 104). Perhaps most important for his career, Steinlen met the singer and songwriter Aristide Bruant at the Chat Noir. When Bruant opened his own cabaret in 1885, Steinlen became his unofficial artist, contributing many drawings to Bruant's journal *Le Mirliton* (fig. 111, 108, 109, 110, 33) and illustrating song sheets and monologues (fig. 107).

Like other Montmartre artists, Steinlen was a close observer of the café-concert and its stars, creating a poster for Yvette Guilbert (fig. 182) as well as drawings of the diva in action (fig. 183). He also captured the daily life of the street. His massive poster *La Rue* (The Street) (fig. 13) depicts the mix of laundresses, workmen, and fashionably dressed bourgeois men and women who frequented Montmartre. Steinlen was also known for his sympathies for the poor of Paris, and hundreds of drawings, prints, and book illustrations chronicle his humanitarian concerns.

"Caillou," a pseudonym occasionally used by Steinlen, means "pebble" in French, corresponding to *stein* (stone) in German. He used this nom de plume for his cover for *Le Mirliton* of 15 January 1886 (fig. 111).

13

La Rue (The Street), 1896, color lithograph on wove paper, mounted on canvas, 236.3 x 302.3 cm (93 ¹/₁₆ x 119). National Gallery of Canada, Ottawa. Purchased 1976, NGC 18679

33

"Les Quat'Pattes," cover for *Le Mirliton,* 9 June 1893, color photorelief, 39 x 28.5 cm (15 ⅜ x 11 ¼). The Jane Voorhees Zimmerli Art Museum, Rutgers, The State University of New Jersey, Herbert D. and Ruth Schimmel Museum Library Fund, 1990.0736.002

98

Gaudeamus (Be Joyful), 1890, oil on canvas, 172 x 84 cm (67 ¹¹/₁₆ x 33 ¹/₁₆). Petit Palais, Musée d'art moderne, Geneva, 1559

99

Apotheosis of Cats, by 1897, oil on canvas, 164.5 x 300 cm (64 ¾ x 118 ⅛). Petit Palais, Musée d'art moderne, Geneva, 15887

104

Tournée du Chat Noir, 1896, color lithograph, 135.9 x 95.9 cm (53 ½ x 37 ¾). The Jane Voorhees Zimmerli Art Museum, Rutgers, The State University of New Jersey, Gift of Susan Schimmel Goldstein, 77.050.003

107

"Fins de siècle: Monologue par Aristide Bruant," c. 1894–1895, black crayon, watercolor and oil with white heightening on tracing paper, mounted on cardboard, 46 x 30.5 cm (18 ⅛ x 12). Arthur E. Vershbow

109

"La Vigne au vin," cover for *Le Mirliton,* 20 January 1893, color photorelief, 29.2 x 20 cm (11 ½ x 7 ⅞). The Jane Voorhees Zimmerli Art Museum, Rutgers, The State University of New Jersey, Herbert D. and Ruth Schimmel Museum Library Fund, 1990.0736.001

111

Sainte Marmite, (signed Jean Caillou), cover for *Le Mirliton,* 15 January 1886, color photorelief, 29.2 x 20 cm (11 ½ x 7 ⅞). The Jane Voorhees Zimmerli Art Museum, Rutgers, The State University of New Jersey, Herbert D. and Ruth Schimmel Museum Library Fund, 1990.0736.001

119

Aristide Bruant, cover for Oscar Méténier's *Aristide Bruant,* 1893, color photorelief, 18.5 x 11.5 cm (7 ⁵/₁₆ x 4 ½). The Jane Voorhees Zimmerli Art Museum, Rutgers, The State University of New Jersey, Gift of Norma D. Bartman, 2001.0928

182

Yvette Guilbert, 1894, lithograph in vermilion, yellow, brown olive, dark blue, and black, on two sheets, 179.4 x 75.9 cm (70 ⅝ x 29 ⅞). Los Angeles County Museum of Art, Kurt J. Wagner, M.D., and C. Kathleen Wagner Collection, M.87.294.53

183

Yvette Guilbert, 1896, blue and black chalk with grey wash on paper, 36.1 x 27.5 cm (14 ³/₁₆ x 10 ¹³/₁₆). Sterling and Francine Clark Art Institute, Williamstown, Massachusetts, 1955.1842

Louis Valtat

French; Dieppe 1869 – Paris 1952

Valtat began his artistic studies in 1887 as a student of Gustave Moreau at the Ecole des Beaux-Arts and completed them at the Académie Julian, where he met Bonnard, Vuillard, and the Nabis. A postimpressionist who painted in a colorful and expressive style related to the work of Gauguin and Van Gogh, Valtat exhibited at the Salon des Indépendants beginning in 1893. In 1894 he exhibited paintings and prints at the Salon des Cent, and that same year he collaborated with Lautrec to create scenery for Aurélien Lugné-Poe's production of *Le Chariot de terre cuite* (The Terracotta Chariot) at the Théâtre de l'Oeuvre.

Influenced by Lautrec in the 1890s, Valtat chose to paint similar subjects, among them cafés-concerts, cabarets, and dance halls. In compositions like *The Couple at the Lapin Agile Cabaret* (fig. 112) he emulated the flattened, simplified shapes seen in Lautrec's work. And his use of dark silhouettes against a bright background can be associated as well with the shadow plays shown at the Chat Noir and elsewhere.

Hoping to improve his poor health, Valtat moved to the south in 1899, and thereafter his work became more intimate in character.

112

The Couple at the Lapin Agile Cabaret, c. 1895, oil on paper, 79.9 x 62.1 cm (31 ⁷⁄₁₆ x 24 ⁷⁄₁₆). Collection, Art Gallery of Ontario, Toronto; Gift of Sam and Ayala Zacks, 1970, 71/355

Jean Veber

French; Paris 1868—Paris 1928

A painter, printmaker, and illustrator, Jean Veber trained in the atelier of Théodore Maillot, then enrolled at the Ecole des Beaux-Arts under the direction of Alexandre Cabanel. He painted genre scenes, portraits, and religious subjects; his first submission to the state-sponsored Salon—*Saint Sebastian*—earned him an honorable mention in 1890. Although he always considered himself a painter first, Veber is best known as a printmaker and caricaturist. His caricatures of politicians were published in illustrated journals including *Gil Blas, Le Journal,* and *Le Rire.* His watercolor of Yvette Guilbert from around 1895 may have been a design for an unrealized album devoted to the café-concert celebrity (fig. 191).

191

Yvette Guilbert, 1895, pencil and watercolor, 27 x 23.4 cm (10 ⁵⁄₈ x 9 ³⁄₁₆). The Jane Voorhees Zimmerli Art Museum, Rutgers, The State University of New Jersey, Gift of Carleton A. Holstrom, 1986.0710

Edouard Vuillard

French; Cuiseaux 1868—La Baule 1940

A painter, printmaker, and photographer, Vuillard moved to Paris in 1877 and enrolled in the Académie Julian in 1888; he also studied briefly at the Ecole des Beaux-Arts under Jean-Léon Gérôme. Vuillard was soon drawn into the group of young artists who called themselves the Nabis and adopted a bold visual style inspired in part by the work of Paul Gauguin. In contrast to his fellow Nabis, who prized a more mystical and abstract approach to art, Vuillard remained firmly grounded in the world around him, in particular the private domestic tableaux within the homes of his family and closest friends.

Vuillard and Toulouse-Lautrec first became acquainted through the circle of *La Revue blanche,* the avant-garde literary journal founded in 1891. Both artists contributed prints and designed posters promoting the publication. They also became intimates of the journal's coeditor Thadée Natanson and his wife Misia, who often invited them, along with other artistic acquaintances like Pierre Bonnard and Félix Vallotton, as guests to their country homes in Valvins and later Villeneuve-sur-Yonne.

Vuillard and Lautrec also shared a passion for the stage. Vuillard was actively involved in the avant-garde theater in Paris, designing sets, posters, and programs for the Théâtre de l'Art, the Théâtre Libre, and most important the Théâtre de l'Oeuvre, a company he cofounded with his friend the playwright Aurélien Lugné-Poe. When the Théâtre de l'Oeuvre staged Alfred Jarry's play *Ubu Roi* in 1896, Lautrec was among the artists who designed sets. Although Vuillard appreciated the intellectualism of the theater, he shared Lautrec's love of the more boisterous cafés-concerts, which he frequented throughout the 1890s. Vuillard produced several paintings and pastels depicting stage performers, including Yvette Guilbert, Jane Avril, and May Belfort, as well as paintings of Lautrec himself.

Although he continued to paint scenes inspired by the life of Montmartre, after 1900 Vuillard increasingly devoted himself to large-scale decorative works and portraiture for a sophisticated and affluent clientele.

94

Paul's Sin (Le Péché de Paul), 1895, oil on canvas, 65.5 x 54 cm (25 ¹³⁄₁₆ x 21 ¼). Courtesy of Galerie Schmit, Paris, Cogeval v-74

199

At the Café-Concert, May Belfort, c. 1895, oil on cardboard, 32 x 51 cm (12 ⁵⁄₈ x 20 ¹⁄₁₆). A. Carter Pottash, Cogeval iii-54

Théophile Pierre Wagner

French; active late nineteenth century

Wagner was an academically trained artist whose studies at the Ecole des Beaux-Arts in the late 1870s coincided roughly with Seurat's. He exhibited at the Salon des Indépendants in the 1880s, but little else is known of his career. Wagner was an amateur circus performer, an avocation illustrated in his *Self-Portrait in the Dressing Room of the Cirque Molier* (Jane Voorhees Zimmerli Art Museum, Rutgers, The State University of New Jersey).

265

Circus Scene, c. 1886–1888, pastel on canvas, 66 x 78.7 cm (26 x 31) in the original frame. The Jane Voorhees Zimmerli Art Museum, Rutgers, The State University of New Jersey, David A. and Mildred H. Morse Art Acquisition Fund, 1982.068.001

Adolphe Léon Willette

French; Châlons-sur-Marne 1857—Paris 1926

In 1875 Willette studied with Alexandre Cabanel at the Ecole des Beaux-Arts in Paris, where he met Rodolphe Salis, who later became one of the artist's most important patrons. Willette was a member of Emile Goudeau's Hydropathes group (see Dennis Cate's essay in the present catalogue) and moved with it to the Chat Noir when Salis opened the new cabaret in 1881. The Hydropathes and the Incohérents—a second group to which Willette adhered, using biting wit to flout academic norms—were the avant-garde core of the Chat Noir crowd.

Willette was closely associated with Steinlen and Henry Somm in the early project to decorate the Chat Noir; he was responsible for the signboard (which showed a cat on a crescent moon), a stained-glass version of his painting *The Virgin with a Cat* (also known as *The Green Virgin*) (fig. 97), and the painting *Parce Domine* (fig. 6). Artist's balls and processions, popular in the 1880s and 1890s, were a point of departure for Willette's *Parce Domine*, with a riotous stream of revelers spilling from the hilltop windmills of Montmartre across the night sky of Paris. Appropriately, by the time the Chat Noir moved in 1885, the painting had become a symbol of the establishment and was carried in an elaborate procession to the new location.

Willette designed a window for the new Chat Noir: *Le Veau d'or* (*The Golden Calf*, also known as *Te Deum Laudamus*) (Musée Carnavalet, Paris). He also collaborated with Somm and Henri Rivière to create the shadow plays for which the cabaret became famous. He founded the journals *Le Pierrot* (1888–1891) and *La Vache enragée* (1896–1897)—Lautrec's 1896 poster *La Vache enragée* is an advertisement—and his illustrations appeared in *Le Chat Noir, Le Courrier français, Le Rire, L'Escarmouche, La Plume,* and *L'Estampe originale,* and other publications.

Early in the twentieth century Willette embraced Roman Catholicism and renounced the risqué, often sacrilegious subjects he had favored. He participated in the creation of a Mass for artists, a memorial service that became known as the "Willette mass" (messe de Willette).

6

Parce Domine, c. 1884, oil on canvas, 200 x 390 cm (78 ¾ x 153 ⁹/₁₆). Musée Carnavalet—Histoire de Paris

97

The Virgin with Cat (also known as *The Green Virgin*), c. 1882, oil on canvas, 199 x 57.5 cm (78 ⅜ x 22 ⅝). The Jane Voorhees Zimmerli Art Museum, Rutgers, The State University of New Jersey, Regina Best Heldrich Art Acquisition Fund, 2001.0371

124

Bal des femmes (invitation), 1892, photorelief, 12.6 x 16.1 cm (4 ¹⁵/₁₆ x 6 ⁵/₁₆). The Jane Voorhees Zimmerli Art Museum, Rutgers, The State University of New Jersey, Gift of Herbert D. and Ruth Schimmel, 1988.0963

Anonymous

59

La Goulue, 1891, photograph. The Jane Voorhees Zimmerli Art Museum, Rutgers, The State University of New Jersey, Gift of Herbert D. and Ruth Schimmel, 1994.0089.001

60

La Goulue, c. 1889, photograph. The Jane Voorhees Zimmerli Art Museum, Rutgers, The State University of New Jersey, Gift of Herbert D. and Ruth Schimmel, 1994.0089.002

61

La Goulue, c. 1889, photograph. The Jane Voorhees Zimmerli Art Museum, Rutgers, The State University of New Jersey, Gift of Herbert D. and Ruth Schimmel, 1994.0089.003

101b

Old Lady, silhouette for an unidentified shadow play, c. 1890–1895, zinc, 44.5 x 24.4 cm (17 ½ x 9 ⅝). The Jane Voorhees Zimmerli Art Museum, Rutgers, The State University of New Jersey, Norma B. Bartman Purchase Fund, 1990.0717

101c

Young Woman, silhouette for an unidentified shadow play, c. 1890–1895, zinc, 37 x 14 cm (14 ⁹/₁₆ x 5 ½). The Jane Voorhees Zimmerli Art Museum, Rutgers, The State University of New Jersey, Mindy and Ramon Tublitz Purchase Fund, 1990.0716

114

Ambassadeurs: Aristide Bruant in His Cabaret, c. 1890, color lithograph, 122.8 x 87 cm (48 ⅜ x 34 ¼); 128 x 91 cm (50 ⅜ x 35 ¹³/₁₆) with mount. Collection Musée de Montmartre, Paris, A/5246.AF

120

Aristide Bruant, c. 1892, color lithograph, 27 x 18 cm (10 ⅝ x 7 ¹/₁₆). The Jane Voorhees Zimmerli Art Museum, Rutgers, The State University of New Jersey, Gift of Herbert D. and Ruth Schimmel, 1995.0179

122

Jardin de Paris: Fête de Nuit—Bal (invitation), n.d., color photorelief, 18.1 x 34.5 cm (7 ⅛ x 13 ⁹/₁₆). The Jane Voorhees Zimmerli Art Museum, Rutgers, The State University of New Jersey, Gift of Herbert D. and Ruth Schimmel, 1987.0456

139

The Dance Hall of the Moulin Rouge, illustration in *Le Panorama: Paris la Nuit,* c. 1898, photorelief, 28 x 70 cm (11 x 27 ⁹/₁₆); 28 x 35 x 20 cm (11 x 13 ¾ x 7 ⅞) closed. The Jane Voorhees Zimmerli Art Museum, Rutgers, The State University of New Jersey, Anonymous Donation, 2004.0021

158

Photographs of Yvette Guilbert, illustration in *La Panorama,* 1897, photorelief, 27 x 69 cm (10 ⅝ x 27 ³/₁₆). The Jane Voorhees Zimmerli Art Museum, Rutgers, The State University of New Jersey, Herbert D. and Ruth Schimmel Museum Library Fund, 1991.0023

detail

Henri de Toulouse-Lautrec, *Rousse (Redhead),* **also known as** *La Toilette,* **1889 (fig. 84)**

Abelès, Luce. "Les Silhouettes du Chat Noir." *48/14,* no. 17 (Autumn 2003): 36–47.

Adhémar, Jean. "Toulouse-Lautrec et son photographe habituel." *Aesculape* 12 (December 1951): 229–234.

Adriani, Götz. *Toulouse-Lautrec: The Complete Graphic Works.* Translated by Eileen Martin. New York, 1988.

Alexandre, Arsène. "Chronique d'aujourd'hui: Henri de Toulouse-Lautrec." *Paris* (8 January 1892): 2.

Anonymous. "Choses et autres." *La Vie parisienne* (5 October 1878): 581.

Anonymous. "Les Théâtres de Paris 1893–1894." *Figaro illustré* 2, no. 42 (September 1893), n.p.

Arnould, A. (7 rue Racine). *Catalogue d'affiches artistiques, françaises, étrangères.* Paris, 1896.

Avril, Jane. "Mes Mémoires." *Paris-Midi* (7 August 1933 et seq.).

Bass, Jacquelynn. "The Origins of L'Estampe originale." *Bulletin of the University of Michigan Museums of Art and Archaeology* 5 (1982–1983): 12–27.

Beauté, Georges. *Toulouse-Lautrec vu par les photographes.* Lausanne, 1988.

Bennett, Arnold. *The Journals.* Edited by Frank Swinnerton. Harmondsworth, England, 1971.

Berck, Armand. *Quelques Aperçus sur la prostitution au point de vue social, économique et morale.* Paris, 1885.

Berlanstein, Lenard R. *Daughters of Eve: A Cultural History of French Theater Women from the Old Regime to the Fin de Siècle.* Cambridge, MA, 2001.

Bernard, Tristan. "Du Symbole dans le chanson de café-concert." *Revue blanche* 1 (October 1891): 48–53.

Bernheimer, Charles. *Figures of Ill-Repute: Representing Prostitution in Nineteenth-Century France.* Cambridge, MA, and London, 1989.

Bloch, L., and Louis Sagari. *Paris qui danse.* Paris, c. 1890.

Bouchot, Henry. "Propos sur l'affiche." *Art et décoration* 3 (January–June 1898): 115–120.

Bourget, Paul. *Physiologie de l'amour moderne.* Paris, 1891.

Broido, Lucy. *The Posters of Jules Chéret.* New York, 1980.

Bruant, Aristide. *L'Argot au XXe siècle. Dictionnaire français = argot.* 2nd ed. with supplement. Paris, 1905.

Callen, Anthea. *The Spectacular Body: Science, Method, and Meaning in the Work of Degas.* New Haven and London, 1995.

Carlier, F. *Les Deux Prostitutions.* Paris, 1887.

Carrère, Jean. "Quelques opinions sur les affiches illustrées." *La Plume,* no. 110 (15 November 1893): 495–499.

Casselaer, Catherine van. *Lot's Wife. Lesbian Paris, 1890–1914.* Liverpool, 1986.

Catalogue de la Collection du Chat Noir "Rodolphe Salis." Auction catalogue, Hôtel Drouot, 16–20 May 1898. Preface by Georges Montorgueil.

Chapin, Mary Weaver. "Henri de Toulouse-Lautrec and the Café-Concert: Printmaking, Publicity, and Celebrity in Fin-de-Siècle Paris." Ph.D., New York University, 2002.

Clark, T.J. *The Painting of Modern Life: Paris in the Art of Manet and His Followers.* Princeton, 1984.

Clayson, Hollis. *Painted Love: Prostitution in French Art of the Impressionist Era.* New Haven and London, 1991.

Coman, Florence E. *Toulouse-Lautrec: "Marcelle Lender in 'Chilpéric.'"* National Gallery of Art, Washington, 1994.

Condemi, Concetta. *Les Cafés-concerts. Histoire d'un divertissement (1849–1914).* Paris, 1992.

Coolus, Romain. "Souvenirs sur Toulouse-Lautrec." *L'Amour de l'art* 12, no. 4 (April 1931): 137–139.

Coquiot, Gustave. *Lautrec, ou quinze ans de moeurs parisiennes, 1885–1900.* Paris, 1921.

Corbin, Alain. *Women for Hire: Prostitution and Sexuality in France after 1850.* Cambridge, MA, and London, 1990.

Corlieu, A. *La Prostitution à Paris.* Paris, 1887.

Dalsème, Antoine-Jean. *Le Cirque à pied et à cheval.* Paris, 1888.

Darzens, Rodolphe. Illustrations by Adolphe Willette. *Nuits à Paris.* Paris, 1889.

Devoisins, A.-J. *La Femme et l'alcoolisme.* Paris, 1885.

Dillaz, Serge. *La Chanson sous la Troisième République, 1870–1940, avec un dictionnaire des auteurs, compositeurs, interprètes.* Paris, 1991.

Donnay, Maurice. *Autour du Chat Noir.* Paris, 1926.

Dortu, M.-G. *Toulouse-Lautrec et son oeuvre.* 6 vols. New York, 1971.

Druick, Douglas. "Toulouse-Lautrec: Notes on an Exhibition." *Print Collector's Newsletter* 18 (May–June 1986): 41–47.

Duret, Théodore. *Manet.* Paris, 1919.

Epstein, Julia, and Kristina Straub, eds. *Body Guards: The Cultural Politics of Gender Ambiguity.* New York and London, 1991.

Fénéon, Félix. *Oeuvres plus que complètes.* Edited by Joan Ungersma Halperin. 2 vols. Geneva, 1970.

Forgione, Nancy. "'The Shadow Only': Shadow and Silhouette in Late Nineteenth-Century Paris." *Art Bulletin* 81, no. 3 (September 1999): 490–512.

Fouillée, Alfred. "Dégénérescence? Le Passé et le présent de notre race." *Revue des deux mondes* 65 (15 October 1896): 793–824.

Frey, Julia. *Toulouse-Lautrec. A Life.* London, 1994.

Gauthier-Villars, Henry. "Le Salon des Indépendants." *Revue indépendante,* no. 19 (April 1891): 107–113.

Gauzi, François. *Lautrec et son temps.* Paris, 1954.

Geffroy, Gustave. *La Vie artistique.* Vol. 6. Paris, 1900.

——. *Yvette Guilbert,* with lithographs by Toulouse-Lautrec. Paris, 1894.

Giret, Noëlle. *Les Arts du cirque au XIXe siècle.* Paris, 2001.

Goudeau, Emile. "Cabarets artistiques." *Revue illustrée* 2 (1886): 449–456.

——. *Dix Ans de Bohème.* Paris, 1888.

Goujon, Jean-Pau. *Jean de Tinan.* Paris, 1991.

Guilbert, Yvette. *La Chanson de ma vie. Mes Mémoires.* Paris, 1927. [English translation by Béatrice de Holthoir in London, 1929.]

——. "Comment on devient étoile." *Revue illustré,* no. 15 (15 July 1897): 79–81.

Guyot, Yves. *Etudes de physiologie sociale. La Prostitution.* Paris, 1882.

Haitt, Charles. "La Loie Fuller and Her Artistic Advertisements." *The Poster* 2, no. 8 (February 1899): 69–74.

Halpern, Joan Ungersma. *Félix Fénéon: Aesthete and Anarchist in Fin-de-Siècle Paris.* New Haven, 1988.

Heller, Reinhold. "Rediscovering Toulouse-Lautrec's *At the Moulin Rouge.*" *Art Institute of Chicago Museum Studies* 12, no. 2 (1986): 51–80.

Herbert, Robert L. *Seurat: Drawings and Paintings.* New Haven and London, 2001.

Hewitt, Nicholas. "From *lieu de plaisir* to *lieu de mémoire:* Montmartre and Parisian Cultural Topography." *French Studies,* no. 54 (March 2000): 453–469.

Hoche, Jules. *Les Parisiens chez eux.* Paris, 1883.

Houchin, John. "The Origins of the *Cabaret Aristique.*" *The Drama Review* 28, no. 1 (Spring 1984): 5–14.

Huc, Arthur [Homodei] . "Nos Expositions. L'Art nouveau." *La Dépêche de Toulouse* (20 May 1894).

——. "Nos Expositions; Les Oeuvres." *La Dépêche de Toulouse* (21 May 1894).

——. "Une Ame d'artiste." *La Dépêche de Toulouse* (21 September 1922).

Hungerford, Constance Cain. *Ernest Meissonier: Master in His Genre.* Cambridge, 1999.

Huret, Jules. *Enquête sur l'évolution littéraire.* Paris, 1891; new ed. 1999.

Jarrassé, Dominique. *Henri de Toulouse-Lautrec-Monfa. Entre le mythe et la modernité.* [Paris], 1991.

Jourdain, Francis, with Jean Adhémar. *Toulouse-Lautrec.* Paris, 1952.

Jourdain, Frantz. "L'Affiche moderne et Henri de Toulouse-Lautrec." *La Plume* (15 November 1893): 488–493.

——. *Les Décorés: Ce qui ne le sont pas.* Paris, 1895.

Joyant, Maurice. *Henri de Toulouse-Lautrec, 1864–1901.* Vol. 1, *Peintre.* Paris, 1926. Vol. 2, *Dessins, estampes, affiches,* Paris, 1927.

Jullian, Philippe. *Montmartre.* New York, 1977.

Knapp, Bettina, and Myra Chipman. *That Was Yvette: The Biography of the Great Diseuse.* New York, 1964.

Leclercq, Paul. *Autour de Toulouse-Lautrec.* Paris, 1921; repr. Geneva, 1954.

Lelieur, Anne-Claude, and Raymond Bachollet. *Célébrités à l'affiche.* Lausanne, 1989.

Leyret, Henry. *En Plein Faubourg.* Paris, 1895; new ed. Paris, 2000.

Le Men, Ségolène. *Jules Chéret. Le Cirque et la vie foraine.* Paris, 2002.

——. *Seurat et Chéret. Le Peintre, le cirque, et l'affiche.* Paris, 2003.

Le Roux, Hugues. *Les Jeux du cirque et la vie foraine.* Paris, 1889.

Littré, Emile. *Dictionnaire de la langue française.* 7th ed. Paris, 1883.

Lorrain, Jean. *Femmes de 1900.* Paris, 1932.

Louis, Pierre [Maurice Denis]. "Notes d'art. Définition du néo-traditionnisme." *Art et critique,* no. 65 (23 August 1890), 540–542.

Loyrette, Henri, ed. *Degas inédit.* Paris, 1989.

Marc, Henri. *Aristide Bruant. Le Maître de la rue.* Paris, 1989.

Mermeix. "Chronique de la semaine." *Le Courrier français* (13 June 1886): 2.

Merson, Olivier. "Exposition de la Société Nationale des Beaux-Arts." *Le Monde illustré* (13 May 1893), 303–306.

Méténier, Oscar. *Aristide Bruant.* Paris, 1893.

——. "Aristide Bruant." *La Plume,* no. 43 (1 February 1891): 39–42. [Méténier 1891b]

——. *La Lutte pour l'amour. Etudes d'argot.* Paris, 1891. [Méténier 1891a]

Meusy, Victor, and Edmond Depas. *Guide de l'étranger à Montmartre.* Paris, 1900.

Milner, John. *The Studios of Paris.* New Haven and London, 1988.

Montorgeuil, Georges. *Paris dansant.* Paris, 1898.

Mouloudji, Marcel. *Aristide Bruant.* Paris, 1972.

Murray, Gale B. *Toulouse-Lautrec: The Formative Years, 1878–1891.* Oxford, 1991.

——. *Toulouse-Lautrec: A Retrospective.* New York, 1992.

——. "The Theme of the Naturalist Quadrille in the Art of Toulouse-Lautrec: Its Origins, Meaning, Evolution, and Relationship to Later Realism." *Arts Magazine* (December 1980).

Natanson, Thadée. *Un Henri de Toulouse-Lautrec.* Geneva, 1951.

Néret, Giles. *Toulouse-Lautrec.* Paris, 1991.

Nocq, Henry. *Tendances nouvelles. Enquête sur l'évolution des industries d'art.* Paris, 1896.

Nye, Robert. *Masculinity and Male Codes of Honour in Modern France.* Oxford, 1993.

Oberthur, Mariel. *Montmartre en liesse, 1880–1900.* Paris, 1994.

Olin, Pierre-M. "Les XX." *Mercure de France* 4, no. 28 (April 1892): 343–344.

Patrick, Emmanuel. "Les Bals de Paris. Le Jardin de Paris." *Le Courrier français* (28 February 1886): 6.

Perrot, Michèle, ed. *A History of Private Life.* Vol. 4. Cambridge, MA, and London, 1990.

Pinkney, David H. *Napoleon III and the Rebuilding of Paris.* Princeton, 1958.

Petit Bottin des lettres et des arts. Paris, 1886.

Rearick, Charles. *Pleasures of the Belle Epoque: Entertainment and Festivity in Turn-of-the-Century France.* New Haven and London, 1985.

Renoy, Georges. *Montmartre de A à Z.* Paris, 1795.

Retté, Adolphe. "Septième Exposition des artistes Indépendants. Notes cursives." *L'Ermitage,* no. 5 (May 1891), 293–301.

Richard, E. *La Prostitution à Paris.* Paris, 1890.

Richer, Paul. *Etudes cliniques sur la grande hystérie ou hystéro-épilepsie.* Paris, 1881; 2nd ed. 1885.

Rigolboche, *Mémoires de Rigolboche.* Paris, 1860.

Robida, Michel. *Le Salon Charpentier et les impressionnistes.* Paris, 1958.

Rodrigues, Eugène [Erastène Ramiro]. *Cours de danse fin-de-siècle.* Paris, 1892.

Roques, Jules. "Cirque Fernando." *Le Courrier français* (13 January 1889): 4.

———. "L'Elysée-Montmartre." *Le Courrier français* (20 June 1886): 6.

———. "Pour les aspirantes-étoiles." *Le Courrier français* (June 1892): 2–3.

Roux, Xavier. "Autour du Café-concert." *La Vie contemporaine* 4 (1 October 1894): 100–107.

Sagne, Jean. "Toulouse-Lautrec photographe." *Prestige de la photographie* 10 (October 1980): 48–67.

Saint-Germier, Marie-Claire. "'Elles,' les douze heures du jour, et l'esthétique du calque." *Revue de la Bibliothèque Nationale* 43 (1992): 74–83.

Sallée, André, and Philippe Chauveau. *Music-hall et café-concert.* Paris, 1985.

Sauvage, Anne-Marie. "A propos des affiches de Lautrec pour Bruant." *Nouvelles de l'estampe,* no. 121 (January–March 1992): 6–13.

Schimmel, Herbert, ed. *The Letters of Henri de Toulouse-Lautrec.* Oxford, 1991.

Schmid, Marion. "From Decadence to Health: Zola's *Paris.*" *Romance Studies* 18, no. 2 (December 2000): 99–111.

Schwartz, Vanessa R. *Spectacular Realities: Early Mass Culture in Fin-de-Siecle Paris.* Berkeley, 1998.

Schwob, Marcel. *Chroniques.* Edited by John Alden Green. Geneva, 1981.

Sertat, Raoul. "Artistes Indépendants." *Revue encyclopédique* (1 June 1891): 549.

Silverman, Debora L. *Art Nouveau in Fin-de-Siècle France: Politics, Psychology and Style.* Berkeley, 1989.

Smith, Paul. *Seurat and the Avant-Garde.* New Haven and London, 1997.

Stein, Donna M., and Donald H. Karshan. *L'Estampe originale: A Catalogue Raisonné.* New York, 1970.

Symons, Arthur. *From Toulouse-Lautrec to Rodin, with Some Personal Impressions.* New York, 1930.

Talmeyr, Maurice. "L'Age de l'affiche." *Revue des deux mondes* 137 (September 1896): 210–216.

———. "Cafes-concerts et music-halls." *Revue des deux mondes* (1 July 1902): 159–184.

Taxil, Léo. *La Corruption fin-de-siècle.* Paris, 1891.

Thalasso, Adolphe. *Le Théâtre Libre.* Paris, 1909.

Thiébault-Sisson. "L'Art décoratif aux Salons, ou en est le nouveau style?" *Art et décoration* 1 (January–July 1897): 97–104.

Thomson, Belinda. *Van Gogh: The Art Institute of Chicago Artists in Focus.* Chicago, 2001.

Thomson, Richard. "A propos de lesbianisme clandestin en plein Paris. La Décadence et *Le Rond-Point des Champs-Elysées* de Louis Anquetin." *Histoire de l'art,* no. 50 (June 2002): 77–84.

———. *Degas: The Nudes.* London, 1988.

———. *Seurat.* Oxford, 1985.

———. "Styling the City. Observation and Perception in Print Albums of the 1890s." In Washington 2000, 48–59.

———. *Toulouse-Lautrec.* London, 1977.

———. "Toulouse-Lautrec, Arthur Huc, et le 'Néo-Réalisme.'" In *Actes du colloque Toulouse-Lautrec. Albi, mai 1992,* edited by Danièle Devynck, 117–131. Albi, 1994.

———. *The Troubled Republic: Visual Culture and Social Debate in France, 1889–1900.* New Haven and London, 2004.

Tiersten, Lisa. *Marianne on the Market. Envisioning Consumer Society in Fin-de-Siècle France.* Berkeley, Los Angeles, and London, 2001.

Valter, Jehan. "Gazette parisienne. Le Cirque Fernando." *Paris-Journal,* no. 131 (13 May 1874): 1–2.

Vauclair, Maurice. "Les Cafés-Concerts." *Paris illustré* 50 (August 1886).

Velter, André. *Les Poètes du Chat Noir.* Paris, 1996.

Verhagen, Marcus. "The Poster in Fin-de-Siècle Paris: 'That Mobile and Degenerate Art.'" In *Cinema and the Invention of Modern Life,* 103–129. Edited by Leo Charney and Vanessa R. Schwartz. Berkeley, 1995.

———. "Whipstrokes." *Representations,* no. 58 (Spring 1997): 115–140.

Virmaître, Charles. *Paris impur.* Paris, 1889.

Ward, Martha. *Pissarro, Neo-Impressionism, and the Spaces of the Avant-Garde.* Chicago, 1996.

Weisberg, Gabriel P. *Montmartre and the Making of Mass Culture.* New Brunswick, NJ, 2001.

Willette, Adolphe. *Feu Pierrot, 1857–19??.* Paris, 1919.

Willy [Henry Gauthier-Villars]. *Maîtresse d'Esthètes.* Edited by Jean-Paul Goujon. Paris, 1897; new ed., Paris, 1995.

Wittrock, Wolfgang. *Toulouse-Lautrec. The Complete Prints.* Edited and translated by Catherine E. Kueh. 2 vols. London, 1985.

Zévaes, Alexandre. *Aristide Bruant.* Paris, 1943.

EXHIBITION CATALOGUES

Albi 1994
Yvette Guilbert. Diseuse fin de siècle. Musée Toulouse-Lautrec, Albi, 1994.

Brisbane 1991
Toulouse-Lautrec: Prints and Posters from the Bibliothèque Nationale. Queensland Art Gallery, Brisbane, 1991.

Cambridge 2002
Three Women: Early Portraits by Henri de Toulouse-Lautrec. Catalogue by Sarah B. Kianovsky. Fogg Art Museum, Cambridge, MA, 2002.

Chicago 1979
Toulouse-Lautrec: Paintings. Catalogue by Charles Stuckey. The Art Institute of Chicago, 1979.

London and Paris 1991
Toulouse-Lautrec. Catalogue by Richard Thomson, Claire Frèches-Thory, Anne Roquebert, and Danièle Devynck. Hayward Gallery, London, and Grand Palais, Paris, 1991.

Los Angeles 1985
Toulouse-Lautrec and His Contemporaries: Posters of the Belle Epoque from the Wagner Collection. Catalogue by Ebria Feinblatt and Bruce Davis. Los Angeles County Museum of Art, Los Angeles, 1985.

Madrid and Barcelona 1997
Santiago Rusiñol, 1861–1931. Museu d'Art Modern, Madrid, and Fundación Mapfre Vida, Barcelona, 1997.

Munich 1995
Loïe Fuller—Getanzter Jugendstil. Edited by Jo-Anne Birnie Danzker. Museum Villa Stuck, Munich, 1995.

Namur, Corbeil-Essonnes, Quebec 1998
Félicien Rops. Catalogue by Bernadette Bonnier, Véronique Leblanc, Didier Prioul, Hélène Védrine. Maison de la Culture, Namur; Commanderie Saint-Jean, Corbeil-Essonnes; and Musée de Québec, 1998.

Nancy 1999
Peinture et art nouveau. Catalogue by Jean-Paul Midant, Gabriel P. Weisberg, and Michèle Leinen. Musée des Beaux-Arts. Nancy, 1999.

New Brunswick 1978
The Color Revolution: Color Lithography in France, 1890–1900. Catalogue by Phillip Dennis Cate and Sinclair Hamilton Hitchings. Rutgers University Art Gallery, New Brunswick, NJ, 1978.

New Brunswick 1985
The Circle of Toulouse-Lautrec. Catalogue by Phillip Dennis Cate and Patricia Eckert Boyer. The Jane Voorhees Zimmerli Art Museum, New Brunswick, NJ, 1985.

New Brunswick 1988a
The Graphic Arts and French Society, 1871–1914. Edited by Phillip Dennis Cate. Jane Voorhees Zimmerli Art Museum, New Brunswick, NJ, 1988.

New Brunswick 1988b
Emile Bernard: Bordellos and Prostitutes in Turn-of-the-Century French Art. Catalogue by Phillip Dennis Cate and Bogomilla Welsh-Ovcharov. The Jane Voorhees Zimmerli Art Museum, New Brunswick, NJ, 1988.

New Brunswick 1988c
The Nabis and the Parisian Avant-Garde. Catalogue by Patricia Eckert Boyer. The Jane Voorhees Zimmerli Art Museum, New Brunswick, NJ, 1988.

New Brunswick 1991
L'Estampe originale: Artistic Printmaking in France, 1893–1895. Catalogue by Patricia Eckert Boyer and Phillip Dennis Cate. The Jane Voorhees Zimmerli Art Museum, New Brunswick, NJ, 1991.

New Brunswick 1996
The Spirit of Montmartre: Cabarets, Humor, and the Avant-Garde, 1875–1905. Catalogue by Phillip Dennis Cate and Mary Shaw. The Jane Voorhees Zimmerli Art Museum, New Brunswick, NJ, 1996.

Paris 1982
Erik Satie à Montmartre. Catalogue by Ornella Volta, Mariel Oberthür, and Robert Caby. Musée de Montmartre, Paris, 1982.

Paris 1986
La Leçon de Charcot. Voyage dans une toile. Catalogue by Nadine Simon-Dhouailly. Musée de l'Assistance Publique, Paris, 1986.

Paris 1992
Le Chat Noir, 1881–1897. Catalogue by Mariel Oberthür. Musée d'Orsay, Paris, 1992.

Richmond 1979
Loïe Fuller: Magician of Light. Catalogue by Margaret Haile Harris. Virginia Museum of Art, Richmond, 1979.

Santa Barbara 1993
Le Chat Noir: A Montmartre Cabaret and Its Artists in Turn-of-the-Century Paris. Catalogue by Armond Fields. Santa Barbara Museum of Art, 1993.

St. Louis 2001
Vincent van Gogh and the Painters of the Petit Boulevard. Catalogue by Cornelia Homburg, Richard Thomson, Elizabeth C. Childs, John House. St. Louis Art Museum and Städelsches Kunstinstitut, Frankfurt, 2001.

Washington 1998
Artists and the Avant-Garde Theater in Paris, 1887–1900. Catalogue by Patricia Eckert Boyer. National Gallery of Art, Washington, 1998.

Washington 2000
Prints Abound: Paris in the 1890s. Essays by Phillip Dennis Cate, Richard Thomson, and Gale B. Murray. Catalogue by Judith Brodie. National Gallery of Art, Washington, 2000.

PHOTOGRAPHY CREDITS

The following numbers refer to figures in the catalogue.

Toulouse-Lautrec and Montmartre: Depicting Decadence in Fin-de-Siècle Paris

I: Victoria & Albert Museum, London/Art Resource, NY

2: Réunion des Musées Nationaux/Art Resource, NY, photograph by Rene-Gabriel Ojeda

3, 19, 25: © 2004 Board of Trustees, National Gallery of Art, Washington

4: Calveras/Mérida/Sagristà

6: Musée du Vieux Montmartre, Paris/Archives Charmet/Bridgeman Art Library

10, 16, 20: Photography © The Art Institute of Chicago

12: © photo du Musée des Beaux-Arts de la Ville de Reims, photograph by C. Devleeschauwer

13: © National Gallery of Canada, Ottawa

14, 26: Photograph by Jack Abraham

15: Photograph by Antonio Caetano

17: Central Art Archives/ Antti Kuivalainen

18: Photograph © 2004 Museum of Fine Arts, Boston

21: Photograph by Bruce M. White

23: Erich Lessing/Art Resource, NY

The Social Menagerie of Toulouse-Lautrec's Montmartre

28–45: Photograph by Jack Abraham

44: © 2004 Artists Rights Society (ARS), New York/ ADAGP, Paris

Toulouse-Lautrec and the Culture of Celebrity

48, 49, 55, 59–61: Photograph by Jack Abraham

51, 57, 64, 66: Photography © The Art Institute of Chicago

52: © Courtesy of the J. Paul Getty Museum

56: Photograph © Museum Associates/LACMA

63: Photograph by Joseph Szaszfai

65: © 2004 Board of Trustees, National Gallery of Art, Washington, photograph by Dean Beasom

68: Digital image © The Museum of Modern Art/Licensed by Scala/Art Resource, NY

Introducing Montmartre

70: Studio Monique Bernaz, Genève

72: Photography © The Art Institute of Chicago

75: © Musées de la Ville de Rouen. Photograph by Catharine Lancien, Carole Loisel

76: Northwestern University Library

77: © Museo Thyssen-Bornemisza. Madrid

79: Photograph © 2004 The Metropolitan Museum of Art

80: Scala/Art Resource, NY

82: © 2004 Board of Trustees, National Gallery of Art, Washington

84: Erich Lessing/Art Resource, NY

85: © 2004 Board of Trustees, National Gallery of Art, Washington, photograph by Lyle Peterzell

92: © 2003 President and Fellows of Harvard College

95, 96: Photograph by Jack Abraham

The Chat Noir and Cabarets

97, 100, 101a–d, 102, 103, 106, 108–111, 118–120: Photograph by Jack Abraham

98, 99: Studio Monique Bernaz, Genève

104: Photograph by Victor Pustai

107: Photograph by Charles Mayer

113, 115–117: Photography © The Art Institute of Chicago

Dance Halls

121, 126, 142, 149: Photography © The Art Institute of Chicago

122–124, 132–140: Photograph by Jack Abraham

129: Calveras/Mérida/Sagristà

141: Photograph © 2004 The Metropolitan Museum of Art

144: © 2004 Board of Trustees, National Gallery of Art, Washington, photograph by Jose A. Naranjo

145, 148: © 2004 Board of Trustees, National Gallery of Art, Washington

146: Luiz Hossaka

Stars of the Café-Concert

153, 154, 155, 179, 223, 224, 225: Photograph © 2004 Museum Associates/LACMA

156–158, 163, 166–168, 170, 171, 180, 181, 184, 191, 196, 218a–f, 219–221, 226: Photograph by Jack Abraham

156, 166–168, 170, 171, 181, 194: © 2004 Artists Rights Society (ARS), New York/ ADAGP, Paris

160, 161, 164, 165a–v, 175–178, 187 recto (left and right), 187 verso (left and right), 197, 200–202, 206, 215: Photography © The Art Institute of Chicago

162, 172, 205: © 2004 Board of Trustees, National Gallery of Art, Washington, photograph by Dean Beasom

174, 216: Photograph © 2004 The Metropolitan Museum of Art

182: Photograph © 2005 Museum Associates/LACMA

186: Photograph by Erik Gould

189: all rights reserved: Musée Toulouse-Lautrec— Albi—Tarn—France

190a–q, 204: © 2004 Board of Trustees, National Gallery of Art, Washington

192: Erich Lessing/Art Resource, NY

193: Réunion des Musée Nationaux/Art Resource, NY, photograph by R. G. Ojeda

194: Réunion des Musée Nationaux/Art Resource, NY, photograph by Hervé Lewansowski

213: Photograph by Stephen Petegorsky

222: Photothèque des Musées de la Ville de Paris (ou PMVP) cliché: Philippe Joffre

227: © 2004 Board of Trustees, National Gallery of Art, Washington, photograph by Philip A. Charles

Roedel, Auguste, 42, 275; *Moulin Rouge: A qui la Pomme?* (fig. 135), 123; *Moulin Rouge: La Bohème Artistique*, invitation (fig. 134), 123; *Moulin Rouge: Noël à Montmartre*, invitation (fig. 133), 123; *Moulin Rouge: Reprise de la Fête du Printemps*, invitation (fig. 136), *124*

Rollinat, Maurice, 27

Rops, Félicien, 56, 209

Roques, Jules, 49–50

Rousse (Redhead) (fig. 84), 68, *79*

Roussel, Ker-Xavier, 18

Royer, Henri Paul, *A pequena colina de Montmartre (On the Slope)* (fig. 15), 13, *13*

Rue des Moulins. See Medical Inspection (fig. 249)

Rusiñol i Prats, Santiago, 4, III; biography, 275; *The Garden of the Moulin de la Galette* (fig. 125), 4, III, *117*; *The Kitchen of the Moulin de la Galette* (fig. 129), III, *120*

S

Sacré-Coeur, 41, 66; *The Sacré-Coeur, Montmartre* (Casas) (fig. 4), 4, *5*, 65

Saint-Senoch, Edgar de, *Yvette Guilbert* (fig. 26), 20, *21*

Salis, Rodolphe, 17, 27, 29–30, 33, 36, *38*, 39, 40, 41, 43, 49, 67, 89–91

Salon des Incohérents, 17

Salon des Indépendants, 7, 14, 16, 56, 68, 69, 109, 110, III, 112, 113, 238

Salon Nationale des Beaux-Arts, 67

Salon of the Rue des Moulins (fig. 248), 208, 209, 222

Salon of the Société des Artistes Français, 16, 31

Sapeck. *See* Bataille, Eugène

Sarcey, Francisque, 40

Satie, Erik, *Erik Satie* (Casas) (fig. 75), 67, *74*

Saupiguet Sardines, 141

La Sauterelle (dancer), 41

Scévola, Guirand de, 42

Schwob, Marcel, 66, 110, 114

Science, II, 19–20

The Seated Clowness (Mademoiselle Cha-u-ka-o) (fig. 259c), 231, 240

Seated Woman from Behind: Study for "At the Moulin Rouge" (fig. 65), 58, *59*

Segatori, Agostina, 69; *Agostina Segatori at the Café du Tambourin* (Van Gogh) (fig. 90), 69, *83*

Sémelaigne (doctor), 240

Sertat, Raoul, 18

Sérusier, Paul, 39

Sescau, Paul, 62; *At the Moulin Rouge* (Toulouse-Lautrec) (fig. 66), 58, *59*; *Paul Sescau* (Toulouse-Lautrec) (fig. 77), 68, *75*; *Toulouse-Lautrec* (fig. 67), *61*

Seurat, Georges, 32, 36, 39; *Chahut* (fig. 7), 7, *7*, 112; *Cirque*, 239; cover for Victor Joze's *L'Homme à femmes* (fig. 36), *36*; *Parade du cirque*, 237, 238

Shadow theater, 2, 7, 37–39, 91

Signac, Paul, 39

Sihouettes, 7

Sivry, Charles de, 27, 42

Société des Artistes Indépendants, 26

Somm, Henry, 7, 30, 37, 39, 40, 275; *Divan Japonais* (fig. 163), 138, *149*; *Le Fils de l'eunuque*, 37; *Five Female Figures with a Dog*, silhouettes for the shadow plan *Le Fils de l'eunuque* (fig. 101a), 91, *97*; *Henry Somm, alias "Elie Calmé"* (Tiret-Bognet) (fig. 42), *40*

A Spectator (fig. 165u), *160*

Steinlen, Théophile-Alexandre, 17, 30, 39, 40, 92, 93; *Apotheosis of Cats* (fig. 99), 39, 90, *96*; biography, 276; *"Dans la rue,"* cover for *Le Mirliton* (fig. 108), 92, *100*; *"Fins de siècle: Monologue par Aristide Bruant"* (fig. 107), 92, *100*; *Gaudeamus (Be Joyful)* (fig. 98), 90, *95*; *"Les Quat'Pattes,"* cover of *Le Mirliton* (fig. 33), *32*, 93; *La Rue (The Street)* (fig. 13), 11, *12*; *Sainte Marmite*, cover for *Le Mirliton* (fig. III), 92, *101*; *"Tha-ma-ra-boum-de-hé,"* cover for *Le Mirliton* (fig. 110), 92, *101*; *Tournée du Chat Noir* (fig. 104), 88 (det.), 91, *99*; *"La Vigne*

au vin," cover for *Le Mirliton* (fig. 109), 92, *101*; *Yvette Guilbert* (fig. 182), 140, *170*; *Yvette Guilbert* (fig. 183), *171*

Stéphani, Camilla, 21

Stevens, Alfred, 27

Study for "Moulin de la Galette" (fig. 127), 110, *119*

Symbolism, 32, 39

Symons, Arthur, 139

Synthetism, 32

T

Talmeyr, Maurice, 5, 112

Tanguy, Père, 66

Tapié de Céleyran, Gabriel, *At the Moulin Rouge* (Toulouse-Lautrec) (fig. 66), 58, 113

Taverne du Bagne, 10

Terrasse, Claude, 39, 40

Teulet, Edmond, 42

Théâtre Libre, 39

Théâtre de l'Oeuvre, 39

Théâtre des Pantins, 39

Théâtre des Variétés, 142

Thérésa (singer), 48

Thibaud, Anna, *Anna Thibaud (Ibels)* (fig. 165g), *153*

Thiébault-Sisson, François, 19

Third Republic: decadence of, 4–6, 13, 67, 112; social and political life of, 3–4

Thomson, Richard, 36

Three-Quarter-Length Study of Yvette Guilbert (fig. 188), *173*

Tiffany, Louis Comfort, 240

Tinchant (Chat Noir personality), 39

Tiret-Bognet, Georges, 40; *Henry Somm, alias "Elie Calmé"* (fig. 42), *40*

La Toilette. See Rousse (Redhead) (fig. 84)

La Tonkinoise (dancer), 41

Toulouse-Lautrec, Henri de, *52*, *61*; alcoholism of, 237, 240; artistic training of, 2; biographical sketch of, 255; birth of, vii, 3; exhibition of work by, 60; health of, vii, 60, 237, 240; as illustrator, vii; personality of, 18; physical appearance of, 60, 62; as printmaker, vii, 51, 53, 55; pseudonym of, 40; public behavior of, 60; social life of, vii

Tréclau (pseudonym of Toulouse-Lautrec), 40

Trombert, François, 40, 42

Trouchet, Abel, 42

The Two Friends (fig. 250), 208, 224

The Two Friends (fig. 252), 209, 225

Les Types de Paris, II

Typology of individuals, II–16, 67

U

Utrillo, Miguel, 38

V

La Vache enragée (magazine), 33

Valadon, Suzanne, 69, 239

Vallotton, Félix, 38

Valtat, Louis: biography, 276–277; *The Couple at the Lapin Agile Cabaret* (fig. 112), *102*

Van Gogh. *See* Gogh

Vary, Hélène, 69; *Hélène Vary* (Toulouse-Lautrec) (fig. 87), 17, 69, *81*

Veber, Jean, 277; *Yvette Guilbert* (fig. 191), 140, *180*

Verneau, Charles, II

Vernet, Carle, 27

Vicaire, Gabriel, 40

Vidal, Pierre, cover for Georges Montorgueil's *La Vie à Montmartre* (fig. 14), 12, *13*

La Vie parisienne (journal), 140

Vincent van Gogh (fig. 88), 17, 69, *82*

Vuillard, Edouard, 18, 38, 39, 40; *At the Café-Concert, May Belfort* (fig. 199), *185*; biography, 277; *Paul's Sin (Le Péché du Paul)* (fig. 94), 69–70, *86*

W

Wagner, Richard, 30

Wagner, Théophile Pierre, 39, 277; *Circus Scene* (fig. 265), 239–240, 244

Warrener, William, 112

Weber, Louise. *See* La Goulue

Wenz, Jeanne, *"A la Bastille" (Jeanne Wenz)* (Toulouse-Lautrec) (fig. 3), 4, *4*, 17

Whistler, James Abbott McNeill, 67

283

Louis Anquetin, *Henri de Toulouse-Lautrec*, c. 1886, oil on canvas, 40.3 x 32.5 cm, private collection, Paris

Anquetin's impressionist portrait of his friend shows Lautrec as he probably appeared in the studio and on the streets of Montmartre at the outset of his career.